CITY CHOREOGRAPHER

CITY CHOREOGRAPHER
LAWRENCE HALPRIN IN
URBAN RENEWAL AMERICA

ALISON BICK HIRSCH

UNIVERSITY OF MINNESOTA PRESS
MINNEAPOLIS • LONDON

This book is supported by a grant from the Graham Foundation
for Advanced Studies in the Fine Arts.

Frontispieces for the Introduction, chapter 2, and chapter 4 from Lawrence Halprin Collection,
The Architectural Archives, University of Pennsylvania.

The University of Minnesota Press gratefully acknowledges financial
assistance provided for the publication of this book by the David R. Coffin
Publication Grant of the Foundation for Landscape Studies, New York.

Published by the University of Minnesota Press
111 Third Avenue South, Suite 290
Minneapolis, MN 55401-2520
http://www.upress.umn.edu

Library of Congress Cataloging-in-Publication Data
Hirsch, Alison Bick.
    City choreographer : Lawrence Halprin in urban renewal America / Alison Bick Hirsch.
        Includes bibliographical references and index.
    ISBN 978-0-8166-7978-2 (hc) — ISBN 978-0-8166-7979-9 (pb)
    1. Halprin, Lawrence—Philosophy. 2. Architects and community—United States. 3. Lawrence
Halprin & Associates. 4. City planning—United States—History—20th century. 5. Urban landscape
architecture—United States—History—20th century. I. Title.
    NA9085.H35H57 2014
    720.92—dc23   2014001581

Printed in the United States of America on acid-free paper

The University of Minnesota is an equal-opportunity educator and employer.

20 19 18 17 16 15 14   10 9 8 7 6 5 4 3 2 1

For my parents

CONTENTS

ACKNOWLEDGMENTS

This project was first inspired by a seminar I took with John Dixon Hunt and Emily Cooperman in the University of Pennsylvania's Architectural Archives, and I am grateful for this initial exposure to the infinite richness of the Lawrence Halprin Collection. With John Dixon Hunt's encouragement and rigorous feedback, the seeds of this project grew into a doctoral dissertation at the University of Pennsylvania. John Dixon Hunt is my model for disciplined and brilliant scholarship, and I aspire to produce works that exhibit the integrity he embodies as a scholar. My dissertation committee (John Dixon Hunt, Randy Mason, Emily Cooperman, and David Leatherbarrow) played a central role in the project's evolution from thesis to book. Randy Mason has remained a consistent advisor, mentor, champion, and friend and has contributed to the book and my academic development in too many ways to list; for this and for his unwavering confidence in my work, I am deeply indebted to him. David Leatherbarrow's encouragement, support, and generous response to multitudinous solicitations for advice have persisted throughout the years, and I owe him endless thanks for all he has done to ensure my success as a scholar.

I am extremely fortunate to have studied at the university where Lawrence Halprin donated his archive, and I am infinitely grateful for the assistance, feedback, and support of Nancy Thorne and Bill Whitaker at the Architectural Archives. They accommodated my countless requests, shared new discoveries, and allowed me to nearly take up residence in the collection.

As the book is based on the work of Lawrence Halprin and the impact Anna Halprin had on his work, I extend my humblest gratitude to them not only for our conversations but for the immeasurable impact they have had on my scholarly, creative, and personal pursuits. I was blessed to have the opportunity to spend time with Larry before he died, interviewing him and hearing his reflections on his career of more than sixty years. I sincerely thank Anna Halprin for speaking with me and for conducting the movement workshops I participated in on the Dance Deck and as part of her retrospective at the Yerba Buena Center for the Arts in 2008. Janice Ross, Anna's biographer and a dance scholar, provided invaluable feedback, shared resources, and guided me through Anna's archive at the Museum of Performance and Design. I also thank Larry's longtime office manager, Dee Mullen, for her availability and generosity throughout the book's progress, as well as Larry's colleague and employee Dai Williams, who gave me fascinating insights into office culture and projects.

I encountered many helpful individuals while studying Halprin's public spaces that faced demolitions threats. Susan Kline, historian and preservationist in Fort Worth, kept me abreast of the status of Heritage Park Plaza; her updates on the preservation progress were critical to the section of this book devoted to this special place.

Scholar and friend Beth Meyer consistently provided generous feedback and opportunities to enrich my research, and I think of her as a true mentor. John Beardsley, director of Garden and Landscape Studies at Dumbarton Oaks, granted me the opportunity to work in the Research Collection there as a postdoctoral fellow. This time proved pivotal to the transformation of my dissertation into something much closer to a book manuscript. Urban historian Alison Isenberg generously reviewed the book's early structure and content and pushed me to consider underlying gender implications of Lawrence Halprin's work. Landscape architect Laurie Olin, a longtime colleague and friend of Larry, offered guidance and served as a sounding board for the project. He offered me valuable insight into Larry's idiosyncratic design methodology and output, and, with John

Beardsley, he served as a reference for the Foundation for Landscape Studies David R. Coffin Grant, which proved extremely beneficial to the book's production.

Inspired by the Halprins' creative process, I decided to continue at the University of Pennsylvania to acquire my own degree in landscape architecture and pursue a hybrid career in academia and practice. This design education enriched the book's development tremendously, and I am grateful to Anu Mathur and Dilip da Dunha, who supported and nurtured my work on Halprin and taught me how to see in ways that significantly impacted how I assessed Halprin's creative process, as well as shaped me as a landscape architect. Jim Corner has also been a palpable champion of my research and design studies, and I am tremendously grateful for his encouragement and support.

I express my thanks to Pieter Martin and Kristian Tvedten at the University of Minnesota Press. Together with their team, they ensured a transparent and seamless publication process. The two reviewers they commissioned provided thoughtful and constructive input that was extremely beneficial to the book's structure and more focused content. In addition, Leigha Delbusso, graduate student in landscape architecture at the University of Southern California, provided invaluable assistance on the index.

I dedicate this book to my parents, Joyce and Jerry Hirsch, who have been an unwavering source of love and encouragement. Not only has this been essential to the book's success but it has fueled me (and made it possible for me) to pursue what I love. For this kind of gratitude there are no words, but I hope dedicating the book to them conveys some of this overwhelming sentiment. Paul Hirsch and Laura Lambert also provided love and positive energy throughout this project and beyond; they served as willing sounding boards for important decisions that directly and indirectly affected the success of the book. Finally, I recognize Aroussiak Gabrielian for her constant love, support, patience, brilliant feedback, and uncanny ability to keep me laughing, even in the midst of hard work. I could not have completed the book without her extraordinary presence in my life.

CITY CHOREOGRAPHER

SCORING THE PARTICIPATORY CITY

LANDSCAPE ARCHITECT LAWRENCE HALPRIN'S nearly sixty-five-year career reflects the story of postwar American urban development—from his residential work in the booming Pacific coast suburbs, to his designs for regional shopping malls as substitutes for downtown public life, to his counterattempts to restore the social life of the city after disorienting change, primarily caused by federal policies such as Title I of the Housing Act of 1949 and the Highway Act of 1956. After vast swaths of central cities were razed, severing deep roots that had grounded communities in their physical environment, new and unfamiliar landscapes rapidly appeared that altered the skyline and the way people occupied and inhabited urban space. Halprin's most noteworthy contribution responded to the nation's densely settled metropolitan areas during this time of urban "crisis" and "renewal."

Paralleling and reacting to a broader public demand for social and political participation in the 1960s, Halprin formulated a creative process he called the "RSVP Cycles" to stimulate a participatory environmental experience. He did not work alone, however.

His success depended on collaboration, particularly the artistic symbiosis that existed between him and his wife, the avant-garde dancer and choreographer Anna Halprin (née Ann Schuman).

During the 1960s, a progressive liberation of the spectator from observer to active participant occurred in the visual and performing arts, which were reciprocally informed by participatory forms of social protest and performance, such as marches, sit-ins, and riots. Anna, with her San Francisco Dancers' Workshop, was directly involved in these developments, and their experiments soon infiltrated her husband's work. Like "Happenings," emerging from the teachings of musician John Cage in New York, Anna organized interactive events in which environmental situations and loose action guidelines were proposed or "scored," but the ultimate performance was left open ended and typically involved the audience.[1] From these new art forms, the "open score" became the major tool for stimulating action and involving the public. Lawrence (Larry) Halprin applied these emerging performance theories to his work first by designing public spaces as "scores" intended to stimulate open-ended kinesthetic response, and second by adopting the temporal-situational guidelines of performance events to structure public participation workshops, which he called the "Take Part Process." Part 1 of this book, "Built Work," and part 2, "Community Workshops," respectively trace these two applications of choreographic scores that Halprin used to reactivate public life in the city. In addition, they each projectively consider how such a reflection on his work might enrich contemporary approaches to shaping the city.

This study began as an exploration of Halprin's bold formal gestures in designs for public spaces, which offered stimulating counterpoints to their often bleak urban contexts, and also as an investigation of why so many of these public spaces were being removed and replaced by "safer" and more passive redesigns. Yet studying his work from the preservation perspective revealed that not only are his designed forms striking but that his creative process was groundbreaking. The process represents an overlooked antecedent to today's approach to landscape and urban design, which emphasizes infrastructural networks, ecological processes, multidisciplinary collaboration, and public participation. And yet, Halprin's work is consistently considered dated, a relic of 1960s social circumstances, and therefore worthy of redesign. In this book I trace the degree to which his theories and projects have continued relevance or if they are too enmeshed in the immediacy of the times to have lasting social value today. My ultimate objective is to demonstrate that Halprin's work represents a lot more than "brutalist" concrete forms and obsolete mechanical systems.

With this overarching agenda in mind, my intentions are really threefold. First and foremost, I attempt to demonstrate that Halprin's most consequential legacy is not the built work he left behind but the creative process he developed and deployed. Most evaluations of Halprin consider his built products and undervalue the theory that drives their development. These evaluations either myopically criticize his heavy-handed designs or blindly celebrate the work simply because it was authored by the heroic Lawrence Halprin. Though many such evaluations mention his collaborative relationship with his choreographer wife, none comprehensively address how Anna's work informed Larry's creative process. This book assesses his writing on the RSVP Cycles and places it in the context of his built work, thereby revealing contrasts and contradictions that may be as informative to today's urbanists as the structure of the process itself.

My second aim is to demonstrate that Halprin's creative process precedes many theories driving landscape and urban design today yet has been overlooked as an instructive precursor. Today's designers value landscape architecture as a process-based practice—emphasizing the medium's temporal or durational dimension as much as its physical one. The vocabulary, methodology, and intentions of Halprin's open-ended scoring approach have only recently become part of accepted disciplinary discourse, yet with little recognition of Halprin's pioneering efforts. This oversight has occurred most primarily because his built forms, which are today considered largely outdated, have overshadowed the richness of the process Halprin deployed to generate them.

Finally, my third objective is to prove that the inconsistency between process and product, or why the process did not yield more timeless results, is related to Halprin's inability to relinquish control to the degree his theory proposes. Larry and Anna's artistic relationship was unique and immensely fruitful, yet rather than being an effortless life-long collaboration (it was often competitive and inequitable), their work was at times deliberately collaborative (particularly in the 1950s and 1960s) and at times simply mutually symbiotic, with each benefitting and expanding from exposure to the other's medium and method. Yet their process and product also often diverged, partly owing to the circumstances of their medium and partly to fundamental differences in attitude. Many of the contradictions of Larry's career (the irresolution between openness and control), however, relate to problems consistently encountered in planning in a democracy.

CONTENT AND CONTEXT

In the 1960s, at the climax of the couple's collaborative experimentation, Larry, with Anna, structured the RSVP Cycles, a creative approach meant to guide the development of both his formal designs and his participatory process. As he explains in his book *The RSVP Cycles: Creative Processes in the Human Environment* (1969), RSVP stands for Resources, Scores, Valuaction, and Performance (Figure I.1). Though these four components conveniently correspond to the French acronym, which invites response or feedback, they are meant to occur in any order and in a cyclical ongoing fashion rather than a linear one. "Resources" refers to the preexisting site conditions and the act of inventorying them in order to determine their potential for informing design or the structure of the Scores. "Scores" are temporal-situational guidelines that structure the unfolding Performance. A closed score implies choreographic control and an open score invites participation by allowing for a range of response. "Valuaction" is a term Halprin coined for the critical feedback process that leads to the consistent revision of the Scores or the workshop activities. Because Scores are intended to be "nonjudgmental," Valuaction embodies the analytical or judgmental component of the process. Finally, "Performance" represents the acting out of the Scores. The use of these abstract terms will become clearer in examples of their application, but the theoretical intention was the emergence of a creative outcome during the process rather than the imposition of a predetermined solution. Scores are most fundamental to achieving this aim.

The RSVP Cycles

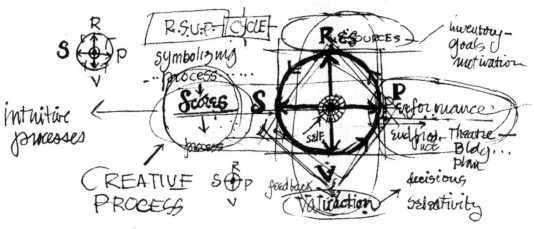

Figure I.1. The original version of this diagram—sketched on a cocktail napkin—was recently discovered in the Lawrence Halprin Collection. It was published as the cover image of Lawrence Halprin, *The RSVP Cycles* (1969). Lawrence Halprin Collection, The Architectural Archives, University of Pennsylvania.

In this book I focus on the years of Lawrence Halprin & Associates (1960–76) when he was most rigorously and self-consciously experimenting with the theories of choreographic scores. Though Halprin made significant contributions to the field beginning in the 1940s and continued to make an impact on the direction of landscape architecture until his death in 2009, the multidisciplinary firm's interventions in American cities, which were then characterized by disturbance, discontinuity, and unrest, were most responsive to the dynamic social circumstances of those decades. The estrangement of the city inhabitant caused by the rapidly shifting environment of urban renewal America presented the most complex challenges faced by Halprin and his firm. This book is thus about bold interventions that respond to the city during a time of massive change.

Scores imply time, process, and change, thereby challenging the Modernist desire to control and order urban space by imposing reductive formal values usually applied in totalizing and fixed "master plans" (Figure I.2). Yet Halprin insists he is a Modernist, and rightly so since his artistic foundation was formed by the pedagogy of the Bauhaus

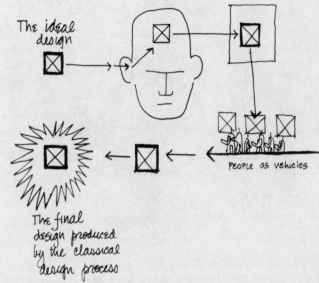

The ideal design

People as vehicles

The final design produced by the classical design process

The traditional design approach is most frequently a closed score, in which the designer (architect, choreographer, artist, planner, composer) conceives and creates his work and displays it to people without their involvement in the creative process.

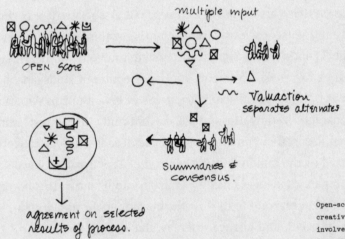

OPEN SCORE

multiple input

Valuaction separates alternates

Summaries & consensus.

agreement on selected results of process.

Open-score processes of collective creativity allow people to become involved in the creative process from the beginning, make their inputs continually, arrive at decisions and alternatives together, and finally agree on what they want to do.

Figure I.2. The open score versus the closed score. Published in Lawrence Halprin and Jim Burns, *Taking Part* (1974), 74. Lawrence Halprin Collection, The Architectural Archives, University of Pennsylvania.

(brought to Harvard), which was based on addressing immediate social needs and a culture of collaboration. Halprin considered Scores a reassertion of Modernist ideals after they had devolved.[2] The retitling of his 1974 unpublished manuscript from "Environment as Art Experience" to "The New Modernism: Art of the Environment" is indicative of his insistent belief in continuing this tradition of supporting positive social change through design.[3] By the use of the word "new," however, he is claiming that environmental values must be part of this effort.

In addition, Halprin's exposure to the European artistic avant-garde and his earlier life experience living on a kibbutz, immersed in its socialist ideals, fueled his lifetime quest for "collective creativity" and consensus. His commitment to unearthing fundamental human commonality and his faith in a universal collective builds on this Modernist legacy. Halprin, who himself underwent Jungian psychoanalysis, consistently cites Jung's theories of the "collective unconscious." He believed in "universal man" bound together by "archetypal needs." Yet the artistic avant-garde, reacting to marginalized groups asserting their position in society, began to shift its focus in the late 1960s from aesthetic essentialism to endless pluralities of human and cultural experience. Although Anna incorporated this shift into her work, Larry continued his search for universal forms of expression.

Halprin's widely acclaimed and revolutionary work on the Sea Ranch, the residential community along the rugged coast of Sonoma County, California, and his passionate connection to the "wildness" of the High Sierra inescapably shaped his attitude toward open space in the city. In this study, these landscapes are presented as aesthetic sources for his urban work. To further clarify my focus in this book, though Halprin wrote *Freeways* in 1966 to demonstrate how proliferating automobile infrastructure might be sensitively integrated in the city, my emphasis here is bodily movement through the city. Yet Halprin's work on freeways certainly guided his approach to a number of spaces designed for the human scale, such as San Francisco's Embarcadero Plaza and Seattle Freeway Park, and is treated accordingly. My aim in this book is also to provide a lens through which to assess Halprin's well-known work developed after dismantling Lawrence Halprin & Associates, such as the Franklin Delano Roosevelt Memorial in Washington, D.C., and Levi's Plaza in San Francisco.

In California the Halprins felt free from the stiff, long-standing stylistic traditions and institutions that they thought stifled creativity in the East. The immediacy represented by the closeness of nature and the freedom offered by the open landscape encouraged limitless possibilities for new modes of inquisition and action. Clearly the legacy of the Beats was part of San Francisco's culture, and the liberation the Bay Area presented from what Anna considered the contrived intellectualism of the East Coast allowed for artistic experimentation out of the spotlight. Anna's contributions to the avant-garde were tremendous. With Merce Cunningham, she may be considered the most innovative figure in what is termed "postmodern dance." Rather than following stylistic trends or seeking shock value, her work in the 1960s was driven by the troubling distinctions between that which was commercially and culturally valued as "art" and the movements of the everyday. To dissolve those distinctions, Anna's "goal was to reengage the gestural vocabulary of everyday life as art and to cast the spectator as a more active participant," in the words of her biographer Janice Ross.[4]

As early as the late 1930s, Anna was exposed to the phenomenological writings of John Dewey while studying under one of his pupils, dance educator Margaret H'Doubler, who wrote *Dance: A Creative Art Experience* (1940) in direct response to Dewey's *Art as Experience* (1934). This initial exposure helped catalyze Anna's lifetime interest in creative intuition and ritual performance. Optimizing aesthetic experience, and particularly kinesthetic awareness, fueled both Anna and Larry's work throughout their careers. The extraordinary impact of Dewey is palpable in the work of both of the Halprins. As an educator and a choreographer, Anna stimulated "creative intuition" by setting up environmental situations, or scores, and encouraging her dancers to respond relying entirely on their kinesthetic sense, without "preconceived notion to direct the action."[5] She studied rituals as the origins of art, thus common to all, to facilitate open communication. She considered the prereflexive mind–body a state of "supreme authenticity" in which one could communicate with others without the barriers of cultural conditioning. Through this common language Anna also sought to achieve "collective creativity," believing in the power of art derived from a group. Larry Halprin absorbed and informed these pursuits; it was kinesthetic awareness, rather than the visual or scopic, and stimulating the collective through the prerational language of "archetypal" forms and expressions that drove his design agenda.

Anna, and later Larry, looked to the emergence of Gestalt therapy to unleash this "prerational" state. Anna worked within the developing field particularly through her close relationship with Dr. Frederick (Fritz) Perls. Just prior to their first meeting in 1964, Perls had been in California developing his Gestalt theories by the reading of emotions through bodily movement and studying the mind and body as an integrated whole.[6] *Gestalt Therapy: Excitement and Growth in the Human Personality* (1951) by Perls with Paul Goodman and Ralph Hefferline focuses on experience in the present moment and the immediate environmental and social contexts that cause self-regulating adjustments, shaping the overall experience. Its cultivation of an awareness of the immediate present and its noninterpretive approach appealed to Anna, who recoiled from the modern dance practices on the East Coast led by Martha Graham, whose style Anna considered "portraying not being."[7] Fritz Perls and his followers, working with Anna, contrived experiments that would lead to greater environmental, emotional, sensory, and bodily awareness, enabling one to experience situations more immediately, and thus more "authentically," through trained liberation from inhibitions, fears, and stereotypes that had been culturally and socially constructed in the past.

Paul Goodman, though not from the Bay Area, advanced Gestalt therapy to its fullest form through his contributions to the publication he coauthored. Simultaneous to his work on *Gestalt Therapy*, he published, with his architect brother Percival Goodman, the seminal text on city planning in postwar America, *Communitas: Means of Livelihood and Ways of Life* (1947). In the words of the counterculture historian Theodore Roszak, "The city emerges from the pages of *Communitas* not as a depersonalized amalgam of technicalities—real estate values, traffic and utilities control, zoning legalities, etc.—but rather as the arena of human drama: 'a choreography of society in motion and in rest.'"[8] Such a comprehensive view would have appealed to Larry Halprin and his choreographic attempts to enhance public life in the city.

In *The RSVP Cycles*, Halprin draws parallels between Gestalt psychology and the encompassing field of ecology, claiming they both "[deal] with relationships between things as much as with the things themselves. The two are in fact very related . . . , ecology dealing with the physical world and Gestalt psychology with the emotional world."[9] As Roszak continues in *The Making of a Counter Culture: Reflections on the Technocratic Society and Its Youthful Opposition* (1969), "Since Gestalt begins by postulating a primal unity which is spontaneously self-regulating, it must of necessity defend the universality of nature. Nature must emerge always as the all-embracing whole." This primal universality of nature is exactly what Halprin attempts to harness in his designed forms, to be addressed in the chapters following. Finally, according to Roszak, "We have lost touch with the self-regulation of a symbiotic system and have given over to a compulsive need to control, under pressure of which the organism freezes up and seems to become unutterably stupid. The major therapeutic technique of Gestalt, therefore, is an ingenious form of directed physical activity which aims at locating and thawing frozen organic energy."[10] Larry Halprin attempts to develop a similar therapeutic device by engaging immediate response to his finely tuned designed environments. By stimulating imagination, direct awareness, and a kind of primal spontaneity and impulse, he hopes to free city dwellers from the restraints ingrained by the conditioning of a regimented culture.

Environmental psychology also developed during this time, largely in response to the impact of urban renewal displacements and relocations. Lawrence Halprin & Associates included environmental psychologists, as well as other social scientists, in the firm's efforts to alleviate these impacts and reestablish a sense of environmental belonging. The studies of the urban planner Kevin Lynch that were synthesized in his book *The Image of the City* (1960) influenced the development of environmental psychology. Like Halprin, Lynch investigated aesthetic experience in the city, yet Lynch and his colleagues at MIT studied aesthetics and environmental perception through empirical research, attempting to establish codified principles for optimal urban form or "legibility." Like Anna, Larry relied on creative intuition rather than data collection and analysis and the formulation of ubiquitous standards.

With Donald Appleyard and John Myer, Lynch also developed a graphic language for the experience of movement in his book *The View from the Road* (1964). While the notational system is meant for driving at fast speeds on proliferating American highways to generate better design principles, Halprin simultaneously developed a movement notation system ("Motation"), which was most intended for the human body. Halprin's graphic "scores" were drawings intended to embody process and instigate change (Figure I.3), as represented by those he generated for Anna's performances of *The Five-Legged Stool* (1962) and *Parades and Changes* (1965), both included in *The RSVP Cycles* (Figure I.4).[11]

Larry Halprin proposed "Motation" as an alternative to traditional representational devices such as plans and elevations, which he considered too static. Motation was intended to be more than a descriptive recording device, as Halprin considers the function of Labanotation, the best-known notational system for dance choreography.[12] Instead, he developed it as a means through which a designer might use movement as a starting point to generate form. As he explains, "Since movement and the complex interrelations which it generates are an essential part of the life of a city, urban design should have the choice of starting from movement as the core—the essential element of the plan. Only after programming the movement and graphically expressing it should the environment—an envelope within

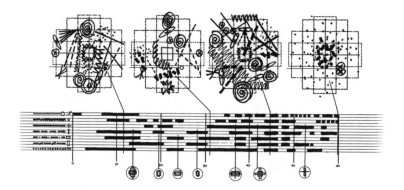

Figure I.3. Lawrence Halprin's graphic score for the Seattle Center Fountain, circa 1962. Published in Lawrence Halprin, *The RSVP Cycles*, 56. Lawrence Halprin Collection, The Architectural Archives, University of Pennsylvania.

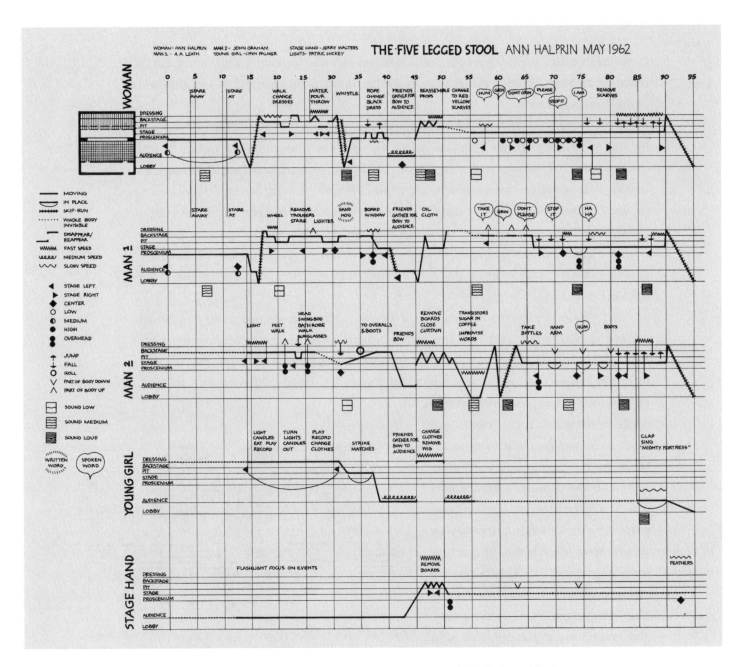

Figure I.4. Lawrence Halprin's graphic score for Anna Halprin's performance of *The Five-Legged Stool*, May 1962. Published in Lawrence Halprin, *The RSVP Cycles*, 34. Lawrence Halprin Collection, The Architectural Archives, University of Pennsylvania.

which movement takes place—be designed. The environment exists for the purpose of movement."[13] Though it seems simple, this idea—of programming (or choreographing) movement first and generating a graphic score with which to design a framework to catalyze or sustain such movement—is still not part of general design discourse. This is just one of Halprin's many ideas that practitioners today would benefit from revisiting.

British architect Philip Thiel also explored notational systems as an environmental design tool, particularly in his 1961 essay "A Sequence-Experience Notation" appearing in *Town Planning Review*. However, his work in this arena is primarily intended to provide a descriptive language rather than a generative one.[14] Even so, in recognizing the proliferation of research in movement perception within the field of environmental design, Thiel invited Halprin, Lynch, and others to create a direct comparison between methodologies by notating "the *same* sequence-environment."[15] Though Halprin eagerly accepted this invitation, the comparison unfortunately never occurred.

In Halprin's 1965 article "Motation," published in *Progressive Architecture* (and in *Impulse* dance magazine in 1966), he explains the original method. He uses a series of film-like "frames" to represent progression through space (Figure I.5). These frames present plans and perspectives in sequence in the horizontal and vertical tracks respectively.[16] Though he is critical of other approaches that privilege vision over the other senses, Motation also most relies on the primacy of sight, while providing smaller spaces for the symbolization of other sensory stimuli.

Though Halprin ultimately did not employ a rigorous Motation process in the designs for his own urban environments, he proposed it as a tool for design pedagogy and practice.[17] The notational approaches of Halprin and his contemporaries are technical; they require fluency in the language of symbols and most likely presented more of an obstacle to the intuitive or creative approaches Halprin inherently applied. The importance of Motation, however, is not its success or its degree of use but rather its implications of how Halprin attempted to use scored movement to (successfully and not) derive form. This is significant because such generative drawing practices have served as a point of reference for current landscape designers, such as James Corner as well as Anuradha

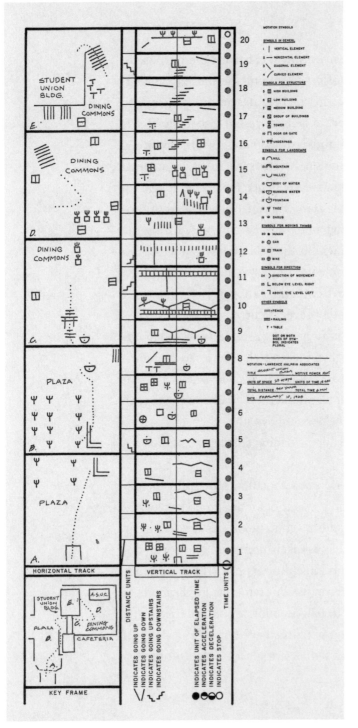

Figure I.5. Motation for Student Union Plaza, University of California, Berkeley, 1965. Published in Lawrence Halprin, "Motation," *Progressive Architecture* (1965). Lawrence Halprin Collection, The Architectural Archives, University of Pennsylvania.

Mathur and Dilip da Cunha, who situate representation—or the act of drawing—as integral to the inventive process rather than simply a means for visual communication.[18]

Larry Halprin's comprehensive environmental design approach may also be linked to the regional planning tradition, often attributed to the lineage composed of Patrick Geddes, Lewis Mumford, Benton MacKaye, and Ian McHarg. Interrelationships between dynamic social and biophysical processes were integral to the approaches of each of these individuals. Yet with the exclusion of Geddes, each largely dismissed the inherited city. In addition, though Halprin remained fiercely devoted to McHarg as a friend and colleague, McHarg and his followers were soon criticized for their design passivity. Halprin is a pivotal figure because he is impacted by this lineage emphasizing process and relationships, but he is also clearly a designer and not nearly as passive as he might admit and as the projects presented should reveal. He is thus a unique and overlooked example of a landscape architect who stitched the gap between ecological analysis and formal design at a time this divide was widening. Furthermore, his emphasis remained on the dynamic possibilities of the historic city and on the inevitability of their "disclimax" or disturbances, to which he responded through environmental adjustments meant to sustain enhanced urban experience.

Just as the social sciences rose in reaction to the dissociative effects of dramatic forces of modernization, environmentalism emerged as a reactive movement in the 1960s. Environmentalists of the decade embraced ecology as the "subversive science," as coined by Paul Sears (1964) and proliferated by Paul Shepard (1969). The biologist Rachel Carson's *Silent Spring* (1962) instigated the attack against the technologically engineered control of nature. Though Ian McHarg is rightfully considered the father of ecological planning, Halprin was intricately involved in the introduction of ecology into the practice of designing the environment. Yet while he highly regarded McHarg and his book *Design with Nature* (1969), Halprin's interest in ecology differed significantly.

According to Roszak in *Where the Wasteland Ends: Politics and Transcendence in Postindustrial Society* (1972):

> Ecology has been called "the subversive science"—and with good reason. Its sensibility—wholistic, receptive . . . deeply grounded in aesthetic intuition—is a radical deviation from traditional science. Ecology does not systematize by mathematical generalization or materialist reductionism, but by the almost sensuous intuiting of natural harmonies on the largest scale. Its patterns are not those of numbers, but of unity in process . . . Ecology is the closest our science has yet come to an integrative wisdom. It . . . deserves to become the *basic* science of the future.

Though Roszak welcomes McHarg's use of ecology in planning, he finds fault in McHarg's thesis: "Where else can we turn for an accurate model of the world and ourselves but to science?" Roszak claims that a positivist analysis perpetuates the objectification of nature, noting that "the question remains open: which will ecology be, the last of the old sciences or the first of the new?"[19] Though ecological study has been primarily practiced as a mechanistic science in order to sustain credibility, Halprin's embrace of ecology was much closer to Roszak's interest in its ideal use. Halprin, whose academic background was in the plant sciences followed by the collaborative artistic training under Bauhaus instructors who had emigrated to Harvard, welcomed the comprehensive holism of ecology versus the fragmentation of expertise practiced in the traditional sciences.

McHarg's rational method, on the other hand, was deterministic, following what is referred to as the "equilibrium paradigm" or ecosystem ecology. In this paradigm, according to the biologist Robert Cook, "the healthy ecosystem is an integrated, efficiently functioning entity that can be defined, described, and measured quantitatively." Cook defines the four elements of the "equilibrium paradigm" as follows:

> First, ecological systems in their natural state are closed, self-regulating systems ... Second, the system in its most mature state is in a condition of balance or equilibrium ... Third, when the system is disturbed by outside forces and degraded to an earlier developmental, less efficient state, an ecological process known as succession changes the system through a sequence of predictable stages to restore the original conditions and return the system to an equilibrium condition ... Finally, the activities of humans are not part of the natural world and are in conflict with its operation.[20]

McHarg adopted this philosophy. He focused on the closed predictable behavior of the "biosphere" acting as a single "superorganism." Yet Halprin preempted an evolutionary shift in the field that began to acknowledge the dynamic nature of communities and ecosystems (Figure I.6). According to Cook, "These systems are no longer seen

Figure I.6. Lawrence Halprin's Sea Ranch "Ecoscore," 1960s. Lawrence Halprin Collection, The Architectural Archives, University of Pennsylvania.

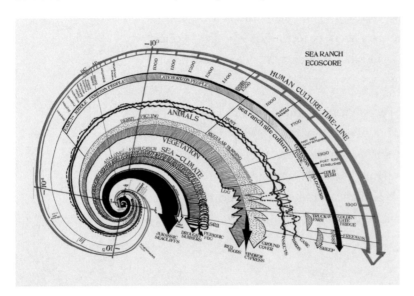

as closed, self-regulating entities . . . Disturbance is a frequent, intrinsic characteristic of ecosystems . . . and species exhibit a wide range of adaptations to disturbance." By the 1980s, ecologists began to readily accept the significant role that chance played in the way the natural world works, ultimately depending more on probability than on determinism.[21] Halprin, who studied natural processes in the academy and in the field, for which he obsessively observed his surroundings through repeated sketching, recognized that nature did not necessarily behave in a way that was consistent with the ideal model and predictions of the old paradigm. He also found the vocabulary of disturbance and disclimax applicable to the dramatically shifting urban landscape.

Environmental, social, political, and artistic activism coalesced during the 1960s, linked by a public insistence on participation. The Bay Area, and Berkeley in particular, became a center for institutional subversions and student protests. On Halprin-designed Sproul Plaza, students at the University of California at Berkeley initiated the Free Speech Movement, demanding the right to public gathering and political organization. Nationally, the struggle for civil rights, women's liberation, the protest of the war in Vietnam, and reaction to urban renewal policies aggressively challenged the long-established power structure that dictated how one was to perform in society.

Though clearly interested in social reform, Anna Halprin's work was not fundamentally driven by politics but by enhancing bodily experience of the environment and enacting the rituals of the everyday with deeper perceptual awareness. Performances of ordinary activities, such as eating lunch (*Lunch,* 1968) and taking a bath (*The Bath,* 1966), were explored separate from the more self-consciously political Fluxus "events" on the East Coast that engaged the public in simple performances of mundane activities as a means of frustrating the high culture of academic and market-driven art.

Beginning in the late 1960s, however, Anna took dance and performance into the streets. In 1968, the San Francisco Dancers' Workshop performed the *Blank Placard Dance* on Market Street as a procession through the city, where the performers marched holding blank signs as a "ritual" based on street demonstrations, which was symbolic of protest "but without any specific cause."[22] Her street dances climaxed in *Citydance* (1976–77). For *Citydance*, the San Francisco Dancers' Workshop presented "A City Score," for which the poster announcement advertised: "Create a Dance & Dance It Through San Francisco." The event, free and open to the public, was presented in two parts: the first, in which Larry would guide the participants on how to create their own city score; and the second, a meeting on Twin Peaks at sunrise to start the performance of the score, which ended at the Halprin-designed Plaza at the Embarcadero.

In Roszak's *The Making of a Counter Culture,* he distinguishes between the two currents of the countercultural movement: one composed of the Beats and hippies, or Beat–hip bohemianism, whose "trip" is inward toward deeper levels of self-examination; and the other of the New Left student political activists, aimed at the restructuring of public life. What relates and allies these two styles, however different they may seem, is their common response to estrangement caused by the technocracy as defined by Roszak. Both ends of the countercultural spectrum, therefore, were seeking a social liberation from the mechanical order through participatory democracy (New Left) and participatory culture (Beat–hip bohemians).

The subject of this analysis, choreographing a participatory environmental experience through the Halprins' creative process, is entirely related to the dissolution of the alienating separations established by a mechanistic culture. The Halprins were more than a generation older than the "youthful opposition" and worked only in parallel to some of its pursuits. Yet they sought to reestablish an organic wholeness between life, art, politics, philosophy, and so on. To reconstruct this interconnected life, and to dissolve the power structure that infused a sense of deep alienation into overall society, Larry employed both strategies of the counterculture by exploring the inward potential of the unconscious, demonstrated by his design interest in "archetypal forms" in the 1960s (see part 1, "Built Works"), as well as the outward possibilities of public statement and participation, demonstrated by his Take Part Process of the 1970s (see part 2 "Workshops"). Yet while Anna began to respond directly to causes for political reform, Larry was most consistently driven by enhancing the quality of human inhabitation.

The virgin soils of the California landscape allowed the Halprins to return to what they considered "primordial origins," to harness the inherent honesty of man and his relationship with nature and other humans without the rationality and control of technocratic society. Frustrated with all that they had to overcome, Larry Halprin claimed that

> it is not art but product that we [society] are supporting. It is a clear expression of an industrialized and specialized society. It is the same attitude sold to us daily that the essential elements of our lives are manufactured for us *by someone else for our use. . . .* We are users, not makers! . . . We have been living in a society which has become increasingly insulated from sources . . . from, if you wish, reality. Reality, that is, if you accept that reality involves personal experience . . . Not second hand. Second hand-ism afflicts us.[23]

In referring to Dewey's distinction between artistic methods, the Halprins clearly allied themselves with the "esthetic" (or what they call "sensuous") rather the "intellectual" approach, which they associated with East Coast art and culture.[24] To both of the Halprins, the isolation of the arts from everyday life was exactly what their respective professional work attempted to counteract. The (devolved) Modernist notion of art had become based on "no touching, no trespassing. The museum as temple, the artist as prophet, the work as relic and cult object, the halo restored," in the words of the cultural historian Andreas Huyssen.[25] The Halprins, like John Dewey, defined the problem as "that of recovering continuity of esthetic experience with normal processes of living."[26]

Despite Anna's and Larry's common aims, the following chapters will reveal Larry's consistent ambivalence regarding choreographic authority. Though he offhandedly claims in *The RSVP Cycles,* "I do not feel that any score is too open," he recognizes situations that require varying levels of control (Figure I.7). He seemed most comfortable not with

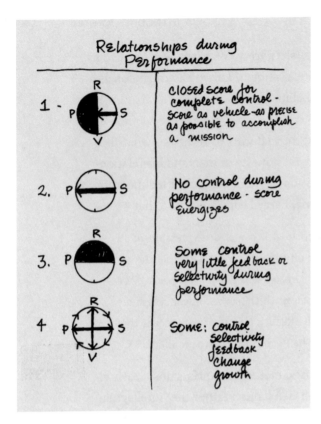

Figure I.7. Degrees of openness of the score.
Published in Lawrence Halprin, *The RSVP Cycles*, 192.
Lawrence Halprin Collection, The Architectural Archives,
University of Pennsylvania.

complete control or utter openness to chance or singularities of response, but with providing an opportunity for choice. In fact, he defines creativity in his book *Cities* (1963) as "freedom of choice." Choice (rather than chance) became a simultaneous theme in Anna's work, which will be addressed in subsequent chapters. This is not to say that Larry never designed spaces that left room for open improvisation or embodied the kind of *opera aperta* or "open work" that Umberto Eco defined in his 1962 book.[27] In some of his most successful built works, in fact, Halprin deployed number two in the diagram illustrated as Figure I.7, such as in his open space sequence for Portland, Oregon (see chapter 3).

In the following chapters, Larry Halprin's dominant theories on scoring, particularly as expressed in *The RSVP Cycles* and in *Taking Part: A Workshop Approach to Collective Creativity* (1974), are interpreted through the critical presentation of a number of his projects and thus reveal how successful he was at executing his stated objectives. The project studies show contradictions and inconsistencies caused primarily by his inability to resolve the degree of choreographic authority or control over the work.

PLAN OF THE BOOK

The first chapter, on "creative origins," presents a selective biography of Halprin by assessing the early life and career experiences that influenced the development of his creative process. Those experiences include his work on a kibbutz, his studies in horticulture, his work with Bauhaus émigrés at Harvard's Graduate School of Design, the Halprins' move west, Larry's work in the private garden initially under Thomas Church, and the incorporation of his office Lawrence Halprin & Associates in 1960. Larry's posthumously published autobiography, *A Life Spent Changing Places* (2011), offers a more comprehensive (and less critical) overview of his life, whereas chapter 1 is intended to focus on those aspects of his life that may have contributed to his unique approach at designing for the changing American city.

Chapters 2 through 5 are split into two parts, "Built Work" and "Workshops," as a way of clarifying and distinguishing Halprin's two applications of choreographic "scores" or the two ways he impacted the shape and the shaping of the American city. Part 1, "Built Work," assesses the process behind the most pivotal projects constructed by Lawrence Halprin & Associates in cities across the nation. Halprin designed forms in space to act as scoring devices that would guide movement. In order for his designs to have the communicative power to resonate throughout the culturally diverse urban public, he spent much of his career searching for "archetypal images," or Resources (R) fundamental to all urban inhabitants, which he discovered in human ritual and nature. Part 1 is organized accordingly. Chapter 2 on "ritual frameworks" introduces Anna's investigation of ritual by setting it in contrast to experiments in chance performed by Merce Cunningham and John Cage, and then discusses Larry's book *Cities* as a catalogue of elements that create the framework for everyday and ceremonial urban rituals. This assessment of *Cities* is situated in relationship to his built work intended to facilitate and choreograph such rituals, including shopping malls and main streets. "Main Street" as infrastructure for civic procession transitions into an analysis of the design for Heritage Park Plaza (Fort Worth) as a processional space that informs Halprin's proposal for the FDR Memorial in Washington, D.C.

To Halprin, the Sierra Nevada represented a primordial environment to which all humans have a fundamental connection or an inescapably primal response. Evidence of its powerful natural processes became the foundation and inspiration for all his land-shaping endeavors. Chapter 3 on nature as "archetypal precedent" presents Halprin's insistence on humans' common origin in nature to reorient people to their environment and reduce the increasing barriers between humans and the natural world. The pioneering open space sequence in Portland, Oregon, is the primary case study in this chapter, as it represents one of the best examples of his choreographic approach. Seattle Freeway Park serves as a comparative study of a later attempt to fulfill similar ideals.

Using Manhattan Square Park (Rochester, New York) as the condensation of many of Halprin's ideas on choreography, choice, and the transmutation of nature, the chapter culminates with a critical synthesis of the inconsistencies between his theory and practice, the most recognizable of which is Halprin's inability to resolve the issue of flexibility. Flexibility to Halprin implies both ability to receive and to react to participatory input over time, as well as to withstand cultural change and remain culturally relevant. Considering the projects' adaptability to people's evolving needs and tastes or the openness of Halprin's choreography to improvisation or indeterminate input is important, not only because he was so vocal about its embodiment in his work but also because so many of the designs that supposedly embody these ideas are being blamed today for being too inflexible, thus justifying their demolition.

Part 2, "Workshops," focuses on the Take Part Process, which Halprin "scored" to engage community participation in urban design. "Taking Part" was developed by Lawrence Halprin & Associates to counteract the top-down approach to urban renewal, which led to the homogenization of urban space and the psychological alienation of the subjugated communities. Building on performance theories, scores were most fundamental to the Take Part Process, since they served as frameworks for action. Scores for the Take Part workshop activities offered "temporal–situational guidelines" for a series of cumulative experiences that were deliberately organized in a sequential and progressive manner to build up a mutual foundation for the diversity of participants. Because participants were chosen as a representative cross-section of a community, many did not share a common background. Therefore, the activities scored for the two- to three-day workshops were intended to foster a shared experience from which a group could develop a common language and thus move forward in a collective way. Using Gestalt techniques and performance practices, scored activities emphasized environmental awareness and perception.

Once a "consensus plan" was collaboratively achieved, if Halprin was also commissioned to implement the findings, he would again assume the role of the designer and create a choreographic form that attempted to incorporate community input.

Chapter 4 places the Take Part Process in the context of other participatory planning methods, both government sanctioned and grassroots. In addition, it situates the workshop process in the trajectory of Halprin's work by examining those fundamental projects that led to the ultimate formulation of Taking Part. These projects include the collaborative workshops Larry and Anna called "Experiments in Environment," as well as the firm's 1968 report titled *New York, New York: A Study of the Quality, Character, and Meaning of Open Space in Urban Design,* which stresses citizen participation and begins to develop a methodology.

Chapter 5, "Facilitation and/or Manipulation," considers Taking Part in Fort Worth (Texas), Everett (Washington), Charlottesville (Virginia), and Cleveland (Ohio). Despite claims that the process was open-ended, Halprin and his firm clearly had preconceived objectives, yet they guided the participants to reach these conclusions themselves. While this might seem counter to the principles of participation, the firm often succeeded in reshaping shortsighted attitudes toward the city that diminished its quality of experience. The chapter ends with an assessment of what might be learned from this tension between facilitation and manipulation, particularly as it relates to widespread debates on participatory planning ongoing today.

The Conclusion summarizes the broad arguments of the book and projects them forward. The concluding analysis demonstrates, in particular, how Halprin's open choreographic method (in ideal application) anticipated the theories that currently drive the practice of landscape architecture and how those aspects of his process that have long been overlooked might enrich a contemporary approach to designing the city. With the powerful forces of urbanization continuing to shape globalizing cities throughout the world, reflecting on a process that attempts to mitigate some of the disorienting effects and to reinstate a robust public life becomes especially urgent.

1. THE CREATIVE ORIGINS OF LARRY AND ANNA HALPRIN

LAWRENCE HALPRIN was born July 1, 1916, and grew up in Brooklyn, New York. The social concerns that distinguish his career were founded on family values. His mother, Rose Luria Halprin, worked with the Women's Zionist Organization of America, Hadassah, and served as its president for multiple terms beginning in 1932. Her tireless activism would shape Halprin's childhood experience and inform his lifelong pursuits. His father, Samuel W. Halprin, initially owned a wholesale women's clothing business, but later became president of a scientific instruments export firm that traded between the United States and what was then the struggling Jewish population in Palestine. Before Samuel lost his fortune in the 1929 stock market crash, his financial success enabled him to take his family on a year-long trip to Europe and the Middle East. Larry's maternal uncle, Sydney Luria, who was invited to accompany the family to keep Larry and his younger sister up to date with their studies, dispensed of traditional lesson plans and took them outside to explore their surroundings in France, Italy, Egypt, and finally Palestine where they stayed for four months. According to Luria, he gave a pad and gouache to

Larry, who immediately began drawing and painting everything he saw.[1] The family traveled throughout Palestine, yet Halprin recalls most vividly their house on the outskirts of Jerusalem fronted by a wheat field through which camels would be led on the path from the desert to the city. This "archetypal" imagery or "parade of fantasies" moving past his window was "like stepping back into . . . Biblical times" for Halprin, whose profound awareness and appreciation of the past consistently impacted his approach to designing for the present.[2]

In the summer of 1933, Halprin returned to Palestine to live until 1935. About this experience, Halprin recalled, "I was going back to a place that I loved. I was looking for adventure. I worked in the building trade; I worked in gardens; I worked in a factory extracting potash from the Dead Sea. I worked in orange groves." He also helped to found what became Kibbutz Ein Hashofet, near Haifa, where he lived for several months.[3] While immersed in the kibbutz movement, he participated in the land's transformation from barren and austere to microclimates more habitable and productive for human occupation. Though this agricultural setting is where, as many have noted, Halprin's connection to the land originated, it was also the ideals of the kibbutz that had significant impact on his interest in the productive nature of what he and Anna called "collective creativity." Prior to his kibbutz experience Halprin had considered becoming a painter, yet later recalled, "I thought that the most relevant thing to do was not to be a painter but somehow to get into something which had some meaning for the development of the country . . . With that as an idea I went to Cornell to study agriculture in a social context."[4]

Halprin returned to the United States to begin pursuing his B.S. in plant sciences at Cornell University School of Agriculture, and he spent his summers working on farms in the Midwest and New England. His research was most focused on how plants adapted to shifting natural environments; concepts derived from this experience no doubt informed his lifelong passion for understanding not just plants' adaptability but the biological, psychological, and social response of humans to different environmental conditions. Outside of academics, while at Cornell Halprin also became involved in social reform and labor organizing. He enthusiastically recognized parallels between the social aspirations of the kibbutz and New Deal programs in the United States.[5] Just as he was finishing his degree in 1939, a professor informed him that a plant researcher at the University of Wisconsin needed help in work related to Halprin's studies. Thus the fall after he graduated from Cornell, postponing his return to the kibbutz because the war had begun, Halprin set out for the Midwest, apparently ready to pursue a Ph.D. in plant physiology. He graduated, however, in 1941 with an M.S. in horticulture, completing a thesis on photoperiod (the optimum length of daylight hours needed for normal plant growth) and its effect on flowering plants. At both Cornell and Wisconsin, Halprin chose an assortment of courses considered unique at the time, including botany, geology, and geography. "I studied what amounted to ecology, but of course no one called it that," Halprin explained in a 1988 interview.[6]

It was in Madison, Wisconsin, that Larry Halprin met Ann Schuman. In 1938, Anna, as she was later called, had moved from a middle-class Chicago suburb to the University of Wisconsin, the first university to offer a dance degree program, which was led by the pioneering dance educator Margaret H'Doubler. In 1924, the university had established one of the nation's first Hillel Foundations, the Jewish organization that provided college students opportunities for gathering to worship, socialize, and partake in cultural and political activities. Anna was extremely active in the university's Hillel, particularly as a leader of its dance group. During her sophomore year, she met Larry after one of her performances at the Hillel. The two were married by September 1940, initiating a lifelong creative collaboration.

Two more events in 1940 had significant impact on Larry Halprin's future career and creative process. First was a visit, inspired by Anna's suggestion, to Frank Lloyd Wright's Taliesin in Spring Green, about thirty miles from Madison. Larry was immediately impressed with the Taliesin Fellowship program, a residential scholarship where students of design participated fully in sustaining the six-hundred-acre estate in a collective existence that must have reminded him of life on the kibbutz. This trip inspired him to return home and immediately find the section on architecture in the campus library, where he discovered a small subsection labeled landscape architecture. A book by the landscape architect Christopher Tunnard, *Gardens in the Modern Landscape* (1938), caught Larry Halprin's attention and imagination, affecting him like a "bolt of lightning," as he found within it his passionate interests in art, science, and human settlement, all "brilliantly interrelated."[7] In the book he would have read passages such as:

> In a sick and suffering world . . . we have come to realize that the earthly paradise is unobtainable without the planner of garden and landscape. Society cannot afford to overlook his power to contribute to the life of the community. In his own medium he dispenses the two chief anodynes of life—art and play—without which we perish as surely as if we lack bread. That medium, the landscape, has taken on a new meaning which he alone, with his own special art and knowledge, can make especially clear to us. Let us give him the opportunity for creation.[8]

Though Halprin had been previously unfamiliar with the existence of such a professional field, he explains,

> By the time I had finished reading I had decided to become whatever it was that the author of this book was, in order to devote myself to all those things he spoke of in his book: the art of gardens, the aesthetics of design in the broader landscape and perhaps, most importantly, how social conditions could become an integral factor in design (how land and people's lives in communities were related and how you could enhance and improve people's lives in communities through design).[9]

He immediately sought out the only landscape architecture course on campus, which was in the horticulture department at the time. Apparently his instructor was so impressed with Halprin's passionate dedication and intuitive understanding that the department successfully sought a scholarship for him to attend Harvard's Graduate School of Design, where Tunnard was a professor.[10]

Christopher Tunnard, a Canadian who wrote *Gardens in the Modern Landscape* while living in London, was committed to linking social responsibility and design. He joined the London-based Modern Architectural Research Group (MARS Group), which focused on social problem-solving by searching for new ways to structure the industrialized city to enhance livability. He was responsible for building a series of gardens in 1930s England, for which he collaborated with the architects Serge Chermayeff and Raymond McGrath who were strongly influenced by European Modernism. *Gardens in the Modern Landscape* proposed an alternative to what Tunnard considered the continued inheritance of the nineteenth-century debasement of earlier landscape traditions. His manifesto required modern gardens and the public landscape be: *functional*, evoking the words of Adolf Loos and Le Corbusier to declare that beauty is derived from utility, not ornament, sentimental expressionism, or intellectual classicism; *empathic* to site and the tactile and rhythmic qualities of nature while using "modern" materials, such as concrete, steel, and glass; and *artistic*, looking to experiments in sculpture and painting to generate new forms expressive of the modern age. The social project that defines Tunnard's early career was his 1939 All-Europe House, designed in collaboration with architect Elizabeth Denby, also a member of the MARS Group, as an offshoot study to the MARS plan for the growth of London. The scheme called for the spatial reduction of rear gardens that typically existed between two rows of houses to allow room for a communal strip of land to which everyone had access and which was maintained cooperatively by the residents.[11] In 1939, Tunnard accepted Gropius's invitation to teach at Harvard's Graduate School of Design. Tunnard was drafted into the Canadian army in 1943, during Halprin's first year at Harvard, so the two had only a limited chance to work together. When Tunnard returned to the United States in 1945 he joined the faculty of Yale University's city planning program, thereby expanding his focus well beyond the garden and subsequently largely dropping from the discourse of landscape architecture, at least until recently.[12]

Despite limited contact with Tunnard, Halprin's time at Harvard impacted every aspect of his subsequent sixty-year career. Though Halprin arrived just after Garrett Eckbo, Dan Kiley, and James Rose had completed their studies in the mid-1930s, these designers had made strides in the reframing of landscape architecture as an agent for social change.[13] During the late 1930s, scores of artists fled Europe for the United States, including many designers and architects from the Bauhaus, which the Nazis had closed in 1933. László Moholy-Nagy, Ludwig Mies van der Rohe, Marcel Breuer, Lyonel Feininger, Herbert Bayer, and Walter Gropius, the founder and director of the Bauhaus from 1919 to 1928, were among those who arrived on American soil during this time. In 1937, Gropius accepted Dean Joseph Hudnut's invitation to chair Harvard's Department of Architecture, yet his impact spread well beyond architecture into the other departments of the Graduate School of Design (GSD). After Tunnard's departure, Halprin sought feedback predominantly from Gropius and Breuer, while lectures by Moholy-Nagy, occasionally visiting from the Illinois Institute of Technology, additionally impacted his studies.

Gropius's pedagogic goal was to unify the fine and practical arts to structure positive social change. He actively encouraged collaboration between students in architecture, city planning, and landscape architecture. All students matriculating at the Graduate School of Design were required to take a general design course modeled after those taught at the Bauhaus. About this course, Halprin reflected, "The Bauhaus always started with a general course in design . . . and it wasn't the history of it, it was doing it . . . And it took me a great leap to the point where I understood the relationship of all the arts together. It was like somebody had opened a curtain and there was this great world of fantasy in front of me, with dancers and painters and set designers and music."[14]

The opening of this curtain would have permanent impact on Halprin, indicated by both his comprehensive approach to environmental design and his Take Part community workshops that would integrate performance, drawing, and choreographed movement. He adamantly defends the Bauhaus pedagogy as "nothing to do with the form of things" but instead about the collaborative process that abolished unproductive distinctions between the arts and between design and craft.[15] Reminiscent of the kibbutz, Halprin recognized at Harvard the power of a collective approach.

Though critics of the International Style or European Modernism typically attack the Bauhaus for proliferating an austere formal language, Halprin correctly asserts that the school (originally) emphasized *form* much less than a creative *method* based on the synthesis of the arts. However, this comprehensive approach might be considered as much about control as it was about collaboration. Gropius and his followers took a totalizing approach, seeking authorship over all aspects of the constructed environment in encompassing architectural schemes. An emphasis on flexibility or adaptability represented attempts to anticipate all possible desired arrangements, such as is exemplified by Gropius's Total Theater (1927) and its three stage configurations.[16] It is worth noting that although Halprin defends the Bauhaus from critics of what became a codified notion of Modernism, he also criticizes the idea of artist–author imposing a totalizing view. Yet the potential of these adaptive designs must have appealed to Halprin, since they provided choice but did not require that he relinquish control. This ambiguous stance remains unresolved in almost all of Halprin's design and theory as he struggled to loosen control and invite open-ended response.

Gropius was familiar with the integration of performance and design from his days at the Bauhaus in Weimar in 1922 when Oskar Schlemmer choreographed *The Triadic Ballet* as a study of the relationships of forms in motion. Appealing to Anna, the performance had no narrative or dialogue. However, Schlemmer's dancers "[symbolized] eternal types of human character and their different moods," in Gropius's words.[17] His costumes simplified the dancers' forms into elemental shapes and limited their gestures to a predictable range or geometry of movement. In other words, though playful in essence Schlemmer was interested in objective standardization, rather than subjective experience, and in imposing control. Despite Larry Halprin's criticism of a rationalist approach that disregarded human experience, Schlemmer's reductionist techniques might be compared to Halprin's search for "primordial" or "archetypal" expression.

The Theater of the Bauhaus, a book edited by Gropius, originally published in 1924–25 and translated into English in 1961, includes an essay by Schlemmer on his approach, as well as one by Moholy-Nagy titled "Theater, Circus, Variety," which is particularly interesting to consider through the lens of the Halprins' development. In the essay Moholy-Nagy includes notational scores and focuses on the future of the theater as "The Theater of Totality," embodying a "Gestaltung" or "organism" made up of the "multifarious complexities of light, space, plane, form, motion, sound, man . . . [and] all the possibilities for varying and combining these elements."[18] Again, this reflects a kind of controlled flex-ibility—the type of score with which Larry became most comfortable (as will be more thoroughly addressed at the end of chapter 3). Though Moholy-Nagy was very much interested in the extremist "elimination of the human actor in favor of a theater of total mechanization,"[19] it is in this essay that he also calls for the dissolved separation between stage and spectator, which he considers "too obviously divided into active and passive, to be able to produce creative relationships and reciprocal tensions." He continues by not-ing, "It is time to produce a kind of stage activity which will no longer permit the masses to be silent spectators, which . . . will let them *take hold and participate*—actually allow them to fuse with the action on the stage at the peak of cathartic ecstasy."[20] Building on the legacy of the European avant-garde, a passionate desire for such participation likewise drove Larry and Anna's creative careers.

Halprin's experience at the GSD seems to have laid the foundation for his lifelong experiments in the choreography of dynamic movement. Johannes Itten had introduced the preliminary design course at the Bauhaus in 1921 with actual gymnastic exercises that heightened awareness of the kinesthetic sense. Paul Klee, who taught "Elemental Design Theory" as a supplement to this preliminary course, focused his career on the intersec-tion of music and the visual arts with particular emphasis on rhythm and notation or the visual representation of temporal processes. Though Klee died in 1940, never making it to Harvard, his impact on the direction of the GSD pedagogy, as well as Halprin's pur-suits, is clear. Klee's book *Das Bildnerische Denken (The Thinking Eye)*, published in 1956 and translated in 1961, stresses creative process over product ("Do not think of form but formation"), emphasizing Gestalt as the process of *developing* form versus form itself, which he defines as "nature morte."[21] Klee considers the dynamic act of walking through the landscape and how to represent the shifting perspective of relational movement, par-ticularly in his "Creative Credo," used in his early teaching at the Bauhaus and origi-nally published in 1920. Many of Halprin's early drawings for garden designs resemble illustrations in this book with their "multi-dimensional simultaneity of projection" (plan, elevation, and movement notation specifically). Klee's work also clearly informed Halprin's development of Motation, and one of his notational drawings thus appears in *The RSVP Cycles*.[22] In addition, in 1947 Moholy-Nagy published his book *Vision in Motion* on "space–time" and seeing while moving. These individuals and their collective impact, with Gropius leading the group in social consciousness and design for enhanced human inhabitation, shaped Larry Halprin's career.

Anna Halprin participated in Larry's education at Harvard, attending public lectures and social gatherings and sitting in on classes, including the general design seminar, which inspired her initial investigations in the spatial dimension of choreography. As an educator herself by this time, teaching dance simultaneously at an elite private high school in Cambridge and at the South End Settlement House in a low-income area of Boston, she absorbed the Bauhaus creative and social ideals into her own pedagogy.

In 1943, Anna began offering dance classes to architecture and design students two nights a week in a studio she rented. Gropius was apparently supportive of these classes, which explored how different spatial arrangements affected one's physical and emotional response. The classes were structured as "problem-solving situations" for which Anna asked the architects to use the materials of the room, such as chairs and tables, to "build an environment." She then asked them to "move" in the environments they constructed. About the course, Anna explained to her biographer Janice Ross:

> We would continuously be working with creating these temporary environments and then moving in them. Because as architects, if you are building a house or a building, how is this going to affect the people living in it? . . . What is the difference in feeling between designing something that goes around in one way or another? What does a curve feel like to experience in your body as opposed to an angle? So I translated what I understood about space into movement for the architects and into conscious use of space for the dancers.[23]

Sibyl Moholy-Nagy, László's wife, contributed to the 1951 issue of *Impulse*, the annual dance magazine founded in 1948 by Anna and the students and faculty of the Halprin-Lathrop (Welland Lathrop) dance studio. In her article, "Modern Art and Modern Dance," she heralds the European avant-garde's success at fusing "All man's creative potentialities": painting and sculpture, as well as "architecture, photography, applied design, music, dance, poetry, and dramatics." She continues to lament the "cultural lag" in America in recognizing the power of this "all-embracing goal." In the essay, Moholy-Nagy celebrates the potential of the dancer as an "integrator" who achieves "a four-dimensional interplay of volume in space moving through time," and, she continues, the potential of dance to discover and represent basic human emotions that "cannot be mechanized."[24]

I have included this extensive section on the Bauhaus influence on the GSD because both Larry and Anna Halprin were deeply impacted by this formative exposure. The goals of the Bauhaus to eliminate art elitism and to dissolve the distinctions between art and the craft of necessities of everyday life permanently influenced the Halprins, as did its culture of collaboration and its emphasis on process and social participation. Yet, as a consequence, Larry Halprin additionally inherited the contradictions and inconsistencies latent in Gropius's theory and pedagogy.

In *The Scope of Total Architecture* (1962), a publication of Gropius's articles and lectures from 1937 to 1952, Gropius never resolves what he sets forth as his main agenda: to reconcile the "two opposites" of "individual variety and a common denominator for all." Instead, he remains devoted to creating "cultural standards" from a "selective process of seeking out the essential and the typical."[25] Halprin, in most ways, perpetuated this desire to find a "common denominator of regional expression" or a "common language of visual communication" (the latter in Gropius's words),[26] as will be particularly exemplified by his study of "archetypes" and by attempts by the Take Part Process to achieve "consensus." Especially in the case of Taking Part, Halprin adopts Gropius's belief that "only the collaboration of many can succeed in finding solutions which transcend the individual aspect—which will retain their validity for many years to come."[27]

Gropius is quite critical of the overspecialization of "our scientific age," calling for "participation in the arts as an essential counterpart of science in order to stop its atomistic effect on us."[28] Yet the rational objective approach he consistently endorsed was derived from the scientific method. The struggle is thus one of objective standardization versus subjective experience. To resolve this tension, Halprin used an "archetypal" formal vocabulary to provoke response yet did not anticipate or script what that response might be. Yet this formative moment in Halprin's life is where so much of his ongoing struggle between the open and closed score originates. Gropius fleetingly states a possibility that Halprin seems to ultimately accept: "Cultural standards . . . far from producing dull uniformity, should give many individuals a chance to contribute their own individual variation of a common theme."[29]

Halprin's training in landscape architecture began when the war was well underway in Europe. His instructors had strong residual ties to friends, families, and colleagues who were still suffering abroad under the threat of Nazi oppression and violence. The gravity of this global condition shaped the direction of the Harvard design curriculum that focused mainly on large-scale social problems, such as housing for war-effort workers and reconstruction. Halprin accelerated his degree so that he could enlist in the U.S. Navy in December 1943, and in March 1944 he was sent to the Central Pacific aboard the flagship destroyer USS *Morris VII*. He served as a Lieutenant Junior Grade, applying his technical skills in architecture and landscape to work predominantly on navigational systems. In April 1945, when his ship was cut in half by a kamikaze carrying a torpedo just before the invasion of Okinawa, Halprin was sent to San Francisco on survivor's leave.

During Larry Halprin's last year at Harvard, William Wurster, who had become one of the premier "Bay Region" architects, and his wife, Catherine Bauer Wurster, the social planner and activist whose writings included the book *Modern Housing* (1934), arrived in Cambridge. Bill Wurster had been appointed Dean of the School of Architecture at the Massachusetts Institute of Technology (MIT) and the Halprins and Wursters quickly became close friends. According to Larry, the Wursters had lent him and Anna their apartment on Telegraph Hill in 1944 when he was waiting to join his ship. He later returned to the city on survivor's leave, joined Anna in New York briefly, was sent to Hawaii for a few additional weeks of naval duty, and then returned yet again to San Francisco. It was at this moment in 1945 that William Wurster asked his office, which was still active during his tenure at MIT, to intercept Halprin and invite him to the firm headquarters. When Halprin arrived he was offered a job, but was additionally directed, at the request of Wurster, to the landscape architecture office of Thomas Dolliver Church who worked in the same building. As Halprin recalls, when Church also offered him a position, he had to make the life-defining decision whether to be an architect or a landscape architect.[30]

Accepting either job meant that Anna had to make some significant career changes. While Larry was at war, she had been in New York living with his parents and performing as a dancer in the Broadway show *Sing Out, Sweet Land*, choreographed by one of her childhood heroines, Doris Humphrey (with Charles Weidman). Though she was initially hesitant to leave New York City, the nucleus of modern dance, she was soon writing to her college friend,

> Now I'm glad I'm going to California—I want to be left alone, live a normal resourceful life with a connection to the soil and to the common pulse of ordinary people. I'm not interested in acclaim—I'm only interested in creating out of the soil and the people a healthy fresh dance that is alive and vital. I'm getting so sick and tired of New York dance—it's neurotic, eccentric and in many cases stale and in most cases uninspired . . . New York itself breeds a warped kind of dance.[31]

Anna, in her abandonment of the East Coast and the "Graham style," which she claimed had "become very much a conformity," was able to harness the "new territory of immediacy" offered by the West Coast.[32] As recognized by Ross, though Anna expressed relief to escape the rational and contrived intellectualism of modern dance in New York, her willingness to move to San Francisco must have also been motivated by the emergence of two dance pioneers out of California—Isadora Duncan and Martha Graham (despite Anna's frustration with Graham's ubiquitous influence). Isadora Duncan, though she never gained great acclaim in the United States, consistently declared the powerful impact of the California landscape on her approach to movement, which was based on improvisation, emotion, and the natural motion and rhythms of the human body. She celebrated the forces of gravity in reaction to the rigid constraints of posture and form imposed by classical ballet. In her autobiography, she claimed, "I bring you the dance. I bring you the idea that is going to revolutionise our entire epoch. Where have I discovered it? By the Pacific Ocean, by the waving pine-forests of Sierra Nevada. I have seen the ideal figure of youthful America dancing over the top of the Rockies."[33]

Duncan's attribution of the freedom of her movement to the openness, power, and virgin quality of the California landscape is very much parallel to Anna's recognition of the transformative potential of this environment to recapture a fundamental or "authentic" quality of movement. Larry responded to these same opportunities provided by this new western frontier. The immediacy of the dramatic terrain—mountains, forest, and ocean—present from all sides, and a climate that offered opportunities for year-round living, working, and playing in the outdoors, convinced him to settle in the Bay Area. The vast scale of the landscape, in sharp contrast to the confines of his warship and the density of New York, had significant impact on both of the Halprins' conceptions of space and how a human being responds to its varied definitions.

Larry Halprin was particularly impressed by the rapid and dynamic changes from sea to mountain that defined the varied ecology of the California landscape. In a lecture in 1957, he explained,

> California . . . starts at the Pacific water's edge with great cliffs of sculptured rock . . . It then moves inland across a coastal range of rolling hills covered with live oak and chaparral on the exposed flanks and redwood, madrone and bay in the protected valleys. Inland, the coastal ranges flatten out into the broad reaches of our great agricultural valleys with their deep soil and deciduous scattered oak trees and ordered irrigated fields, and finally it climbs fast into the range of light—that great up-ended knife edge of rocks and small glacial lakes and mountain meadows called the Sierra Nevada. All this change happens in a comparatively short space, so that we are particularly aware of these changing landscapes in the environment all around us.[34]

The mountains, flatlands, forests, and valleys of this dramatic culmination of the western frontier had been the creative source of inspiration for writers, poets, artists, and naturalists since before the mid-nineteenth century, when the region was annexed into the United States. California historian Kevin Starr describes this terrain that so strongly impacted Halprin: "Seas, convulsions, lava, and glaciers had left their record in monuments of stone which seemed to the imagination imminent of release, as if once again there could be a time of seething birth."[35]

This geomorphological drama and potential for rebirth translated into a comprehensive sense of limitless opportunity in California. Daria Halprin later reflected on her parents' arrival into this setting: "They're both very big people. They needed the kind of space that California allowed them in that time to create their own stages. California was virgin land."[36] The Halprins arrived in this largely undeveloped territory during a period of extreme wealth and optimism when the possibilities seemed endless.

In the Bay Area, Larry discovered a culture of regionalism that had emerged in designed form at the turn of the century. The new housing constructed in mass quantities to respond to the state's nearly one million additional inhabitants after the war reflected the informality of the California lifestyle and, subsequently, so did the gardens. In the early 1900s, Henry and Charles Greene had introduced a renewed form of domestic architecture to Southern California, which included porches and terraces related to rooms of the house, harkening back to Spanish and Mexican patterns. Developments in Southern California, as well as local work by Bernard Maybeck who emphasized the interpenetration of interior and exterior space, influenced the approach of midcentury architects in the Bay Area. In 1949, the San Francisco Museum of Art presented an exhibition entitled *Domestic Architecture of the San Francisco Bay Region*, which recognized the achievements of local architects including William Wurster and his firm Wurster Bernardi & Emmons, as well as Gardner Dailey, Joseph Esherick, George Rockrise, and John Funk. The exhibition catalogue includes an essay by Lewis Mumford in which he claims:

> The Bay Region architects have given form to their very informality . . . A few years ago . . . I characterized the buildings that have been assembled for this exhibition as examples of the "Bay Region Style," and contrasted it with the restrictive and arid formulas of the so-

called "International Style" . . . It was a steady organic growth, producing modern forms accepted as natural and appropriate by both client and architect . . . Here the architects have absorbed the universal lessons of science and the machine, and have reconciled them with human wants and human desires, with full regard for the setting of nature, the climate and topography and vegetation, with all those regional qualities.[37]

In addition to this "organic" approach to design, Halprin was also immediately attracted to the "incompleteness" of San Francisco, which to him had "a feeling like a forest with young seedlings growing up in the underbrush and that there was lots of change about to happen. San Francisco just seemed ripe for growth. Ripe for opportunity."[38] At the announcement of V-J Day (victory over Japan), the city exploded in celebration and public performance of "euphoria and anarchy." As Ross notes, "For a choreographer and a landscape architect, both on the dawn of their professional careers, these responses to V-J Day must have seemed like an inauguration of the performance potential of the city itself, making use of its public open spaces, its geography, its architecture, its citizens. In the decade ahead, these aspects of the city would become elements of a new theater of life for both Halprins."[39]

The postwar wealth and optimism, coupled with a population surge caused particularly by GIs who had left from Pacific ports and returned to its temperate climate, relaxed lifestyle, and open landscape, provided the perfect stage upon which the Halprins concentrated their creative attention. When in 1945 Halprin made the decision to go into landscape architecture with Thomas Church, the Halprins purchased a modest ranch-style house in a rural community in Marin's Mill Valley. It was originally constructed to house wartime workers in the nearby shipyards of Sausalito. By recycling materials already existing on the site, including the sod, grapestake fence, and hedges, Larry transformed this average subdivision lot into an environment for outdoor living.[40] The garden was particularly significant because it served as an example of how to transform mass housing constructed to support the war effort into a private suburban house accessible and appealing to the new middle class. Church's influence is evident in the design of

Halprin's Mill Valley property, particularly by the clean sweeping lines between hardscape and softscape. In one early drawing by Halprin, a centrally located tree is included as a garden anchor, one of Church's preferred spatial devices (Figure 1.1).

Church's lifelong emphasis remained, according to Halprin, on "how people can enlarge their lives through their gardens,"[41] which Church later spelled out in simple basic concepts in his book *Gardens Are for People* (1955). By the time Halprin joined Church's office, the recognized Bay Area landscape architects Robert Royston and Douglas Baylis had already worked in the office and moved on. Beginning in the 1930s, Church had been immensely prolific, and he was actively endorsed by popular magazines such as *House Beautiful* and *Sunset: The Magazine for Western Living*. Church reused formal devices such as simple planes, flowing lines, and a multiplicity of viewpoints, and placed an emphasis on texture, color, space, and form. Most of his gardens incorporated a basic "kit of parts," including a terrace, lawn, screens, barbecue, shade structure, play spaces, service yard, and tool shed, which were typically anchored around an old tree. Despite the standard forms and functions, Church was best known for developing relationships with his clients and creating environments individualized to their preferences. In fact, garden design became a means by which homeowners could safely assert their individuality, a right of democracy, in the face of postwar conformity. Articles such as "A Garden Can Banish Subdivi-

Figure 1.1. Drawing by Lawrence Halprin of the garden he designed for the Halprin home in Mill Valley, California, c. 1946. Lawrence Halprin Collection, The Architectural Archives, University of Pennsylvania (014.II.A.067).

sion Monotony" began appearing in popular magazines, making claims such as "You must give your personal expression, your taste, free play—or you will emerge like an end-product on an assembly line of canned culture."[42] Rather than a front yard for public view and two unusable strips of land on either side of the house, Bay Region landscape architects devoted every exterior inch of the small lots to work, play, and living in the outdoors. In 1949, in fact, Halprin and Church coauthored an article in *House Beautiful* titled "You Have a Goldmine in Your Backyard," with a number of drawings by Halprin, presenting the "golden assets" of a well-considered garden for outdoor living. Just like the architects of the time and region, these landscape architects emphasized "function, beauty, adaptability, convenience and economy of upkeep," according to Church.[43]

Halprin claimed that Church "made no forward movement after 1948 or '49 or '50, and stopped innovating anything after that . . . I think he said what he wanted to say; he was not a deeply theoretical person at all; he was very pragmatic."[44] It was in 1949, then, that Halprin left the firm and started out on his own, determined to continue innovating—theoretically and pragmatically. He was increasingly aware of his tugging desire to make a broader social impact, which he had developed after reading Tunnard and studying at Harvard, while retaining vivid memories of the kibbutz.

In addition to Church, Halprin is frequently grouped with a number of landscape architects working in California at the time, including Garrett Eckbo, Robert Royston, Theodore Osmundson, and Douglas Baylis. Because of Eckbo's progressive social agenda, he is often associated with Halprin, though the two had little personal or professional interaction. He was one of Halprin's early competitors as part of the firm Eckbo, Royston & Williams, which existed from 1945 through 1958, working predominantly out of Southern California. Halprin admired Eckbo's early career as a landscape architect for the New Deal's Farm Security Administration (FSA), designing the physical framework for housing, sanitation, and education for migrant workers across the western states.[45]

After the rationalist landscape planning essays Eckbo published with James Rose and Dan Kiley in *Architectural Record* (1939–40), he authored a series of socially minded books, the most manifesto-like of which was his first, *Landscape for Living* (1950). Like

Tunnard's *Gardens in the Modern Landscape* (1938), Eckbo rejects the inheritance of a sentimental landscape design tradition, yet when the later book is compared to its predecessor, some fundamental differences arise. Eckbo's text demands the adoption of the scientific method, which he describes as "the process of rational analysis and creative synthesis, of continuous research, hypothesis, and experiment to prove or disprove such hypotheses."[46] He calls for the integration of "the spatial arts" into "site-planning," an "art based in science rather than mysticism."[47] Technology and science, including biology and psychology, are driving forces behind Eckbo's manifesto, allying him closely with architects with whom he collaborated and whom he admired, such as Richard Neutra. Despite his comprehensive interests in the integrated design fields focused on the establishment of "relations between man and the land," Eckbo's book is quite different from Halprin's writings and practice. Eckbo is much more self-consciously "Modern" than Halprin, emphasizing volume, form, and materials as planning instruments. Like Eckbo, Halprin adopts Tunnard's insistence on functionalism and art, but unlike Eckbo, Halprin also seizes the third criterion—empathy. With an intuitive sensitivity toward the forces of nature, Halprin created landscapes inspired by these processes as well as human's inherent biological and social needs, thereby deriving forms that were "empathic" to nature as well as to human experience.

In addition, while composition was not one of Halprin's primary concerns, Eckbo studied the compositional techniques of modern painting, particularly of the artist Wassily Kandinsky and his studies of relationships between objects in space. Eckbo seems to have been impacted by the gardens presented in the 1925 Exposition Internationale des Arts Décoratifs et Industriels Modernes, particularly Gabriel Guevrekian's Garden of Water and Light, which became a cited turning point for the profession.[48] Yet Guevrekian's work also borrowed devices adopted from painting, particularly Cubism. Halprin accuses Eckbo in a later interview of being "decorative" and "formalistic," and also "paying a great deal of attention to shapes, little angles, and very derivative from painting rather than from the essence of landscape architecture."[49]

Throughout his early career, Halprin remained critical of those who adopted compositional elements directly from modern painting. Though he admired Roberto Burle Marx, Halprin critiques his direct adaptation of painterly experiments in biomorphism and free-form abstraction, which became extremely popular in the Bay Area in the 1940s. In an interview about Halprin's relationship with Thomas Church, Halprin explains,

> I hardly knew about Burle Marx. But I was influenced by Miró, and Picasso and Arp. And so was Burle Marx. I think Burle carried it to its ultimate conclusion, and . . . what he did was to take it and use it as a palette, and just sort of plant it down on the ground. What he was doing was painting in the landscape . . . Although I love it dearly, it's not the same way that I work, or Tommy works. . . . The issue for Tommy was to evolve an aesthetic out of the nature of the site, the users, and the materials of the garden art, not to impose painterly concerns on it. He was searching for a garden art to enhance people's lives and enrich them.[50]

Halprin, employing an "empathic" approach, was much more aligned with how he describes Church in this passage, demonstrating the influence of his former employer, despite the gap in their overall bodies of work (with Church remaining in the private sphere and Halprin exploding into the public arena).

Halprin often contrasts the reliance of other practitioners primarily on compositional and visual effects with his emphasis on bodily experience. In "Education for a Landscape Aesthetic," an unpublished essay from 1955, Halprin traces the origins of the "mechanical" practice of "transferring" painterly compositions onto the landscape to the eighteenth-century picturesque:

> The fact is that we all know of the historically close and constant interrelationships between paintings and the landscape arts. The development of the picturesque in painting paralleled the picturesque gardens of Capability Brown and Vanbrugh; and the paintings of Chinese landscapes so closely paralleled their gardens as to make them seem identical. In our times Miró replaces Claude Lorraine in his influence on some landscape architects as does Mondrian on others.[51]

Oddly enough, Halprin seems ignorant of the similarities between his interests and the maturation of the English Picturesque with its emphasis on triggering varied aesthetic response experienced through movement. Tunnard's *Gardens in the Modern Landscape*, Eckbo's *Landscape for Living*, and Ian McHarg's *Design with Nature* (1969), a book that had enormous impact on Halprin, all include sections on the history of landscape design, each offering interpretations that contextualize the strategies of their counterpoint approach. Like Tunnard, Eckbo, and McHarg, Halprin is additionally critical of the consideration of the garden as a prettying afterthought, "very much the same way as parsley is placed around a roast," in the words of Bay Region architect Gardner Dailey.[52] Halprin often associates this "prettying" with the "picturesque," which he considers simply "scenery" or the re-creation of pictures or paintings.[53] This limited reading of the Picturesque, which in the eighteenth century was driven by temporal change, spatial sequence, memory, and association (all elements Halprin attempts to evoke), is most likely owing to its devolution into "little more than 'a pleasing scene'" that landscape scholar Elizabeth Meyer argues is a result of its filtering through nineteenth- and twentieth-century treatises and handbooks depicting illustrations of "placeless decorative vignettes."[54] Tunnard, in his 1938 manifesto, seems aware of this devolution, when he lauds the "early Picturesque" as stimulating and creative, versus its later incarnation as "sentimental and sterile."[55]

Halprin is also critical of Renaissance stasis and monumentality, yet he admires the High Renaissance gardens of Rome particularly for their playful experimentation with water, producing delight and surprise (he does not, however, mention the introduction of a multiplicity of perspectives or unfolding experiences in these gardens). He considers the elaboration of the Italian tradition in French Baroque gardens such as Versailles, which broke through the bounds of their Italian precedents and attempted to "control" infinite space. In *The RSVP Cycles*, he associates this degree of control with "master planning" by European Modernists including Lúcio Costa and Oscar Niemeyer at Brasilia and Le Corbusier at Chandigarh. He criticizes the City Beautiful movement for being similarly controlling, monumental, and singularly perspectival. In *Cities*, he claims that Renaissance and Beaux-Arts planning was structured on the "static, axially-oriented point of view":

Their spaces were all laid out as if viewed in perspective from a fixed point. Cities, as well as paintings, were designed to be seen from one place in a one point perspective, as if movement did not exist. But this is giving way in our time to the understanding of the changing point of view, the mobile, non-fixed ever-shifting viewpoint. Even when designing for pedestrians who move at comparatively slow speeds, the environment relates to the person constantly in motion with a varied viewpoint and a constantly changing position.[56]

The private garden provided the perfect laboratory to begin experimenting with these choreographic principles. Before Halprin left Church's office he contributed significantly to the design of the Donnell Garden in Sonoma County, which became "a national icon of postwar leisure and home ownership."[57] Halprin was involved in the design of the kidney-shaped pool, but, more important, he was responsible for the carefully choreographed approach road and the siting of its terminus—the garden at the top of the hill. Describing this pivotal moment in his career, Halprin explains that

a major effort [at Donnell] was using the site . . . It was thought of starting from the road, the main road: you came in, opened the gate, drove up, and that road up was very carefully designed so you came up below the swimming pool area, the bath house, and then you came around it to the upper area, and then there was a path that comes down, around, and goes down in through some rocks, and then you come into the space. And that's a long, intricate, choreographed sequence, which was the major effort. Then when you're in it, the thing itself starts spiraling around, moving and so on.[58]

Such early experiments in the garden, focused especially on the processional sequence through a number of unfolding spatial experiences, were important to the development of choreographic concepts applied on the urban scale a decade later.

A year after Halprin worked on the Donnell Garden, he published "The Choreography of Gardens" in *Impulse*. In the article, Halprin explains how he designed gardens as stage sets for the dance of life:

Our lives have changed over the years. So have our dances, and our gardens. We are no longer content to sit stiffly in the garden in our best Sunday clothes, protected from the sun by a frilled umbrella. Our gardens have become more dynamic and should be designed with the moving person in mind. Our garden space has become a framework within which activities of all sorts take place—games, barbecues, walks, swimming and even at times lounging. As a framework for movement activities the garden can influence our lives tremendously. If it flows easily in interesting patterns of terraces and paths, varying its texture of paving underfoot, and its foliage backgrounds, and fences, all rhythmically united, then it can influence people's movement patterns through its spaces taking on the fine sense of a dance.[59]

Figure 1.2. Merce Cunningham on the Dance Deck, Kentfield, California, 1957.
Lawrence Halprin Collection, The Architectural Archives, University of Pennsylvania (unstamped).

Though his conception of the garden in history is not entirely accurate, Halprin's response reflects his exposure to his wife's breakthrough experiments in the body's kinesthetic response to environmental conditions and the rapid physical and social changes of postwar urbanization.

In addition to the Donnell Garden, the pivotal project in Halprin's early career was his design, in collaboration with Arch Lauterer, lighting designer for Martha Graham, for an outdoor "dance deck" on the Halprins' four-acre wooded property in Kentfield, Marin County, where they moved in 1952 (Figure 1.2). Bill Wurster designed the main house with views to the peak of Mount Tamalpais to the south and across the San Francisco Bay to Berkeley to the east. Halprin configured the approach to the deck as a choreographed sequence from the house, down the steps and through the woods (Figures 1.3 and 1.4). In an article appearing in *Progressive Architecture* in 1958, he carefully explained the procession through their property:

We are at the end of a narrow road which has no other houses and winds down the cliff's edge to a turn-around. One parks outside a fence and, walking through the low entrance gate, sees the house for the first time, ahead. This entrance garden is a space confined on three sides . . . But the space explodes outward to the view on the downhill side—it is, in effect, an outdoor room opening across a broad expanse of treetops forming a green, almost level carpet to the view. This entrance garden is paved in red brick and the trunks of birch form a sequence of space markers along its edge. The house too has much the same sequence of space configurations. You enter by the front door into a low-ceilinged, confined entrance under the stair and, to the right, the glass-enclosed living room extends out into the view with a high ceiling which moves the space vertically as well . . . The back garden. . . can be reached by a path in back of the house or through it. Along the north bank is a narrow garden passage which then opens up into the shady north terrace. This area is less architecturally controlled; the space is confined more by plantings than structure . . . The views are into the deep forest, and the brick terrace reaches out past the summer house to a path through the woods. The screened summer house is in lieu of a porch attached to the house; it floats, on deck and stilts, above the sloping hillside . . .

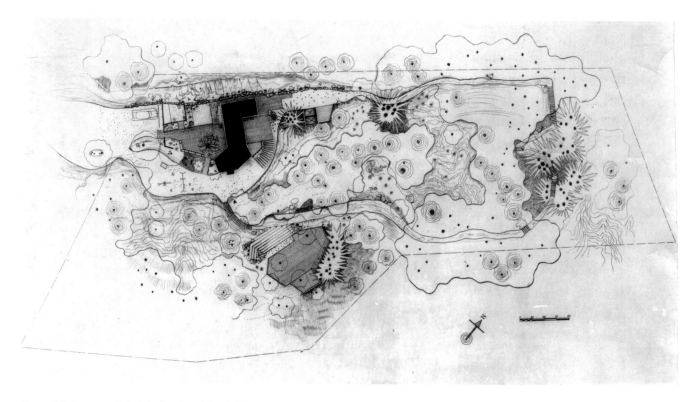

Figure 1.3. Lawrence Halprin's site plan of the Halprin residence in Kentfield, California, 1950s.
Lawrence Halprin Collection, The Architectural Archives, University of Pennsylvania.

The garden then extends from the terrace into the woods on a long needle-covered path which skirts a grove of redwoods through the dense enclosed spaces of the evergreen forest. It too has a series of spatial progressions because at the wood's beginning it is closed by the heavily leafed and close growing red barked madrone trees; moving into it is almost like passing through a gate. But after a while the path turns down a series of wooden plank steps through a grove of redwoods which are very tall and very thin and whose leaves form a light canopy 150 feet in the air and the forest space is much more open. Finally it leads to the dance deck which creates a broad flat open plane in the forest . . . The movement through the woods to the deck creates a time sequence which is very pleasant. The deck has its own qualities of kinetics.[60]

The Dance Deck stands isolated in the forest of madrone, oak, and redwood trees below the house. It incorporates existing tree trunks as anchor points and extends out from the slope so that at its highest point it hangs thirty feet in the air. Small changes in elevation were designed to provide opportunities for functional variation or somatic response. The deck enabled Anna to experiment with her pioneering improvisational techniques and teach workshops while remaining at home to raise her two children. In an article published in *Impulse* featuring the deck, she explains:

Figure 1.4. Descent from house to Dance Deck, c. 1955. Photograph by Ernest Braun.

Since there is ever changing form and texture and light around you, a certain drive develops toward constant experimentation and change in dance itself. In a sense one becomes less introverted, less dependent on sheer invention, and more out going and receptive to environmental change . . . The non-rectangular form of the deck forces a complete reorientation on the dancer. The customary points of reference are gone and in place of a cubic space . . . the space explodes and becomes mobile. Movement within a moving space, I have found, is different than movement within a static cube.[61]

Figure 1.5. The Caygill Garden in Orinda, California, designed by Lawrence Halprin, 1950–51. Courtesy of Rondal Partridge Archives. Copyright 2013 Rondal Partridge Archives.

The construction of the Dance Deck became a turning point for Anna's career, heightening her awareness of the "raw" elements of the environment: wind, light, heat, and the active physicality of trees, mountains, birds, and other members of the natural world. This rawness often inspired nudity in her dances and workshops and stimulated her exploration of human instinct and creative intuition in immediate response to dynamic environmental conditions.

Larry Halprin's gardens from the 1950s demonstrate his primary interest in designing environments that stimulate the body, the senses, and the emotions; in other words, activating such "creative intuition."[62] Textures, sequence and transitions, directing views, water features, and spatial definition were all explored under the easy conditions of residential projects and then later applied in adapted forms to the public environments of shopping malls, parks, and downtowns.

Halprin paid careful attention to the behavioral response he might evoke in various garden spaces, such as quiet contemplation within an enclosed water garden or engaged social interaction around a swimming pool. Water, which he first explores in his early gardens, becomes a choreographic force that remains consistent throughout his entire oeuvre. He experiments with its sounds and its movement in an infinite range of design possibilities. Of course, Halprin is best known for his interactive fountains in public spaces, but it was in the private California garden that he had the opportunity to experiment with water's potential. The Caygill Garden in Orinda (1950–51), for instance, was the first design in which Halprin used running water—in a wading pool with a fountain washed over river stones from Big Sur (Figure 1.5).[63] The later McIntyre garden in Hillsborough (1958–61), on a much grander scale, is a melodic composition of water responding to steps, channels, cascades, and pools (Figure 1.6).

Halprin's planting plans, produced through the significant contribution of his early associate Jean Walton, were richer and more experimental than those of his contemporaries. Walton and Halprin composed stimulating tapestries of tactility and texture particularly through the use of xerophytes and other native plants (Figure 1.7). Halprin considered the feeling of different ground surfaces underfoot and how these different

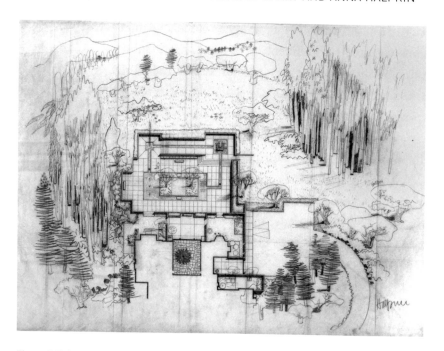

Figure 1.6. Lawrence Halprin & Associates, drawing of the McIntyre Garden, Hillsborough, California, 1958–61. Lawrence Halprin Collection, The Architectural Archives, University of Pennsylvania (014.II.A.113).

sensations were appropriate to the mood of their setting. He was particularly sensitive to transitions and sequence, often creating processional schemes to be experienced as an unfolding of shifting opportunities. These sequences directed the garden visitor to different outlooks and views, ranging from foreground details to vast "borrowed landscape" scenes beyond the garden walls. Steps and other climbing features would entice movement up or down and open up new prospects.

After the firm's initial years working in the private garden, it started getting commissions for more complex projects, which required a larger staff. Halprin's early associates included Jean Walton who joined him in 1949, Don Ray Carter in 1950, then Satoru Nishita in 1951 and Richard Vignolo in 1955.[64] During this decade the firm began planning university campuses; the siting and organizing of university buildings and open spaces prepared Halprin for urban-scale projects.[65] However, his most lucrative focus during this period remained on the burgeoning suburbs, particularly the development of the regional shopping mall as an alternative to the public spaces of what was then the dying urban downtown. The shopping center, a typology developed primarily by architect Victor Gruen, emerged as part of the culture of consumerism that characterized the 1950s. As Gruen's biographer, M. Jeffrey Hardwick, explains, "With kiosks, shop windows, cafés, streets, fountains, sculpture, crowds, benches, and trees, Gruen consciously re-created an aura of urbanity for white suburbanites." The shopping center came to represent a distillation of all the magnetic qualities of downtown, "the variety, the individuality, the lights, the color, even the crowds," yet without being "noisy and dirty and chaotic."[66]

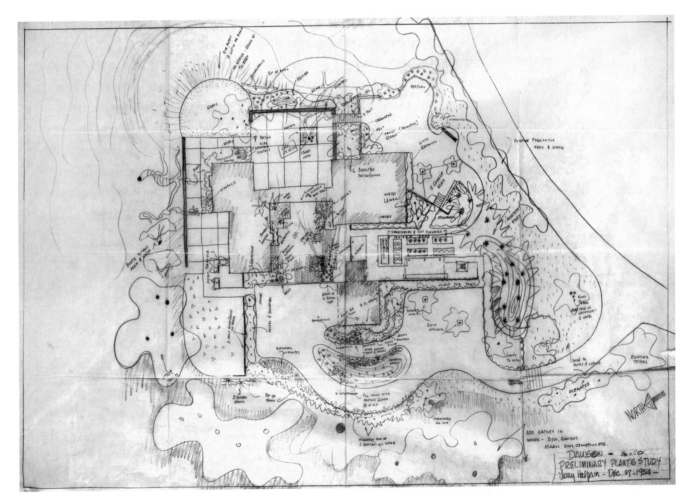

Figure 1.7. Lawrence Halprin's preliminary planting plan for the Dawson Garden, Los Altos, California, 1953–55. Lawrence Halprin Collection, The Architectural Archives, University of Pennsylvania (014.II.A.37).

Halprin reflects on this aspect of his career with mixed emotions. To him the shopping center served as a "testing ground for many urban solutions," particularly street furniture, paving, as well as movement choreography.[67] The Old Orchard Shopping Center in Skokie, Illinois, provided the first of these testing grounds. He considered the experience of the mall as one originating on the freeway emptying onto a ring road that directs customers to the parking lot. Rather than a "sea of cars," the parking lot was divided by "great long pedestrian arms" which guided the shopper on foot from an "orderly and comprehensible" parking area designed at "human scale," into the encompassing pedestrian environment of the mall itself. In these consumer spaces, which he called "gardens for shopping" in a 1970s office brochure, Halprin designed interactive fountains, furniture, playgrounds, and plantings to provide a stimulating environment. Most significantly, the landscape structure was established first, creating a framework for the architecture, which defined the edges and enclosed the outdoor spaces to ensure a pleasant shopping experience stripped of the hassles of shopping downtown.[68] Yet in 1968, Halprin claimed that what the shopping center type had not done was to get enough variety:

> The average shopping center is pretty uni-purpose. It provides shopping, a handsome environment but does not provide the kind of downtown quality that most of us enjoy. That's why they tend to become sterile. They don't provide things like churches, few of them provide real means of going to the movies, or clubs. There is very little acceptable sin in a shopping center. They tend to cater to a kind of uniform level of income and uniform level of people. Middle class people.[69]

In 1975, his views became even more critical:

> During the early Fifties, God help me, I designed some of the early major shopping centers in this country, for which I've always been very regretful. Old Orchard, Oak Brook, around Chicago—some of the prototypical ones. I haven't been involved in designing

shopping centers in ten years. If I were offered one now, I wouldn't design it . . . I think they're a crock of shit . . . because they draw everything out where it shouldn't be. They cater to a kind of a strange upper-middle class. They siphon off from the downtown area. They do all kinds of bad things, in my view.[70]

Nevertheless, this type of commission provided a lucrative means of building the firm and plenty of experience to learn about the collective rituals of shopping and the sequencing of space.

Between 1960 and 1965, the population of California surged dramatically, creating demands for new housing developments and related facilities to support them. Appropriately timed, Halprin incorporated his office into the interdisciplinary design firm Lawrence Halprin & Associates in 1960, and its emphasis became the larger public environment. Halprin's fundamental concerns—designing stimulating environments to inspire human participation—did not change, however.

The award-winning St. Francis Square, for instance, designed with architects Marquis & Stoller (1960–63), offered 299 housing units sold on a "racially-integrated basis," according to racial quotas set by the sponsor (Pension Fund jointly administered by the International Longshoremen's and Warehousemen's Union and the Pacific Maritime Association) and income limitations established by the Federal Housing Administration.[71] The development was located in San Francisco's Western Addition, a previously African American neighborhood that authorities declared a "Negro slum" and had systematically razed beginning in the early 1950s. Halprin's firm developed the master plan and landscape design for the super-block development.[72] The outdoor space served as the comprehensive framework or "continuous park," tying together the housing, school, and YMCA on the site. By situating the parking at the periphery and facing the buildings inward rather than toward the street, the walkways, courts, plazas, play areas, and gardens became the central feature and allowed for a range of creative appropriations (not that different from the shopping center). This modestly funded project served as a prototype for much of Halprin's work to come. With the landscape operating as organizational framework, the network of "linkages" and varied spaces provided enriching opportunities for choice. The introversion of these schemes, however, had social implications that soon made them outmoded urbanistically.

In reflecting on the increasing scale of his work, Halprin claimed that

the progression of problems which I have been solving has been important. I started with issues of personal relationships:—gardens & houses—evocative of private family needs, tract houses & gardens after the war. After that I attempted to link these together: group housing, suburban villages, shopping centers. Gradually these issues have aggregated into larger ones—how people, in regions, can live together in towns & villages without raping the land & destroying the very environment they live in.[73]

Halprin embraced environmental design as the "potentially most inclusive of all the arts of man—the design of his ecosystem for the future."[74] With his background in plant sciences, and specifically the adaptability of plants to natural environments, Halprin wove the developing field of ecology into his approach to human habitats. The dynamism and interconnection of the ecological model, accepting and responding to change, was foundational to his encompassing method. In a speech titled "The Human Community as an Ecosystem," given at the 1963 American Institute of Architects (AIA) Northwest Regional Conference, he compared the climax and disclimax conditions of plant and animal communities to the evolutionary forces of human settlements and the disruptions caused by natural disaster, and more important, by human-generated changes such as the proliferation of the automobile and its associated parking lots and freeways. In a polemic reminiscent of McHarg, Halprin addresses two other "blind, inexorable forces." The first is urban redevelopment, which he claims "demolishes whole areas, whole sections of a community . . . and in place of the established order evolved over years of development, must quickly [impose] its own will and its own esthetic and sociological character on the ecosystem." The second is "the disruption, in our ecosystem, of the countryside surrounding our cities—the proliferation of suburban communities into what were previously farmlands serving the city . . . The suburb, itself, often so pleasant to live in, is a sinister agent for disclimax; shifting the balance and destroying the very countryside its inhabitants went out to be in." Halprin's stance on "disclimax" conditions caused by rapid redevelopment remains ambiguous throughout his career, however. He profits from these conditions and is most innovative in his design responses to the "disturbances" caused by such redevelopment, yet he was deeply devoted to social and physical preservation to sustain a sense of urban continuity. The St. Francis Square example is thus particularly revealing, as it illustrates Halprin's equivocal stance on urban renewal. After witnessing a number of displacement campaigns, he began developing the Take Part Process, but his early career in the public sector was largely mitigatory; he accepted the inevitability of redevelopment and worked to provide stimulating environments that often counteracted the deadening effects of bleak architectural ensembles.

The task of Lawrence Halprin & Associates, therefore, was the application of a comprehensive approach to safeguard the human livability and ecological sustainability of the urban environment. The firm embraced ecological planning, made most accessible to the design professions through Ian McHarg, and applied it in expanded form to address the web of interrelationships between social and biophysical systems. Halprin was one of the first designers to implement this form of environmental planning—in 1960 at Peacock Gap in the San Francisco Bay and then at Sea Ranch. For Peacock Gap, a three-thousand-acre site on a peninsula projecting into the San Francisco Bay, the firm produced a schematic development plan and impact study for proposed housing. In the foreword to this study, Halprin declares "that man can not only preserve, but often can improve upon the natural order. We believe that all nature is in process and man has been a key part of this process for many millennia."[75] Throughout his subsequent career, whether designing a small park or a regional plan, his consistent emphasis remained on the interrelationships of all the working parts, physical, social, and experiential. He considered his life's work the attempt "to evolve a symbiotic relationship between the environment and people so they mutually enhance each other and develop a way of life that enhances creativity."[76] Networks of movement and linkages to enrich interconnections and limitless kinesthetic potential remained the firm's focus. Working at all scales, the firm consistently looked well beyond site boundaries. As Halprin explains,

> [Our] involvement is not limited to the City, or Suburbia alone. The linkages need to include entire regions—into choreographed sequences and kinesthetically conceived regional scores, which will enable people to savor them all—each for its own interactive potential. These area-wide linkages will permit and encourage uses at every scale—it will avoid the segregation of urban life from the country and vice-versa. For this to happen we need to perceive the urban, suburban, and natural environments as entire linkages, designed for a diversity of interactive needs.[77]

In order to work at this increasingly comprehensive scale, by 1969 the firm had grown to nearly fifty employees divided between two offices in San Francisco and New York. Yet a "radical reorganization" occurred that year, primarily through the initiative of younger members of the firm protesting what had become a hierarchical environment in which Halprin retained ultimate authority. As the firm grew throughout the 1960s, Halprin became less directly involved in design development and took on the role of more of a "conceptualizer," yet he continued to have final say in decisions.[78] This tense arrangement serves as a critical example of Larry Halprin's inability to relinquish control, despite his proclaimed commitment to facilitating the creativity of others.

In 1969, through the guidance of psychologist Jim Creighton, Lawrence Halprin & Associates thus underwent a difficult transformation that resulted in the departure of nearly twenty-five employees. The establishment of a Policy Council attempted to diminish the office hierarchy. After the restructuring, Halprin began to bring in new types of people who were "more intellectuals rather than design types, and not related to specific expertise." By employing a creative group of "planners, ecologists, social anthropologists, architects, landscape architects, urban designers, community designers, community activators, political scientists, writers, media artists, and others," under the as-necessary consultation of those in "economics, market analysis, governmental interrelationships, zoning, transportation, all aspects of engineering, psychology, sociology, and other specialists," the firm identified its practice as truly "synergistic":

> Our interests and professional abilities encompass a broad scope of habitats. At the largest scale we work in comprehensive conservation, in the planning of national and regional parks and the exploration of large-scale regional systems. At the city-scale, our work has been heavily involved in urban planning and design from the replanning of existing cities to the design of entirely new communities . . .
>
> Working in eroding, existing cities we have replanned and designed entire central business districts and gone on to design exciting and inviting plazas, malls, shopping areas, parks, residential areas, and playgrounds and transit systems to serve them. At each scale we relate the specific back to the general with the deep conviction that various parts of the environment have a profound effect on all the others. Our hope is always to implement what we do, so that ideas and creativity get carried into reality—in legal and zoning terms as well as in built form.
>
> Many of the vanguard problems of our time are just beginning to be clearly perceived: population impact, mobility, demands for increased and new forms of energy, new forms of group living—land ownership and controls and democratic forms for control of development—development patterns themselves; new techniques for natural resource preservation, urban living patterns, equitable distribution of amenities. We understand our environment to include our social, economic and cultural environment as well as our physical one. At Lawrence Halprin & Associates we are prepared as a firm, and in conjunction with expert specialist consultants, to deal synergistically with all these problems.[79]

Despite the 1969–70 restructuring, Halprin disbanded Lawrence Halprin & Associates in 1976 when he began again feeling increasingly isolated from daily and direct involvement in projects. At this point, he turned his full attention to RoundHouse, a "studio/think-tank" he established with his longtime colleague Sue Yung Li Ikeda. Rather than commissioned projects, with RoundHouse Halprin began experimenting with film and continued organizing multidisciplinary creativity workshops. He reentered practice when he was commissioned to design Levi's Plaza in 1978.

This largely biographical chapter is intended to situate Halprin's choreographic process within the context of his own life and career, as well as the historical moment in which he was practicing. Clearly his artistic dialogue with Anna played the most significant role, but his early life experience on the kibbutz, his studies in horticulture and ecology, his work under Bauhaus émigrés at Harvard, and his move west also impacted and shaped his process. In addition to the idiosyncracies of his own life and career, the rapid and alienating forces of urbanization that caused significant physical restructuring of the city—as it was occupied, inhabited, and appropriated—provided the challenges that stimulated the development of Halprin's unique design approach. As massive urban restructuring perpetuates, as well as a reawakening of participatory demands begins to permeate our globalized society, a renewed examination of this process and practice becomes especially revealing.

Before moving forward, one clarification on crediting firm employees must be noted. Since Halprin worked amid a firm of diverse professionals, he depended strongly on collaboration with those in his office as well as consultants and clients without. Though he retained ultimate authority over design decisions even after the 1969 office restructuring, his associates and principals played significant and sometimes dominant roles in the designs and the management of these projects. The chapters that follow attempt to highlight the nature of this collaborative process but will not dissect the intricacies of each person's individualized input into the projects. Of course, when associates, principals, consultants, and the like are known to have made significant contributions, they are recognized. However, the firm will generally be considered as a totality and "Halprin" typically refers both to him plus the input of his numerous employees and consultants.

PART I. BUILT WORK

2. FRAMING CIVIC RITUALS

MARKET STREET, NICOLLET MALL, HERITAGE PARK PLAZA

PART I ON LAWRENCE HALPRIN'S BUILT WORK focuses less on formal prod-
ucts than on the process that generated them, as well as how those forms invited human
interaction and enhanced public life in cities undergoing urban renewal. To stimulate
this participatory response, Halprin searched for "archetypal forms" or Resources (R)
fundamental to all urban inhabitants—which he discovered in nature and human ritual.

More specifically, "built work" implies the tangible embodiment of Halprin's cho-
reographic concepts at two scales: first, the intimate experiences created by designed
elements in the landscape and their ability to provoke or stimulate a range of sensory
(including kinesthetic) responses; and second, the broader organizational structuring
of movement through the city. In his 1960 lecture to the International Federation of
Landscape Architects titled "The Role of the Twentieth-Century Landscape Architect,"
Halprin stated that the landscape architect must "strive continually to emphasize the
importance of landscape open space as the very matrix of life, as the *dominant* part of

the environment and structures as simply part of the complex relationship occurring *within* it."[1] This inversion of the long-accepted hierarchy of the organizational potential of the figure over ground came before Colin Rowe's "Crisis of the Object" (1978), before Kenneth Frampton's "Toward an Urban Landscape" (1995), and before the current trend called "Landscape Urbanism."[2] Halprin is often overlooked for pioneering this terrain. Though he stresses the organization of relationships within the complex city, he continues in this lecture to emphasize that focusing on site organization is not enough and the landscape architect must additionally "design [the environment] in all its detail as the medium within which life occurs." He is therefore stressing both scales of intervention.

Halprin is able to address both scales through design for enhanced social rituals in the city. The focus of this chapter is Halprin's infrastructural interventions that choreograph movement through the city as ritualistic procession, as well as his designs for the body that elevate the experience of habitual urban activities to the art of ritual. Rituals imply performative and collective action, in which "the transmitter, receiver and message become fused in the participant," according to the anthropologist Roy Rappaport.[3]

Activists during the 1960s trusted physical engagement over discursive rhetoric, relying on the persuasive power of action over words. The cultural anthropologist Victor Turner theorized about the ritual process in 1969 and its relationship to the counterculture of the 1960s. Though the Halprins were most likely not aware of Turner's studies in Britain, his contextual analysis is revealing. Turner elaborated on the discussion of the liminal from the French ethnographer Arnold van Gennep's phases of ritual action. During ritual, a person exists in ambiguous territory between one state and the next. Turner celebrated this ambiguous yet liberating "antistructure" as a release from the restraints of quotidian life and as a temporary immersion in a creative "communitas." He believed the solidarity and equality of *communitas* freed ritual comrades from the imposed social order, thus finding themselves bound together, as an undifferentiated authentic whole, by their common experience of being human. Though the Halprins embraced the potential of ritual to heighten the experience of everyday tasks and actions, rather than directly as a means to disrupt the accepted social order, Turner's notion of *communitas* is particularly applicable to their mutual desire to unleash "authentic" human response to harness "collective creativity."

While both of the Halprins looked to ritual practice in "preindustrial societies," particularly Native American cultures, their different experiences with Judaism offered much to be creatively mined. Ross fittingly initiates Anna Halprin's biography with Anna's memory of her grandfather in ecstatic prayer, enacting a Hassidic ritual dance. Though Anna was raised more culturally than religiously Jewish, witnessing her Orthodox grandfather expressing his fervor through moving prayer inspired her life's work. Larry's exposure to Zionism and his early life experience in Palestine, "a place of origins," clearly impacted his quest for ritualistic beginnings, and for the achievement of a kind of *communitas* that paralleled Turner's theoretical model.

The title of the annual issue of *Impulse* dance magazine for 1951 is "Dance in Relation to the Individual and Society." The opening article, "The Unconscious Origin of Dance," is authored by the Halprins' longtime friend and psychotherapist, Joseph Henderson, an analytical psychologist who trained under Carl Jung.[4] Jung believed that observing preindustrial cultures would offer modern man a glimpse of the essence of his own rational existence. In the article, Henderson argues that "dance had its origin in a primitive ritual drama" by tracing the "Summer Corn Dance" as performed within the Zuni pueblo. This ritual, he describes, was derived from the rhythms of nature–wind, water, movement of the sun, birds, and the "beating heart of man"—and was a participatory act—the spectators were "quietly absorbed in the dance as if they were also on the stage, as . . . commentators and participants all in one." Henderson presents this ritual, exhibiting an "organic unity with nature" and a "deep willingness of primitive Man to lose his personal identity in the quest for a common good," as an expression of the collective psyche of man. He continues by noting that "Jung has called these contents of the unconscious archetypes, by which he means the eternal forms or images originating in a primordial level of the psyche and specifically elaborated into complex cultural units or patterns by a process of mediation between Man as a conscious individual and Man as a participant in a collective unconscious."

After criticism of the "superficiality" of classical ballet, Henderson concludes with an analysis of what he refers to as "so-called Modern Dance," emerging from the work of individuals such as Isadora Duncan, Mary Wigman, and Martha Graham, as an attempt to "recapture the fundamental primitive content of the unconscious." He claims that to achieve the "inward serenity and sustained strength of movement" of the primitive dancer, one must remain aware "that dance is not performance, not style, not form, but pure feeling as it reproduces those eternally valid images of the right relations between Man, the group to which he belongs and the world of nature."

Anna, who welcomed the idea of moving to California to reestablish a fundamental connection to sources of creativity, namely the rhythms of nature, looked to ancient ritual and myth, studying their eternal forms, to recapture immediacy and "authenticity." Martha Graham, and her teachers Ruth St. Denis and Ted Shawn, also integrated "primitive" ritual and myth into their work, but more literally and theatrically to inform narrative structure. Anna, instead, looked to these rituals as a model, but encouraged her dancers to invent their own vocabulary of movement symbols.

The invention of rituals and myths, as well as the elevation of prosaic activities to the art of ritual, appear time and again in Anna's work, whether performed on the stage, on the coast of the Sea Ranch, or in the streets. *Planetary Dance*, which Anna originally scored in 1981, is still enacted internationally as an "annual all-day ritual of healing and community."[5] In attempting to uncover the sources of creativity unfiltered by "secondhandism," Anna looked to "ritualistic beginnings of art as a sharpened expression of life."[6] In her breakthrough piece *Parades and Changes* (premiering in 1965), performers enacted mundane tasks such as undressing and dressing with slow deliberate movement. The process of enacting these tasks in response to shifting environmental conditions, as scored by composer Morton Subotnick, became the performance. "Process becomes the form," according to Larry Halprin's notes on the piece, which he helped visualize graphically.[7] In 1966 Anna performed *The Bath* at the Wadsworth Atheneum in Hartford, Connecticut. Within its courtyard fountain, she and her dancers "ritualized the commonplace" by performing the simple task of bathing. By elevating habitual action to ritual, Anna hoped to endow a "heightened state of consciousness" or "a way of experiencing your life rather than routinely going through it or having it imposed on you."[8] Because anyone could perform these acts, Anna used them in her public dance workshops, such as *Ten Myths*, which occurred on ten nights in 1967–68. For each event, Anna's San Francisco Dancers' Workshop invited the public to participate in a ritualistic response to an idea, or myth, that was basic to everyone, such as creation, atonement, and dreams. Environmental conditions were carefully and elaborately constructed as part of the score. The intention was for the group to explore these basic ideas with heightened awareness of oneself freed from socialized inhibitions, as well as oneself as part of a collective body, sharing in the same process of ritualistic discovery and "mutual creation."[9] The correspondence with Turner's parallel work on the ritual process thus becomes particularly acute.

Rituals are active participatory events and require a framework for their reiterative performance. Larry Halprin, in his symbiotic artistic relationship with Anna, sought to structure such a framework in the city that would "elicit actions and responses" and serve as a "self-directing score," words used to describe the environments of *Ten Myths*.[10] To the Halprins, a ritual represented "the formalized expression of universal human qualities," "binding us together" in our "common humanity." Of course, the particularities of rituals are more culturally idiosyncratic than universal per se, but the Halprins seemed to be optimistically (and perhaps idealistically) considering those fundamental rituals that are widely shared as a collective experience. In an unpublished essay called "The City as a Spiritual Center for Modern Myths and Rituals," they state: "We need more time together out in the streets in joyful interaction in our cities, experiencing together our past as well as our present, ritualizing the events which bind us together more than the ones which divide us."[11]

Though not always "joyful," the streets and public spaces of the 1960s city were appropriated as a stage for the enactment of public protest and performance. Marches, riots, sit-ins, celebrations, and other forms of occupation ensured a vibrant yet tense public life of encounter, confrontation, and exchange. The Great March on Washington of 1963, the initiation of the Free Speech Movement on the University of California, Berkeley's Sproul Plaza in 1964–65, the Summer of Love in Haight–Ashbury in 1967, the riotous backlash to racial discrimination and the assassination of Martin Luther King Jr. in 1968, the first Earth Day celebrations of 1970 (and on and on) clearly impacted Larry Halprin, who hoped to provide enhanced infrastructure to enable such collective events and aggressive assertions of public life. Today, with global expressions of discontent over the distribution of wealth in efforts such as "Occupy Wall Street," with lessons learned from the Arab Spring, and with protests of recent wars in the Middle East, as well as new forms of spontaneously claiming the street catalyzed by expanding social media networks, the city once again has become a proper stage for public performance and collective ritual, making Halprin's relevance seem more acute.

In his book *Cities* (1963), Halprin presents design possibilities for the facilitation of such collective events as dynamic social rituals. His book offers a global taxonomy of urban forms to demonstrate commonalities as well as cultural distinctions. Cities, he discovered, are structured by a system of universal elements, such as ceremonial gateways, grand boulevards for processions and parades, and public spaces for gathering, often with steps and platforms as stages with architectural backdrops. This urban framework enabled an enriched sense of theater in the streets. Despite the "unnatural" qualities of such urban elements, Halprin considers their integrated or choreographed composition essential for a healthy urban ecosystem. More fundamental than these specific physical components that comprise city structure, in a later essay Halprin lists a series of primal human needs that provide a deeper foundation for human settlement and ritual expression:

> The sense of shelter . . . is basic to us all—the nurturing quality of protection and privacy, of territoriality and personal space . . . a primordial and pre-natal need shared by all.
>
> Another example of a basic need is water . . . as it links us to our sources (erosion, wave actions, irrigation of crops, a multitude of interactions in nature, and from our common pre-natal experience of a nourishing liquid environment *in utero*). Water as part

of the made landscape relates us in profound ways to the origins of our beginnings. Its sounds and shapes and feel in parks and plazas call up deep emotional responses in us.

Gateways and entrances link us back to origins as well—how we come into the world and the dark mysterious ways in which we react to the change of day and night as well as to the seasons . . . How we step through from space to space, the transitions from outward to inward, lies at the core of deep emotion.

These needs to which we respond . . . belong to the human species. They are "of nature, innate, transpersonal, pre-rational and (when alerted) compulsive."[12]

Larry Halprin's career is defined by the search for these "origins of our beginnings" to return us to our immediate creative sources. The rational and functionalist modern city was what Larry hoped to transform through a reconnection to these common origins. To him the city had become "sensuously deprived" or sterilized:

It permits no interaction, no opportunities for physically becoming involved . . . Think for a moment of the city *core*, primarily. Here are vast areas whose sensuous characteristics have consciously been eradicated, stifled and neutralized wherever they tend to crop up. Floors and pavements underfoot are made of concrete and asphalt . . . so as to be as flat as possible with as little variation as possible . . . Usually any sign of living things are kept to a minimum, rivers are enclosed in culverts, sun and light is obscured, sidewalks are narrow, sitting or loitering is prohibited . . . color is limited, views of the sky are obscured by tall buildings . . . It is an eminently sterilized unsensual and biologically stultifying environment. There is no way for us to interact with the environment—when we do, it destroys us—cars pollute the air and run us down; in the vast cavernous underground subways the press of bodies, the filth, the queasy, unsanitary atmosphere haunts the lives of those who must use them. The city offends every sense! The city *can* become a delight when it caters to people's real needs on a biological level. This does not mean greening the city or suburbanizing it by poking plants at it. It *does* mean concern about people's interaction with it—their use of it, other than their practical economically-based use.[13]

Larry Halprin's response to this deprivation is an interactive environment that intensified kinesthetic awareness and the performance of everyday life.

Most significantly, Halprin attempted to elevate habitual movement through the city to a kind of ceremonial procession. Joseph Henderson, in his essay "Psychology and the Roots of Design," appearing in the *Lawrence Halprin: Changing Places* exhibition catalogue (1986), presents his interpretation of two types of archetypal images, which he defines as those that "emerge from the unconscious as preformed abstractions," discovered through his study of dreams.[14] They include the "centered image" having a formative influence on the design of houses, temples, formal gardens, and the like, which have a fixed point from which everything else is relatively placed. The other type is "an image of liberated movement," which is associated with sequential processions that include bridges, tunnels, stairways, and labyrinthine passages, and "always move beyond any fixed points in the search for new and different levels of experience." As he notes further, "For me [Halprin's] designs seem to depend on the creation of a moving line as an ordering principle by which people can experience nature archetypally." He adds that these linear forms remain "open ended, never to be perfected or finalized." In theory, this is exactly what Halprin's scores intend to provoke—a progressive movement sequence that enables people to experience their environment with a kind of primal immediacy.

In *Cities*, Halprin states that "the essence of our urban experiences is the process of movement through a sequential and variegated series of spaces" (197). The open spaces of the city, Halprin claims, should provide the organizational framework for moving through it and provide the stage upon which public life can unfold. These open spaces that lace the city include "streets, alleyways, passageways, malls, boulevards, avenues, marketplaces, plazas, underground shopping malls, parking spaces, arcades, leftover triangles, parks, playgrounds, waterfronts, railroad yards, tracks, rooftops, hills, valleys, freeways, bridges, interchanges." The choreography of these spaces create "an ordering of movement through which we ... live our urban lives."[15]

All the fundamental urban elements Halprin explores in *Cities* facilitate this modern landscape of motion, change, and choice. As Halprin states within the first few pages of the book:

> The city comes alive through movement and its rhythmic structure. The elements are no longer merely inanimate. They play a vital role, they become modulators of activity and are seen in juxtaposition with other moving objects. Within the spaces, movement flows, the paving and ramps become platforms for action, the street furniture is used, the sculpture in the street is seen and enjoyed. And the whole city landscape comes alive through movement as a total environment for the creative process of living.

Halprin accepts the dynamism and flux of the modern city. Because he recognizes the inevitability of the city's transformative speed, his emphasis remained on sustaining continuity through aesthetics as a means of grounding and orienting the city's inhabitants. Additionally, he tries to counter the cultural obsolescence of his own work through catering to human's basic and fundamental needs. Like his experiments in the garden, Halprin's attempts to score movement, rhythm, and facilitate unexpected occurrence, unfolding opportunity, environmental choice, and engagement in the city were guided by an interest in the same basic elements: transitions, sequence, topography, textures, materials, and seasonal and diurnal change.

The choreography of this ritualistic movement through the city began with the street. The city street is the stage on which the props and sets prompt a series of spontaneous theatrical events as well as unfolding ritualistic dramas. According to Halprin,

> It is, after all, only on streets that people meet face to face, where interaction occurs, where shopping and visiting and eating and festivals occur . . . It is in the city street in fact that community life is carried on (as distinguished from family and private life) . . . The street *is* the city for many people—only the middle-aged avoid it . . . It is on the streets that demonstrations occur, where peace marches can happen, where confrontations with the establishment take place . . . The street exists for *activity*, and activity is more than

visual. It involves many other senses including the kinesthetic, and, primarily, it involves the *interactions of people* which cannot be prescored . . . The street score can open possibilities, it can make things available, it can energize the potentiality of events.[16]

Halprin reasserted Main Street as a ceremonial passage through the city. He was interested in its potential for inspiring ritualistic procession and providing a sequence of diverse experiences as well as opportunities for social interaction and exchange along its length. After his success designing suburban shopping centers, cities began commissioning his firm to restore their commercial cores. Throughout the 1960s, though predominantly in the earlier half of the decade, Halprin was simultaneously involved in shopping center design and downtown renewal to counteract the former's draining effects. As an insider in the development of the alluring shopping center typology, he was properly suited to lead its counter-opposition in the downtown.

Before moving on to an analysis of Halprin's Main Street scores for San Francisco and Minneapolis, his involvement in the "recycling" of San Francisco's Ghirardelli chocolate factory into a retail environment deserves mention, since it served as a kind of intermediary project that provided the contained and introverted conditions of the shopping center but was intended to stimulate reinvestment in the city.[17] It also introduces the question of Halprin's authorial control. Deemed "one of his finest examples of creating space as theater" in the San Francisco Museum of Modern Art's retrospective catalogue on Halprin (1986), Ghirardelli Square's terraces, ramps, steps, street furniture, planting, lights, kiosk, fountain, and framed views of the Bay ensured an interactive and enticing environment for San Francisco consumers (Figure 2.1). In 1962, simultaneous with the aforementioned Main Street scores, the developer William Roth hired Lawrence Halprin & Associates for master planning and for the design of all the public areas, and Wurster, Bernardi & Emmons for the architecture of the square. The innovative civic–commercial development combining arts (theater), retail, dining, and entertainment came well before festival marketplaces such as Faneuil Hall in Boston and South Street Seaport in New York. The ramps and stepped terraces staged multidimensional pedestrian movement and constantly shifting views of the consumer environment and the dramatic landscape

Figure 2.1. Central fountain in Ghirardelli Square before Ruth Asawa's sculpture was installed in 1968. Photograph by Ernest Braun.

beyond. Though the development is located within the city, it is closer to Halprin's sub-urban shopping centers rather than the scores for urban retail streets because of the isolation and insularity of the complex. Instead of opening the development to the sur-rounding North Beach neighborhood, composed largely of Italian businesses, go-go bars, and residual Beat culture, all the buildings and activities of the square are oriented inward toward the central plaza (built on top of a multistory parking garage) and toward the panorama of the Bay.

In addition to the project's insularity, Halprin demonstrated his difficulty relinquish-ing control to future accretion when the central fountain, whose base he had designed (pictured in Figure 2.1), was surmounted by a sculpture of two bronze mermaids sur-rounded by sea turtles and frogs. According to Halprin, the representational sculpture was out of character with the square and even "violated" it.[18] Though he had agreed that an artist would be commissioned to create the fountain's central feature, when sculptor Ruth Asawa had her bronze mermaids installed in March 1968, Halprin sent an immedi-ate response to the media and design community. In it, he argues that the sculpture does not invite participatory response or interaction, and because of its figurative character the range of interpretation is limited. It is thus a "static form . . . which people would look at curiously and then leave," rather than "something open-ended, engaging their imagi-nation—something one could come back to and each time derive something new from." Though these assertions are reasonable, Halprin's statement culminates with the reveal-ing evocation of the "principle of the second man" derived from Ed Bacon's explanation in *Design of Cities* (1967). Halprin claims the first designer (himself in this case) "sets the framework, establishes the character, works out an idea . . . The second man [owes] a re-sponsibility to the first, not to him personally but to his idea, to his seminal concept. That principle has been violated here. The second man has given no thought to the idea or the concept or the purpose. He has done only what has pleased him and his own ego. He has not been able to work within the overall concept and its basic intention." Clearly much can be said about Halprin's perspectives on gender when assessing this statement, yet it is included here to introduce the consistent paradox in Halprin's work: his supposed desire for open-endedness and flexibility repeatedly challenged by his inability to release control.

MARKET STREET, SAN FRANCISCO, CALIFORNIA

At the same time he was designing Ghirardelli Square, Halprin began what became decades of work on the grand boulevard of his city, an experience that informed his more successful street interventions in places like Minneapolis. Beginning in the early 1960s, Halprin and his associates collaborated with a team of designers to address downtown San Francisco with a major focus on Market Street as the city's organizational and economic "spine."[19] Unlike the challenges presented by regional shopping centers and Ghirardelli Square, on Market Street the firm had to negotiate with particular social complexities since it ran through a diverse transect of the city. Lawrence Halprin & Associates designed the street furniture, paving, and plazas along its length, providing the framework or score that sought to facilitate an interactive public life of meaningful collective rituals—both ceremonial and quotidian.

The opportunity to rebuild the street, characterized then (and parts still now) as "sleazy," "seedy," and "tawdry," arose with plans to tear it up to run the new subway (BART) underneath. Halprin initially proposed a "multi-dimensional system" along Market Street in five levels of progressive movement (see four levels in Figure 2.2): two levels for the new subway line, one for street cars that would be removed from the surface and burrowed, not directly below the street surface but below a continuous pedestrian mezzanine extending from Front Street to Van Ness.[20] The four

Figure 2.2. Lawrence Halprin & Associates, proposed section through Market Street, 1962. Published in the study "What to Do about Market Street?" (1962), 24. Lawrence Halprin Collection, The Architectural Archives, University of Pennsylvania.

underground tunnels would be topped with a street that would most cater to the pedestrian. Such a segregation of modes of transport was a tenet of the 1933 Athens Charter issued by the Congrès Internationaux d'Architecture Moderne (CIAM), which was organized by Le Corbusier and composed of the key figures of European Modernism, including Walter Gropius. By adopting such principles, Halprin is clearly expressing his Modernist foundations.

The collaborative study "What to Do about Market Street?" (October 1962) indicated "Five Market Streets" of varying character: the Gateway Sector starting at the Ferry Building and moving southwest through the Financial Sector, the Central Retail Sector, the Amusement Sector, and the General Commercial Sector. Halprin's major contribution to the report is his description of "A Walk Up Market Street" in its current condition and his hopes for its renewal. The writing is similar to the thoughts that occur to Halprin as he is sketching in his notebooks. The description is included in its near entirety to demonstrate his interest in the narrative unfolding of experience as one proceeded down the length of the ceremonial street:

Start at the Embarcadero. The waterfront is almost a misnomer, for the Freeway and Ferry Building have created an impenetrable barrier, at street level, to one of San Francisco's most priceless assets—its marine setting. If rapport with the Bay cannot be established by removing one or both wings of the Ferry Building, as suggested in an early Ferry Park study by Mario Ciampi, at least there should be a ground level arcade . . . It is important that the "beginning" of Market Street have a unique and special flavor . . . Is there a way that the romance and color of our lusty waterfront can be recreated without tawdryness? The Ferry Park could be a great open space with canals, lagoons, and fountains that would revive the marine flavor by actually bringing the Bay back into the area. The atmosphere of European parks could be injected with handsome paving, sidewalk cafes, and fine restaurants. The freeway should be painted dark, and large trees should be planted to suppress its sight and its sounds. Difficult as this may be, establish the Ferry Park area as a vibrant, alive, colorful place, used by day and at night, and it will send a tingle up the spine of Market Street . . . As one enters the financial sector, the block between Spear and

Main Streets on the south side of Market would be an ideal location for a plaza about 100 feet deep . . . Distinctive landscape treatment of each block would greatly enhance the appearance of the street . . . No one uniform, parkway-type treatment would be appropriate on Market Street. It should have a series of carefully designed urban landscape incidents, integrated and organized, but not unified as on New York's Park Avenue . . . The Crown Zellerbach Plaza is a delight . . . The triangular island at Sansome and Sutter should be landscaped and, possibly, connected with the block to the east. Need it only be a concrete roosting place for the weary walker? . . . The Market–Montgomery–Post Street intersection is one of the busiest. It deserves a fountain, a piece of sculpture, planting . . . How pleasant it would be if all the merchants on this block got together and put up awnings of harmonious color and design! . . . The ugly new façade of Woolworths . . . murders the lower stories of the once elegant Flood Building. This is only one of many handsome, classic buildings that have been remodeled insensitively, causing Market Street to lose much of its distinctive, lordly character. When stores are given new fronts or entire buildings new skins, care should be taken to ensure that the new has a sympathetic relationship with the old . . . And now we arrive at the amusement sector. Even the mood and make-up of the crowds here is different . . . Let's organize it so it really has the daytime gaiety and the nighttime fantasy an amusement district should have. The refreshment stands and other small establishments that abound here could be clustered and recessed in arcades to create intimate pockets out of the current of the street . . . From here west, Market is in need of major rehabilitation. The answer may be the much discussed, but never implemented, effort to link the Civic Center with Market Street. To do this effectively, sweeping views into the Civic Center must be created, and, conversely, the vistas from the Center to Market Street must not terminate in junk. Opposite the Market–Fulton intersection, why not a plaza on the south side of the street surrounded by important commercial buildings or government offices? If the Civic Center Plan is carried out, the 2 blocks between Jones & Hyde will be opened up, and when the Hyde–Larkin block is reconstructed (as proposed in the plan), views in the Civic Center should be created. Thus our Civic Center, one of the most beautiful in America, could give tremendous support to Market Street.[21]

The Market Street Design Plan (1967), prepared for the city by a team led by the architect Mario Ciampi, with Halprin as a primary consultant, emerged as a response to the "What to Do about Market Street?" report.[22] Halprin paid careful attention to the pedestrian connections and "leftover" triangular spaces where the diagonal Market Street intersected with the angled streets to the north (Figure 2.3). To rationalize traffic flow, the plan called for the closure of some of these streets, resulting in the Fulton–Leavenworth and Powell Street malls.

In 1967, Halprin, Ciampi, and the architect John C. Warnecke were granted the

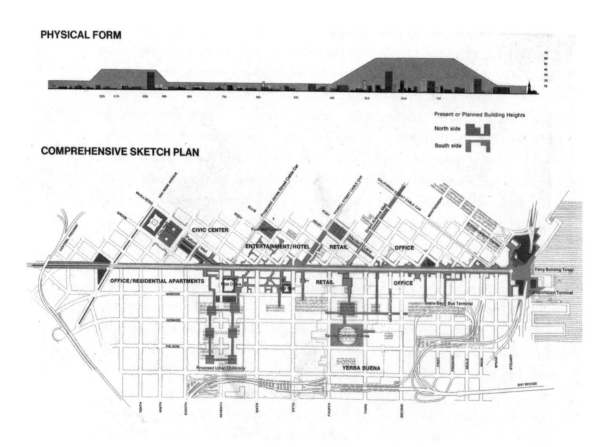

Figure 2.3. Proposed Market Street open space network. Published in *The Market Street Design Plan* (1967). Lawrence Halprin Collection, The Architectural Archives, University of Pennsylvania.

commission to execute the design of the reconceived Market Street. Rather than enhance the street's variety, Halprin's Market Street is more uniform than the series of "landscape incidents" he recommended in 1962. Yet its uniformity serves to "knit together all the various uses" of the diverse street. Halprin's conception of Market Street as a long linear promenade or grand boulevard integrated the malls and plazas as part of a comprehensive design all interconnected by the hierarchically dominant spine.[23] Thus, areas for movement (the malls and the widened sidewalks) and for pause (the plazas) were carefully choreographed in a rhythmic sequence along the length of the street.

One of Halprin's most significant concerns was the experience of emerging from the subway underground into the light and air. His earlier conceptions for continuous underground mezzanines that were open to the sky through cuts in the median strip (see Figure 2.2) were scaled back to modest pedestrian concourses of varying extent at the subway stations, so the multidimensional system diminished significantly. Three major plazas, interspersed with smaller ones, were designed and built along the street's length: Embarcadero Plaza, Andrew Hallidie Plaza (formerly Powell Plaza), and the Civic Center Plaza. The latter two were situated at subway stations while a more minor plaza was designed at the Montgomery Street Station, each to serve as "new gateways to the City," according to the 1967 report. Embarcadero Plaza was not part of the Market Street development but served as the anchor to the sequence, or the "Ferry Park" Halprin wrote about in 1962 as the "beginning of Market Street," in an attempt to connect the street to the Ferry Building and the waterfront despite the freeway obstruction.

The true anchoring element of the sequence is the Embarcadero Fountain, designed by the Canadian André Vaillancourt and overseen by Halprin. While certainly not as extravagant as the canals, lagoons, and fountains Halprin recommended for this park in 1962, the fountain caused much lively public and media debate upon its dedication in 1971, questioning its visual appeal and artistic merit. The driving intention of the massive form of concrete, steel, and water was to respond to and better integrate the adjacent freeway into the context of the city (Figure 2.4). Halprin situated the sculpture in the bend of the freeway ramp, so the ramp and the corner fountain enclose the large open space that comprises the rest of the plaza. According to one article printed just after its dedication: "Whizzing vehicles on the freeway seem to weave through the concrete sculpture, giving it a kinetic urban essence and, at the same time, embracing and adding dimension to the freeway."[24] Water, stepping-stones, and stairs invite active participation in the dynamic structure Halprin called an "environmental event." The remainder of the four-acre plaza (later renamed after Justin Herman, the dynamic director of San Francisco's Redevelopment Agency) provided a gathering place for large civic ritual events, including political rallies, speeches, ceremonies, concerts, and parade culmination or

Figure 2.4. Embarcadero Plaza, fountain, and freeway in context, 1970s.
Lawrence Halprin Collection, The Architectural Archives, University of
Pennsylvania (detail of slide D-C702, stamped by Lawrence Halprin & Associates).

initiation. The plaza and fountain as its focal point was deliberately situated off-axis to "avoid the Renaissance quality of objects in visually static relationship," explains Halprin.[25]

Hallidie Plaza at Fifth Street, extending east to Powell Street, acts as the gateway to the retail section of Market Street (Figure 2.5). It is entered from the most sizeable underground concourse that opens into the plaza, which is sunken below street level and accessed from the street by stairs and escalators. This vertical movement was desirable to Halprin to vary the potential monotony of walking along the flat ground-plane of Market Street. However, the architectural critics Allan Temko and Paul Goldberg reviewed the mundane plaza in 1979 as a $2 million "hole in the ground,"[26] since very little was done to activate or entice

Figure 2.5. Hallidie Plaza on Market Street in San Francisco. Photograph by Paul Ryan, November 1975.

Figure 2.6. United Nations Plaza and City Hall
from the San Francisco Federal Building, 2005.
Photograph courtesy of U.S. General Services Administration.

shoppers to descend into the sunken space that was obscured from the "eyes on the street" (about which Jane Jacobs wrote just before the street's design in *The Death and Life of Great American Cities*).

The Civic Center Plaza was to be dominated by a major sculpture, or what became the United Nations Plaza and Fountain, and was to direct views, ceremonial processions, or parade events off Market Street and toward City Hall—one of Halprin's major recommendations in the 1962 report (Figure 2.6). Originally intended as another multidimensional environment from station to street level, the plan was diminished and it became an uninterrupted civic space. Though not ultimately multileveled, as Lawrence Halprin & Associates state in a press document: "The UN Plaza is the pivot of the renovated Market Street . . . Market has always been the route of parades. The new Market will serve, too, as a processional way where parades can march on what will be one of the world's most beautiful urban boulevards turning at the UN Plaza to continue up the Mall to the City Hall."[27] In reality, the fountain became a well-used public toilet and bath for the abundant homeless population that gathers in this portion of Market Street, causing the city to chain it off in 2003.

Unlike Minneapolis's Nicollet Avenue, more attention seemed to be paid to uniformity than to complexity along Market Street, since the preexisting street characteristics already exhibited significant diversity. Therefore, the linear sequence with its lateral plazas opening up shifting perspectives was made consistent through brick paving patterns and more regularized tree plantings, including approximately six hundred London plane trees.[28] Perhaps the most physically notable element of the mediocre result is Halprin's street furniture, including benches, bus shelters, kiosks, telephone booths, newspaper racks, vending stands, traffic signals, drinking fountains, trash receptacles, planters, emergency call boxes, and so on. Only the fire hydrants and lamp standards were not redesigned.[29] The arrangement of these common elements created the stage and props intended to support everyday rituals and stimulate public interaction. Though the plazas are certainly underwhelming, as an organizational datum for the burgeoning city and a ceremonial passage now culminating to the east in a cleared view of the Ferry Building, Market Street provided a hometown laboratory for Halprin to develop techniques he was simultaneously considering for other projects. It also provided a stage for Anna: she scored *Blank Placard Dance* and *Citydance*, among other more spontaneous "events," along the city's more sharply defined ceremonial way.

NICOLLET AVENUE TRANSIT MALL, MINNEAPOLIS, MINNESOTA

Like Market Street, Nicollet Avenue was historically Minneapolis's "parade street."[30] For both these projects, Halprin was given the chance to enhance the quality of civic rituals as collective participatory events. Nicollet Mall (Figure 2.7) is one of the few projects for which Halprin draws a Motational sequence (Figure 2.8).[31] The notational study, depicting stationary elements designed by the firm as well as moving objects and people, was most likely used as a "testing-out device" to experiment with projected movement through the conceived design, rather than starting with abstracted movement to generate form.[32] This is most likely due to the project's constraints and the complexity of the inherited urban condition.

The transitway scheme and the signature undulation of Nicollet Avenue cannot be attributed to the Halprin firm. The fate of the street was determined by the formation of the Downtown Council of Minneapolis in 1955. The council, composed of top executive officers of major corporations, retailers, and property owners, soon formed a subcommittee to plan for the retail street, recognizing its potential for sharp decline as it had started experiencing the draining effects of suburban development.[33] By 1958, the Downtown Council had hired the engineering and planning firm Barton Aschman Associates of Chicago to create what became the *Nicollet Avenue Study: Principles and Techniques for Retail Street Improvement* (1960). This study presented five alternative scenarios for Nicollet Avenue, the fifth of which, "Mall and Transitway," was ultimately selected. The serpentine nature of the transitway became a key element of the early conceptual planning. According to Frederick Aschman, planners and traffic engineers collaboratively conceived of the serpentine plan to reduce the visual monotony of the linear street. The ultimate aim was to transform the downtown motorist into a promenading shopper.

Why Halprin jumped at the opportunity to design this project should be evident, especially with the funding and support available for design with top-quality materials and expert construction and with traffic planners agreeable to this new and interesting street pattern amid the Minneapolis grid (Figure 2.9). Halprin was most likely also retained in Minneapolis for his success in designing midwestern regional shopping centers,

Figure 2.7. Nicollet Avenue Transit Mall, Minneapolis, Minnesota. Published in Lawrence Halprin, *The RSVP Cycles*, 73. Photograph by Paul Ryan.

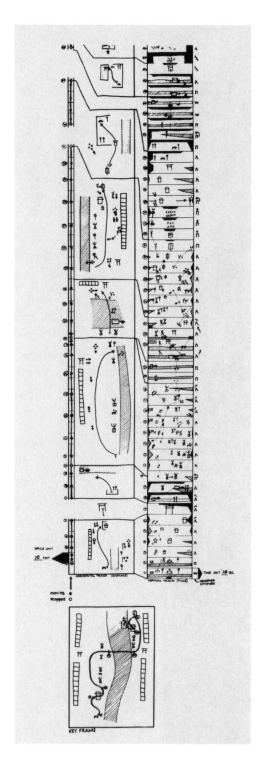

Figure 2.8. Nicollet Avenue "Motation."
Published in Lawrence Halprin,
The RSVP Cycles, 68–69.

including Old Orchard and Oakbrook Shopping Centers on the outskirts of Chicago. In the unpublished manuscript titled *The Environment as Art Experience* (1974), Halprin explains,

The great contribution that the suburban shopping center has made to the 20th century is that it has forced the city to re-think its own qualities. The environmental competition of the suburban shopping center more than any abstract philosophy has had a profound impact on the downtown environment. Insufficient and limited as they are, suburban shopping centers have attempted to provide participatory environments for their customers. For that reason alone, downtown has had to re-think itself in order to "survive."[34]

Halprin was the perfect candidate, in this case, for the generation of such a survival plan. In a small illustration included in *Cities*, Halprin depicts "the shopping street as evaluated by a shopping center developer" (Figure 2.10). The diagrammatic sketch demonstrates optimized merchandizing frontage configurations for "impulse buying." Adjacent to these plans, he explains how urban designers would benefit from studying the accomplishments of merchants and store designers who have carefully evaluated "pedestrian movement geared to salesmanship" (194).

In the shopping center, Halprin did not have to battle with preexisting street patterns, specifically the grid that he so often claimed stultified the senses. He could create an entirely new "fantasy environment" (his phrase), catered to the suburbanites who gathered there as a social ritual, and perhaps to fill the void created by the loss of public life since deserting the city. One of the major caveats presented by the Downtown Council, however, was that Nicollet Avenue must be "urbane, and not patterned after suburban shopping centers ... provided with the fullest safeguards against garishness and commercialism."[35]

Lawrence Halprin & Associates's Thomas Brown was named the associate in charge and Richard Vignolo the principal in charge of the Nicollet project. After Halprin's original 1962–1963 ideas and schematic plans, the later process documents can be attributed to both of these individuals (most primarily Tom Brown).[36] The year 1962 was an extremely busy one for the firm and included the initiation of the Sea Ranch master plan, Ghirardelli Square, the Market Street study, and the San Francisco Freeways report. In addition, Halprin was finishing his book *Cities*, many sections of which he applies directly to his original concepts for Nicollet Avenue. Therefore, it is important to consider passages in *Cities* to fully understand his points of theoretical departure in Minneapolis.

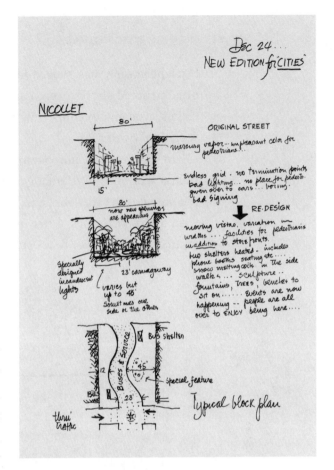

Figure 2.9. Lawrence Halprin's sketch of Nicollet Mall for the second edition of *Cities* (1972). Lawrence Halprin Collection, The Architectural Archives, University of Pennsylvania (scan from photo print, 014.IV.A.105).

The serpentine street directly responded to what Halprin would later write about the controlling nature of "street scores" in *The RSVP Cycles* (82–93). The street presented the greatest choreographic challenge to Halprin because "more than any other urban pattern the street system scores the quality and character of the life pattern of its inhabitants for centuries" (85). He had started to consider the controlling versus choreographic potential of street patterns in *Cities*, published a year after he started on the Nicollet project.

Straight linear vistas viewed in single-point perspective, as well as undifferentiated or uninterrupted streets, were conditions embodied by the ubiquitous grid, and, Halprin claims, "become too uniformly dull" and "achieve a nightmarish quality of personal dissociation" (193).

In his chapter "Choreography" in *Cities*, he was just beginning to work out his theories on scoring in a systematic manner, after applying it intuitively to gardens throughout the previous decade. The book is most primarily focused on the potential of the pedestrian to experience his or her environment at a human scale and walking speed, "a maximum of four miles per hour" (193). The book's pages are filled with images, particularly of sites in Europe, and especially of medieval cities whose streets were not intended for fast-moving vehicles and thus provided "the stage on which all the life of the city was played."[37]

Halprin's emphasis on the segregation of modes of travel is integral to the plans for Nicollet Mall and, more generally, to all his city-scale projects during the 1960s and 1970s.[38] In *Cities* he proclaims that the automobile "will destroy the very essence of downtown" (201–2). As stated, Halprin's conception of a multidimensional system of movement, at its most extreme, separated all forms of travel in a way reminiscent of some of the early twentieth-century European avant-gardes. Like his proposal for Market Street, he states that "the new local street, choreographically designed, will be multileveled—the ma-

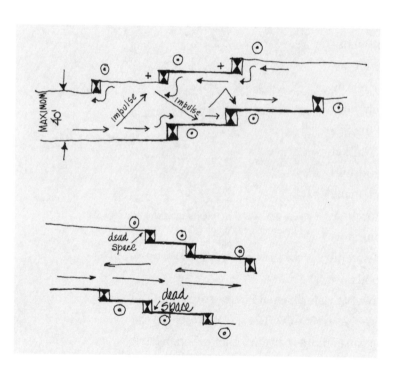

Figure 2.10. Lawrence Halprin's sketch of "the shopping street as evaluated by a shopping center developer." Published in Lawrence Halprin, *Cities* (1972), 194. Lawrence Halprin Collection, The Architectural Archives, University of Pennsylvania.

chines at ground level, rapid transit at a still lower level, and pedestrian raised above both, on upper decks and bridges closer to the sky and free from the dangers and impediments of high speed vehicles" (207).

Halprin was also a supporter of the superblock, deemed another Modernist failure, particularly after his success at St. Francis Square, since it added variety to the relentless grid and offered a pedestrianized territory for the city's inhabitants. However, as his study *New York, New York: A Study of the Quality, Character, and Meaning of Open Space in Urban Design* (1968) reveals, he supported the superblock more for its potential to provide a shared gathering space uninterrupted by automobile traffic, similar to Tunnard's urban schemes for the "All-Europe House" or Clarence Stein and Henry Wright's Radburn, then the barren and alienating tower-in-the-park public housing superblock model. Though certainly not a downtown block, Halprin's design (with William Wurster) for Greenwood Common in the Berkeley Hills (1955–58) arranges individual houses and their small personal gardens around a shared open space and sets parking at the periphery (Figure 2.11). The pedestrianized "common" had to be humanly scaled to support social gathering separate from the interference of vehicles, other good examples of which are integrated into Halprin's Open Space Sequence in Portland, Oregon, to be considered in chapter 3. In addition to Ghirardelli Square, Halprin's regional shopping centers are clearly another example of pedestrianized environments separated from automobiles. Visitors leave their cars in the surrounding parking lot and enter an enclosed court landscaped to provide interactive "public" spaces and an optimized environment for leisurely shopping.

Devoted to such separation, Halprin's interest in downtown Minneapolis was largely inspired by its "skyway" system—enclosed (and heated) overhead pedestrian connectors or bridges—which began in 1962 and proliferated throughout the subsequent decades. Halprin eagerly anticipated the developing complexity of this system, considering the mall a catalyst that would generate the skyways' growth into a complex multidimensional network for which the mall would act as the connective spine.[39]

Halprin's avid interest in this skyway development as an augmentation to his unilevel mall is ironic, since rather than enhance the mall it contributed significantly to its demise.

Figure 2.11. Lawrence Halprin's drawing of Greenwood Common, Berkeley, California, designed 1955–58. Lawrence Halprin Collection, The Architectural Archives, University of Pennsylvania (scan from colored photo print).

Apparently, the skyway system was conceived in 1958 but was stalled because of merchants' concerns over potential losses from street-level stores. The ultimate deterioration and demolition of Halprin's Nicollet Mall in 1990 was attributed to just such losses and the diminishment of concentrated street life where people are forced to interact on the same plane.

The serpentine street pattern excited Halprin for both the variety of views and rhythms it provided as well as the spaces it created for diverse activities. Twenty-four feet was the standard width allotted for the transit bus system, but the street's undulation made it possible to design sizeable pedestrian plazas and walkways of varying widths. Meanwhile, the northernmost two-and-half blocks were straightened to offer a clear view to the Northwestern Life Insurance Building, designed by Minoru Yamasaki, which visually terminated the mall, additionally breaking the grid.[40]

The concept of a "transitway," conceived by the Downtown Council with Barton Aschman Associates, had not yet been pioneered in the United States. The bus system added another movement dimension to the sequenced experience of the mall. Buses were required to travel five to six miles per hour during peak hours and eight to nine at off-peak. Therefore, although none of the design had to cater to the perceptual experience of rapid movement, the mall's design recognizes the experiential and durational distinctions between walking and riding the bus. The buses were also intended to improve access to the area; all downtown routes ran across, on, or parallel to and within one block of the mall.[41] This reconfigured bus system was intended to bring large numbers of people from all over the city to the retail street to collectively conduct common social rituals—shopping, eating, and so forth.

In many ways Nicollet Mall served as a tangible embodiment of the *Cities* publication. Because so much of the project was predeveloped when it was handed over to Halprin and his associates, their emphasis remained on the street paving, furniture, plantings, and the treatment of building facades, all composed to appeal to the shopper's senses. Just as Halprin included sections in the book devoted to bollards, drains, kiosks, clocks, and the like, he controlled the design of each of these elements on Nicollet Avenue, paying careful attention to their rhythmic placement. The inventory of such elements integrated in Minneapolis is extensive. Halprin's firm designed standardized forms, including incandescent street lights, benches, bollards, drinking fountains (of Minnesota granite), flower pots (Halprin's signature cast-stone pots), trash containers, bronze-anodized aluminum

Figure 2.12. Paving patterns and furniture on Nicollet Avenue in Minneapolis, 1968. Photograph by Paul Ryan.

signal housings with integrated street name signs and traffic instructions, sixteen heated bus shelters, flag poles, directories to orient pedestrians to the retail choices on the mall, and tree planter boxes and grates of varying shapes and patterns.

These standardized forms offered some uniformity to what was also a plan constituting deliberate diversity. For instance, the arrangement of these elements along the mall was composed to appear haphazard, as if it were the organic outcome of accretional development over time, qualities that Halprin admired in medieval cities (yet had trouble accepting if this meant alterations to his own design). In addition, he designed other street features that were unique, yet related. For instance, paving patterns varied but used the same palette of materials: terrazzo accented with red tile bands, brick, and granite (Figure 2.12), with each street intersection demarcated by a unique and colorful inlaid tile medallion (see Figure 2.7). As another example, the approximately one hundred trees in nearly twenty varieties were selected for both their urban survival and contrasting characteristics. Halprin lists possible tree species in his notebooks: "(a) Tall arching—locust, (b) Medium dense—green ash, sycamore, (c) Flowering—cherries, crabs, etc., (d) Evergreens—some—risky."[42] These trees, according to Tom Brown, were arranged to "define areas, break up vistas down the street and to provide the major vertical element in the otherwise two-dimensional composition," and "to hide unsightly facades and to throw upon and add interest to pleasing but overly plain facades."[43]

Beyond the subtle variations in standard forms, the changing paving patterns and the different tree specimens arranged irregularly, each block contained a distinctive "focal point" or "special feature" that existed "within the strong framework of the whole."[44] These were intended to give each block a unique character of its own, to stimulate interactive response and gathering, and to provide orientation as "landmarks" (they may be compared to the unique plazas along Market Street).[45] These included fountains and clocks, as well as a self-service post office and a "weather station" (a small interactive structure with temperature, humidity, barometer, wind speed, and precipitation gauges). Finally, the "crown jewel" of such landmarks was a Calder stabile donated to the city by Dayton's department store and situated outside it on Seventh Street (Figure 2.13). Photographs of the mall reveal that the base of the Calder is set flush with terrazzo pavement around it, and a manhole cover is even integrated into the base. Its prominence was deliberately subdued in order to diminish its monumentality and the look-don't-touch nature of public sculpture often placed as unintegrated objects, particularly in corporate plazas during this time. It was thus made to appear as if the stabile had always existed on the street as part of a long process of accretion.[46]

In the "Statement by Lawrence Halprin & Associates," dated November 1967, the Nicollet Mall design team writes, "We wanted the new elements to relate, to feel as if they grew into the street in a natural way, not as a superimposed design."[47] Yet the very same month this statement was devised, Halprin proclaimed in his dedication speech that "a whole new vocabulary of street furniture has been built to replace the chaotic hardware of the past." These two statements, considered together, imply that Halprin believed his

intervention created the image of the continual passage of time better than the actual evolutionary development of the street.

Other elements of the design by Lawrence Halprin & Associates aid in enhancing the rhythms of street life. For instance, aerial photographs reveal the complexity and attention paid to the mall's pavement patterns.[48] On Nicollet Avenue the bands of tile set within the larger terrazzo slabs infuse the experience of the walking surface with a rhythmic beat. The medallions set within the asphalt of the cross-street intersections provide an alternative rhythm that distinguishes the speed and distance of the buses in contrast to the tempo of the pedestrian. Finally, the areas paved in diverse and textured patterns of granite and brick

Figure 2.13. Alexander Calder stabile on Nicollet Avenue in Minneapolis, 1968. Photograph by Paul Ryan.

for the sitting or gathering areas, separate from the directional stream of people, enforce Halprin's interest in the segregation of movement. Where people are still or slowed, more attention is freed for recognition of such intricacies of pattern and texture. Again, the qualities of speed and perceptual experience determine the composition.

The street furniture acts as another tempo device. "The city," Halprin explains in *Cities*, "like a stage set, demands modulators for people in motion—objects of use and comfort and artistry—guides for activity, shelters for incidental but necessary events, semi-buildings, signs, symbols, places for sitting—a whole universe of objects" (51). Halprin anticipates the types of users on the street—the window shopper, the weary shopper, the downtown office worker or commuter, the tourist or conventioneer, the child, and so on—and provides what he considers optimal situations for each to enact their daily rituals. As Halprin continues, "The modern city is a kaleidoscope of overlapping activities and people in motion. As the people eddy and move in a multifaceted series of actions, the furniture in the street becomes the fixed point which can guide and enrich their movements" (51).

Yet Halprin does not necessarily conceive of these elements as merely static, despite their fixity into the ground. They are perceived by the moving person and, as the Motational sequence indicates, they move in relationship to an individual's changing perspectives and progression. The "special features" serve as orienting elements or "pivots" around which the drama unfolds. They both generate and serve as spectacle. Their individuality entices or propels shoppers to continue forward to discover what each block has to offer to their curiosity and sense of delight.

The temporal dimension of the street was structured by a longer-range score as well. The firm anticipated and optimized diurnal and seasonal change on Nicollet Avenue. In addition, Halprin, in *Cities* and throughout his career, insists on the preservation of old buildings, not necessarily for any momentous historical significance but for their physical manifestation of a temporal continuity integral to his ecological position. "Buildings of different ages, reflecting the taste and culture of different periods, [remind] us of our past as well as our future," he explains (216). The history of the street, written up by the

Hennepin County Historical Society and filed in Halprin's Nicollet Mall materials, best illustrates his interest in this sense of continuity. The street was first established as a "meandering Indian trail," extending from a crossing place of the Mississippi River (the "meandering" quality reiterated in the 1960s design). After it was developed by white settlers, a fire in 1860 ravaged its mostly wooden structures, but by 1890 the street was rebuilt and had become the center of business and "retail dominance." Interestingly, since the mall was being handed back to the pedestrian, the document continues: "One of the many reasons for the retail dominance of Nicollet Avenue was due to the fact there were no street car lines on Nicollet in the downtown section. Business interests deliberately kept car lines off Nicollet, and in the past commonly advertised the convenience and safety to children of old Nicollet!"[49]

Some of the standard private development facilitated by urban renewal policies exists along the length of the mall, as well as "modernized" lower facades, but the general texture and variety represent the visual and temporal continuum Halprin considered essential to the primal need of humans to be rooted or oriented in both time and place. In his statement "The Design of Nicollet Avenue," Halprin declares that "Nicollet Avenue is unique in that, in this major city, all the major shopping facilities have remained on this single street. Our design aims to continue its character and reinforce it."[50] In addition, Nicollet's history as a parade street was undoubtedly attractive to Halprin, whose design sustained and enhanced its role as a site for ceremonial events as well as the "everyday ritual" of shopping as a collective civic activity.

The durational score for Nicollet Mall not only integrates the past but was intended to remain open to the future, a notion partially embodied in the idea that the street is only a stage set, and its life depends on the people who inhabit and activate it. In his dedication speech, Halprin explains: "Remember too that the street itself is only a place. Its life and character, its quality and vitality come from its people and the uses they put it to. This is in *your* hands to expand and enjoy . . . You have given me the wonderful opportunity to design Nicollet Avenue for you. I now give it back to you to bring to life." In addition, Halprin and his employees anticipated the mall as a catalyst for future development, and as such they attempted to design a street that was open enough to allow for adaptation, accretion, and change. Earlier in the dedication speech, he proclaims:

> This is just the beginning. This street itself will inevitably change over the years. The buildings that line it will be altered or rebuilt. The new shops will change its character. Heights will vary. At each point decisions will have to be made of whether to set back from the street or line it; whether to open plazas at corners or fill them in. The work in a city never ends—everything is and should be in process—and I hope that this process has received an initial great emphasis from our design for the street.
>
> But Nicollet alone cannot make your downtown. It must ramify, extend. Arcades must lead to other streets, to other areas. The riverfront—your great untapped natural resource—must be cleaned up, opened up for use and enjoyment, for promenades and parks, restaurants and shops.[51]

Halprin's desire for openness is genuine, yet his approach to achieving this desire in built form is questionable. He foresees the increasing complexity of the skyway system as a positive dimensional scheme enhancing the downtown. He imagines how generated enthusiasm for public space could catalyze interest in other areas of the city, particularly the waterfront. He writes about the private plazas that already exist adjacent to the mall as an enhancement to the open space system or network for which Nicollet serves as the spine. Yet he also states his desire to make the mall *appear* as if it had developed "naturally" rather than by "a superimposed design," but achieves this appearance by replacing the "chaotic hardware of the past" that *had* accrued over time with his single comprehensive intervention. Therefore, the street score is perhaps more closed, and Halprin retains more control than he admits.[52] The critical question is thus whether Halprin left enough room for future adaptation or gradual modification, or if, owing to the mall's lack of "imperfection" or "incompletion" to which he claims to aspire, it does not invite change at all. This question can perhaps be answered by the mall's redesign in 1990, described below. Challenging his intentions or success at applying his theories might be unfair, however, since the mall was an immediate social and financial success that generated millions of dollars of new construction and rehabilitation on the mall or within one block of it.[53] Further, photographs taken during the 1970s reveal people making creative use of the mall. For example, in addition to seating themselves on benches and under bus shelters, they sit on bollard chains, tree planters, and the walls backing the benches, appropriating the space and activating it in open-ended performance.

Despite this initial success, the mall has since been redesigned by BRW, Inc. of Minneapolis and, in September 2013, James Corner Field Operations was selected to revive it once more. BRW's principal in charge, Craig Amundsen, claimed that the mall had become "functionally and aesthetically outdated."[54] The pavings, structures, and lights thus were replaced, the latter by historicist fixtures. The skyway system that Halprin eagerly anticipated as an enhancement to the pedestrian network actually functioned to pull people off the streets and into the heated and "safe" environments. Articles by Amundsen indicate that the physical fabric had deteriorated from use and lack of attention after the second stories became the true retail center. Apparently the twenty-four-hour street life did not permanently materialize. Flexibility is the issue the redesigners of 1990 use as their argument for support of their proposal. They claim the key to the success of the elements included along the new mall is "that they have been designed for successive improvements and change. With few permanent fixtures, they will be periodically updated to respond to changing needs and tastes."[55] This notion seems to be in direct response to Halprin's mall—as a design that did not leave the score open enough for future adaptation. Yet the success of such an attempt at achieving "flexibility" might be revealed by how these impermanent or "throw-away" elements were valued during their short lifespans. In addition, though Amundsen argues that the previous mall would be replaced with one that was "more flexible and usable," his description of the new design appears to be quite similar to Halprin's in the 1960s. Colorful banners, changing flower displays, trees that celebrate the change in seasons, and the inclusion of a "water theme" through the insertion of pools and fountains echo Halprin's original description of the 1960s design. The serpentine pattern was modified by BRW so that the curvature that once created irregular and varied spaces "has been gracefully reconfigured to create a string of symmetrical plazas."[56]

And yet, according to one insightful review of the redesign, the previous mall was "functioning adequately" and was replaced with something perhaps more "flexible" and "safer" but at the expense of becoming "spiritless."[57] The regularized symmetry and the repetitive objects, the elements that are "derivative of the Victorian vernacular," in addition to the "flexibility" of the spaces, all of which represent a kind of "passivity of the redesign," is "all the more painful," the author claims, "because the Mall originally swirled in excitement." While attempting to be flexible enough to appease everyone, including future users, "the new Mall has become 'timeless' at the expense of character." These statements are particularly revealing because although Halprin claimed to create flexible spaces open to adapt to future needs, the ultimate demise of his design was attributed to just the opposite characteristics. Yet the redesign was clearly flawed because its very attempt at being flexible has produced a relatively meaningless result. As a hopeful result, a new design will soon take its place.

HERITAGE PARK PLAZA, FORT WORTH, TEXAS

In Lawrence Halprin's projects in San Francisco and Minneapolis, he worked to enhance preexisting infrastructure as a framework for ceremonial civic ritual. In Fort Worth, however, he and his firm designed a new space intended to guide movement through a new public procession. Halprin believed that rituals bind us to a collective past. He looked not only to the ancient and preindustrial past but hoped to heighten the tangibility of the historical continuum embodied in the physical environment. The palpability of centuries of human history in Jerusalem stirred this fundamental belief. Clearly his work in Ghirardelli Square conveys his interest in the reappropriation of historic fabric, and his drawings for the Sea Ranch demonstrate his integration of the social (in addition to ecological and geological) history of sites into the design process (see Figure I.6). More telling, however, is that in 1967 Lyndon Johnson appointed him as the only West Coast representative to the first President's Advisory Council on Historic Preservation. In addition to situating us temporally, Halprin believed the inherited environment provides the framework for sustained ritualistic expression.

Yet while Heritage Park Plaza (Figure 2.14) in Fort Worth is a new framework for ritualistic experience, it is a commemorative space that recognizes the collective past of the city. It is a processional design that through choreographed movement reveals the narrative of the city's founding. Appropriately, the plaza was funded by the city's Bicentennial Committee (yet it was not dedicated until April 1980).[58]

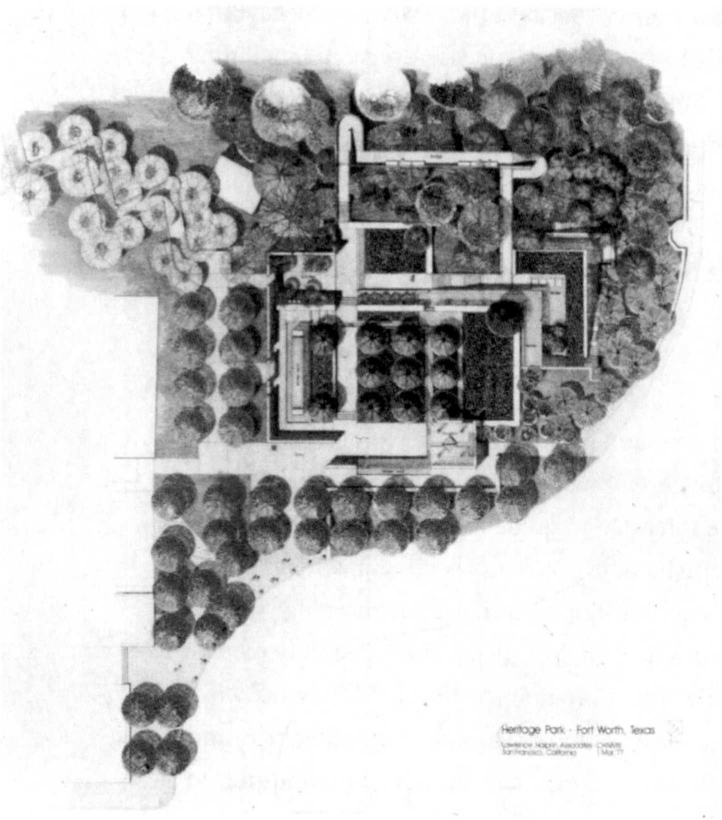

Figure 2.14. Lawrence Halprin & Associates and Carter Hull Nishita McCulley Baxter, Heritage Park Plaza plan, March 1977. The plan directly references the plan of the original fort complex, images of which are included in the Lawrence Halprin & Associates project documents. Lawrence Halprin Collection, The Architectural Archives, University of Pennsylvania (slide B-J417).

Situated on the bluffs overlooking the confluence of the Clear and West forks of the Trinity River, the plaza is at the location of the original fort (1849–53) for which the city is named. The plaza commands sweeping views of the converging river and the land to the east, west, and north, and its plan was largely inspired by the plan of the original fort. The plaza is part of a 112-acre open space network called Heritage Park (plans for which Halprin conceived in 1970), which serves as the link from the Central Business District into an eight-mile stretch of trails along the river. The link acts as an extended threshold between city and river, providing a transformative release from the structure of urban life through progressive movement toward the river—closely recalling Victor Turner's theories on the ritual process.

The terraced site was originally animated by water features that enveloped the visitor and gradually channeled flow downward toward the Trinity River, demonstrating reverence to the topographic feature that made this site historically significant.[59] In the late 1960s, the Streams and Valleys Committee, a newly formed local organization dedicated to reclaiming the abused Trinity River as a historic, scenic, and ecological resource, invited Lawrence Halprin & Associates to develop a plan to fulfill its mission.[60] The firm released the *Fort Worth Trinity River Report* in 1970, while it was also generating a detailed planning study for Fort Worth's Central Business District (CBD).[61] With an initial and primary foundation in Fort Worth's regional river ecology, the two studies unfolded simultaneously and became entirely interdependent. The Texas Highway Department also hired Halprin for a Freeway Corridor Selection in Fort Worth, which additionally progressed as a kind of organic extension of the two other projects. The Trinity River report and the CBD sector report played a significant role in the development of Heritage Park Plaza as a commemorative space, so they both deserve further discussion.

The Trinity River report considered the eight-mile length of the river that loops around downtown Fort Worth and was channeled and leveed in the 1950s for flood control.[62] Generally, the city developed with little or no public connection to the river, which Lawrence Halprin & Associates identified as a major recreational and aesthetic resource. The firm's report thus calls for a "regional open space system" to be structured along the banks, which run through a variety of Fort Worth neighborhoods. The emphasis of the report is on accessibility and orientation, increased recreational opportunities, enhanced flood control using more environmentally responsible methods, and conservation, specifically protecting water quality by erosion and pollution control, protecting wildlife habitats and the entire river ecosystem as the ecological framework of the whole Fort Worth region. Because the firm was working on the CBD report simultaneously and because this part of Fort Worth was developing in a rapid manner similar to other commercial cores in cities previously discussed, the firm concentrated most strongly on the portion of the river abutting the downtown.

Suggestions for this section of the river are proposed in both reports and stress the interdependence and mutually beneficial relationships of the river and the downtown if the latter is developed with sensitivity to the former. The historic and topographic significance of the site of Heritage Park Plaza is enhanced by the adjacency of the late nineteenth-century county courthouse and the landmark Paddock Viaduct built in 1914. Government buildings and businesses appropriately clustered around this primary site and the downtown burgeoned. In conjunction with the Trinity River report, the firm's approach to the CBD was comprehensive, including recommendations for traffic and parking, public transit, open space, a pedestrian network of at-grade malls and elevated enclosed walkways, and retail developments to combat competition from the sprawling suburbs.

The 1970–71 Halprin plan for downtown was developed along similar lines to the famous 1956 (Victor) Gruen Plan for Fort Worth, which had significant impact on American urban planning but was ultimately shelved by the city. "The Gruen Plan for a Greater Fort Worth Tomorrow" called for a freeway loop circling the CBD, which would be entirely pedestrianized as a shopping and commercial center. The Halprin Plan sought a balance between pedestrian and automobile networks and, unlike the Gruen plan, was based on existing regional ecology and urban networks. Though the Halprin team recognizes the predecessor plan's innovation and strengths, they note that it remained a limited land use plan that proposed too much investment in automobile infrastructure rather than enhanced public transit.[63]

The Halprin plan began with a participatory workshop, the first of what would become a standard urban planning approach for the firm, in this case incorporating the inputs primarily of merchants and businessmen, as well as media and public officials (see chapter 5). Six major projects ultimately selected by the Sector Council were to be implemented immediately as a catalyst to "set the framework for future growth in Fort Worth."[64] The projects included: (1) the Loop Road System around the city center; (2) the Off-Street Parking Program; (3) the Houston Street Mall created by narrowing traffic lanes and widening sidewalks enhanced with street furniture and "other coordinated design features" (citing Nicollet Mall as a model); (4) an Enclosed Pedestrian Network of

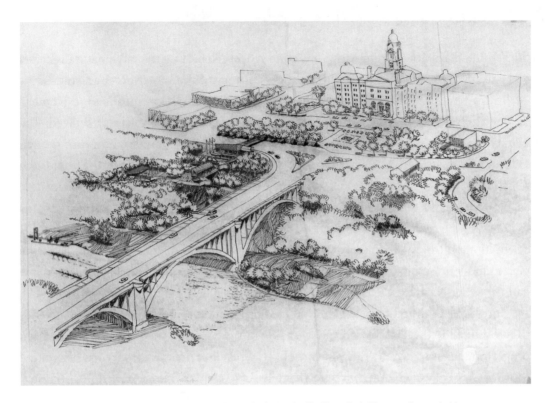

Figure 2.15. Lawrence Halprin & Associates, schematic design for Heritage Park Plaza on the east side of Paddock Viaduct, c. 1973. Lawrence Halprin Collection, The Architectural Archives, University of Pennsylvania.

climate-controlled elevated walkways (like the Minneapolis "skyways"), so that "eventually, shoppers, businessmen and tourists could walk through most of the downtown area without being exposed to cars, rain or heat"; (5) a Major Retail Development, and (6) The Trinity River Overlook and Riverfront Park.[65] The latter was considered in both reports to be developed as "an initial physical link between downtown Fort Worth and the River."[66]

This link was originally conceived to the east of the Paddock Viaduct, also known as the North Main Street Bridge (Figure 2.15). This originally proposed overlook designed as a series of terraces and stairways was to include restaurants and other concessions with historic displays all in an Old West motif.[67] This early conception is worth noting because the as-built plaza is a contemplative, intimate space, celebrating the city's natural, scenic, and cultural resources and commemorating its history, with no consumer amenities.

In the end, despite Halprin's emphasis in the CBD report on means of implementation, the plans fell victim to the economy of the 1970s and were largely shelved. The Trinity River report had significant impact on the city's development, however, though only today are its recommendations being considered comprehensively.[68] Despite the rejection of two major park and recreational capital improvement propositions, some aspects of the river report did materialize in the 1970s, such as the plaza, low water dams to maintain the river flow, more trees along the river banks, bicycle trails, and an annual celebration on the riverbank, Mayfest, which raised money for implementing Halprin's plan in modest increments. During the first such event in 1973, Anna Halprin and fellow dancer Xavier Nash led the children of Fort Worth in a dance around the maypole.[69]

Soon after the Bicentennial Committee adopted the project in 1974 and relocated it to the site of the original fort on the west side of the Viaduct, the plans for commercial programming disappeared. This was most likely a result of pressure from members of the Streams and Valleys Committee who wrote letters, such as one by Mrs. John D. Boon:

> Within the CBD the idea is to achieve respite from a city's inner mechanics—noise, congestion, hot pavements—the sensory pollution always present. Cooling water, the incomparable soothing and function of trees and eye-appealing landscapes all serve great human need in and near a city. Quieting influences and a cleaner urban environment rather than higher activity is in order. The artificial amusement parks, playgrounds, picnic areas and marinas (all contributing much litter) . . . should be planned for the more barren and still rural or residential reaches where urban dwellers can be drawn away from the city's heart.[70]

Lawrence Halprin generated the initial concept and basic design for the plaza, though its development was a collaboration with Satoru (Sat) Nishita, who also managed the project after Halprin split off from the office, which retained its name before becoming Carter Hull Nishita McCulley Baxter (CHNMB).[71] As indicated, the plaza was designed as one element in what was to be a more extensive downtown open space network. The Houston Street Mall in particular would have created a pedestrian environment along this major north–south axis that was initiated to the south by the city's Water Garden (designed by Philip Johnson) and culminated to the north with the plaza and the river trails. Between these two parks that anchor the proposed major retail street, the firm also recommended another central block along this spine be designated as "Public Square Park." Though the Water Garden was built before Heritage Park Plaza, no links between the sites materialized and they remain disconnected despite some interesting parallels and even more compelling divergences—the former representing the "public and social" life of the city and the latter "the private and introverted," both of which Halprin thought were essential for a full urban experience.[72] Without this expected open space matrix structuring a downtown public life, Heritage Park Plaza serves a more confined, but still important, function as the link or gateway between the downtown and the river.

Because of the city's failure to see beyond the scope of the plaza, it remains isolated from downtown by a road system quite inhospitable to pedestrians and, therefore, potential visitors. Though the plaza today is in disrepair and undergoing rehabilitation, water originally fell over the concrete wall marked by mounted letters indicating that behind it is "HERITAGE PARK." The concrete wall serves as the "screen & barrier" that the Halprin firm ultimately recommended because of the degraded pedestrian environment beyond. It encloses the site and directs the oblique angle of entry (Figure 2.16).

Once one enters the plaza the modern city disappears, as the senses are overcome with flowing water and breezes off the river through the leaves of the gridded live oaks (Figure 2.17). To the right of one's angled entry is a wall of water falling over the words "Embrace the Spirit and Preserve the Freedom which inspired those of Vision and Courage to Shape our Heritage." If the plaza entrance had offered straight access into the site, this commemorative inscription would be behind the visitor and the continuation of the movement sequence would have been obscured, so the oblique entrance is deliberate as part of the score. These are the only words inserted into the site, and they are meant to direct consciousness to the power of the place. Just beyond is a source fountain under

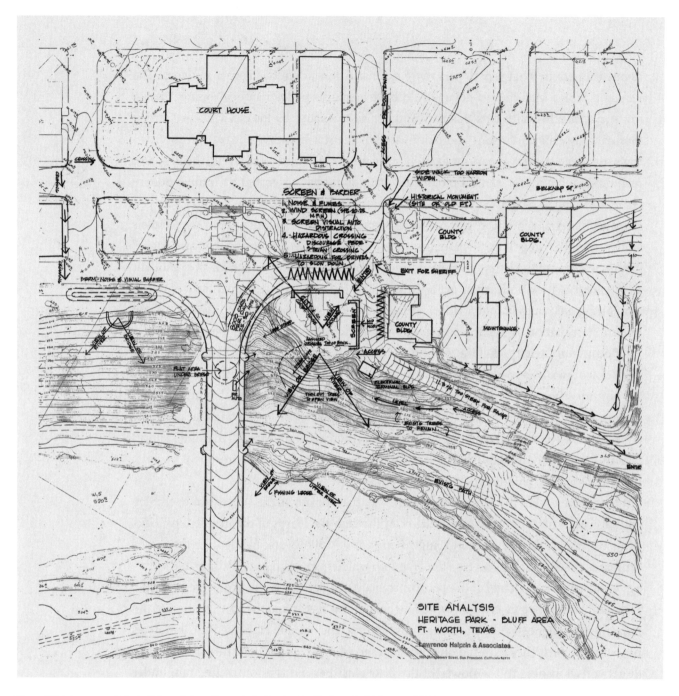

Figure 2.16. Lawrence Halprin & Associates, site analysis drawing for Heritage Park Plaza, c. 1976.
Lawrence Halprin Collection, The Architectural Archives, University of Pennsylvania.

a concrete pavilion, reminiscent of stone water basins placed in Japanese gardens for ritual purification before entering a shrine (Figure 2.18). In fact, much of the restrained sequential quality of the plaza, as well as some of the physical details, reflect Japanese gardening principles, at least partially owing to the design involvement of Sat Nishita and Junji Shirai from Halprin's office.[73] This ritualistic initiation clarifies that this is a site for quiet contemplation to reflect on the history of the city and region. The drawings of the site by Lawrence Halprin & Associates, in Satoru Nishita's hand, depict people visiting the plaza in solitude, with appropriate space between individuals who are there to absorb the meaning of the site's location and program (Figure 2.19).[74]

Inside the plaza one catches glimpses of the open sky from within the deep shade of the live oaks. Water flows over the wall to the west, inciting curiosity to discover its source. On the other

Figure 2.17. Gridded live oaks and the watercourse in Heritage Park Plaza. Photograph by John Roberts, AIA, 2002 (www.fortwortharchitecture.com).

Figure 2.18. The pavilion and "source fountain" in Heritage Park Plaza. Photograph by John Roberts, AIA, 2002 (www.fortwortharchitecture.com).

HERITAGE PARK- FORT WORTH-TEXAS
LAWRENCE HALPRIN ASSOC.- CHNMB S.F.
I MARCH 77

Figure 2.19. Satoru Nishita's drawing of solitary visitors overlooking the Trinity River from Heritage Park Plaza, March 1, 1977. Notice the water that falls from the runnel in the handrail to one along the ground. Lawrence Halprin Collection, The Architectural Archives, University of Pennsylvania.

side of the wall, the mysterious water source is not found (water is pumped up through the wall), but an abstract plan of the forking river and the original fort complex is inlaid into the concrete over which more water falls, revealing the formal inspiration for the configuration of the plaza. Punctured openings in the park's western enclosing wall offer tempting glimpses of the "water wall" and historic plan from the trail up from Lower Heritage Park (Figure 2.20).

Figure 2.20. Entry to Heritage Park Plaza from lower Heritage Park river trails. The plan of Fort Worth is inlaid into the inner wall, over which water used to cascade. Photograph by the author, January 2005.

The channeled water runs down grade toward the river, guiding the visitor's movement in pursuit of the historic view of the river's fork. After stepping down to the next level of the terraced site, one would have originally discovered an intimate "garden" area, planted with sculptural native evergreen yaupons, as well as St. John's wort (*Hypericum calycinum*) and ballerina rhaphiolepis, or pink lady (*Rhaphiolepis indica* "Ballerina"). From the "garden," one can get a glimpse of the river through an opening in the concrete wall, enticing the visitor forward. As one descends through the space, the plantings become less geometrically arranged and more native to the region. In fact, along the switchbacks descending toward the river's edge, the preexisting native vegetation was largely retained when the site was constructed.[75] The visitor is going back in time, from the gridded formality of the modern city, and the planted grove or "garden" space behind, to the untamed lands that were originally discovered by Major Ripley Arnold in 1849. The watercourse leads visitors to the edge of a belvedere (Figure 2.21), which echoes the viewing platforms that jut from the adjacent Paddock Viaduct and offer views to the plaza and bluffs. The park's belvedere is directly across the river from TXU Power's North Main Street Steam Electric Generating Station, which was erected in 1912 by the Fort Worth Power and Light Company. The power plant was instrumental in the early development of the city, and therefore its presence within the viewshed of Heritage Park Plaza represents a significant portion of the park's historical narrative. The structure of the plant, with its towering smokestacks, was recognized in Halprin's 1970 plan for Fort Worth as a "powerful architectural form" and "an enhancing and positive visual element" along the Trinity River, and acted as an orienting landmark before the stacks were recently imploded.[76]

Beyond the power plant, the distant stockyards are visible just off North Main Street. The early development of Fort Worth depended largely on the meat-packing industry, particularly after the establishment of the railroad in 1876. When the city's stockyards closed their doors in the 1960s, plans were made to develop the historic site into a landmark tourist destination, which opened in 1976 just before the completion of Heritage Park Plaza. In 2003, when development along the river began to raise questions about

Figure 2.21.
The view from the approach to the belvedere in Heritage Park Plaza. Photograph by the author, January 2005.

Figure 2.22. The terminal grotto in Heritage Park Plaza.
Photograph by John Roberts, AIA, 2002 (www.fortwortharchitecture.com).

the fate of the plaza, architect Kevin Sloan pointed out that the bridge that guides the visitor away from the belvedere and runs parallel to the bluff "can be perceived as a poured-in-place abstraction of the wood trestles once used by beef traders to view from above the cattle pens of the stockyards."[77] This seems quite possibly deliberate, particularly since letters from Sat Nishita reveal that he had the chance to explore the city and surrounding area and since Halprin had spent substantial time in Fort Worth developing his CBD and Trinity River reports.[78]

Once the suspended walkway ramps back toward the main plaza, the water falls from a runnel in the handrail to one along the ground and then is channeled straight ahead to a "grotto," in which water cascades. The water is then directed toward a pool with concrete stepping stones that guide movement around the corner, disclosing another grotto form that acts as the terminus to the water sequence (Figure 2.22).[79] The path then leads the visitor out of the plaza space and down the stairs to complete the journey along the switchbacks to the river's edge. This culminates the choreographed procession through this transformative space.

The plaza was designed at the same time that Halprin was developing his winning proposal for the Franklin Delano Roosevelt Memorial in Washington, D.C. Heritage Park Plaza is a significant antecedent to that landmark design for which Halprin depended on scoring movement through a sequence of "outdoor rooms" embodying the career of the former president.[80] In his sketch analysis of the FDR project reproduced in *Sketchbooks*, Halprin presents "the memorial as a series of processional spaces" (Figure 2.23):

> The FDR Memorial is conceived as a 1000' long progression of spatial experiences in the landscape—this relates it to all the great archetypal memorials from time immemorial which are based on a series of progressions—Ise Shrine . . . the Acropolis, Peking (the inner city), Gunnar Asplund's cemetery—etc. etc. . . . . Karnak. (74)

In these sketches, movement scores are presented as essential to the design concept and its development. The commemorative plaza in Fort Worth is also a processional sequence yet with a more complex configuration than the FDR Memorial.

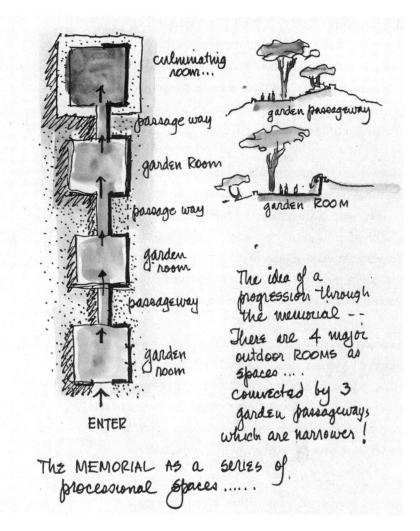

culminating room...

passage way

garden Room

passage way

garden room

passageway

garden room

ENTER

garden passageway

garden ROOM

The idea of a progression through the memorial -- There are 4 major outdoor ROOMS as spaces .... connected by 3 garden passageways which are narrower!

The MEMORIAL AS a series of processional spaces......

Figure 2.23. Lawrence Halprin, concept sketch of the Franklin Delano Roosevelt Memorial, c. 1976. The site, as built, is not axial. Published in *Sketchbooks of Lawrence Halprin* (1981), 79. Lawrence Halprin Collection, The Architectural Archives, University of Pennsylvania.

Volumetric spaces present varying yet interconnected interactive experiences situated on terraces stepping down the bluff. Though the FDR Memorial is not axial, the procession through the more sprawling single-level site is rather simple, and its interpretation of history more literal due to the inclusion of figurative sculpture and the abundance of inscriptions. In Heritage Park Plaza, progressive movement is directed through paths, steps, ramps, views, and the watercourse—leading visitors from one volumetric space to another. Views unfold as they reveal the historical narrative of the city's development. The water is choreographed through weirs, falls, runnels, cascades, and pools, all ultimately running toward the river at its base, and celebrating the significance of the Trinity River as integral to the founding of the city. The "archetypal forms" in this site—the grottoes, groves, various water elements, and the overall enclosure—reflect Jungian principles by reasserting the spiritual mystery of nature that Jung claims has been lost through the rationality of modern science.[81]

The site responds to the historical process, as a landscape defined by movement and flows: the river's flow, of course, but also the frontier and its associated migrations, the abandonment and resettlement of the fort site, the stagecoach line that came through in 1856 ("with the main attraction for stageline passengers being the view from the bluffs" at Bluff and Houston Streets), the Chisholm Cattle Trail (which "began routing hundreds of thousands of Texas Longhorns between the bluffs and Trinity River during the trail driving years of the late 1860's and 1870's"), and the "arrival of the railroad in 1876" (which brought in industries on which the city was economically founded and caused its development on and near these same bluffs). Therefore, "the majority of Fort Worth's early and exciting history occurred around or within view of the blufftop" and the new park, according to Lawrence Halprin & Associates.[82] The firm attempts to integrate the plaza within this historical process. The commemorative narrative subtly unfolds through the choreographed procession as the plaza becomes a transformative space between the modern city and the topographic resource that sparked its growth.

In Fort Worth, therefore, Halprin designed a new ritual framework to memorialize the city's founding and development experienced through progressive movement. While this contemplative space is acutely different from the consumer character of his Main Street scores, he deploys similar devices in each that entice movement and sequence space in a deliberate rhythm. Rituals—as repeated bodily actions or performance that have social significance and require spatial frameworks—are essential to a healthy public life. In addition to the civic and ceremonial, through his physical frameworks Halprin even attempted to elevate the habitual social practices of everyday life to the art of ritual, and he did so to varying levels of success.

In nature, form is not static. It invites choreography . . .
Moving through a city is very similar to moving through a magnificent forest.

—LAWRENCE HALPRIN, MAY 28, 1978

I want a garden which is enhanced by chance occurrences, which is enriched
by weeds & suckering growth & the changing patterns of sunlight and shade
and the branch falling on the terrace.

—LAWRENCE HALPRIN, 1972

3. DESIGNING WITH NATURE AS "ARCHETYPAL PRECEDENT"

PORTLAND OPEN SPACE SEQUENCE, SEATTLE FREEWAY PARK, MANHATTAN SQUARE PARK

RITUALS ARE REPEATED AND COLLECTIVE PERFORMANCE EVENTS. Yet Lawrence Halprin's designs act as the stage (and choreography) for the theater of everyday life, composed of both the consistency of what he calls "living rituals" and the chance occurrences or happenings that are indeterminate but just as significant to full urban experience. By looking to "natural form-making" (particularly erosion) as precedent for design generation, Halprin hoped to create environments that would trigger the kind of unexpected and uncontrolled encounters one might have in "raw" and "elemental" places such as the High Sierra and the Sonoma coast.

Thus in addition to reoccurring ritualistic performance, the Halprins both theoretically welcomed spontaneous and open-ended kinesthetic response to their scores. Like many of their artistic contemporaries experimenting in "chance" performance, particularly John Cage and his followers and collaborators such as Merce Cunningham, Larry Halprin considered the choreographic potential of the ancient Chinese *I Ching*, or "Book of Changes." The *I Ching* is a classic Chinese text, relying on the casting of yarrow sticks

117

or coins to generate divinatory hexagrams, which expressed an acceptance of the inevitability of change. Larry's interest in the *I Ching* filtered through Anna's exposure to the Cage–Cunningham collaboration, as well as his own study of the work of Carl Jung, who wrote a foreword to the translated text in 1949.[1]

According to Larry Halprin in 1969, the absence of intellect in these chance procedures allows us to "release ourselves from preconceptions and hang-ups which prevent and block creativity."[2] Yet just as Anna remained skeptical of this aspect of the Cage–Cunningham collaborations, Larry exhibits little desire to leave public response entirely open to chance. This is due to his ambiguity over how to act both as a designer and as an "enabler" of others' creativity, liberating people from the controlling master plans that were imposed in urban renewal projects across the nation.

To try to keep his scores open, Halprin adopted the notion of archetypes (inspired by but distinct from Jung's images of the "collective unconscious") to stimulate sensuous participation and phenomenal engagement in the environment. Though he later considers imagery emerging from ancient religion and myth, Halprin, first and foremost, turns to biology or ecology for primordial sources of form.

Nature, to Halprin, is "pure process made visible," and nowhere did he think this process more visible than in the High Sierra.[3] He thus looked to the "archetypal" precedent of natural processes, such as erosion, sedimentation or deposition, and succession, as "the biological and ecological origins of things."[4] To Halprin, humans share common origins in Nature; he thus turns to geologic forms and the processes that shape them as humans' shared aesthetic foundation. In one handwritten essay, "In the Beginning," he claims that

the great form making events of nature are caused . . . by what we call earth building forces ie: volcanoes, formations by up-welling of rocks from beneath the earth's surface making of synclines and anticlines. These are followed by wearing down forces—those of erosion by wind, rain, earthquake, watercourses, ice formation & thawing—the eating away of the base rock into new sculptural form. These forms are added to by fracturing, sliding, talus forming . . . by slippage of plates called plate tectonics, by crashing of seas along coastlines, by glaciers dumping their burdens on long glacier carved slopes or as impediments in river beds.

The shapes and forms carved from the base rock by the forces of erosion are sculpture ... they hold within their presence great role models for our criteria of sculptural form. They are for us the absolute demonstration of how things should be—as part of our biologic inheritance—as part of what we are born into and accept as right. They are the very source of our aesthetics ... because they and we as part of nature are born into the same primeval origins.[5]

He continues these ideas in his essay "The Shape of Erosion": "If we penetrate behind outward forms into the basic processes of nature which give rise to form, we have begun to tap the true source of form ... Erosion shapes are clear and simple evidence of this phenomenon. They show the process as visible action."[6]

A performance methodology thus more parallel to Halprin's interest in stimulating participation through archetypal imagery instead of relying on pure chance methods is a series of 1966–67 works by the Bay Area musician Charles Amirkhanian, who is also featured in *The RSVP Cycles*. Rather than look to the *I Ching* to dictate a spontaneous and random composition that he would then perform, Amirkhanian and his collaborator, the painter Ted Greer, each drew visual scores of basic abstract forms placed in parallel rows. Amirkhanian would "play" Greer's score and vice versa.[7] Therefore, instead of a random process, the performer responded subjectively to the open-ended symbols. No one response was correct; there were endless possibilities of performance, and therefore a more similar notion to what Halprin considers the potentials of the urban environment. He thus calls Amirkhanian's music "open environmental events."[8] Just as Halprin uses a vocabulary of forms derived from biological forces meant to inspire basic human sensory and behavioral response (Performance, P), Amirkhanian's symbols are meant to evoke immediate personalized response without an intellectualized filter. Amirkhanian's score, which remains open to infinite singularities of response or reception, is most reflective of number two in Halprin's diagram illustrated as Figure I.7, an approach he was rarely successful at harnessing. Thus while artists and writers began to shift in the late 1960s from universalism and metanarratives to pluralism and difference, Halprin sustained his search for absolute truths, continuously asserting his Modernist heritage.

Halprin sought such absolutes in humans' origins in nature and the natural forces of creation, attempting to reconnect humans to the rhythms of the biophysical world. He, like Jung and Dewey, recognized man's increasing separation and isolation from these rhythms. He claims that the human "need for constant contact with the elements of the natural environment"—"deeply and subconsciously rooted—remains encoded in our biology and in our archetypal patterning."[9] Though the city does not always provide opportunities for "constant contact" with what might be conventionally considered "elements of the natural environment," Halprin made direct associations between the growth and change of the urban environment and the successional transformation of plant communities.

In addition, by making nature's processes palpable, Halprin felt confident that his designs would contain the communicative power to resonate throughout a culturally diverse public and universally invite interaction. His work became most focused on rooting sites in their indigenous or primordial soil, imparting relevance and reorientation to the city inhabitant who had become "sensuously deprived." To him the introduction of what he called the "experiential equivalent" to ecological processes into the then barren urban environment would stimulate engagement similar to how one might experience nature, or what Halprin calls "wildness."[10] Halprin described his theory of "experiential equivalency" as follows:

> The idea that design intention is to provide a kind of experience which is equivalent to & similar to that in nature & therefore taps deep seated human needs & desires ... to accomplish this the focus we design need *not* be 'Natural' but the essence & thus the experience of it should be ... caves, waterfalls, shafts of light, enclosures, exits & entrys, feelings of exhilaration & even danger can be designed to evoke these feelings—without copying the exact forms.[11]

Halprin turns not to imitation but *transmutation*—"of the experience of natural landscape into man-made landscape" to derive new forms that invite human participation—as "the essence of the art of landscape design."[12] His intended interest, therefore, remains on how these forms arise, not their geometric composition as static objects. Processes such as succession and erosion and the behavior of water serve as Halprin's primary vocabulary: "Form follows process," he declares as an alternative to the Modernist principle "form follows function."[13] Such processes become the generating force shaping both form and organization, to stimulate creative environmental engagement. By introducing these processes into the urban environment, starved of the rhythms of nature, they become a palpable and physical presence and an aesthetic experience that reduced barriers between humans and the natural world.

Hydrological processes are a particularly central focus of Halprin's work. As already described, he used water as a choreographic force that triggered sensorial response and guided movement. He spent his life obsessively sketching the behaviors of water in dramatic settings such as Sea Ranch and the High Sierra. From these direct observations, he designed complex water features throughout his career that maximized on the element's variable natures. Water could be scored to stimulate movement; curiously looking for its source, seeking out its sound, playing in its mist and sprays and splashing in its pools were considered universal human responses that Halprin anticipated. He harnessed water's potential as an elemental force and "atavistic need" that is fundamental to the survival of man, to incite such primal response, believing that "even in a city, the sound and sight of water stirs the most elemental and basic roots of our human natures."[14]

PORTLAND OPEN SPACE SEQUENCE, PORTLAND, OREGON

Water is what guides visitors through the narrative sequence of open spaces in Portland, Oregon, which Lawrence Halprin & Associates designed in the 1960s as a matrix of dynamic counterpoints to the bleakness of the surrounding urban renewal development. The sequence unfolds as an ecological narrative from mountain spring to roaring cascade (Figure 3.1). Though a narrative intent might imply a closed score or heavy-handed

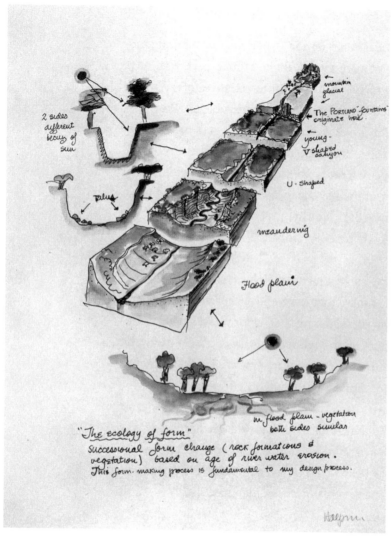

Labels on drawing:

2 sides different becuz of sun

mountain glacial

The PORTLAND "fountains" originate here.

young-V shaped canyon

talus

U-Shaped

meandering

Flood plain

in flood plain - vegetation both sides similar

"The ecology of form"
Successional form change (rock formations & vegetation) based on age of river water erosion.
This form-making process is fundamental to my design process.

Halprin

Figure 3.1. Lawrence Halprin's drawing of "the ecology of form" as it relates to the Portland Open Space Sequence, c. 1960s. Published in *Sketchbooks of Lawrence Halprin*, 62. In this drawing, he diagrams the transect of a watercourse from mountain glacial runoff to a wide floodplain valley, emphasizing water's erosive force in shaping land and vegetation over time. An arrow points to the origination of the Portland sequence, just before cascading powerfully from its mountain source to carve a young streambed. Lawrence Halprin Collection, The Architectural Archives, University of Pennsylvania.

choreography, Halprin's involvement in Portland is one of the best illustrations of his choreographic approach and represents one of his most open scores.

The participation of Lawrence Halprin & Associates in Portland was partly simultaneous with the firm's work on Nicollet Mall, yet it differed rather significantly in concept and execution. Like Minneapolis, downtown Portland was not a classic example of 1950s urban decline. Though city officials began to recognize signs of "blight" and the loss of the middle class to the fringes,[15] the firm's intervention was an attempt to remedy the situation early, thereby preempting accelerated losses. In 1958, Portland voters approved the creation of an urban renewal agency, called the Portland Development Commission (PDC), which instituted a significant redevelopment campaign led by chairman Ira Keller, chief executive and founder of the wood products company Western Kraft, and executive director John Kenward, formerly a member of the city's planning staff.

The PDC's first attempt to stem the outflow of the middle class was the redevelopment of the 83.5–acre area on the southern fringe of the downtown, which became known as the South Auditorium Urban Renewal Area.[16] By 1963, the approximately four hundred buildings of the preexisting predominantly Jewish and immigrant mixed-use neighborhood had been wiped clean and their residents relocated. This is noteworthy, since Halprin was often invited to reinvent areas that had already been razed and cleansed of the "natural" growth he considered essential to proper and humane place-making. These early projects that displaced thousands of powerless residents ultimately inspired him to develop the Take Part Process.

The urban renewal plan for this area, developed predominantly by Skidmore, Owings and Merrill (SOM) in 1961, reconceived it as a mix of offices, commercial and retail services, high-rise apartments, parking structures, a hotel, parks, and pedestrian malls.[17] The PDC partnered with the newly created Portland Center Redevelopment Corporation, who initially hired SOM and later also Lawrence Halprin & Associates to work on this mixed-use complex, which became known as Portland Center. In 1965, the South Auditorium Renewal Area was extended another twenty-six acres northward (SW Market to SW Jefferson streets), then encompassing the actual Civic Auditorium in front of which Halprin's firm designed Auditorium Forecourt (later renamed Ira Keller Fountain), thus crowning the open space sequence with this most dramatic contribution.

In June 1970, the *New York Times* critic Ada Louise Huxtable retrospectively criticized the transformation of the "renewed" Portland into a "scattered bomb-site" formed by the all-too-typical proliferation of asphalt parking lots. She continues:

Portland has urban renewal in the shiny, scaleless, Chamber-of-Commerce-image, and a better-than-average assortment of the Anywhere, USA products of the large national big-city architectural firms, with their interchangeable towers and plazas multiplying a slick, redundant, formula . . . No one has stopped looking at the tops of these buildings long enough to see what is happening on the ground. Each one is contributing to the devitalization of the city. Virtually all of them eliminate the life of the street. There is nothing on each square block on which these buildings rise—where there should be windows, shops, pedestrian attractions and activities—but a corporate entrance and a parking garage. This deadly design usually employs the most foolproof city-wrecking device ever adopted by architects . . . It is the tower on an elevated plaza, or podium . . . which puts a concrete or marble bunker on the street—a blind, insolent, formidable fortress raised against pedestrian humanity . . . The new Portland, then, consists of largely towers, bunkers and bomb sites.[18]

The exception she cites is the Lawrence Halprin & Associates intervention at Portland Center, which is "brought to life by Lovejoy Park" as "the area's social center." She is also the same critic who, only two days later, exclaimed that Auditorium Forecourt was "what may be one of the most important urban spaces since the Renaissance."[19] It seems that the PDC knew it would require a designer sensitive to human needs to ameliorate the dissociation caused by the "deadly design" of Anywhere, USA, so Halprin was invited partly as mitigator. Rooting the development in its regional soil, instating relevance and connection between these interchangeable or placeless elements and the site upon which they sit, was Halprin's challenging role in Portland, and subsequently in many other places.

John Kenward therefore invited Halprin in February 1963 to discuss the renewal project already underway with the PDC, the Design Advisory Council to the PDC,[20] and SOM. By June, Kenward had started working out the contracts whereby Halprin and his firm would jointly serve the PDC, for landscape "treatment" of the public areas, and the Portland Center Redevelopment Corporation, for work on the private development.[21] Halprin thus became responsible for developing the planting and landscape plans for the open spaces structuring the SOM-designed private office, commercial, and residential buildings as well for all public parks, streets, and malls in the redevelopment area.

The focus for this project was, again, primarily the experience of the pedestrian, separated from the automobile by converting the grid street pattern into a superblock system with interior promenades and open public spaces serving the new residents and office workers.[22] Though SOM and the city had instituted the superblock system for this area, the grid was retained by the pedestrian promenades, which divided the large lots into more a comprehensible scale.

Halprin's scoring method was applied on two scales in Portland: first, the wide organizational framework of the expandable pedestrian system, which followed Henderson's "image of liberated movement" through a "sequential and variegated series of spaces"; and second, the intimate human scale, integrating nodes within the larger system that offer the "experiential equivalency" to indigenous natural phenomena and thus connect the people of Portland to their foundational ecology. These two scales are best described by Halprin in his graphic summary of the project presented in *Sketchbooks*:

> In Portland, I attempted to do 2 things:
>
> The first of these was to develop a long eight block sequence of open spaces...promenades, nodes of plazas & parks with a mix of public space & private space interwoven... Along this progression are a diversity of uses—housing, apartments, shops, restaurants, offices, auditorium. The space is choreographed for movement with nodes for quiet & contemplation, action & inaction, hard & soft, YIN & YANG...
>
> The second basic approach was to bring into the downtown activities which related in a very real way to the environment of the Portland area—the Columbia River, the Cascade mountains, the streams, rivers & mountain meadows. These symbolic elements are very much part of Portlanders' psyche—they glory in the natural environment & escape to it as often as possible. But it seemed important to acknowledge the urban character of these places as well as their origins—so the designs deal with the *origins* of form: the process by which natural form is created.[23]

Therefore, though much existing analysis is dedicated specifically to Halprin's impressive fountains, one must consider the entirety of his phased intervention to understand the broader implications of his scoring approach.

The 1962 "Land Use Map" of the South Auditorium Urban Renewal Area issued by the PDC (Figure 3.2), locates what became Pettygrove Park and Lovejoy Plaza at the core of Blocks A and B (respectively) with the malls interlinking them and the rest of the

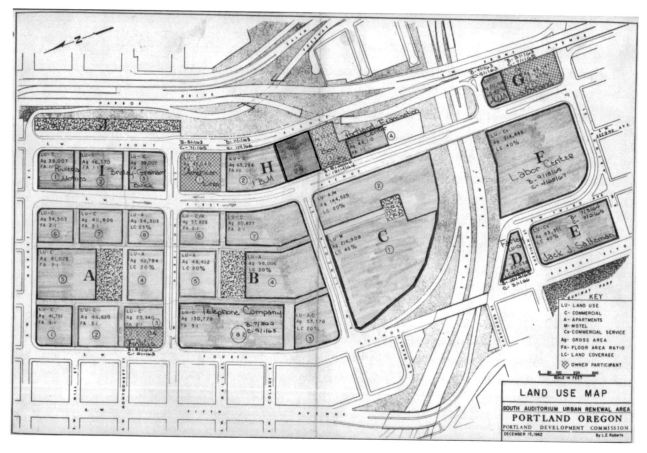

Figure 3.2. Land Use Map issued by the Portland Development Commission for the South Auditorium Urban Renewal Area, December 1962. Lawrence Halprin Collection, The Architectural Archives, University of Pennsylvania.

development features. The pedestrian network, especially once it had expanded to include Auditorium Forecourt to the north, became a kind of urban microcosm of Halprin's ideal city: one in which a web of linked open spaces becomes "the very matrix of life."[24] Halprin envisioned his intervention would behave as a "living connective tissue" that would grow to structure more of the surrounding city through time.[25] Consequently, in 1973 the city commissioned him to design the Portland Transit Mall situated on Fifth and Sixth avenues, north of the sequence and in the heart of downtown, giving him the chance to build on the system he had initiated.

The connective malls were conceived with a simple palette of materials that balanced uniformity with diversity, though much more modestly than in Minneapolis. In Portland, it was clear the malls were part of the same overall scheme but each offered a slightly different movement experience. Some are stepped in a rhythmic sequence; some have planters situated in the middle at even intervals to enliven the strong axiality; some are compressed and then released into small plazas typically with benches and some variation in the pavement and planting.[26] The plantings on either side are typically dense and tree allées (*Tilia euchlora* along Second Avenue and *Aesculus carnea* along Third Avenue) protect pedestrians from Portland's frequent rains, as well as direct movement onward toward the next "node" in the sequence. Though the malls are organized nonhierarchically, Halprin clearly emphasized a particular sequence that revealed a specific narrative. Because he presents the entirety of the project as a progressive score, the following descriptive analysis will trace that sequential experience to reveal the unfolding narrative.

From the intended entry into Portland Center at Lincoln Street and Second Avenue, the sequence unfolds primarily in the northward direction.[27] This modest and indistinct entry almost immediately widens into a brick plaza containing a central corbelled brick fountain that appears to emerge from underneath the plaza (Figure 3.3). Though constructed after Lovejoy, the fountain was conceived as the "source," the "experiential equivalent" to a spring from which groundwater flows out of the earth and initiates a watercourse. While in one drawing Halprin labels this fountain "source" (Figure 3.4), in another drawing of the sequence reproduced in his *Sketchbooks* volume, he graphically notes the "hills" that rise to the southwest of the site as an indication of the potential of the actual topography to generate the power of this watercourse, which cascades forcefully in Lovejoy Plaza (Figure 3.5). Also in *Sketchbooks*, he includes a diagram of the erosive force of flowing water shaping rock and vegetation over time (see Figure 3.1). In this diagram an arrow points to the moment within this natural process from which the Portland sequence originates—just before cascading powerfully from its mountain source to carve a young streambed. Sources, as the origin and instigator of process, are critical to Halprin's scoring approach.[28] The "source fountain" is modest, however, most likely to reflect the quiet surging spring that only later, under forces of gravity and perhaps the conjoining of other springs, generates the power that the visitor discovers as one emerges onto Lovejoy Plaza.[29]

In the early planning document, just north of the source fountain the firm proposes a "central shopping place" where the pedestrian mall would widen to form a small plaza surrounded by a restaurant, shops and a market (Figure 3.6). The drawing representing this area is similar to sketches by the firm of interior courtyards of suburban shopping centers, though the shops drawn, including a "tabak," or newsstand, and a sizeable

Figure 3.3. The "Source Fountain" in Portland Center, c. 1970. Photograph by Paul Ryan.

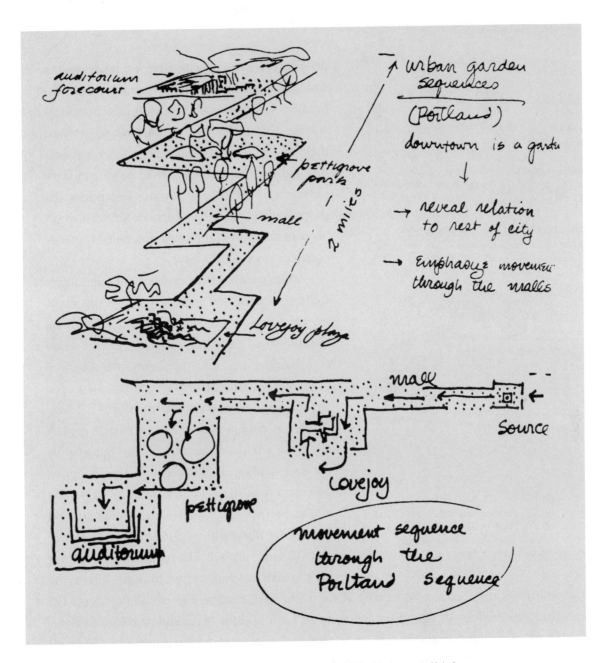

Figure 3.4. The "movement sequence through the Portland sequence." Published in *Lawrence Halprin: Changing Places* (1986), 23. Lawrence Halprin Collection, The Architectural Archives, University of Pennsylvania.

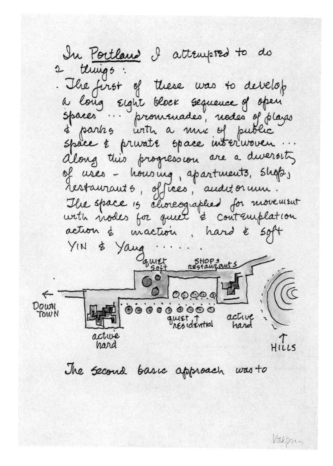

In <u>Portland</u> I attempted to do
2 things:
. The first of these was to develop
a long Eight block sequence of open
spaces ... promenades, nodes of plazas
& parks with a mix of public
space & private space interwoven ...
along this progression are a diversity
of uses - housing, apartments, shops,
restaurants, offices, auditorium.
The space is choreographed for movement
with nodes for quiet & contemplation
action & inaction, hard & soft
YIN & Yang .....

quiet
soft

SHOPS
restaurants

←

DownTown

quiet & residential

active hard

active hard

↑ HILLS

The second basic approach was to

Figure 3.5. Lawrence Halprin's Portland Open Space Sequence sketch and notes, c. 1968. Published in *Sketchbooks of Lawrence Halprin* (1981), 61. Lawrence Halprin Collection, The Architectural Archives, University of Pennsylvania.

drugstore, were to provide basic essentials for the surrounding residents rather than serve as a destination shopping mall.[30] Providing such services ensures that residents did not have to get into their cars to drive for basic necessities, yet neither did they have to leave their private enclave to interact with the city beyond. Regardless, the shops and restaurants, which Halprin notes on his plan sketches of the sequence, failed to materialize in any significant way.[31]

After passing the modest but significant source fountain, and moving through this commercial segment along the Second Avenue mall, visitors would experience a great spatial release at Lovejoy Plaza, finding themselves below a monumental cascade of water to the west. The "active" and "hard," what was then called "South Park," was designed as an open concrete gathering place protected from traffic and industry by the surrounding development. It was designed by a team consisting of Larry Halprin, Sat Nishita as the partner in charge, James Coleman, and Byron McCulley, with architects Charles Moore and William Turnbull. The natural topography of the sloped site, which angled from the hills to the southwest down to the Willamette River to the east, became one of the Resources (R) that informed the design of the fountains in both Lovejoy Plaza and Auditorium Forecourt. As Halprin claims in a letter to Gyorgy Kepes, author of a number of books on visual communication that marry art and technology, the Resources (R) that influenced the Portland score include "the essential nature of the site . . its ecological relations, the topography . . . views, relations to the city, etc."[32] The entirety of the concrete plaza is stepped in an irregular configuration that strongly resembles a topographic contour model and, other than the fountain, remains open—awaiting people to activate it through creative appropriation (Figure 3.7).

Lovejoy Fountain embodied the accelerated force of mountain springs as they crashed over rock forms which they shape by erosion. The fountain was designed predominantly by Halprin with Charles Moore (Figure 3.8).[33] Reflecting on their successful collaboration, Charles Moore notes with amazement Halprin's extraordinary ability at convincing his clients in Portland to accept such forms that had never been seen before in the designed environment. Though Halprin was proposing the introduction of "nature" into the city, here the (concrete) forms were evocative of violent forces rather than pastoral scenes.[34]

For this "active" plaza, Halprin clearly wanted a dynamic fountain informed by his studies of the High Sierra backcountry and the qualities of water falling, streaming, flowing, and crashing through it. Halprin's sketches of the watercourses of the High Sierra are not static or merely visual. Arrows indicate how water behaves or falls against different rock faces or boulders in its way. Sound descriptions like "ch-ch-ch" and "tic-tic" and "grrrr" are notated where they were heard. In another drawing of the High Sierra, he notes the

Figure 3.6. The "central shopping place" within the Portland Center development. Printed in the master plan report by Lawrence Halprin & Associates, *South Auditorium, Portland Oregon*, c. 1963. Lawrence Halprin Collection, The Architectural Archives, University of Pennsylvania (014.I.B.2656).

Figure 3.7. Lovejoy Plaza just after its completion, 1960s. Lawrence Halprin Collection, The Architectural Archives, University of Pennsylvania (slide E-F530, unstamped).

multiple responses of water to different physical conditions, using the terms leap, bounce, bubble, surge, eddy, boil, and glide, with graphic gestures representing these varied dynamic qualities (Figure 3.9). In these studies, Halprin claims:

> I observed the effects of constriction on speed of flow; the effects of obstructions and how they break up sheetings of water; the effect of different drops from heights; of sound effects and light qualities; and notated all these in their natural habitat. These came under R in the RSVP cycles. From these field observations, I developed scores and then combined them into the final waterfall design which coordinated the structural elements and the water effects into a total composition as Performance (P). Not quite total, however.

The open-ended element remains the people for whom the plaza fountain was designed. The fountain, once built, became, itself, a *score* for movement. The Performance (P) was not an end but a beginning in the cycle again.[35]

Halprin wanted this fountain to be a translation of these studies into urban form, as well as a means to evoke the region's origins or "symbolic elements," including the Columbia River and the Cascade Mountains.

So that the fledgling architectural firm of Moore & Turnbull would receive credit

Figure 3.8. Activity in Lovejoy Fountain, 1960s. Photograph by Maude Dorr.

Figure 3.9. Sketch by Lawrence Halprin of the High Sierras with notations for sound and movement of water, 1960s. Published in *Sketchbooks of Lawrence Halprin* (1981), 64. Lawrence Halprin Collection, The Architectural Archives, University of Pennsylvania.

for contributing to the project, Halprin invited them to design the park shelter behind the cascade where one could sit, protected from the elements, and participate more passively. The dynamic form of the timber pavilion, which created a material complement to the concrete surrounds and made reference to regional tradition, provides a strong contrast to the static severity of the tower that rose above it (Figure 3.10).

He explains to Kepes that the RSVP process unfolds here in an ongoing and cyclical way, thereby aligning this project most closely with his theoretical writings of the 1960s and 1970s. Halprin uses Resources (R) such as the native topography of the region to feed into a Score (S) (really just a design proposal) whose "Performance" is the form that both the static elements (concrete, etc.) and the fluid water eventually take—all refined through an evaluative process (Valuaction, V). While this "cycle" of the process is a rather standard means of generating a design, more uniquely, the creative team intended for the forms themselves to act as an open score, inviting environmental participation without dictating what kind. "(P) becomes (S)," according to Halprin, describing it most lucidly in his letter to Gyorgy Kepes: "Thus once we as designers had gone through the process of R–S–V–P, the resulting P, that is, the *actual fountains*, become themselves an open score allowing for participation and recycling into a SCORE themselves." The steps up to the fountain's pinnacle, for instance, are almost irresistible in their invitation to climb and explore. The "atavistic" need that water represents, according to Halprin, in conjunction with the alluring forms, seems to provoke a primordial urge to participate through play.[36] As the architect Donlyn Lyndon, who also contributed to the Sea Ranch, claimed in 1966 about Lovejoy Fountain: "On a hot day there is usually someone to be found in a state of ecstatic immersion."[37]

.10. Lovejoy Plaza pavilion by William Turnbull
rles Moore. Photograph by the author, 2008.

In *The RSVP Cycles*, Halprin describes Lovejoy Plaza as follows:

> This is as much a theatre where events can occur, as it is a more formalized theatrical en-
> vironment . . . I hoped that they would use the water, climb the cascade, wade in the pool,
> listen to the sounds, and use the entire composition as a giant play sculpture which would
> heighten and enrich the normal everyday life-activity in the neighborhood. (P) becomes
> (S) . . . The composition was unfulfilled until it was occupied (58).

Halprin's intention for the fountain was to serve as an interactive theater to invite im-
provisation, as well as to provide a stage for events or "living rituals" to occur.[38] His wish
became reality and a series of "hippie weddings" even apparently occurred within the
cascade. He also intended for the plaza to serve as an actual theatrical space for "dancers
all over AND arriving to center space from above . . ." (Figure 3.11).

Beyond weddings and mystical events staged by counterculture youth, the reception
of the space was as open as Halprin hoped and anticipated for his score. One unsolicited
letter from an early park visitor to the Halprin firm recorded the varied responses she
observed during its first summer:

> Here are remarks I've gathered over the summer. I hope they bring you pleasure.
> Thank you for the fountain.   —A wet Shirley Volz

> Guy, age 17: "It's real, like me, with so many personalities! I groove here."

> Young girl, 13: "I'm sort of scared of people, here I can do my thing, and if I have to
> talk to someone we can talk about the fountain."

> Boy, 16: "Wow! It's just like Wow!"

> Woman, 45 or so: "I came to the fountain just to see it. I put my toe in and I was lost.
> I had to walk up the steps, dress, nylons, who cares? What a feeling! Such freedom."

> Little girl, 4: she steps into the lower pond, comes right out, runs fast while looking over
> her shoulder. She steps. She runs back into the pond. Repeats same over and over. I ask,
> "What are you doing?" She points to her foot pattern on the cement and says,
> "The wet likes to follow me."

Girl, 9 (in Sunday dress): "It's okay if I get wet, it's okay. Mommy likes me to be wet."

Boy, 8: "I hate baths. When I come here she doesn't make me take one."

Woman, 30: "If I couldn't see, I'd come here just to listen and touch. It's a living creature, giving something of life to everyone."

Father, 48?: "I take the kids to the park, first I gotta push them on the swing, then down the slide, up the jungle gym. You think I relax. Hell, no! The fountain, it plays with them. Me, I relax. What more could I want, heh?"

Boy, 17: "It's groovy, it sings, it screams, it whispers. I can touch them all. Wow!"

Girl, 8: "Take me up the steps. Take me up the steps. Just this once. Now take me down, oh, please!"

My thoughts, age 24: "The fountain is a special gift you give a friend who has never been there. I like to give presents but I don't have any money so I bring them to the fountain. It's nice to give something you can't buy."[39]

Figure 3.11. Lawrence Halprin's sketch of Lovejoy Fountain, 1960s. Published in *Sketchbooks of Lawrence Halprin* (1981), 72. Lawrence Halprin Collection, The Architectural Archives, University of Pennsylvania.

Despite such euphoric response, within a few months of its opening, contentions emerged over who should have a right to this new kind of public space, as journalist Randy Gragg notes. Tensions grew over the "hippie" presence in the plaza, inspiring the parks commission to prohibit "wading, swimming, and bathing." Enforcement remained lax, however, causing continued attempts to control what City Commissioner William Bowes referred to as "sex bums, punks, pushers, and rabble rousers."[40] Confrontation and exchange are essential to a healthy public realm, and Halprin knew this. He was no doubt pleased by the debate his park inspired.

From Lovejoy Plaza, the narrative continues. Both tree-lined linkages open up into a quiet "park" of mounded woody knolls, or "mountain foothills," called Pettygrove Park, which Halprin hoped would provide a "peaceful oasis in the middle of downtown

Figure 3.12. Aerial view of Pettygrove Park, Portland, Oregon, c. 1970. Photograph by Paul Ryan.

Portland" (Figure 3.12).[41] Basalt from the Columbia River Gorge is used for stone detailing, embedding the park in its place. Halprin claimed that the contrast between the "active" and "hard" (Lovejoy) *plaza* and the "quiet" and "soft" (Pettygrove) *park* embodied the "Yin and Yang" (see Figure 3.5). Since "Yin" qualities are characterized as active, light, and upward-seeking and "Yang" as passive and dark, Halprin does seem conscious of the implications of this contrast. While Lovejoy Plaza is open, with the fountain reaching upward in dynamic force, Pettygrove is shaded and planted and the soft mounds invite passive activity. In one drawing included in *Sketchbooks*, Halprin notes, "Keep trees off top & sides of mounds—place at base of mounds only" in order for the mounds to remain clear enough for sitting, picnicking, and quieter socialization (Figures 3.13 and 3.14).[42] The "two-fold life" Halprin writes about in *Cities* is therefore perfectly realized here in Portland. Urban open spaces, he believes, should facilitate the one side of city life that is "public and social, extroverted and inter-related," the other that is "private and introverted, the personal, individual, self-oriented life which ... needs enclosure and quiet, removal from crowds and a quality of calm and relaxation" (11).

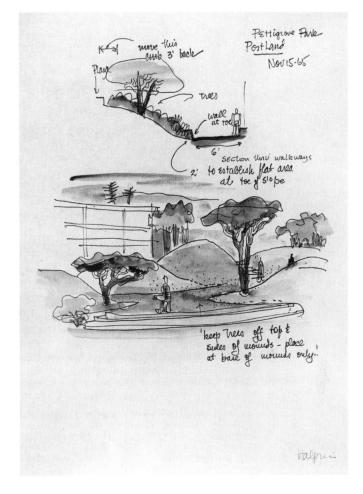

Figure 3.13. Lawrence Halprin's sketches for Pettygrove Park, November 1965. Published in *Sketchbooks of Lawrence Halprin* (1981), 70. Lawrence Halprin Collection, The Architectural Archives, University of Pennsylvania.

Figure 3.14. Quiet activity in Pettygrove Park, 1967. Lawrence Halprin Collection, The Architectural Archives, University of Pennsylvania (slide E·l536, stamped by Lawrence Halprin & Associates).

Halprin had experimented with the contrast of soft and hard to induce different moods in the private garden—associating the former with intimate and quiet experiences and the latter with social and dynamic opportunities.[43] Later, in Levi's Plaza in San Francisco, Halprin juxtaposed a hardscaped plaza containing a dynamic and monumental fountain with a vegetated space across the street that incorporates a quiet meandering "stream." Of course, Halprin is not the first to create such contrasting conditions for the city dweller. Just as he intended these enclosed plazas to be separated from traffic and city bustle beyond, in the 1860s Frederick Law Olmsted with Calvert Vaux created one of their most refined projects, Prospect Park in Brooklyn, to act as a protected oasis composed of a variety of experiential opportunities informed by the qualities of nature not typically found in the city—the pastoral meadow, the serene lake, and the wooded and dramatic ravine. The lake, the "Ravine" (an abstracted compression of this natural feature as found in the Adirondack Mountains), and the "Long Meadow" (the undulating pastoral lawn) were structured by an elaborately constructed watercourse that started from a designated source, at Fallkill, and took on different characters along its length—quite similar to the concept in Portland. Though Halprin is obviously working within the same tradition, his forms are more highly abstracted and more recognizably contrived than Olmsted's designs, which are often mistaken as "natural."

From Pettygrove, the sequential journey continues along the Third Avenue Mall, out of the superblocks and onto the city streets once again. From the corner of SW Market Street and the Third Avenue Mall, a foreboding office tower rises on a tall podium to the right, but straight ahead views open to the Civic Auditorium and its Forecourt.

In 1965, while Halprin was still working on Portland Center, the city sanctioned the area north, directly around the Civic Auditorium, to be "renewed" as a cultural area, and again SOM was commissioned to plan it. One local journalist recently reflected that the SOM design was so offensive that citizen groups formed a committee to generate alternatives.[44] In the same series of reflections on the project, John Kenward explained that early on he had casually asked Halprin what to do with this "blighted" block, since it supposedly contained the "four of the worst buildings in town." According to Kenward, Halprin had suggested that they "tear it down and just plant grass," which is apparently exactly what the PDC did, using a kind of "clean and green" strategy applied in many shrinking cities today.[45] As Kenward continues,

> We tore them all down and I can remember sitting out there one day when the grass was growing nicely and a beautiful summer day and Larry was sketching on a pad how we could develop . . . falls and pools and so on of the fountain that is there. And I said to Larry, you really shouldn't be here, you should be in the auditorium because Lady Bird

Johnson is making a speech to the National Association of Landscape Architects, a national convention. And he says, No, I don't need to be there. I wrote her speech. And he did, he had written her speech. But he suggested that we come up with pretty much the kind of thing that is there now.[46]

One notebook sketch from a discussion with Kenward includes the basic layout (Figure 3.15), yet a series of studies indicates that the schematic development was not as spontaneously generated (Figure 3.16). An outdoor amphitheater related to the Civic Auditorium seems to be the consistent theme among these numerous early studies, as well as the presence of a monumental fountain to tie the area together as a "major civic scene." In a letter from Halprin firm associate Sat Nishita to John Kenward on December 15, 1966, Nishita explains:

We feel it extremely important to make the auditorium area more significant as a major civic scene, not only spatially and architecturally but also in terms of the additional facilities and uses. Such a civic complex would greatly enhance the South Auditorium Urban Renewal Project . . . [and] Portland as a whole. A small theater can, in our opinion, be located on this parcel leaving the major open space between it and the auditorium. A similar example to this can be cited in the Court of Honor in San Francisco between the Opera House and Veteran's Building . . . A comparative example in architectural scale and use is the theater by Paul Kirk in Seattle adjoining the Opera House. Another similar example in an urban renewal area is the theater in Washington, DC by Harry Weiss.[47]

The studies seem to correspond to a sketch Halprin presents in the *Sketchbooks* series of a swimming hole within a waterfall in the Tuolumne River (Figure 3.17). The deep basin of pooled water is surrounded by "swelling granite sides around to lie on." Another drawing by Halprin included in the *Sketchbooks* series depicts a granite rock face at eleven thousand feet in the High Sierra (Figure 3.18). The multiplanar wall of varying texture and color was, according to Halprin's note, a "possible wall for Portland fountain." By October 1968, Kenward authorized Halprin to proceed with his work on the Auditorium Forecourt:

It is the hope of our Commission and others that you will achieve the softer, more natural qualities of the High Sierra granite country that you showed in your slides as your work progresses. It is the understanding of our Commission that you will be working very closely with this project as it proceeds in order to achieve the best possible results.[48]

Halprin did not seem to pursue any such "softness" in his continued concept sketches, because he clearly did not think it appropriate for a civic plaza. A final drawing included in *Sketchbooks* compares a "usual waterfall as at Portland" which looks similar to Lovejoy, to an innovative "*idea for a fountain . . . concrete planes in many dimensions*" from which water would surge and collect into a bowl at its base (Figure 3.19). Halprin conceives this scheme as a series of large masses, surrounded by water, to be climbed from below. In the second edition of *Cities*, published in 1972, well after the project was complete, he claims that "the strong concrete slabs, steles, and slanted forms of Auditorium Forecourt create a man-made reference to the cliffs and mesas of the American West."[49] Mesas are forms uplifted by tectonic forces and appear similar to the masses in the drawing reproduced in *Sketchbooks* (pictured as Figure 3.19), yet they are typical of arid climates and are not indigenous to the Pacific Northwest. Further, they are not the immediate image evoked by the built form of the Forecourt. Using this kind of "archetypal" language without grounding it in its real specificity of place actually represents a contradiction that appears often in Halprin's work. Rather, the Forecourt's plummeting water over the one-hundred-foot-wide

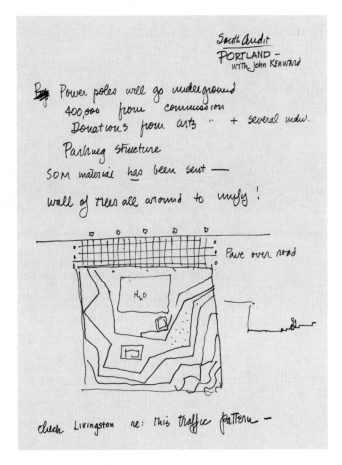

Figure 3.15. Lawrence Halprin, notebook page of conversation with John Kenward about Auditorium Forecourt, 1964. Lawrence Halprin Collection, The Architectural Archives, University of Pennsylvania.

Figure 3.16.
Lawrence Halprin
& Associates,
schematic sketches
for Auditorium
Forecourt, Portland,
1960s. Lawrence
Halprin Collection,
The Architectural
Archives, University
of Pennsylvania.

cliff face is more reflective of the abundant and dramatic waterfalls of the Pacific Northwest (Figure 3.20), specifically the powerful streams of the nearby Cascade Range and the heavy flow of the Columbia River, whose elevation drop over a short distance serves as a major source of hydroelectricity in the region. In fact, the Columbia River, in whose watershed Portland is located, is unquestionably part of the primordial regionalism ingrained in the "psyche" of the city's inhabitants. By integrating this kind of symbol and force into the public urban context, Halprin attempted to "transmute the images & fantasies of nature into a life-nourishing form people can relate to in the cities."[50]

The ultimate design of the Forecourt, begun in 1968 and dedicated in June 1970, which extended the sequence and created a link onward to the downtown just north, was conceived in its complexity by Angela Danadjieva, appointed the project designer. Sat Nishita was the partner-in-charge and Byron McCulley the project director. Halprin's role consisted of initial concept sketches and some guiding principles, but Danadjieva's hand is most recognizable in the final scheme, despite Kenward's obvious desire for Halprin's full attention. Danadjieva, who had only been at Lawrence Halprin & Associates for one year before developing comprehensive sketches of the Forecourt, was a critical addition to Halprin's firm and the application of his choreographic techniques. Prior to joining Halprin, she had worked in her home country of Bulgaria as a movie set designer for the Bulgarian State Film industry. Her training was in architecture, but her work "compos[ing] the sets for the motion of the camera" was perfectly aligned with Halprin's theoretical focus.[51] Although she achieved more refinement in her design for Seattle Freeway Park in terms of the application of her cinematic background, her contribution to Portland made it clear that she was accomplished at creating dramatic environments with varied emotional impact condensed into small space. For the Portland project, according to Danadjieva, PDC chairman Ira Keller referred her to a book on the waterfalls of the Columbia River Gorge, which became the primary inspiration in developing the project.[52]

Just as Halprin, in the Portland Center development, offered a diversity of choice for outdoor living in the active "plaza," the

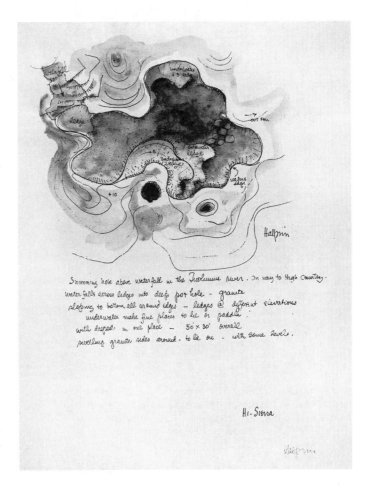

Figure 3.17. Lawrence Halprin's drawing of a swimming hole in the Tuolumne River, 1960s. Published in *Sketchbooks of Lawrence Halprin* (1981), 67. Lawrence Halprin Collection, The Architectural Archives, University of Pennsylvania.

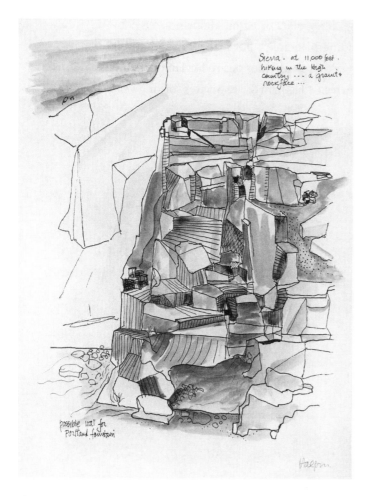

Sierra. at 11,000 feet.
hiking in the High
country ... a granite
rockface ...

possible wall for
Portland fountain

Figure 3.18. Lawrence Halprin's drawing of a "possible wall for Portland fountain," August 28, 1968. Published in *Sketchbooks of Lawrence Halprin* (1981), 66. Lawrence Halprin Collection, The Architectural Archives, University of Pennsylvania.

quiet "park," and the interconnective links, the Auditorium Forecourt presents a series of experiential opportunities concentrated in one block. What makes the Forecourt distinct from the previous "nodes" within the sequence is its relative degree of openness to the street. The Forecourt is not enclosed by peripheral superblock development, though berms and thick plantings along three of the perimeter edges create a desired screen. The design, like Lovejoy, follows the natural topography of the site by directing the waterflow in small quiet "streams" through a grove of pines that then suddenly plummet over the eighteen-foot concrete edge into a sunken pool below.

The edge that is not bermed or planted faces the Civic Auditorium, a theater that was considered a city monument despite its subdued architectural character. Its unimpressiveness, however, enhances the excitement of the Forecourt by serving as a neutral backdrop similar to the Portland Center buildings. The cascading sheets of water face the Civic Auditorium, competing with the dramas that take place within it. The Forecourt was, itself, designed to be a theater inviting both the improvisations of the everyday as well as formal productions. The pools at the base of the cascade are dropped below street level to enhance the drama of the cliff faces and to create a protective enclosure separate from the traffic above. Stairs descending from the street into the sunken plaza offer places to sit and watch the drama unfold in and around the fountain in an amphitheatrical arrangement. The concrete pads set within the lower pool serve as the stage with the waterfall as the uproarious background. Originally, programming for the park included performances for this outdoor theater. Images of the Joffrey Ballet and Portland's Ballet Workshop, ironically a form of dance that Halprin considered "too closed," appear in the press during the park's first decade (Figures 3.21).[53]

This theatrical stage invited participation in even more multidimensional ways (Figure 3.22). In 1971 the city of Portland contacted the Halprin firm with concerns over the potential danger of the fountain. The firm subsequently made studies of a system of railings drawn over a photograph of the fountain, most likely to demonstrate how ludicrous this addition would be perceived by park users.[54] The thrill of danger provided in nature is re-created here in the city and becomes part of the fountain's primal allure. In his 1970 letter to Gyorgy Kepes, Halprin explained his intentions for participation in the Portland fountains: "The design could not have railings or for that matter any constraining elements

Figure 3.19. Lawrence Halprin's drawing of an "idea for a fountain," 1960s. Published in *Sketchbooks of Lawrence Halprin* (1981), 68. Lawrence Halprin Collection, The Architectural Archives, University of Pennsylvania.

Figure 3.20. Aerial view of Auditorium Forecourt, c. 1970.
Lawrence Halprin Collection, The Architectural Archives, University of
Pennsylvania (slide E-H405, stamped by Lawrence Halprin & Associates).

that would by implication say STAY OUT . . . The very nature of the forms and the boundaries had to imply: COME IN, PARTICIPATE, GET INVOLVED, PLEASE USE. The design needed to be permissive and inclusive."

A diversity of experiential opportunities abstracted from the surrounding natural environment—the swimming hole, mountain glade, and waterfall—is provided by the fountain to engage such participation by a wide cross-section of people. As one journalist noted in 1970, within the quieter upstream street-level portion of the block "elderly people sit and talk and babies dabble in the shallow water," while "the brink of the falls is . . . for the more adventurous."[55] The fountain both is the spectacle or the Performance (P) and inspires the spectacle as the Score (S), stimulating people to climb the water stairs, enter the "caves" behind the waterfalls, and wade or jump in the pools. In addition, in the fountain's early years every day at 11:00 a.m. expectant crowds would assemble to watch the drama of the waterfall being turned on as a new urban ritual.

A tense theatricality defined the Forecourt's opening day in June 1970. As noted in a pamphlet generated by the recently formed Lawrence Halprin Landscape Conservancy, the fountain's dedication occurred just days after the Kent State shootings, which was followed by a violent clash between Portland police and student protestors at Portland State University in the city's most violent antiwar protests. The tension between the students attending and the police patrolling was so palpable that Halprin took the microphone and exclaimed, "These very straight people somehow understand what people can be all about . . . So as you play in this garden,

Figure 3.21. Joffrey Ballet performing in Auditorium Forecourt, 1975. Lawrence Halprin Collection, The Architectural Archives, University of Pennsylvania (slide E-H631, stamped by Lawrence Halprin & Associates).

please try to remember that we're all in this together." He then jumped into the fountain, demonstrating the joy and relief the fountain might offer in such smoldering times.[56]

Halprin's involvement in Portland is one of the best illustrations of his choreographic approach, and it represents one of his most open scores. "The nodal experience of the progression through the Portland sequence" guides movement, providing enough choice to avoid dictating it.[57] As he hoped, Halprin's sequence, particularly the Auditorium Forecourt since it is surrounded by city streets and is situated just south of downtown in this civic and cultural area, did stimulate a growing park network as well as instill a deeper public value for open space in the city. Halprin's influence is palpable in the city's Down-

Figure 3.22. Activity in Auditorium Forecourt on opening day, July 1970.
Unlike the ballerinas, others enact their own improvised dance,
fully submerged in the pools. Photograph by Jim Hallas/*The Oregonian*.

town Plan of 1972, which emphasized public open space and environmental relationships by "connect[ing] open spaces with pedestrian and bicycle linkages" in a complex system of "pedestrianways." Further, it proposed many "traffic free" environments and demonstrated a concern for views both into the city and from the city to landmark features such as Mt. Hood.[58] In addition, the Downtown Plan insists on the development of the Transit Mall and on opening up the city to the waterfront, including dismantling Harbor Drive to build Tom McCall Waterfront Park.

Public fountains, in particular, have been built throughout downtown Portland since Halprin's involvement. The writer Randy Gragg, recognizing the impact of Halprin's work on the city's open space system, claimed in 2003 that "from Halprin's Source Fountain essentially springs everything, from Pioneer Courthouse Square to the soon-to-be constructed North Park Square in the Pearl District."[59] The fact that the sequence seems to have generated this larger network of public spaces, activated by water, is demonstrative of Halprin's success at structuring an open-ended score. His intervention stimulated a wider network for continued movement and everyday performance that may have spread the population more thinly among open spaces;[60] however, the enhanced sense of urban choice ensures a more creative and participatory lifestyle in which people can improvise rather than feel constrained or controlled by limited options.

The score of the individual parts or "nodes" of the overall sequence also remains open. The Score (S) and Performance (P) of water unfolds as the most dynamic invitation to participate. The powerful Columbia River and the Cascades, glimpses of which are visible even from downtown as timeless reminders of the regional landscape, are inevitably part of the "psyche" of Portlanders, a city of inhabitants who have since proved themselves more environmentally conscious than any city in the United States. The open space sequence of their downtown, initiated by Halprin and his firm, follows the structure of these ever-present reminders and successfully inspires environmental curiosity and creative movement. On a smaller scale, Halprin's score of water's behavior over abstracted but recognizable forms triggers response in "open-ended participatory events."[61] In Lovejoy, water twists and tumbles over erosion forms constructed in materials recognizable in the urban environment (i.e., concrete). In Auditorium Forecourt, in contrast, it rushes and cascades over cliff faces unidirectionally and monumentally, making a unique civic statement. Although the contrast invites different forms of participation—climbing, swimming, scaling the steps, dancing, jumping, dangling feet, listening, touching, and so on—both fountains invoke the dynamic, even violent, forces of nature in a bold new urban gesture.

Yet though the Portland Sequence is an impressive and precedent-setting endeavor, it is not totally successful in achieving the objectives Halprin originally intended. For instance, whether due to the city's weakness of follow through or the firm's oversight, the sense of connection to the larger city grid by the kind of "linkages" Halprin considered so essential remains rather weak.[62] As a result, the Portland Center spaces in particular are introverted and isolated from the city street. One journalist's criticism of the Portland Center project in 1989 considers the inner-block "haven" more alienating than inviting: "To some extent the project is an anachronism, a relic of another time and another philosophy. Today, the need for a haven from such a livable city is much less clear."[63]

Halprin's 1991–92 report for Auditorium Forecourt (by then renamed the Ira Keller Fountain) addresses its "introversion" as detrimental to the life of the space, thus recognizing and embracing changes in attitude about public spaces since the urban tumult of the 1960s. Despite its public exposure surrounded on all sides by through streets, the Forecourt provided another "oasis from the sounds and forms of the rest of the city" by the powerful roar of falling water, the bermed and thickly planted perimeters, and the sunken basin at the foot of the Auditorium.[64] By the 1990s, its isolation from the street invited not positive participation but apparently "vandalism and undesirable behavior." To address the park's introversion, Halprin claimed that "no changes to the basic design were needed." Instead, he recommended a tree-thinning program as well as the rehabilitation of the original night-lighting scheme that had since failed due to inadequate maintenance. In addition, Halprin uncharacteristically suggested policing the site at night and reactivating the programs, such as the performances, concerts, and ballets, that had originally enlivened it.[65]

Not surprising is Halprin's insistence on no physical change to the original design. Even earlier, in 1971, Halprin's firm inspected the sequence "to critique any elements or practices not in keeping with the intent and design of the project," which included the insertion of "incompatible" trashcans, ash urns, and bike racks.[66] Since the firm seemed to prohibit accretions, the project might be easily compared to Nicollet Mall. However, though critical of the "incompatible" insertions, Halprin remained open to what he considered "natural" change over time. In his 1990s report on Auditorium Forecourt, subtitled "Recapturing the Magic," he claims:

> If anything it has improved with age—the trees have grown, framed the fountain, the concrete color has softened, moss has ameliorated the initial starkness of the construction & a warm patina has infused the paving & walls. The berms & surrounding plantings of trees have stretched a veil between the park & the surrounding traffic . . . & the poetic qualities of nature: water, plantings, the sense of wilderness (so important in cities) has increased over the years. These were the original intentions.

In Portland, the scores for citywide movement experience, as well as kinesthetic or performative response to individualized nodes, invite indeterminate futures. By structuring the score using the "archetypal" Resources (R) of indigenous ecologies, Lawrence Halprin & Associates provoked strong yet variable response, instilling a sense of spontaneity within the city fabric. The score, in this case, is certainly more similar to Amirkanian's than to Bach's—a comparison Halprin makes in *The RSVP Cycles*.

Though Portland is perhaps the most successful example of Halprin's attempt at scoring a creative and dynamic public life, particularly owing to the city's obvious concern for environmental quality and its positive effects on the city inhabitant, the firm used regional ecologies as "archetypes" to stimulate participation in many other cities undergoing change. At Skyline Park in Denver, for instance, the long narrow configuration of the given site extending over three blocks inspired the abstracted introduction of an erosive streambed into the city similarly (yet less dramatically) transitioning from mountain to wooded foothills. The park became a stylized version of an arroyo, a gully formation native to the Southwest, including Colorado, resulting mainly from excessive seasonal rainfall. Such a reference was particularly appropriate, because the park was also designed in 1970–74 as a site for stormwater retention, a priority after the destructive Platte River flood of 1965 that had affected much of what became the Skyline Urban Renewal Area. While the tripartite park was made cohesive through the narrative sequence and material continuity, including the pink-red cast-stone forms that were inspired by Halprin's tour of Denver's Red Rock Mountain Park, to break up the park's linear monotony the stream appeared to carve out sunken spaces that created a rhythm for human movement and rest (Figure 3.23).[67]

Figure 3.23. Block 18 of Skyline Park in Denver, Colorado, with sunken areas directing movement and rest, c. 1974. Lawrence Halprin Collection, The Architectural Archives, University of Pennsylvania (slide B-E335, unstamped).

Figure 3.24. Aerial view of Seattle Freeway Park, c. 1976. The park appears in the foreground at the base of the Park Place Building (left), bridging Interstate 5. Lawrence Halprin Collection, The Architectural Archives, University of Pennsylvania (slide F-J607, stamped by Lawrence Halprin & Associates).

SEATTLE FREEWAY PARK, SEATTLE, WASHINGTON

A chapter on Halprin's commitment to "ecologies of form" to stimulate human participation would not be complete without an assessment of Seattle Freeway Park. The forest fragment that hovers over Interstate 5 (I-5) in Seattle is a reminder of the city's prehistory. It bridges the chasm created by the concrete riverbed to connect the severed neighborhoods, as well as to connect the city dweller to these remote origins (Figure 3.24). Yet at no point does the visitor mistake the forest for a relic; instead, the highway below and the city surrounds become part of the fantasy of this unique experience. As a transitional space, restitching the city together in another remediative intervention, movement is primary. Rather than a legible narrative from one end to the other, the "experiential equivalent" of a wander through a wooded mountain landscape is the applied choreographic device, with stretches of heightened drama interspersed with serene moments for pause.

It is no wonder why Lawrence Halprin & Associates was selected in 1970 to address the challenges presented by the twelve-lane depressed freeway that cut through Seattle's grid, severing residential neighborhoods from their downtown (Figure 3.25). Halprin had published his book *Freeways* in 1966 to address just the problem Seattle now had to face—how to reconnect the city after inflicting this open wound (Figure 3.26). And yet, *Freeways* was more about city foresight, how to build transportation infrastructure as an integrated part of the "vast and complex functioning organism" or the "enormous megastructure" that is "the city of the future" (154). Despite public protest, as soon as funds became available, with help from the Highway Act of 1956, Seattle built the extension of I-5 to facilitate travel amid the region's sprawling development.

Seattle was unique, however, since the construction catalyzed a fierce campaign to seek creative amenity from what was otherwise destructive to urban life. As early as 1961 when the freeway was proposed, local architect Paul Thiry, who at the time was working with Halprin on the grounds for the Seattle World's Fair, recommended a seven-block concrete "lid" over it. When open space funds became available in 1968, the city and the Forward Thrust organization, a civic group formed in reaction to the region's sprawling development, found themselves ill-equipped to pursue this unprecedented concept, and became instead committed to a linear park along the freeway.[68] Yet James Ellis, the founder of Forward Thrust and the individual primarily responsible for securing the funds, suggested extending this park across the freeway, thus instigating a complex collaboration of dedicated public and private entities that worked to make a portion of this "lid" concept feasible.

From 1962 through 1964, Halprin continued to work with Thiry to convert the fairgrounds into a permanent park and cultural center for the city. By 1966, the year *Freeways* was published, the city was completing the interstate. According to numerous accounts, a Seattle Park Commission official discovered Halprin's book and realized that Seattle's freeway had been largely underconceived. Simultaneous to I-5's construction and its re-

Figure 3.25.
Interstate
5 divides
downtown
Seattle (right)
from First Hill
(left), c. 1970.
Seattle Municipal
Archives (series
5804–04, box 1).

sponse in Seattle, Halprin's work in nearby Portland was receiving highest praises. Selecting Lawrence Halprin & Associates for the design of the multiacre amenity that would bridge the freeway could not therefore have been a difficult decision.[69] *Freeways* was a culmination of the work Halprin had done from 1962 to 1964 for the city of San Francisco, studying the impact of transportation infrastructure on cities and the possibilities for the mutually beneficial integration of freeways into the urban setting. The difference between his work on what became the *San Francisco Freeways Report* and the *Panhandle Freeway Plan and Report* and the project presented in Seattle was that in the former two he was part of the preconstruction planning, whereas in the latter he was invited to mitigate

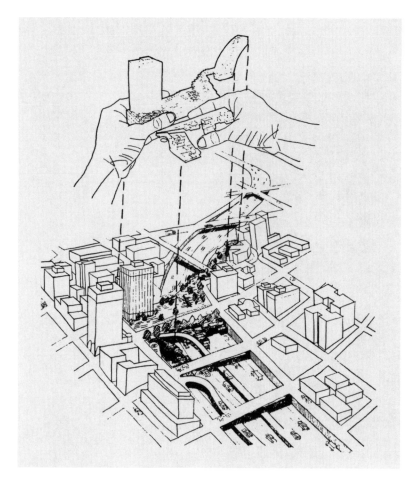

Figure 3.26. Concept drawing by Lawrence Halprin & Associates for Seattle Freeway Park, early 1970s. Published in *Process Architecture* (1984): 229. Lawrence Halprin Collection, The Architectural Archives, University of Pennsylvania.

the effects after freeway construction was complete. The interstate severed long-established relationships that likened the city to, as described in *Freeways*, a "biological ecosystem" (85). Halprin's interest was in integrating new transportation methods that enhance or give form to these relationships rather than destroy them. *Freeways* emphasizes the wonders and thrills of fast-speed travel but also insists that the infrastructure that facilitates this travel must enrich the places it passes through as "a new traffic architecture whose ultimate aim is to enhance people's lives as well as move them about" (149).

Halprin was pioneering these concepts just as the city of Seattle was daringly generating funds to transform this roadway liability into a partial amenity. Not only were the funding sources an example of the incredible complexity of the collaboration that generated Seattle Freeway Park, but the design team (led by Angela Danadjieva as project designer) and its consultants comprised a vastly complex network of relationships that was well worth more than the sum of its parts.[70] In *Freeways*, Halprin declares that to properly integrate a freeway into the city in a mutually beneficial relationship, "planners, sociologists, architects, landscape architects, economists, acoustical experts and engineers must be involved" (134). In Seattle, such a collaboration was made possible through the enthusiasm, dedication, and support of the city and some of its forward-thinking private entities.

As part of their elaborate "Reconnaissance and Program" phase, the firm collected extensive site Resources (R), particularly "Ecological and Environmental" and "Human Needs."[71] The firm conducted a "visual analysis of site and surrounding area," which included assessing views, topography, access, and pedestrian and vehicular traffic and movement patterns, as well as defining the character of the area, inventorying local construction materials, and finally, studying "existing patterns of behavioral and human uses of peripheral area."[72] Increased reliance on social science in urban design and planning is reflected in the firm's projects of the 1970s. Survey questionnaires developed by firm-member Simon Nicholson were distributed within the IBM Building (at Fifth Avenue and Seneca Street), the Exeter (a retirement complex abutting the site), the local Garfield High School, and the adjacent Olympic and Hilton hotels. Rather than conduct costly workshops for projects of limited scale and scope, the firm occasionally relied on questionnaires. Halprin had become critical of the limitations of questionnaires by this time, partly because they did not allow him opportunity to shape public values but rather only synthesize data in a much more linear approach than the Take Part Process. According to Bob Mendelsohn, previously the San Francisco supervisor who joined Halprin in 1970 to lead the office's community involvement initiatives, those surveyed gave the firm "a reasonable cross-section of the groups likely to use the park (area residents, many of them elderly, young people, office workers, and hotel guests)." In the same report, Mendelsohn concluded "that the park must have regional as well as community appeal, accommodate young children, the elderly and infirm, and that it should include some dynamic water feature (for which there was overwhelming support)."[73] These rather generic demands were synthesized into what became a truly unique place.

In *Freeways*, Halprin's emphasis is on the experience of rapid movement. He considers "the automobile on the freeway . . . symbolic of the intense dedication of our age of motion" (12). In the city, the freeway opens up entirely new "dimensions of experience—

color, form and shape—seen suddenly through motion" (23). He briefly acknowledges the work of Kevin Lynch, and then presents his early studies in "Motation" as the foundation for the development of "choreographic devices to register movement quality, character, speed, involvement with other mobile (or static) elements, and progressive spatial relationships including vertical and horizontal" (87). It is here that he considers the possibilities of motion picture techniques, which are particularly relevant to the project in Seattle because Danadjieva was the project designer and had spent seven years building sets for the Bulgarian film industry.[74] Her sets had to serve the constant motion of the camera, just as the park she designed had to serve perceptual demands of both the pedestrian and the driver. Danadjieva addressed these contrasting kinetic demands with "different scale impressions," explaining: "The frame of the park is a heavy form (vehicular perception), while the scale of the configuration of the park elements in the interior of the park is smaller in scale (pedestrian perception)."[75] For instance, the giant concrete planter boxes of the "Great Box Garden" cascade toward the freeway below.[76] The large planter boxes and tall mature trees floating above the road create an unforgettable approach into or through the downtown, offering the driver a dramatic sense of arrival into the region's economic and cultural core (Figures 3.27, 3.28, and 3.29).

Danadjieva's choreography is founded not on dance but on the frames of a moving camera, and the close, middle, and distant views that create an environment of varying moods and experiences as one moves through it. In an early site concept document, she explains that

> the variation in distance between viewer and object of interest . . . can help achieve these many experiences. Tight areas with close-up views can be used in attaining a dramatic feeling (for example, standing in a narrow canyon with water splashing all around the viewer). Middle-ground views can be employed for observation and personal reflection. Distant views will offer panoramas and opportunities for sightseeing . . . To help create the strong impression of place, most of the views should be limited to close-ups and those to the middle-ground. In contrast to this natural area, there could be an opening toward the Freeway, giving a striking overview of the motion and noise of the traffic. Then, in

Figure 3.27. The "forest" over Interstate 5. Photograph by the author, 2004.

contrast to this active space, there might be a relatively broad quiet area with middle ground and long views close to the Exeter Hotel . . . Along the 8th Avenue [overpass] or projected above it, there might be some elevated platforms exposed to the wind and noise of the Freeway, and taking advantage of exciting distant views toward the waterfront, Queen Anne Hill and Beacon Hill.[77]

Though this quotation implies Danadjieva was only interested in creating scenes or that she prioritized the visual sense, once inside the park the visitor is immediately immersed in fullest bodily presence. Upon entry from downtown, the sound of moving water overtakes the senses.[78] The Central Plaza's two fountains, the Cascade and particularly the Canyon (Figure 3.30), block out the park's urban surroundings and envelop the visitor in the magical qualities of the forested site. The Cascade Fountain is situated in the western

Figure 3.28. Drawing by Angela Danadjieva of Seattle Freeway Park, c. 1970. Scanned from slide in the Seattle Municipal Archives. Lawrence Halprin Collection, The Architectural Archives, University of Pennsylvania.

Figure 3.29. Drawing by Angela Danadjieva of Seattle Freeway Park from the perspective of the freeway, c. 1970. Scanned from slide in the Seattle Municipal Archives. Lawrence Halprin Collection, The Architectural Archives, University of Pennsylvania.

portion of the Central Plaza adjacent to the Park Place Building (Figure 3.31). Water in this feature pours over a tumbled rock formation abstracted into concrete blocks, and visitors are encouraged to walk within the fountain, surrounding themselves on all sides by falling water. As indicated by numerous office documents and articles responding to the park's development, a restaurant had been originally intended for the ground floor of the Park Place Building, which was supposed to have opened up onto the park and activated the space between the building and the cascade.[79]

To the east of the Cascade is the Canyon Fountain, the true centerpiece of the park and the climax of the drama (Figure 3.32). Danadjieva worked out the sculptural form in various clay models, carefully considering its three-dimensional qualities and psychological effects on the visitor. The top of the structure to the bottom of the canyon floor, which rests upon the freeway's median strip, measures thirty feet. Over the feature's sheer "rock face," many thousands of gallons of recirculated water plummeted per minute.[80] Sharply angled stairways invite visitors to hike to the canyon floor and peer out the large window that frames views of the cars rushing by on the freeway at almost eye level. Reflecting on this feature, Halprin explains: "As you are down in the gorge where the water falls . . . you can look through and see the cars run by, but you can't hear them and then the water goes across it and then it masks it, so that it is a kind of a fantasy of this imagery of the cars going by behind a waterfall looking through."[81] Blind corners within the canyon offer unexpected surprises at every turn, though today they are considered unsafe. A park brochure from 1976 describes the Canyon Fountain as follows: "The freeway has been silenced, bested on its own terms, its power and scale matched and opposed by the natural force of churning water." Danadjieva's theatrical training in Bulgaria was enhanced by a series of trips she took while employed by the Halprin firm to experience the natural wonders of the western United States, including the Grand Canyon, Death Valley, and Bryce Canyon.[82] The Canyon Fountain's upthrust volumes and deeply sunken voids recall such memorable places.

To the east of the fountain, a path meanders through a wooded section vegetated most densely at the edges, blocking out views to the city beyond. Just beyond the Eighth

Figure 3.30. Early photograph of Seattle Freeway Park from the Park Place Building, c. 1976. Photograph by John Pastier.

Avenue overpass from which one can get elevated views into the park, the primary meandering path continues into an open area likened to a "mountain meadow." According to the 1976 brochure, "away from the canyon, grassy retreats and unexpected spaces open among the concrete cliffs. Small spaces restore a sense of human proportion, and shrubs, trees and grass create softness and a sense of belonging. Occasionally the city reasserts itself and architectural details outside the park demand attention—a row of arched windows, the geometry of a downtown tower, the white dome of a church, or the arch of the 8th Avenue overcrossing."

The park is about contrasting moods and varying levels of dramatic intensity.[83] Especially in its current maturity, the park perfectly embodies the manmade "Fantasy Environments" about which Halprin wrote in the early 1970s: "Not only don't [cities] provide adequate housing and transportation and clean air; but they lack a sense of fantasy ... they do not give us a chance to dream, to search out mysteries, to adventure, to imagine the most wonderful things—to fantasize. They lack places to hide, to play." The hanging forest over the deep chasm of the interstate provides such a place that has "an instancy and immediacy of appeal," and "contains secret and private places full of closed womb-like spaces" in its caves, caverns, and other penetrations in the concrete forms.[84]

The freeway divided the First Hill neighborhood from the downtown. As the firm surely uncovered, First Hill was blanketed in old growth forest before the first settlers arrived on Elliott Bay in the 1860s and had it cleared and milled. After the fire of 1889 in what is now downtown Seattle, the area became an elite suburb, particularly because of its plethora of seeps and springs. Freeway Park meant to reorient people to their rapidly changing surrounds. The firm achieved this reorientation through the application of

Figure 3.31. Activity in the Cascade Fountain, Seattle Freeway Park. Lawrence Halprin Collection, The Architectural Archives, University of Pennsylvania (slide F-J201, stamped by Lawrence Halprin & Associates, 1976).

Figure 3.32. Canyon Fountain, Seattle Freeway Park, c.1976. Lawrence Halprin Collection, The Architectural Archives, University of Pennsylvania (slide F-J432, stamped by Lawrence Halprin & Associates).

"primordial expressions" of the old growth forest and the reinsertion of the water that was once bountiful upon the site and uphill to the east, as well as dominant in the distant surrounds of Elliott Bay, Lake Union, and the other water bodies that envelop and shape the city.

When seen from the air, the meandering freeway, cutting through the city grid, appears as a powerfully erosive force that does not look alien in the city entirely shaped by water (see Figure 3.25). The park's forms and flows respond to this "concrete river-bed," activated by the steady stream of cars. The original planting scheme corresponded to park topography as it referenced places like the Olympic Mountains, sometimes visible from the city on clear days. Rhododendrons, azaleas, and alders were planted in the lower southwestern portions of the park, and Douglas fir and upland trees were placed in the upper park, which is nearly ninety feet higher. The wooded site is also a direct response to the forests of First Hill that were milled into planks in the late nineteenth century. Whether intended or not, the milled timber board forms used to cast in place the site's concrete structures reference this historic consumption of timber in the immediate region.

"Experiential equivalency" is used as a choreographic device in Seattle in its most advanced form (Figure 3.33).[85] The dramatic peaks represented in the park provide moments of sublime drama juxtaposed with serene and beautiful qualities of open mountain meadows, again embodying the "yin" and "yang," effects Halprin explored at Pettygrove Park and Lovejoy Plaza. The extremes in mood and "emotional effects" were part of the primary program for the park. The contrasts—"swift motion of cars and calm movement of strollers; noisy atmosphere of the freeway and streets and the peaceful sounds of water, wind, and trees; hard edges of freeway concrete and automobile metal and the soft outlines of landscaping and changeable nature of water shapes"[86]—were meant to instill a deep sense of environmental awareness. This new range of experiences introduced into the city as a series of linked spaces along the primary path create the true transition from First Hill to the Central Business District. This "choreographed sequence of varied spaces and uses in the heart of the city" starts quiet at either end and builds in intensity toward the central features when it hits a climax and then slows.[87]

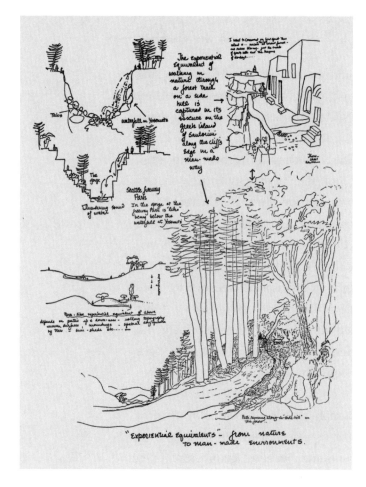

Figure 3.33. Lawrence Halprin's sketch of "experiential equivalency" as applied to Seattle Freeway Park, 1970s. Published in *Sketchbooks of Lawrence Halprin* (1981), 31. Lawrence Halprin Collection, The Architectural Archives, University of Pennsylvania.

In addition to introducing the "primordial" experience of the Pacific Northwest forest, the park's vertical concrete elements also respond to the burgeoning downtown to the west of the park. Similar to how Halprin balances the violent force of the Embarcadero freeway in San Francisco by the powerful drama of the plaza fountain, Seattle Freeway Park was built as an equally dynamic counterpoint to the freeway and city surrounds as well as a continuation of some of its materials and moods.

Concrete was deliberately used here, as well as in many other Halprin parks, as an indication that this space is, in fact, urban and not simply a passive palliative offering a soothing retreat.[88] As Danadjieva indicates in her "Design Notes on Freeway Park": "Seattle is characterized by strong changes in elevation—both natural and man-made forms: First Hill, Queen Anne Hill, the Freeway Canyon, the elevated Alaskan Freeway, suspended off-ramps and on-ramps, pedestrian overpasses and many bridges. I feel the proposed park should reflect this character."[89] The park incorporates the speeding automobile into the experience of its design and responds by "set[ing] against the surrounding dynamism a new dynamic," according to Danadjieva, and consequently a completely new form for an urban public space.[90] While the recent "Big Dig" in Boston, which tunneled the Central Artery (Interstate 93) through the city, integrates a park that makes no reference to the massive feat of engineering below, Halprin and his firm not only make reference but amplify the experiential effects of this powerful urban infrastructure. Not until the construction of Seattle's Olympic Sculpture Park (opened 2007)—complexly straddling a highway and train tracks along Elliott Bay less than two miles from Freeway Park—has such a relationship been established in any U.S. city. The fact that both projects are situated in Seattle suggests the city's clear commitment to innovation in public space and infrastructural design.[91]

The configuration of the original park was thirteen hundred feet long and its irregular width varied from four hundred feet to less than sixty. But the park has since grown. The insertion of the American Legion's Freedom Plaza now acts as an access point to the newer Washington State Convention and Trade Center, opening up onto a large concrete-paved plaza fronted by the structure's irregular glass facade.[92] Just after the park was completed, Danadjieva left Lawrence Halprin & Associates and established the firm Danadjieva & Koenig, which was responsible for the Convention Center as well as the Pigott Corridor. The Pigott Memorial Corridor acted as a new entrance to the park from the retirement community above it by accommodating the change of grade in a series of ADA (American Disabilities Act) switchback ramps, as well as short flights of stairs, with a watercourse flowing along one side.[93]

The Halprin firm had intended for the park to serve as the kind of open score that could accept these additions and growths over time. This gradual layering of updates, reflective of the evolution of attitudes and urban needs, makes Seattle Freeway Park a rich cultural document. In addition to the accretions that extend immediately from it, the firm considered the park only "the potential beginning of a great green network for Seattle," and as such a catalyst for an extending system at the scale of the city and even region.[94] In another document by the firm titled "Seattle Freeway Park: New Dimensions for Freeways," the project is described as one that would

> connect sections of the city rent asunder by the construction of the freeway, and, if the designers achieve their ultimate goal, will act as the energizing element in an eventual large-scale system of landscaped plazas, walkways, and terraces interrelating many areas of Seattle over the freeway and streets down to the waterfront . . . If it can continue to

proliferate in size and be realized as an eventual living green skein of terraces, parks, rec-
reation areas, and planted overhangs integrating many areas of Seattle and its waterfront
over the freeways and streets, an extremely important statement about returning to a
vital relationship between men, the city, and natural things will have been accomplished,
and other cities will take heart and follow Seattle's example.[95]

At the time, there were no major parks in Seattle's downtown. The courtyard to the
Seattle Public Library and the U.S. Courthouse lawn a few blocks south, the firm discov-
ered, were the only outdoor gathering spaces in the nearby vicinity. The density and con-
struction of the central business core was increasing dramatically during the 1960s and
1970s, so creative planning for open space was crucial during this period. With the con-
struction of the Alaskan Way Viaduct along the waterfront and the rapid development of
the business district, the firm recognized the possibility of the city losing the connection
to its dramatic natural sea setting. They therefore considered the park a "generator of
more systems," so that "the whole development will appear as a green necklace" tying the
city together and to its regional ecology.[96]

The establishment of a network of green spaces is consistent with plans for Seat-
tle created by the Olmsted Brothers in the early twentieth century. The Olmsted firm
planned for a network of parks linked by boulevards and parkways, forming a "Green
Ring" around the city. During this period, the sprawling and multiuse Woodland Park
and Green Lake Park were developed. In a synopsis of the Lawrence Halprin & Associates
survey responses to the question asking which Seattle parks people particularly enjoyed,
Simon Nicholson summarized that although adults commonly preferred the Olmsted
parks, the high school students, as well as many workers from the IBM building, favored
the Washington Park Arboretum. He considered this fact "extremely interesting because
it is not a 'park' in the traditional sense."[97] Perhaps this justified the untraditional nature
of the place that Halprin & Associates eventually developed in Seattle. The unique op-
portunities that Freeway Park provides offer a heightened sense of diversity and choice
in the city.

In 2002 the city initiated a parks campaign called "The Blue Ring," which was meant to link the central city's open spaces and create a continuous open space network that includes Seattle Freeway Park and Seattle Center. Its objectives were nearly identical to those desired by the Halprin firm, acting well ahead of its time:

> Large portions of the Blue Ring will help bridge the physical gaps between neighborhoods resulting from I-5 and the Alaskan Way Viaduct . . . The most challenging improvement will be physical changes to the Waterfront and a lid over I-5 . . . The Blue Ring is not only a path, but an organizing principle . . . The Blue Ring will not be one continuous place but rather the aggregation of varied and interconnected places and spaces that will add up to the equivalent of a much larger open space . . . The Blue Ring strategy is intended to serve as a means to coordinate projects conceived long ago with others yet to come. It will connect these projects to the city fabric, and make the whole far greater than sum of the parts.[98]

The above quotation above could have believably been taken from Lawrence Halprin & Associates documents. The firm's intention was for the park to catalyze a spreading system, just as the Blue Ring campaign proposed "Catalyst Projects" to achieve the same goal. The Alaskan Way Viaduct, for instance, which long separated Seattle from its waterfront, will soon be replaced with a tunnel, thus providing new land for public space and a renewed relationship with Elliott Bay, a relationship the Halprin firm had urged forty years prior.

Seattle Freeway Park in its maturity now fully embodies one of Halprin's "Fantasy Environments"—a floating forest of mystery, discovery, and an unfolding diversity of spaces experienced through movement. Forms serve as the score generating performance—as official theater,[99] as ritual, and as spontaneous interactive response to designed triggers and prompts. Integrating the freeway into the preestablished network of the city and creating a transition from one neighborhood to the next while also providing a place worth remaining were the programmatic stimuli for the project. Only through movement does the park reveal its complexity and full range of spatial and qualitative effects as the "experiential equivalent" to the primordial surrounds that were deeply embedded in the psyche of the city's residents. The park's intensifying drama unfolds as the visitor travels the primary path and experiences finely manipulated views as part of this narrative. Along that path, the park's spaces invite interactive participation with "the three dimensional kinetic possibilities of the place."[100]

Halprin and his firm had undeniable foresight and, in many ways, were well ahead of their time. They recommended that cities open themselves up to their waterfronts, enhance their public space network as green infrastructure, and embrace the inherited city for its dynamic and diverse opportunities for social interaction. Yet the built works, though intended as spaces that would adapt to shifting social circumstances as an open score, might be considered relics of a particular time in the history of American urban development. While they were never passive or neutral "open spaces," the parks and plazas typically offered protective enclaves from the "sensuously deprived" private development emerging in downtowns at this time. Today, however, healthy cities pride themselves on vibrant street life and opportunities for public exchange. Thus while Halprin hoped for enhanced social life after dissociative change, his spaces often do not invite the public life of the street to permeate their bounds. However, while I argue that it is Halprin's creative process that has potential to impact city-shaping today (rather than the forms themselves), these built works enrich today's city by offering another opportunity to choose how we appropriate and use open space.

MANHATTAN SQUARE PARK, ROCHESTER, NEW YORK

Manhattan Square Park (1971–76) provides a kind of condensation of ideas that Lawrence Halprin & Associates simultaneously applied in other cities, but in a much more compressed multiuse park. Rather than a horizontal extension as in Portland, where the matrix of open space knits urban fragments together, here the movement was directed in the vertical dimension, emphasizing the park's section over its plan, the latter of which is a relatively mundane composition of programmatic zones. Within its five acres, Lawrence Halprin & Associates, with Jim Coleman of the New York office in charge, condensed a fountain and associated amphitheater plaza, a 100' by 100' by 50' space-frame with an overlook tower, a restaurant, a sunken playground, a raised playfield, a berm garden, a promenade, and recreational courts that converted into a skating rink in the winter (Figures 3.34, 3.35).

The story is similar despite the unique result. The park was developed as the centerpiece in the first (and only) phase of another ambitious redevelopment scheme, the Southeast Loop Urban Renewal Area (Figure 3.36). The sixty-acre area was to encompass a high-density, mixed-income residential neighborhood with services and entertainment facilities to serve the seventy-five hundred intended new residents and the workers from the nearby Xerox and Marine Midland offices and Midtown Plaza.[101] The previous dense neighborhood fabric had been designated "blighted" and cleared. Streets were removed and rerouted as part of the construction of the Inner Loop, the expressway that circles downtown. Completed in 1965, the Inner Loop severed downtown from adjacent neighborhoods and made it possible for motorists to entirely bypass the city's core, contributing to the surrounding sprawl. When the New York State Urban Development Corporation (UDC) threatened bankruptcy in 1975, urban renewal progress halted, leaving the park and 10 Manhattan Square the only executed elements of the plan. The city subsequently began selling off land piecemeal to developers who built without engaging

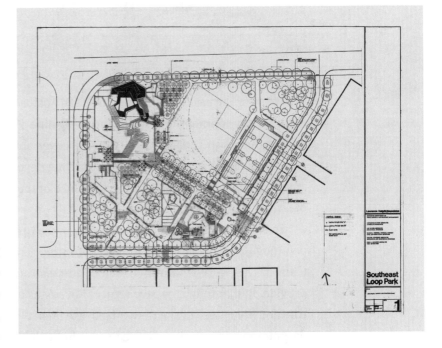

Figure 3.34. Lawrence Halprin & Associates, plan of Manhattan Square Park (Southeast Loop Park), Rochester, New York, 1971. Lawrence Halprin Collection, The Architectural Archives, University of Pennsylvania.

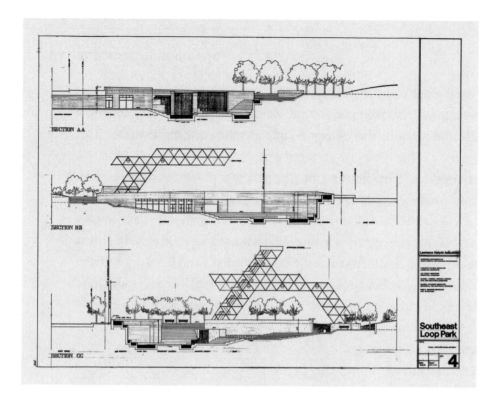

Figure 3.35.
Lawrence Halprin &
Associates, sections
of Manhattan Square
Park (Southeast Loop
Park), Rochester, New
York, 1971. Lawrence
Halprin Collection,
The Architectural
Archives, University
of Pennsylvania.

the street or the park. This story had already played out in Denver, which had a hard time enticing development around Halprin's Skyline Park, designed as the "heart" or "symbol" of the urban renewal area. When Denver abandoned the design guidelines for the renewal area to try and lure reluctant private development, the same disengagement occurred, proving disastrous to the experience of the park as part of a wider urban network of streets, skyways, and open spaces.[102]

In Rochester and other cities, however, the optimism of the early 1970s spurred park planning. City officials with the Rochester branch of the UDC and the Southeast Loop Citizens' Advisory Committee generated a list of activities they hoped the park would provide. Rather than a passive refuge, Rochester uniquely considered this park to be the true activity center of the new mixed-use area. As a response to the city's insistence on programming, the firm generated what they called a "visual score" (really a photographic montage) for the promotional report, illustrating the dynamic array of activities the park would eventually offer.[103]

The temporal-situational aspect of the park (its score) resided in its reference to the earlier street patterns, its rooted connection to the dynamics of the Genessee River, which uniquely runs and dramatically falls through downtown, and the segregated movement systems distinguished by sectional levels. The park's spine, the promenade that runs diagonal to the surrounding grid, links the park's pieces together and grounds it in its context by following the orientation of George Street, which existed before renewal clearance, and by creating a link with the neighborhoods just outside the Inner Loop, which retained the old street orientation (Figure 3.37).[104]

Though, at first glance, the fountain plaza seems like a tired repetition of Lovejoy Plaza (Figure 3.38), a deeper understanding of the park's physical context poses a different possibility. The city was, in fact, enthusiastic of such a signature Halprin element and referenced the parks in Portland, and the firm's promotional report for what was originally called Southeast Loop Park included photographs of Portland's fountain plazas in use. However, the Rochester fountain did also provide what seems like a deliberate response to its own setting.

The Genesee River was essential to the city's development. It powered the gristmills that processed the wheat that earned Rochester the name "the flour city." By maximizing on topographic changes, the mills ran on the hydroelectric power that still provides power to downtown Rochester. A half mile from the park, the river falls dramatically toward its mouth

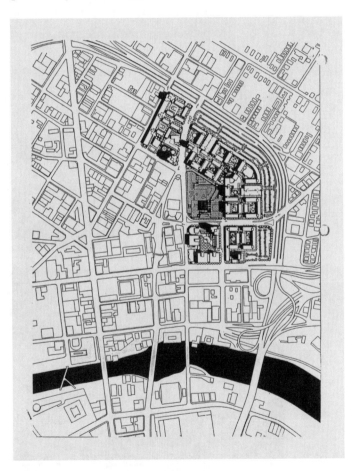

Figure 3.36. Southeast Loop Urban Renewal Area, Rochester, New York, c. 1970. The shaded parcel indicates the location of the planned park. Lawrence Halprin Collection, The Architectural Archives, University of Pennsylvania.

at Lake Ontario, and one may discover the old Erie Canal aqueduct (now the Broad Street bridge), a canal lock, the old Johnson and Seymour spillway, and just another half mile or so downstream, the voluminous High Falls. Thus the drama of the fountain, which rises five feet above street level and descends twenty feet below (see Figure 3.35), is an ecological expression that Halprin would have considered part of the archetypal language shared by the city residents. Using this "ecology of form," the intention behind the fountain was to provoke interactive response.

Figure 3.37. Manhattan Square Park, looking southeast.
From the Rowe Photo Collection, Rochester, New York, August 1975.

Figure 3.38. Fountain plaza in Manhattan Square Park.
Photograph by John Veltri, 1975.

While much of Manhattan Square Park is sunken, its most unique feature is the space-frame and its overlook tower, which rises nearly one hundred feet above the fountain plaza and creates a skyline element, boldly marking the park's presence (Figure 3.39). Halprin built a much more modest space-frame at the Embarcadero in San Francisco, yet the Rochester structure is significantly more interactive.[105] In addition to allowing people to climb in the vertical dimension to view the city and watch the activity in the fountain and park at its base, the structure also supported an elaborate lighting and sound system for performances in the fountain amphitheater.

The multidimensionality of the movement systems was further enhanced by the

Figure 3.39. Manhattan Square Park space-frame. Photograph by John Veltri, 1975.

segregation of vehicular and pedestrian ways by means of grade distinctions, thus complicating the movement choreography through the park and into the surrounding streets. The pedestrian enters the park from a major intersection in a sunken underpass, while the widened Chestnut Street remained at grade. These large-scale infrastructural gestures created complex section profiles that make the park truly distinctive and so uniquely reflective of its particular time in American urban development.

I have included the Manhattan Square Park example in part 1, "Built Work," because it rounds out the comprehensive study of Lawrence Halprin & Associates' most dynamic built work of the urban renewal period. Though some of the features are redundant, the vertical movement score is most unique. In addition, it provides yet another illustration of the tragic optimism of these spaces. Rather than being a vibrant "new town downtown" served by this dynamic park at its core, the surroundings still remain largely vacant and the park has thus declined.

THE PROVOCATIVE CITY

The projects profiled in part 1 represent some of Lawrence Halprin & Associates' most experientially rich urban interventions that react to the "disclimax" conditions of cities at this time. Though Halprin disagreed with many of the destructive forces stimulated by government policies, he rarely countered them with direct action (although in one unique case, he was arrested in 1969 for protesting the flood-control proposal for Tamalpais Creek). Instead, he treated the destructive effects of these policies as a creative opportunity (and clearly benefitted financially from this stance). Though mitigation or amelioration might be acceptable terms for his work in cities at the time, they imply a degree of passivity, which Halprin's projects rarely exhibited.

Instead, his spaces act as infrastructure inviting participation by facilitating both institutionalized and "everyday" rituals whereby people could wait for the bus, eat lunch in the shade, walk to the store, and so on, but with a heightened environmental awareness or sensory engagement. In addition, by understanding natural processes and how humans were deeply embedded in these processes, Halprin attempted to score or catalyze open-ended creative response. While he considered natural process the trigger to universally stimulate this response, he expected that this reception would unfold in infinitely different ways depending on individual interpretation and responsive performance.

Market Street as a hometown laboratory and Nicollet Mall represent Halprin's early attempts at applying to the public urban environment his early thoughts on choreography, which he had integrated less consciously in gardens and shopping centers throughout the 1950s. In both, he enhanced the ritualistic potential of the historic parade street. In San Francisco, he structured a standardized framework to unify the diverse boulevard and provided elements to facilitate an interactive public life. The modest everyday features are complemented by moments of heightened drama. The rhythmic score for Nicollet broke the monotony of the city grid as well as provided spaces for participation and interaction in a setting that had previously only catered to automobiles. The commemorative program of Heritage Park Plaza provided the framework for a new public ritual, recognizing the city's cultural heritage and social connection to its watershed. It is a transformative space experienced through processional movement.

Portland has been presented as Halprin's most comprehensive and successful use of open scores. By structuring movement on an urban and human scale, Halprin provides the links and transitions essential to a healthy urban ecosystem, as well as reconnects people to their fundamental ecology to provoke uninhibited response. Seattle Freeway Park provided the fantasy and mystery associated with the native forests of the Pacific Northwest to reknit the city, reorient the people, "tame" the freeway, and capitalize on its dynamic possibilities. As in Portland, Lawrence Halprin & Associates hoped the park would act as an open score itself catalyzing the infiltration of the city's interstices by a "green skein" connecting Seattle inhabitants to their forests and their waterfronts. In Manhattan Square Park, the focal point for another failed renewal scheme, many of these ideas were compressed into a single space with enhanced sectional diversity. The numerous programs inspired a slightly less comprehensive scheme, but one that was certainly dynamic and offered multiple choices for creative urban living. In all cases, Lawrence Halprin & Associates contributed to an increased public value for urban open space and, in many cases, foretold and catalyzed the future of each city's public space planning. However, many consider these places a failure, a criticism that cannot be entirely attributed to Halprin as a designer but to the fact that the development anticipated to absorb these spaces into a larger urban fabric never materialized.

Halprin used the language of scores to insist his projects invite evolutionary change essential to the natural succession of city development. However, the major tension in his designs is his inability to resolve the issue of flexibility. In fact, as indicated by most of the project studies, the unresolved tension between enabling and imposing exists in all of his work. Though Halprin's theoretical and built work is riddled with inconsistencies and contradictions natural to the questioning or critical mind, what drives or causes most of them is the irresolution of the open versus closed score and the degree of participation Halprin truly wished to invite. The term *choreography*, in place of "master planning" in the order of Le Nôtre or Le Corbusier, two figures he often accused of executing their designs through top-down imposition, implies an interest in guidance rather than control. However, as Halprin repeatedly acknowledges, choreographers exercise varying levels of authority, and he spent the 1960s and 1970s trying to figure out where he stood within this spectrum (see Figure I.5).[106] Whereas Anna Halprin has arguably spent much of her career helping individuals release themselves from cultural inhibitions and unleash personal creativity, Larry Halprin struggled to loosen control. In his defense, however, one might not be able to consider his work landscape architecture if the score were left entirely open; it would simply be too passive, too diluted or weak, as revealed by the more "flexible" redesigns of his projects, specifically Nicollet Mall and Skyline Park. Halprin's struggles are perhaps best illustrated by a November 29, 1967, passage from his *Notebooks* in which he records thoughts discussed with Paul Baum on "Flexibility." He asks, "How can a place be (1) Someplace, (2) NOT completely defined . . . allowing for participation." He continues to list "levels of participation" including "(1) Portland, Play Spaces—Disneyland, etc.—Use & participate but not alter! (2) Stores for potential use but people alter to their taste (3) Allotment gardens in Europe (4) Movable features (5) Each individual designs his own place (6) Build your own house."[107] Halprin experiments with all of these techniques during his career, yet (1) and (2) in the latter quotation are most common. He considers the "imperfect" or "incomplete" work the most inclusive, "allowing for addition or subtraction which enables a person to feel part of it."[108] He consistently references the polarities between the monumental order of the city, that which was imposed as "the official image of how things *ought to be*," and the "city of the people," which is "rambling, complex, individualized, small scale, human, intricate" and whose order is fluid and "expressive of growth" or generated from the people.[109] These polarities appear in Halprin's wide range of projects executed during the height of urban renewal. For instance, the idea of "megastructures" that retain a complete internal order appealed to Halprin, as represented by his enthusiasm for the Yerba Buena Center, the thirty-five-acre redevelopment in downtown San Francisco that was never built because of public protest over the flawed relocation process.[110] The design, to which Halprin contributed working under Kenzo Tange, embodies a higher degree of design control than a project like Portland, which is comprehensive but works within the existing conditions of the city rather than imposing a completely new and autonomous physical order. Though the proposed Yerba Buena Center offered opportunities for choice in movement, all the choices were provided by the designers, making it difficult to conceive as "expressive of growth"—a dilemma also quite present in Nicollet Mall.

Flexibility to Halprin implies both ability to receive and react to participatory input over time, as well as ability to withstand cultural change and remain culturally relevant, which are more or less one and the same. The balance Halprin seems to have sought is the idea of the "interactive container for life,"[111] where his designs act as the stage for the theater of everyday life composed of both the consistency of "living rituals" and the chance occurrences or happenings that are indeterminate but just as significant to the full urban experience. The idea of flexibility or adaptability to people's evolving needs and desires or the openness of his choreography to improvisation is important when considering Halprin's projects, not only because he was so vocal about its embodiment in his work, but because so many of the designs that supposedly resist obsolescence are being blamed today for being too inflexible and inadaptable as justification for their demolition. The urban context and experience has clearly changed since the tumultuous redevelopment of the 1960s and 1970s, perhaps so dramatically that Halprin's work may be considered outdated. Whereas Halprin often conceived downtown parks as protected precincts, shielding the view of surrounding construction by berms or sinking the park below street level and providing dramatic water elements to drown out its noise, today, because of public concern over safety, as well as more reestablished street life, this "haven" concept is no longer viable. Yet Halprin's projects typically add another opportunity for choice amid an increasingly homogenized urban environment, offering the chance to enact new and embedded rituals with enhanced awareness and experience the drama and mystery of forces abstracted from Nature reintroduced in the city.

PART II. COMMUNITY WORKSHOPS

4. THE TAKE PART PROCESS

LAWRENCE HALPRIN & ASSOCIATES IN PARTICIPATORY DESIGN

WHILE LAWRENCE HALPRIN applied the choreographic concept of "open scores" to design public spaces that stimulated movement response and enhanced opportunities for choice, chance, encounter, and exchange, he used the same concept to structure his participatory workshops. His Take Part Process (Figure 4.1) responded to the fierce demands for participation expressed in the mass public mobilizations of the 1960s—protests, demonstrations, rallies, and riots. As cities across the nation erupted in violence largely in reaction to institutionalized racism physically manifested by discriminatory redevelopment policies, urban renewal programs became increasingly suspect.[1] President Lyndon Johnson's "Great Society" programs and his "War on Poverty" attempted to mitigate some of the social and economic damage caused by the lack of comprehensive planning to address the declining urban core. Participation was central to his federal initiatives, such as the Economic Opportunity Act of 1964, which required that community action agencies have "maximum feasible participation," and the Model Cities program, which ambiguously called for "widespread participation." Yet by 1969, Sherry Arnstein, the former

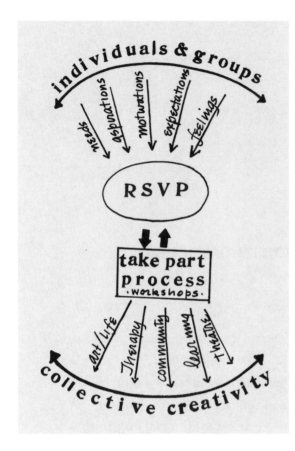

Figure 4.1. Diagram of the Take Part Process in relationship to the RSVP Cycles. Published in Halprin and Burns, *Taking Part*, 3. Lawrence Halprin Collection, The Architectural Archives, University of Pennsylvania.

chief advisor on citizen participation in the Department of Housing and Urban Development's (HUD) Model Cities Administration, claimed these policies intended to placate citizens at best.[2]

Despite its countercultural and avant-garde influences, Lawrence Halprin & Associates applied for HUD funding in 1970 to institute the Take Part Process after witnessing a decade of citizen attempts at thwarting redevelopment projects largely dictated by government and big business. The urban activist Jane Jacobs played a central role in this history; along with fellow-resident and mother Shirley Hayes, she held rallies, staged demonstrations, and attended hearings, successfully blocking Robert Moses's plans for the Lower Manhattan Expressway in the early 1960s. In her 1958 essay "Downtown Is for People," she declared: "You've got to get out and walk" the city and plan according to direct observation of its strengths and shortcomings.[3] Her seminal book *The Death and Life of Great American Cities* (1961) continues to inspire generations of urban planners aiming to optimize the physical and social diversity now recognized as essential to a healthy public life. Her wisdom clearly captured Halprin, who never cites her influence but tellingly invited her to consult on his 1967 commission to evaluate the environmental quality of urban renewal projects in New York City, which will be discussed later in this chapter.

Also in the late 1960s, Halprin's involvement in the master planning of Yerba Buena Center (the South of Market Street Redevelopment Project) prompted his investment in citizen participation. When thousands of households were displaced by the demolition of this massive area of downtown San Francisco and, in turn, experienced an extremely flawed relocation process, residents revolted, stalling the project until the late 1970s. Not only was Halprin a witness to the successes of grassroots community organizing in influencing environmental decisions, but he was also a target. In the early 1960s, citizen and media opposition halted Halprin's plan for a "Panhandle Parkway and Crosstown Tunnel" in San Francisco. Halprin claimed that the fierce opposition occurred because of a misunderstanding of the plan by the media and public.[4] He considered this situation an exemplary reason for participatory processes and a learning experience for his firm. Therefore, Halprin's interest in the collaborative participatory process was not entirely based on the ethics of inclusion, but also on optimizing the potential for the implementation of his designs, as the public became more committed to plans that they helped generate. This is fundamental to a full understanding of the Take Part Process (also simply called "Taking Part").

In 1972, Lawrence Halprin & Associates issued the promotional report *Take Part: A Report on New Ways in Which People Can Participate in Planning their Own Environments*. The process is described more comprehensively in a book Halprin cowrote in 1974 with his associate and friend Jim Burns, called *Taking Part: A Workshop Approach to Collective Creativity*. The book includes chapters by Anna Halprin and the Gestalt psychologist Paul Baum, who were both seminal to the development of the process.

In the ideal application of Taking Part, using the RSVP Cycles as a framework, workshop participants were chosen carefully by the firm after intensive Resource (R) gathering to determine a suitable "microcosm" of the community, or those who would be affected by change. Halprin Scored (S) these workshops by creating guidelines for a set of cumulative experiences, emphasizing environmental awareness, to optimize the creative energy of the group working together. This always began with an Awareness Score, typically a City Walk, to get participants immediately interacting with their environment. The cumulative activity scores, to be Performed (P) by the workshop participants, were deliberately choreographed in a sequential and progressive manner to build up a mutual foundation for the diversity of participants. Because participants were chosen as a community cross-section, many did not share a common background. Therefore, the activities scored for the two- to three-day workshop were intended to foster a shared experience from which a group could develop a "common language of environmental awareness" and move forward in a collective way. Feedback and sharing sessions, or Valu-action (V), would facilitate communication among the participants so that a consensus could ultimately emerge.

Halprin's use of the word creativity in the context of Taking Part implied active involvement in the generation of ideas not encumbered by cultural or social constructs but based on the immediacy of human intuition and instinct. By asking for a kind of primal or "gut-level response" to situations, participants could directly confront their environment on common ground. In a proposal for community workshop funding, the firm states:

> Each man is limited to his own experience . . . A suburban executive may experience the city as an automative traffic pattern. The ghetto dweller's world may be defined by the public transportation system . . . Opportunity must be provided for the citizens to experience the other factors in the environment, and the environment itself as a whole, including other people's experiences.[5]

Thus, for instance, in an early application of the workshop process in Fort Worth that uniquely involved almost entirely community decision-makers, participants were asked to get out of their cars, offices, and suburban dwellings and experience the city in its 102-degree heat. The score, in fact, asked that the participants move around the city in anything but their cars. According to the firm, "after this personal experience of heat, unpleasantness, delay and frustration at the lack of getting about, the workshop consensus was that a superior mass transit system must be built."[6] This was most clearly the firm's predetermined objective, suggesting the process was not as open as Halprin asserts. An unresolved tension between facilitation and manipulation thus becomes particularly evident when the process is applied in practice—an observation that will be considered further in chapter 5.

Scores (S) are most fundamental to the Take Part Process. As agents for growth and change, they served as frameworks and catalysts for action. Scored workshop activities challenged participants to consider their environment with "fresh eyes," to think beyond their cultural stereotypes and respond "creatively" to their immediate situation. As Lawrence Halprin & Associates notes about the participatory method in their March 1971 document "Leadership Training Workshop, General Statement of Objectives": "The basic technique which lies at the core of this approach is one called 'situational'—that is, the learning experience derived from placing people in *situations* from which they learn by experiencing. This differs from more usual teaching in which people are 'instructed.' People will learn by experiencing and then evaluate what they have experienced."[7] In other words, Halprin is relying on the kind of situational or experiential learning promoted by figures such as John Dewey, rather than on the imposition of professional expertise. This is a unique description of the process by Halprin not found in the book *Taking Part*. The use of the word "learning" here is essential, as it sets the tone for the following chapter. Rather than a process that was entirely open to indeterminate input, Taking Part exposed participants to the experience of others through a carefully scripted sequence. This again implies the scores were not as open as Halprin might propose. In fact, workshops were often choreographed to shape or engineer public attitudes toward the environment based on the firm's long-standing principles. Part II introduces the unresolved ambiguity between facilitation and manipulation latent in the process, as well as what might be learned from the tension between facilitation and manipulation in public process planning today. Regardless of the contradictions that emerge between written theory and practical application, Taking Part is a compelling experiment in structuring a shared experience to facilitate communication between diverse constituents who saw their lives in new contexts.

Selecting participants for community workshops was a crucial aspect of preworkshop planning. Appropriately, *Taking Part* includes a significant section on this challenge since it so strongly influences the direction of the workshop and what is supposed to be an inclusionary and pluralistic process. Halprin insists the ideal workshop group of thirty-five to forty participants must be of representative diversity, embodying the range of problems and complexities inherent to the area in question. The only way to determine what this range is and who to recruit for the process was through the Resource (R) gathering phase. When time and funding were available, the firm preferred to conduct interviews with all potential participants, as well as with a contact group that would be able to relay what economic, social, ethnic, age, and other patterns are evident and who might be considered most representative of these groups and interests.

Though the Take Part workshops were intended to maximize inclusion and transparency, the emphasis remained on generating what Larry and Anna called "collective creativity," or the premise that the creative potential of diverse individuals "can be unleashed and enhanced" when they interact in groups. Diversity is a central theme in *Taking Part* and other publications promoting the process. According to the firm, participants in the workshops were not to lose their individual identities for the sake of the group; instead, the collaborative process was supposed to maximize the participants' diversity as a creative force. As Anna explains in her chapter in *Taking Part*: "In most performance companies, especially dance, diversity is replaced by uniformity. Everybody learns to dance like the director or choreographer, everybody is supposed to be young, everyone pretends he is heterosexual, blacks in white companies have to move like whites or form their own all-black companies. But people are not the same. Cohesion is not the same as uniformity, and the melting pot is not our ideal" (154–55).

Yet while Anna Halprin welcomed the pluralism that defined the evolving avant-garde into the 1970s, Larry remained somewhat insistent on the possibility of unearthing a single collective—bound by "archetypal needs." Beginning in the late 1960s, Anna began working with specific marginalized groups, eventually including those infected with HIV and AIDS and the elderly. With race riots erupting in cities across the nation (including San Francisco; see, for instance, the Bayview–Hunters Point race riot of 1966), causing mass flight of the predominantly white middle class to the suburbs, racial tensions largely instigated the "acute urban crisis." Anna became increasingly focused on addressing and exploring such tensions through dance. In 1968, she collaborated with theater artist James Woods and the Studio Watts School of the Arts, situated in the Watts neighborhood of Los Angeles made infamous by the well-publicized Watts riots, to produce a workshop and performance called *Ceremony of Us.* For five months, Anna spent Saturdays in Los Angeles with an all-black dance group created upon her request by Woods. Her counterpart all-white group in San Francisco worked separately with Anna until the two groups came together for the ten-day event in Los Angeles. The charged "physical conversation" they performed addressed the complexity of racial dynamics on a personal and political level—exploring stereotypes, sexual territories, and how cultural values inform movement.[8]

Meanwhile, Larry Halprin remained unresolved on the tense relationship between pluralism and collectivism embedded in his work. He rarely mentions racial dynamics during these charged decades. He and the firm clearly attempt to integrate a "microcosmic" amount of African Americans (then called "Negroes") into the workshops, indicated by the office notes and photographs of participants published in the 1972 report and 1974 book. However, despite applying the process in Cleveland, Ohio, a city fraught with racial violence and inequity, one of Halprin's only references to such discrimination and unrest is printed in his introduction to the report generated for the New York City urban renewal evaluation:

> We sense that Negroes like any other group have come to the conclusion that their salvation lies within their own hands. Black power is, we suspect, a response (as Martin Luther King has said) to the failure of white power. We gather that the black community does not want the white community to impose its own middle class standards . . . What is needed here, as it is elsewhere, is self-determination and complete participation in all phases of planning and programming. The black community must, we believe, structure its own renewal. But open occupancy, opportunities for economic advancement, job opportunities, and increased ability for property ownership must underlie the whole forward thrust.[9]

Though just prior to these remarks Halprin calls racial tension and inequality the "hair shirt of all our cities," he seems disinterested in addressing the complexities of the issue.

Rather than acknowledge the American reality of multiple publics and endless pluralities of experience, Halprin relied on his idealist belief in common humanity and the ability to unearth this common bond through the experience-based process.

Similarly, instead of compromise Halprin hoped the process of shared experience, common language, and communication would generate a collective understanding that would enable a consensus plan agreeable to all. Rather than accomplishing consensus through "discursive democracy"—a process of rational argumentation for which Jürgen Habermas argues in his *Theory of Communicative Action* (1981)—Halprin choreographed the Take Part Workshops so that participants reached consensus through shared action and modes of expression outside conventional deliberation (such as drawing and performance) to free participants from: "(1) communicating in the same ways they always have and leaving the old feelings and messages still covered; (2) intellectualizing and pragmatizing the process they are experiencing together and therefore covering up material that should be shared; (3) being unable to communicate because of differences of age, education, or life styles."[10]

Again, while 1960s antiestablishment culture impacted its development, Halprin sought government support to institutionalize the Take Part Process. In contrast, community organizers such as Saul Alinsky, author of the book *Rules for Radicals* (1971), attempted to provide the powerless with the organizational capacity to mobilize, confront, and negotiate in the process of decision making. In *After the Planners* (1972), Robert Goodman called for "direct action rather than adapting to existing bureaucratic techniques," through "community socialism" and "guerilla architecture," celebrating, for instance, the neighborhood claims to People's Park in Berkeley, California. Instead, Halprin worked within the official structure of urban renewal and public city planning agencies to formalize a process to mediate between economic forces and public interest in the historic and social value of their environments. He did not fight the "disclimax" conditions he often criticized in his writings but rather responded to their inevitability and benefitted from the creative challenges they posed.

Unlike Halprin, most landscape architects continued to work in the burgeoning suburbs. Two other exceptions included Paul Friedberg and especially Karl Linn, who worked through the 1960s with (typically poor black) communities to develop neighborhood open space. Though Halprin acknowledges their achievements, he considered them too localized and, therefore, of limited impact.[11] Slightly later, in the mid-1970s, the activist landscape architect Randy Hester began writing more comprehensively about the organization of neighborhoods for the development of their own open space. Hester's methodology, outlined in *Planning Neighborhood Space with People* (originally published in 1975), included some of the activities proposed in Halprin's workshop scores, such as role-playing. The planner Henry Sanoff, too, in his 1978 book *Designing with Community Participation*, integrates environmental awareness activities to achieve "consensus." Ten years prior, civil rights leader and director of the National Urban League Whitney M. Young Jr. addressed the American Institute of Architects (AIA) national convention where he accused the profession of a "thunderous silence" in response to the injustices of the time. This catalytic speech stimulated the development of the nonprofit Community Design Centers (CDC) around the country. However, the pragmatic and equity-focused methods of the CDCs and individuals such as Hester and Sanoff differed significantly from the carefully choreographed experiential-situational scoring of Halprin's participatory process.[12]

By the mid-1960s, comprehensive physical planning had become increasingly suspect in the urban planning profession.[13] Paul Davidoff's manifesto "Advocacy and Pluralism in Planning" proposed confrontational tactics by planners as advocates for the underrepresented that had widespread impact on participatory approaches. Arnstein's "A Ladder of Citizen Participation" (1969) constructed a framework to evaluate participation programs and "the extent of citizens' power" in effecting decisions. The terms comprising the ladder are: 1. Manipulation, 2. Therapy, 3. Informing, 4. Consultation, 5. Placation, 6. Partnership, 7. Delegated Power, 8. Citizen Control. She defines "Manipulation" as a form of "chicanery" or means of dishonestly "engineering" support (218).

While it is useful to reference Arnstein's evaluative framework, Halprin's process is distinct from other community-based as well as government participation programs because social justice was not his primary motivation. Arnstein sets up her argument based on the power struggle between the haves and "have-nots," just as Davidoff's process challenged power distribution. Advocating for communities was typically practiced by consultants who translated action into dramatic confrontation against "the establishment"—the city, the state, and federal institutions. In a 1970 critique of advocacy planning, Langley Keyes and Edward Teitcher contrast the advocate planner from the generalist planner, who "is concerned with the whole man and with comprehensive interrelationships."[14] The generalist or environmental planner better describes Halprin, though he was most focused on the physical, which advocacy planning typically ignored—choosing to prioritize social and economic issues. In fact, Halprin eventually strongly opposed the confrontational policies of advocacy planning. In *The RSVP Cycles*, he expresses interest in the progress of the advocacy planners, claiming it integrates a "more pluralistic involvement of members of communities." Yet five years later, in *Taking Part*, he equates advocacy planning with "hostile last-ditch arbitration" and critically calls it a "win-lose situation which assumes incompatible goals and is based on power struggles in which one group overcomes the other's point of view" (44).

NEW YORK, NEW YORK

In 1967, Halprin was commissioned to evaluate the environmental quality of six sample renewal projects executed in New York City. The work was funded by the federal Department of Housing and Urban Development and a grant from the New York Foundation. Though Halprin did not develop the full Take Part framework until the early 1970s, he considered the resulting report *New York, New York: A Study of the Quality, Character, and Meaning of Open Space in Urban Design* (March 1968) to be "the first major proposal stressing the importance of citizens participating in what happens to, and in, their own environment."[15]

Mayor John Lindsay initially claimed that the project would be merely focused on planting, lighting, and street furniture, which would "create a more . . . beautiful environment."[16] In the introduction to the report, Halprin himself, who grew up in Brooklyn, states that he thought the firm would "focus on the enriched potential inherent in beautiful pavings, on handsome street furniture, on benches, on lighting fixtures, trash containers, playground equipment, graphics and fountains. We had presumed a study on urban open space aesthetics—a manual of design. We wished to make New York City beautiful. I had written such a book on cities some years ago [*Cities*, 1963] and intended to apply its lessons to New York City in a particular way" (1). Yet, as Halprin soon discovered, aesthetics could not be considered in a vacuum, especially when addressing such a complex place as New York City, and had to be studied as part of an integrated environmental process. As a result, Lawrence Halprin & Associates produced a document within six months that not only critiqued the human psychological and sociological implications of the top-down or impositional shaping of urban space, but presented achievable recommendations for the future of community development. The report was intended to be comprehensible and accessible to city agencies, designers, and the general public. In response, the *New York Times* critic Ada Louise Huxtable claimed that in the document Halprin "offers so much wisdom about cities, so many insights into the urban world and so fine a sense of the special needs of New York that the report should be read by everyone and taped to the forehead of city officials."[17]

Since 1949, when the mayor initiated slum clearance programs, the city had been erecting the ubiquitous tower-in-the-park model to supposedly rehouse the low-income residents who had been uprooted by the demolitions. Robert Moses was chairman of the Mayor's Committee on Slum Clearance from 1949 to 1960, but he was forced to resign when the city began rejecting ideas that his projects embodied, including top-down planning, wholesale clearance, and superblock urbanism. The evolving attitude toward neighborhood preservation was presented most articulately by Jane Jacobs in *The Death and Life of Great American Cities* (1961). Her theories on localized planning and preserving the fine-grained fabric of neighborhood scale were embraced nationally by city agencies but particularly those in New York about which she wrote most extensively. Halprin invited Jacobs to participate as a consultant to his study, and her theories and influence are evident throughout the report:

> The street has been altered. The dense pattern of New York has been opened up. Light and air and open space have been brought into the city. But the change has been a mixed blessing! Though the slums are in process of disappearing, the quality of life in the new projects seems to have become unsatisfactory for their residents. Though overcrowding has been reduced, the quality of the neighborhood is disappearing . . . Though mixed incompatible uses have been stopped, a new uniformity has replaced the old variety. Though open space surrounds the buildings, the open space is sterile, uninviting, windy & lacking in interest. Though children do not have to play in the streets, their playgrounds are made of asphalt and surrounded by cyclone fences. Though light & air penetrate to all rooms, mothers can no longer throw an apple out of the window to a hungry child. Though green lawns surround the houses, the streets are uninteresting, if not unsafe, to walk upon. Though projects are more widely available to different income groups, these groups tend to remain alienated from each other. Though buildings are new and more spacious, the small Mamma–Papa store run by the new immigrant (at low rentals) in his way up has been lost. Though the pushcarts with their attendant confusion and filth on the streets have been removed, their color and vitality and the face to face interaction they made possible is now sadly lacking. The city which is emerging is semi-suburbanized, having neither the good qualities of the suburbs nor the excitement, the color, the variety, and the intense interaction of the former city. We have been asked to review six major new projects which exemplify these changes in various parts of the city. They are in various stages—some are recently completed, some under construction, some are now on the drawing boards. All are changing the face of the city and will make major contributions to living patterns. Each, however, raises serious questions as to whether we are proceeding along the right lines! (6)

In his analysis of each of the six projects, Halprin critiques the diminished balance within the figure–ground relationship. The monumental towers of housing were situated in vacuous expanses of turf. Halprin's diagrams demonstrate how one would reknit these "figures" into the larger urban network through a consideration of the neglected "ground," within which he considered a socialized public life should play out (Figure 4.2).

The project methodology was truly "synergistic," incorporating sociological, psychological, ecological, biological, aesthetic, and legal perspectives. Halprin seemed to deliberately minimize the economic angle, since economics had controlled the redevelopment process until then. The list of consultants reflects his multidisciplinary approach:

Robert Alpern, lawyer and planner, zoning expert

Dr. Paul Baum, director, San Francisco Institute of Gestalt Psychology

Lester Eisner, former regional administrator, Region I, U.S. Department of Housing and Urban Development

Dr. E. T. Hall [behavioral scientist and] author, *The Hidden Dimension* (1966) and *The Silent Language* (1959)

Jane Jacobs, author, *The Death and Life of Great American Cities* (1961)

Dr. A. E. Parr, senior scientist and former director of the American Museum of Natural History, New York, New York

Dr. George Rand, assistant professor, Department of Psychology and Education, Columbia University Teachers College, New York, New York[18]

With these consultants, Lawrence Halprin & Associates created a report that was not complicated by technical jargon but was made deliberately accessible to the general reading public to inspire citizen awareness and action.

In the report, Halprin declares that citizens should have the opportunity to become involved from the very beginning of a "renewal" project: "If the people who are going to live in an area are involved at its inception . . . if they can express in a deep sense their

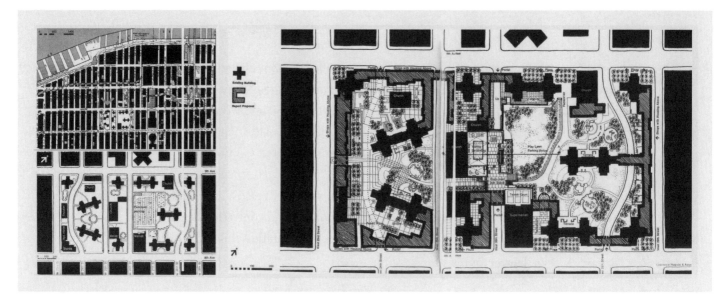

Figure 4.2. The redevelopment of Penn Station South. The figure-ground plans to the left show the new monumental housing towers as they contrast the surrounding dense urban fabric. To the right is Halprin's proposal for reknitting these "figures" into the neglected "ground" around them. Published in Lawrence Halprin & Associates, *New York, New York* (1968), 17–18. Lawrence Halprin Collection, The Architectural Archives, University of Pennsylvania.

real needs and desires; if they can feel that the project is designed for them as people not as abstractions, then the sense of community will have started before the project is even built" (59). Because, he proposes, planning is a never-completed process, open space recommendations must remain flexible enough to allow for perpetual change in response to evolving community needs ("Open spaces must admit for flexibility because use patterns may change, but they also should allow for the flexibility inherent in people's own desire to modify their environment" [48]).

Halprin and the Gestalt psychologist Paul Baum (who contributed to the *Taking Part* publication) were responsible for the questionnaires and "Encounter Groups," which provided specific insight into the successes and failures of the projects on a human scale. Baum proposes means by which such "encounter groups" could be incorporated into the overall planning process. He claims they should be composed as a microcosm of the target area and include "all those groups of people who are likely to be affected by any change in the area and who are in a position to cause some change":

> Examples of these people are: commuter; taxi-driver; . . . cop; pimp; prostitute; hustler; pusher; someone in drag; someone who owns and runs a store in the area, a big store, like Macy's, a small one, like an ethnic restaurant; executive; checking agent from the Greyhound bus terminal; member of an ethnic group; longshoreman; priest; Catholic layman; old person; young person; middle-aged person; a person from the nearest upper class area who is probably worried about his teenage kids using the area; school drop-out, including a drop-out who dropped out to work and one who dropped out to not work; someone from a local militant group; etc. (111).

The idea for such a microcosmic group served as the precedent for participant selection in Taking Part.

In addition, by engaging psychologists and other social scientists, Halprin studied community members' cultural and individual response to the new landscapes and, from the findings, articulated alternatives ("We began a search into the relationships of cultural and ethnic systems to environment and the impact of background on attitudes; then we began to probe into the psychological impact of open spaces on individual human behavior" [2]). In the section "Ethnic Variation," Halprin and his colleagues claim that unique ethnic community structure should be recognized and preserved by renewal planning agencies. Halprin's friend and consultant to the project, the anthropologist Dr. Edward T. Hall, analyzed the cultural patterns of the community space of individual ethnic groups and called for the retention of these patterns in renewal schemes, citing Herbert Gans's *Urban Villagers* (1962) and Nathan Glazer and Daniel P. Moynihan's *Beyond the Melting Pot* (1963).[19] To justify this potentially controversial proposal, the report states: "Though this idea of ethnic individuality may be in conflict with the 'American' concept of integration of cultural and economic groups, we recommend it, if only for its allowance of *choice*—that most important of freedoms. The validity of the melting pot where every group gave up its characteristics in favor of a single uniformity is becoming more questionable" (53). Though Lawrence Halprin devoted his life to unearthing a common sense of "collectivity," he and his team supposedly did not want to impose white, middle-class values on the ethnic tapestry of New York City. This, they feared, would cause a "suburbanization" of the complex urbanity of the city (6, 108). In fact, the biological idea of "Complexification" is featured as one of the report's most significant recommendations. Halprin applies biological theories to the social landscape by explaining how all biotic communities evolve from a state of simplicity to a stable state of complexity (in this case conveniently adopting the "equilibrium paradigm" outlined in the introduction). Just as Jacobs insists on the preservation of urban diversity and mixed uses, about this urban ecosystem Halprin states: "Complexification and diversity are a biological imperative. Isolation and similarity breed stupidity. Interaction and variety encourage creativity" (108–9). In other words, Halprin insisted on preserving and restoring the possibilities of chance and choice in the rapidly homogenizing urban environment.

Halprin's study of New York is a pivotal precursor to the development of Taking Part. Without this commission, Halprin would not have had the same depth of exposure to the far-reaching effects of urban renewal. Though he soon challenged the validity of the questionnaire and survey-based approach, the project inspired him to search for more action-oriented methods. "Scores" and choreography became the ultimate means by which he catalyzed such participatory action.

"EXPERIMENTS IN ENVIRONMENT"

In 1966, just prior to the *New York, New York* commission, Anna and Larry Halprin organized the first of a series of "Experiments in Environment" in an effort to combine the culture of participation with their interest in collectivity. These multiday collaborative workshops involving designers, dancers, musicians, visual artists, writers, teachers, and psychologists were intended to investigate "theories and approaches leading to integrated, cross-professional creativity" and heightened environmental awareness.[20]

Halprin applied lessons learned in these "experiments" to his work in the public arena. Their "scored" structure inspired the framework for Taking Part.

Anna and Larry conducted the 1968 "Experiments in Environment" with Paul Baum, who practiced group therapy and had served as a consultant for the *New York, New York* report, completed only a few months earlier. The workshop was a twenty-four-day event located in downtown San Francisco, in woodland Kentfield in Marin County, and the dramatic coastal Sea Ranch. The three environments were evaluated through "intuitive modes of perception," including kinesthetics and other body-environment awareness techniques. The theme of the workshop was "community." In the announcement letter, the Halprins explained: "We will start with a continued exploration of the individual's awareness and extend this awareness to his interaction with the environment. From this we will develop the idea of group interaction with the environment, which will lead to the development of an understanding of larger communities."[21]

Day one became the prototype for all of the initial awareness activities in subsequent Take Part workshops. "City Map" (Figure 4.3) served as a score to stimulate direct interaction with the physical environment of downtown San Francisco. Guidelines included: "Be as aware of the environment as you can . . . This will include all sounds, smells, textures, tactility, spaces, confining elements, heights, relations of up and down elements. Also your own sense of movement around you, your encounters with people and the environment AND YOUR FEELINGS!" Visual material was distributed, including an actual map with a processional sequence, indicating mode of transportation (walk, cable car ride) and stops along the way (Figure 4.4). The predetermined "tracks" throughout the city ensured that each person's time in each place varied from the next person's. The group was therefore in constant flux, except at 3 p.m. when in Union Square all forty participants were instructed to rise to the sound of chimes and face the sun. To choreograph this complexity, accompanying the map the Halprins distributed a diagram, called the "Master Score," that indicated the sequence in which each participant was to visit the places along the route, the time to get there, and how long to stay.

1

INSTRUCTIONS

This sheet indicates the various places you will visit and the path you must travel.

Sheet No. 2 tells you the sequence in which you will visit these places, the time to get there, and how long you are to be at each place. The activities indicated are those you are to perform at each place.

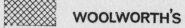 **CABLE CAR BARN**

 WOOLWORTH'S

 UNION SQUARE

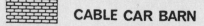 **AQUATIC PARK**

CABLE CAR

WALK

Figure 4.3.
"City Map" score for the first day of the "Experiments in Environment" workshop in 1968. Published in Lawrence Halprin, *The RSVP Cycles*, 78. Lawrence Halprin Collection, The Architectural Archives, University of Pennsylvania.

What "remained unscored and open," according to Larry Halprin, were "the involvements with other people, the adventures, sensitivities, games played, and impressions gained."[22]

Day two of "Experiments in Environment" was situated in Marin and included what was called "Trails Myth." The participants were asked to join hands and perform the movement score blindfolded in order to gain a "direct experience of the kinesthetic sense

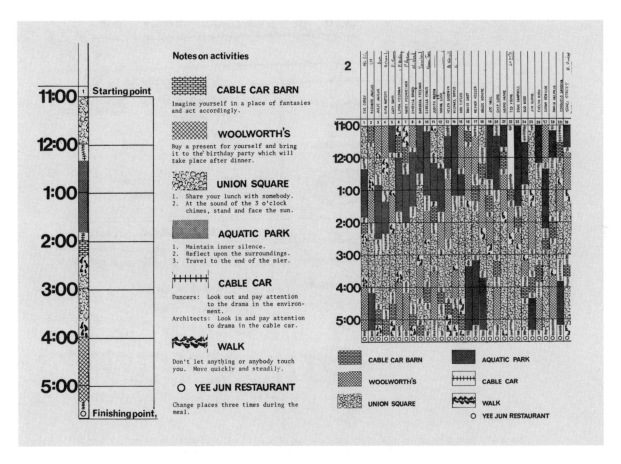

Figure 4.4. "Master Score" for "City Map" conducted on the first day of the "Experiments in Environment" workshop in 1968. Published in Lawrence Halprin, *The RSVP Cycles*, 81. Lawrence Halprin Collection, The Architectural Archives, University of Pennsylvania.

in space." About "Trails Myth" Larry Halprin explained: "When people lose the sense that we all depend on for most of our environmental information—sight—they get lost in space, confused, panicky; the experience of [Trails Myth] . . . brings this disorientation into focus and makes what is a very difficult adjustment for most people into a powerful experience." After "Trails Myth," a "Blindfold Walk" extended the group-movement

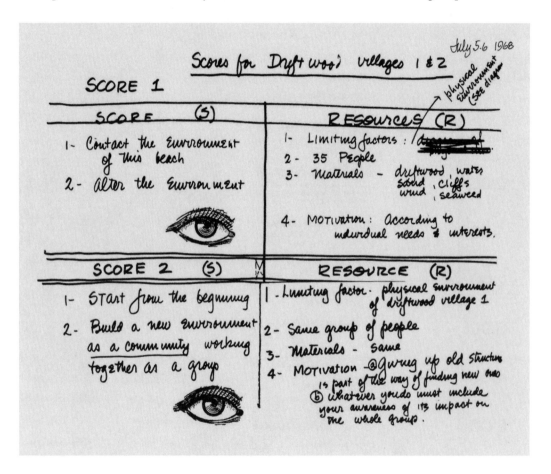

Figure 4.5. "Scores for Driftwood Villages 1 & 2" for days five and six of the "Experiments in Environment" workshop in 1968. Published in Lawrence Halprin, *The RSVP Cycles*, 157. Lawrence Halprin Collection, The Architectural Archives, University of Pennsylvania.

possibilities into the outdoors. Participants were instructed to walk through the woods blindfolded holding onto the shoulder of the person directly in front. The intention was, again, to heighten the other senses. After the blindfolds were removed, participants were asked to draw the experience of their Blindfold Walk and, according to Larry Halprin, "without seeing it in their customary mode of perception, the participants recreated where the open vistas occurred, where the terrain changed, where spaces were narrow or lofty or threatening."[23] Such "sensitivity walks" were adapted for "Taking Part" to instill a stronger awareness of the environment and enhanced perception of movement through it. Although Halprin did not typically use blindfolds, he had Take Part participants isolate their senses while performing the initial awareness scores.

On days five and six at the Sea Ranch, scores were presented for Driftwood Villages 1 and 2 that ambiguously commanded the participants to "make direct use of the resources of the environment to produce expressions of collective creativity" (Figure 4.5).[24] In Driftwood Village 1, participants were asked to use the ocean beach littered with driftwood as the "palette" upon which to create their own structures according to individual needs and desires. The space and materials were chosen because they contained "no 'value system' inherent in them, so were ideal for people to use in a free way to create fantasy . . . environments."[25] Driftwood Village 2 (Figures 4.6 and 4.7) involved the destruction of the previous day's village and the rebuilding of a new environment collaboratively to investigate how building or transforming a place collectively might aid community development.

On the culminating days, the participants were asked to generate a "Community Statement," similar to what became known as the Consensus Report in the Take Part Workshops. According to the workshop analysis, the group was not entirely able to perform this score, mostly owing to a reassertion of some the original group dynamics ("false starts, emotional outbursts").[26] This served as a learning experience for the members of the firm, who committed themselves to "the idea of process and participation, not [getting] hung up on anxiety about the group's producing products. The duty of leaders and facilitators is to help people participate, to encourage them to experience the process

Figure 4.6. "Driftwood Village 2." Published in Lawrence Halprin, *The RSVP Cycles*, 16. Photograph by Joe Ehreth. Copyright 1969 by Lawrence Halprin. Reprinted with permission by George Braziller, Inc. All rights reserved.

Figure 4.7. Dancers in "Driftwood Village," 1960s. Lawrence Halprin Collection, The Architectural Archives, University of Pennsylvania (slide I-G540, unstamped).

together, not to cheerlead them into making some specific statement or evolving some particular result."[27] Such a declaration is interesting to consider while examining the Take Part Process applied in practice in the following chapter.

In a letter in which Halprin reflected on the 1968 workshop, he claimed:

> I have become increasingly convinced of the validity and significance of the pluralistic approach to art processes and the significance of allowing art to emerge from a multiplicity of inputs with scores as guides and catalysts. In this development the artist grows into a community guide, NOT a form maker . . . and takes his rightful place in the future society as a catalyzer and developer of peak experience rather than only as a producer of products.[28]

As the Take Part Process is considered in application, however, it will become clear that Halprin is incapable of taking on the role of merely "guide," ever remaining a true form-maker. In a telling interview with Randy Hester, Halprin reveals: "You know, the odd thing is that on a personality basis, I'm not really suited to do this, to doing participation . . . Like any designer, I want to take a pencil and design the thing. I don't like to be seen as a do-gooder, soft-hearted, sweet man because I'm not any of that. But I learned the hard way."[29]

5. FACILITATION AND/OR MANIPULATION

THE CHALLENGES OF TAKING PART IN FORT WORTH, EVERETT, CHARLOTTESVILLE, AND CLEVELAND

THE COMMUNITY WORKSHOPS in Fort Worth, Texas; Everett, Washington; Charlottesville, Virginia; and Cleveland, Ohio, conducted by Lawrence Halprin & Associates represent the most complex application of the participatory process. The workshops in each of these cities presented different challenges and achieved varying levels of success. The firm conducted other Take Part Processes during the early 1970s in Wilmington, Delaware (regarding the redesign of the city's major retail corridor, Market Street); Morningside Heights, Harlem (for resolution of a long-standing conflict between Columbia University and neighborhood residents over Morningside Park);[1] and Tulsa, Oklahoma (particularly focused on the development of an open space network). Additionally, the firm conducted "Leadership Training Workshops," funded by a federal Housing and Urban Development (HUD) demonstration grant, in San Francisco (predominantly for the Halprin staff) and in Indianapolis (for representatives of poverty programs, Model Cities, and the city and state planning divisions) to instruct individuals how to create, "score," and conduct their own workshops.[2]

TAKING PART IN FORT WORTH, TEXAS

The years 1969 and 1970 posed a major turning point for Halprin and his firm. As described in chapter 1, with a staff of nearly sixty employees Halprin began to feel more and more alienated from everyday decisions at the same time many of his employees began to resent his lack of involvement but retention of final authority.[3] It was at this time (March and April 1970) that the firm underwent the "radical reorganization" that resulted in the exodus of nearly twenty-five employees and a revamped management system aimed at open dialogue. In early June 1970, Halprin hired Robert (Bob) Mendelsohn to head the community participation division of the restructured firm. He had previously served as a San Francisco supervisor, simultaneously teaching political science and community organizing at both San Francisco State College and the University of California, Berkeley, and before that he was a community information chief for the San Francisco Redevelopment Agency, the context in which Halprin most likely met him. The fact that Mendelsohn was a political scientist, not a designer, is indicative of the new directions the firm was taking at this time. Lawrence Halprin & Associates's first workshop in Fort Worth (June 26–27, 1970) became "Mendelsohn's debut as an urban interlocuter," according to Halprin.[4]

Perhaps because of Mendelsohn's background in politics, as one who "hews to traditional views of management,"[5] or perhaps simply because Halprin began the project working with business and government officials rather than everyday citizens, the process in Fort Worth was not as inclusive as the authors of *Taking Part* recommended in 1974 or as "microcosmic" as Paul Baum suggested in his section on "Encounter Groups" in the *New York, New York* report. Yet this may be the reason why consensus seems to have been achieved seamlessly in the Fort Worth case and why Halprin could declare it a "resounding success." The workshop was comprised of twenty-five "community leaders," including "directors of the major banks and insurance corporations, the major city planning officials, the chamber of commerce, managers of the largest retail stores and others."[6] In other words, the participants were members of the city's power structure whose extensive private efforts at "civic betterment" and "beautification" had long proven influential.[7]

Despite the relatively homogenous composition of the group and the city's general conservatism, Halprin's firm used lessons learned from the "Experiments in Environment" to develop a "common language of awareness between the various city leaders (business, financial, and political) and the design team," as stated in the final central business district (CBD) report presented in chapter 2.[8] The process unfolded in the transparent manner the firm intended and generated positive enthusiasm among participants. However, the Fort Worth City Sector Planning Council was resistant to opening up the decision-making process to the general public, as indicated by a memo to Mendelsohn from a Halprin staff member in which he complains about chairman of the Sector Council Burl Hulsey's refusal to distribute a "handout" at a public presentation in the summer of 1971:

> The idea behind the "handout" was to facilitate citizen participation through intelligent written responses and criticisms; and would be an inexpensive key step towards citizen approval of the plan.
>
> Burl felt that he and the Sector Council . . . did not want to proceed with a "handout" for two reasons . . . They would prefer that the invited participants see only the slides and not have a printed document as a record of what they saw . . .
>
> With this attitude expressed by the Sector Council, I feel there is little or no need for a public presentation, and we would be only participating in a token and sham attempt of encouraging citizen participation. I feel we should not attend such a presentation under these conditions as our presence would only endorse their manner.[9]

Regardless of the conservatism of the Sector Council, the workshop did successfully incorporate activities that got the participants to leave the safety and comfort of their habitual routines (Figure 5.1). Beginning with the "City Walk," the workshop members were initiated into a series of firsthand experiences scored to expose participants to different aspects of their downtown as though "for the first time."[10] The day chosen for the "City Walk" was extremely hot and humid and, as explained in chapter 4, the score required participants to move around the city using anything except automobiles. Each of the twenty-five participants moved along a preconceived sequence, but their timing was staggered so that no member encountered another along the way. Similar to the 1968 "City Map," the score was presented in notational form, including a map with the designated journey, the movement systems to be used (walking and riding the subway), the time to be spent in each place, and the assigned tasks at each location (Figure 5.2). Halprin, Mendelsohn, and others from the firm decided on eight locations they most likely considered problem areas (or areas with potential) and integrated them as nodes along the processional journey through the central business district. Choreographed activities included riding the subway and observing the other passengers, accessing the river on foot, and interacting with people on the street while recording sensory and emotive response.

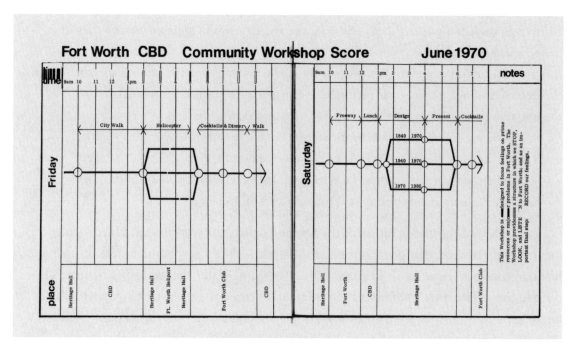

Figure 5.1. Master Score for the Fort Worth Central Business District Community Workshop. Printed in Lawrence Halprin & Associates, *The Fort Worth Central Business District Sector Report* (October 1971): 99–100. Lawrence Halprin Collection, The Architectural Archives, University of Pennsylvania (014.box.362).

Halprin knew that these city representatives would not agree to what he considered necessary interventions if he did not immerse them in these first-hand situations. For example, in addition to considering the inadequacies of the public transit system, the firm recognized the potential for an enhanced retail environment along Main Street. They thus organized the Main Street Walk (number 8 in Figure 5.2) during which the firm asked for observations of storefront activity and the movement patterns of vehicles and pedestrians.

The Friday scores following included a helicopter ride to demonstrate to the participants the interconnection and interdependence of the CBD to the river and the rest of Fort Worth and its outlying region. The second and final day of the workshop included a drive on the freeways and byways servicing the city and a gaming exercise for the Design Session. For this latter activity the firm presented a warm-up fantasy exercise for which they asked participants to design an "ideal city for any place you wish in the world." This was immediately followed by an assignment to design Fort Worth as if it were the years 1870, 1940, and 1970. What made this exercise intriguing is the firm requested that the 1870 and 1940 group "design

Figure 5.2. Fort Worth City Walk Map and "Specific Tasks at Each Location," 1970. Published in Halprin and Burns, *Taking Part*, 78–79. Lawrence Halprin Collection, The Architectural Archives, University of Pennsylvania.

Fort Worth City Walk Map

Sample Track · SPECIFIC TASKS AT EACH LOCATION

10 am

LOCATION 1 COUNTY COURT HOUSE
From the north steps observe the visual environment and the activities and movement of people and cars.
Compare with the view from the south steps.
Record your feelings: Did you like the views? Which did you prefer? Why? What would you change? What would you retain?

LOCATION 2 LEONARDS SUBWAY AND RIVER
Ride subway to parking lot, walk to river and return.
Observe the people and their interactions.
Record your feelings: How did you like riding the subway? Did you like the people on the subway? How do you think the other people on the subway felt about you?
Record your experiences getting to the river.

11

LOCATION 3 COURTYARD FIRST METHODIST CHURCH
Close eyes, listen to the sounds of the city.
Record your feelings while in this place. Did you feel good, sad, lonely, at peace?
Record any interactions with other people while in this place.

LOCATION 4 MOTOR BANK 1ST NATIONAL BANK
Walk through Motor Bank, observe traffic flow and pattern.
Record your experiences as a pedestrian.
Listen for one minute with eyes closed—record your reaction to the sounds.

12 lunch

LOCATION 5 PLAZA 1ST NATIONAL BANK
Remain inconspicuously for five minutes—observe your own activities and activity of others.
Make a list of ten different activities that can be done in this place.
Record your feelings in this place.

LOCATION 6 BURNETT PARK
Change location three times.
Isolate a different sense each time.
Describe your favorite place in the park—record how you feel when you are in that place.
Record any interactions with other people while in this place.

pm 1

LOCATION 7 PLAZA, FEDERAL BUILDING
Walk through lobby.
Stand at each entrance and record your impression of the mood people are in when they enter the building.
Record any differences you felt between the entrances.

LOCATION 8 MAIN STREET WALK
Record your general impressions of the walk, looking north and south.
Observe the storefront activity in a two block strip.
At an intersection observe movements of vehicles and pedestrians.
Record the feelings you experienced during the walk.

2

Fort Worth knowing what you now know but with the givens of the 1840 [or 1940] situation." In 1870, of course, very little of Fort Worth had been developed, so there were few impediments to this group's collective response. For the 1940 group, the participants apparently spent most of their time planning to prevent suburban dispersal. The 1970 group was asked to "design Fort Worth as you would like it to be in 1980." This group spent the most time struggling with the current situation to plan for a better future. The activity was thus intended as an exercise in foresight and the power of thinking in the long term, rather than only about the immediate returns of the here and now.

Though the exercise required participants have some prior knowledge of the city's development history, it was meant to build on the previous day's experiences—now that they were more aware of the city, they could more knowledgeably plan for its improvement. Though the initial fantasy exercise loosened the group's creativity for the Fort Worth–specific exercise that followed, the general ideas in the "Areas of Investigation Recommended by Workshop Participants," presented in the final report, were not particularly innovative. Rather, they offered standard solutions such as mixed uses in the downtown, pedestrianized streets, and enhanced public transit. This generic response might be attributed to what the firm claimed early on:

> In terms of development problems—Fort Worth is no more unique from any other city, than one man with a broken leg is different from another man with a broken leg—the location changes but the problems remain fundamentally the same. Fort Worth exhibits classic problems of cities in general and CBD's in particular.[11]

Therefore, the firm was able to guide the city officials to generate what they considered healthy options for urban development. This statement by the firm is inconsistent, however, since Halprin claimed to be interested in fostering a uniqueness of place based on regional specificity.

The Fort Worth example is included here because it offers an initial glimpse of the issues encountered in the subsequent and more complex applications of the public process to be presented in the following sections. Those issues are related to the actual degree of "openness" of the Take Part score. Fort Worth represented limited participation or "taking part" and a degree of seeming preconception of urban problems and their solutions. Yet despite the apparent control the firm seemed to retain during the workshop, the participants felt as though they were directing their own destiny and the outcome was a general consensus on what the city should explore for the future.

EVERETT, WASHINGTON

Also in 1969, using lessons learned in Fort Worth, Lawrence Halprin & Associates tackled the city of Everett, Washington, where the workshop process (not yet called Taking Part) was applied more comprehensively to address economic, social, and ecological issues in the entire city and its region.[12] As Halprin's scores were intended to catalyze participation rather than impose plans, this nearly three-year project was structured entirely on the theoretical basis of scores, through experience-based "situations" and more conventional means for public input. Yet like in Fort Worth, the scores were not open to indeterminate futures but were carefully choreographed to unfold according to the firm's environmental values. The terminology of scores diminishes in written documents later in the project, since, as the firm claims in their December 1970 Progress Report: "Professional jargon is often confusing to the layman . . . although useful as an 'in house' technique for problem solving."[13] The firm clearly applied this lesson to later projects as the language of choreography no longer appears in reports. However, the concepts behind scores, serving as guides and catalysts to stimulate participation, remain present throughout the Everett project's entirety. The following section will focus on the creative process rather than the final recommendations, though the *Everett Community Plan* (1972) is an extremely rich and innovative document that deserves further examination.[14]

The project in Everett served as another "pilot study," building on the firm's experience in Fort Worth, this time with the help of federal money. The federal Department of Housing and Urban Development (HUD) responded positively to the Lawrence Halprin & Associates's grant proposal, providing two-thirds of the funds for the project, which would demonstrate that a strong community participation program could result in a plan to develop a city set in a healthful relationship with its region.[15] The firm successfully sought full transparency, so that no portion of the process was undertaken behind closed doors, and thus the final product would have the "best possible chance of being implemented," according to Mendelsohn.[16]

In 1969, the city of Everett hired Lawrence Halprin & Associates after recognizing their success in the Pacific Northwest region. The firm was still in the midst of reorganization and downsizing so that Halprin could reestablish his more direct involvement in its multifaceted projects. The complexity of the firm members' contributions to this three-year project demonstrates that the period was particularly tumultuous as the office was restructuring. Halprin himself, invested in the project as a pilot study that he hoped might be officially adopted by HUD, maintained "close surveillance" after his early direct contributions.[17] Initially Felix Warburg was titled project director, and his July 21, 1969, "Reconnaissance Report and Planning Program" incorporated the résumés of those first on the Everett study team. The members included Halprin and himself with the urban planner Alexander Cuthbert, along with Thomas Thorp who had served as "geographer consultant to Lawrence Halprin & Associates performing field and library research and preparing reports on urban and rural environmental planning factors, 1966 to present."[18] Because Warburg was one of the individuals who left the firm in early 1970, the line-up shifted. Mendelsohn became project coordinator, Larason Guthrie took over as the project director and remained in this position through Phase I, after which he was replaced by Tom Koenig who carried the project through to its completion.[19]

Everett was a small city of sixty thousand residents, the northernmost urbanized region along Puget Sound, when the firm was commissioned to address its unregulated development, conflicting infrastructure, and deteriorated downtown. Mayor Robert Anderson and the Everett City Council invited the firm to create a comprehensive program of guidelines to balance the social, economic, and ecological values for future development. The entire process was structured on complete transparency and utmost participation.

The study was divided into two phases. Phase I was most focused on Resource (R) gathering or analyzing the existing conditions and identifying problems, challenges, and potential opportunities within Everett and developing objectives to move forward. This included the initial workshops, widely distributed progress reports to solicit community feedback, and the opening of the Community Planning Office. Phase I culminated in the Final Preliminary Report, which explained Phase II would focus on the development of "carefully conceived implementation methods" to achieve "the strengthening of Everett's central district as a community shopping, economic, social, and cultural center; the conservation or improvement of older residential neighborhoods to maintain investment incentives and desirability; and the creation of an open space–recreational network based on preservation of ecologically valuable lands."[20] Phase II thus considered the means to implement the objectives identified in Phase I. Lawrence Halprin & Associates' Phase II director, Tom Koenig, presented the firm's work as not a final product but a process through which to project the city into the future:

> [It is] not a guaranteed cure for a city's ills, but rather a guide which can enable a city to cure its own ills . . . This plan must be RESPONSIVE to the community and FLEXIBLE and useable for the years ahead. For this reason we have developed a POLICY PLAN, including a land use plan (rather than *just* a land use plan as is all too traditional). By a policy plan, we mean one explaining the processes by which decisions were made and reasons for and thinking behind the recommendations prescribed. Because planning is a long range endeavor, unforeseeable events and changes are inevitable and while a land use plan is very useful in describing solutions to current and foreseeable problems, a policy plan adds the ability to rationally deal with new turns of events.[21]

Thus the intention of the policy plan—as distinguished from the fixed solutions of land use plans—was to provide an open framework that could adapt to unforeseeable futures. This attitude is emergent from the idea of the open score. In August 1970, the psychologist Jim Creighton, who had become a permanent consultant to the office after his involvement during the 1969 restructuring, issued a memorandum titled the "Everett Community Participation Program." This document summarized the firm's broad-based participation program as both a general template for future projects as well as one specific to the issues in Everett. In regard to the former, the firm sought a program that was sensitized to two ubiquitous problems encountered in community participation programs:

1.   People become habituated to their environment and have difficulty identifying problems which they now consider "normal."

2.   People have limited motivation to participate in community planning, and those that do participate sometimes are highly motivated by specific interests that may not include the needs of the entire community.

To address these two problems the firm proposed their workshop process, which was "designed precisely to provide citizens with the opportunity to re-experience their city and articulate the problems they identify."[22] Again, the motivations were to immerse participants in the everyday realities of fellow citizens.

In his analysis, Creighton recommends that the initial Everett workshop involve the city's "power structure," similar to the firm's approach in Fort Worth. However, Creighton clarifies that those identified as "powerful" do not only include members of the official decision-making elite, such as elected officials, but also the "informal power structure including representatives of an identifiable minority." The firm thus chose fifty individuals to participate, each of whom agreed to "facilitate subsequent phases of the program" in a leadership role. The infiltration of original workshop participants to generate broader public enthusiasm and awareness of the project was unique to Everett, perhaps owing to HUD's involvement and financial support.

The early Resource (R) gathering documentation indicates that the city did not have a large racial, ethnic, or economic disparity, therefore a cross-section might be best represented by a diversity in professions or interests, ages, and the balanced inclusion of men and women.[23] The firm's priority was to create such a cross-section so that those involved in this initial workshop could permeate the community and stimulate involvement within the broadest base possible. The firm attempted in Everett to organize a system of "follow-up workshops" so that eventually the process could be completely handed over to the people of Everett. However, just after the first workshop, one of the participants, a female staff writer for the *Everett Herald*, expressed disappointment that the initial workshop did not integrate the creative input of a more diverse constituency:

> I feel very strongly the need to involve individuals who have thus far had no representa-tion . . . I was a little disappointed to see the *Herald* photos play up the participation of those who are known as community & *financial* leaders. What about Joe Kappler, Bob Haggard, Dennis Gregoire, or any of the many others in the workshop who fit more easily into the average citizen group? If we get a country club reputation we're dead before we start . . . Businesses are often willing to release their junior execs for a day, but how do we get someone off the assembly line at Scott [Paper Company]? How do we get mothers with young children when babysitters, if available, cost $8 a day? How do we get people to commit themselves for 2 full days? Can this experience successfully be broken into smaller chunks? . . . Both the Port District and the Economic Development Council are by their very nature interested FIRST in business interests and second, if at all, in community interests . . . It seems to me the people of this community must be DIRECTLY involved in the decisions regarding what direction we will take. At the current time this is not the case, probably because of apathy & ignorance. Those are difficult obstacles to overcome but perhaps the workshop has helped many of us to make this project number one on our list of priorities.[24]

Provisions to reach this wider constituency were made later by the establishment of a Community Planning Office, but the firm did very little active recruiting. This ensured that those who participated were already eagerly interested in the future of their com-munities rather than those who might not have had the awareness, time, or money to become involved.

Another indication of the lack of social conflict in Everett, which simplified the early process, was the situation of the workshop headquarters at the First Baptist Church. In the 1974 publication of *Taking Part*, the authors specify that such headquarters must be accessible and neutral. They particularly address the detrimental effects of locating the workshop in a church, since "it would turn off some members who are of a different belief or people who do not feel comfortable working in a religious environment" (300). Clearly these early workshops, including the one in Everett, were part of the learning experience leading to the conception of the formalized Take Part Process first published in the 1972 report *Take Part*.

The firm also suggested an "Everett Day" event that included a wide-scale awareness score to be televised on local access networks. Though this did not take place, probably owing to funding and organizational limitations, the idea was dependent on a "major public relations effort" that would invite and entice all citizens of Everett to participate in the "broad general score" for another City Walk, which would have been partially devised by the original workshop participants. The firm proposed a "feedback mechanism . . . provided via 1) De-briefing 'Town Meetings'; and 2) T.V. program summarizing town meetings with interchange between Larry Halprin, Senator Jackson, Mayor Anderson."[25] This event would have choreographed the people of Everett in a procession through their city in order to generate an even wider-reaching "common foundation" that would stimulate creative response amid a collective public. Such an idea, integrating an entire city in a single score, was not brought to life until Anna and Larry's collaboration in the organization of *Citydance* in 1976–1977 through the streets of San Francisco.

The first Everett Community Workshop, held on September 25–26, 1970, just three months after the one conducted in Fort Worth, was organized almost identically, with a city walk, drive, and helicopter flight (Figure 5.3). As was apparent in Fort Worth, the firm had already identified the city's flaws prior to the development of the workshop score and structured the first workshop to expose the participants to these predetermined issues. This is clear, for instance, when associate Simon Nicholson, part of the workshop team with Halprin, Mendelsohn, Guthrie, and the ecologist Michael Bowie, explicitly reported that "the walk-score concealed in it what we thought were basic social issues relating to 'downtown,' in the hope that most of the participants would sense and become aware of these issues."[26] The fact that he claims their intentions are "concealed" certainly implies a level of manipulation embedded in the process.

After a workshop introduction, the two-hour "Downtown Walk" (Figure 5.4) directed the participants through eight different locations in the central business district where they were directed to look, listen, feel, move through, and interact with their environment in specific ways. Activity guidelines instructed the participants themselves to act as behavioral scientists, observing "human activities" and uses and asking questions of people on the street. The workbook asked direct questions, such as "What of the things you see would you like to change?" and deliberately open-ended requests, such as "Close your eyes for one minute and listen to the sounds of the city." As suggested, the score for this activity was purposely structured to lead participants to preconceived conclusions. For instance, so that participants would recognize the inaccessibility of the waterfront, the firm required they ask two separate people for directions to it (which they would most likely not know). Or to demonstrate the lack of activity in a certain area, the participants had to ask someone on the street "What there is to see and do here?" (to which they would probably respond, "nothing").

According to the workshop notes by Simon Nicholson and the workbook passages cut and pasted into his summary notebook, the participants generally agreed on the run-down character and the lack of activity in the downtown, the potential rehabilitation of the old buildings, the magnificence of the views, the unacceptable degree of air pollution and visual pollution by billboards and overhead wiring,[27]

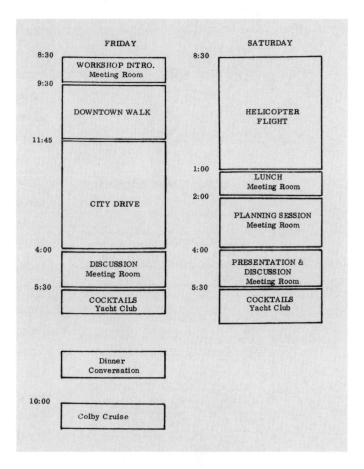

Figure 5.3. Master Score for the Everett Community Workshop, 1970. Lawrence Halprin Collection, The Architectural Archives, University of Pennsylvania (014.I.B.2552).

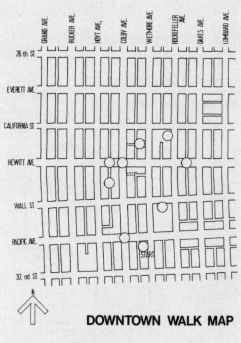

GRAND AVE. RUCKER AVE. HOYT AVE. COLBY AVE. WETMORE AVE. ROCKEFELLER AVE. OAKES AVE. LOMBARD AVE.

26 th ST

EVERETT AVE.

CALIFORNIA ST.

HEWITT AVE.

WALL ST.

PACIFIC AVE.

START

32 nd ST.

N

DOWNTOWN WALK MAP

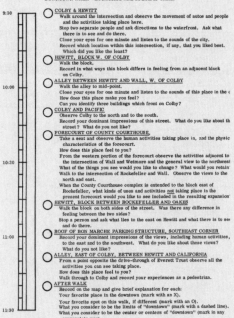

DOWNTOWN WALK - LOCATIONS AND SPECIFIC TASKS

9:30 ○ COLBY & HEWITT
Walk around the intersection and observe the movement of autos and people and the activities taking place here.
Stop two separate people and ask directions to the waterfront. Ask what there is to see and do there.
Close your eyes for one minute and listen to the sounds of the city.
Record which location within this intersection, if any, that you liked best. Which did you like the least?

○ HEWITT, BLOCK W. OF COLBY
Walk the block.
Record in what ways this block differs in feeling from an adjacent block on Colby.

○ ALLEY BETWEEN HEWITT AND WALL, W. OF COLBY
10:00 Walk the alley to mid-point.
Close your eyes for one minute and listen to the sounds of this place in the c
How does this place make you feel?
Can you identify three buildings which front on Colby?

○ COLBY AND PACIFIC
Observe Colby to the north and to the south.
Record your dominant impressions of this street. What do you like about th street? What do you not like?

○ FORECOURT OF COUNTY COURTHOUSE
Take a seat and observe the human activities taking place in, and the physic characteristics of the forecourt.
How does this place feel to you?
10:30 From the western portion of the forecourt observe the activities adjacent to the intersection of Wall and Wetmore and the general view to the northwest
What of the things you see would you like to change? What would you retain'
Walk to the intersection of Rockefeller and Wall. Observe the views to the north and east.
When the County Courthouse complex is extended to the block east of Rockefeller, what kinds of uses and activities not taking place in the present forecourt would you like to see included in the resulting expansion'

○ HEWITT, BLOCK BETWEEN ROCKEFELLER AND OAKES
Walk the block on both sides of the street. Was there any difference in feeling between the two sides?
Stop a person and ask what lies to the east on Hewitt and what there is to se and do there.

11:00 ○ ROOF OF BON MARCHE PARKING STRUCTURE, SOUTHEAST CORNER
Record your dominant impressions of the views, including human activities, to the east and to the southwest. What do you like about those views?
What do you not like?

○ ALLEY, EAST OF COLBY, BETWEEN HEWITT AND CALIFORNIA
From a point opposite the drive-through of Everett Trust observe all the activities you can see taking place.
How does this place feel to you?
Walk through to Colby and record your experiences as a pedestrian.

○ AFTER WALK
Record on the map and give brief explanation for each:
Your favorite place in the downtown (mark with an X).
Your favorite spot on this walk, if different (mark with an O).
11:30 What you consider to be the limits of "downtown" (mark with a dashed line).
What you consider to be the center or centers of "downtown" (mark in any appropriate way).

and the pedestrian unfriendliness of the streets.[28] Not surprisingly, the compilation of these observations satisfied the firm.

The four-hour City Drive, which included shorter city walks at separate locations along the way, enabled participants to explore a much larger area (Figure 5.5). The central business district's situation within and relationship to its urban and regional context was as important to Halprin as the experience of the CBD itself. Though the Downtown Walk was to be conducted alone, the drive was done with partners. During the first stop along the waterfront, participants were asked to split apart to eat lunch, to sketch observations, and to close their eyes and record the sounds and smells of the place in a manner similar to the "Experiments in Environment" blindfold walk. Again, waterfront accessibility was a problem the firm had already identified, indicated by the second stop where the participants had to record how they reached the river, and, if they saw anyone, to engage him in conversation to find out what he was doing there. According to Nicholson's summary, "there was . . . almost unanimously positive reaction to these natural assets with undertones of nostalgia for the past and sadness that pollution and lack of public access have progressed to their present state."[29] The focus for the City Drive was also the strip development along both Broadway and Evergreen Way, the latter of which

Figure 5.4. Downtown Walk Map and Score for the Everett Community Workshop, 1970. Lawrence Halprin Collection, The Architectural Archives, University of Pennsylvania (014.I.B.2552).

the firm clearly considered problematic and unaccommodating to pedestrians. Participants were asked to park along each strip, purchase something for 25 cents or less, then observe the comparisons between the two experiences, after which the score instructed them to exchange driving partners. From the strip, they were led into the South Everett residential neighborhoods where the firm evidently disapproved of what they considered uncontrolled sprawl.

The most unique activity of the first Everett workshop was the late-night "Colby Cruise." The firm recognized a certain social ritual, or what one participant called a "tribal ritual,"[30] that occurred nightly, but most elaborately on Friday and Saturday, when teenagers of Everett would "cruise," or drive the length of Colby Avenue to see and be seen. Cars would drive the same circuit throughout the evening. The ritual was long-standing; one newspaper article records the comments of "Yesteryear Cruisers."[31] Merchants strongly disliked this activity, deeming it a nuisance due to traffic jams, noise, and the simple presence of distrusted teenagers. Many adults in Everett considered "cruising Colby," or "Shooting the Gut," an opportunity for delinquency despite the apparent lack of misconduct.[32] However, the ritual quality of this dynamic activity performed by teenagers, who were marginalized members of the community, was clearly exciting to Halprin. From his record summaries of the "Valuaction" session on Saturday morning, he noted the participants' impassioned response to the cruise and its rhythms of movement. He also recognized, however, that the traffic was frustrating. Simon Nicholson, who created the workshop report, noted that only seven members of the workshop actually participated in the "Cruise Colby" score.

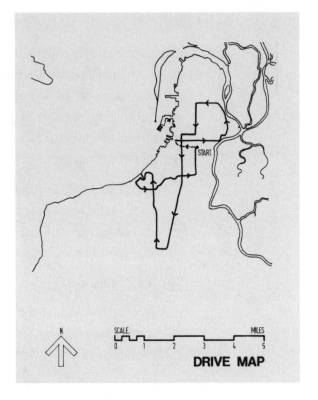

Figure 5.5. Drive Map for the Everett Community Workshop, 1970. Lawrence Halprin Collection, The Architectural Archives, University of Pennsylvania (014.I.B.2552).

Learning from this experience, the book *Taking Part* emphasized the need for full participation in *all* activities in order to build up a carefully orchestrated common language. Nicholson's report incorporated passages from participants' responses to the cruising ritual, including one negative and one positive. The author of the former did not indicate whether he or she actually participated in this score. Instead, the response was a general reaction to the activity:

> I get all MAD trying to drive thru it . . . I get MAD when I see the cans & bottles left on the St. I get MAD when I think that most of the kids don't work—or pay for their cars or gas. I get MAD when, on occasion, I am working late and the damned horns keep blowing & the tires are screeching.

The latter concludes:

> It's incredible! All I can think of is a stampede! It's a stampede of ENERGY! Imagine 1000 honking, radio-blaring cars with 4-TO-A-CAR-AVERAGE (!) on a street six blocks long. It's fantastic! THEY COMMUNICATE WITH THEIR CARS. IT'S A COMMUNAL THING.

Oddly enough, in April 1971 the firm helped structure a Demonstration or Experimental Mall along one block of Colby Avenue, in the middle of the cruise circuit, therefore obstructing and thus dissolving the long-standing ritual. The experiment was called "April Park," a collaborative event organized and funded by the city and merchants of Everett with citizen volunteers. Apparently the city had considered this option for years, and Lawrence Halprin & Associates' involvement helped actually facilitate it. The experiment was intended to identify "changes in human behavioral patterns," including "Cruising Colby," and to demonstrate "what vitality a Mall might give to downtown."[33] According to the summary report, the mall did not cause the relocation of cruisers to Evergreen Way as expected, and the traffic dissipated. The firm's final *Everett Community Plan* recommended that the idea be implemented permanently along Colby from Everett Avenue to Wall Street.[34] Such a recommendation is a complete contradiction to Halprin's claims about the collective and participatory potential of urban rituals and the excitement of youth culture. However, the mall concept seems to be a key component of the firm's "kit of parts" or standardized remedies for urban decline, and clearly the power structure of the city would support its institution along "the long concrete raceway called Colby."[35] Though Nicholson recommended a separate youth workshop (which never occurred), the social needs of this group are not integrated into the final plan.[36] This both denies the firm's supposed commitment to the diverse needs of the public and Halprin's interest in facilitating or enhancing embedded social rituals.

The second day of the workshop began with an additional awareness event, the Helicopter Flight. This gave participants another perspective of the development patterns, topography, and natural features of their region. Participants were asked to observe the regional setting, major topographic features, major surface transportation routes, major building complexes and their locations, as well as the use of water bodies, natural open space areas, and, while over the downtown in particular, to notice the street configurations. The helicopter landed on the jetty island off the shore of the downtown. The future of the jetty was a source of heated tension in the city. Lawrence Halprin & Associates recognized its potential as a public recreational amenity unsuitable for industry since it contained a unique and fragile ecology. Many members of the city's power structure were in favor of earlier plans that recommended that half the jetty be reserved for continued port activity. It seems that most of the participants had never visited the island, since recorded responses convey amazement and a general desire to preserve it entirely as a public resource. The score had thus been appropriately "crafted," aligning the participants with the firm's interests, despite the opposition's claims that the diminishment of industry would increase unemployment, a major problem in Everett.

The workshop score concluded similarly to that of Fort Worth. The participants were asked to break into groups that would tackle one of two scenarios—designing Everett in 1870 and 1970. Of this activity, Nicholson was particularly critical:

> The planning session almost totally ignored the suburbs . . . Some teams were hampered by "experts," and by insufficient planning and design alternatives on which to base their decisions: a typical example of this was Scheme 5 (1870) which was in many ways the most interesting from an SF (science fiction) point of view, and which consisted of an Everett

constructed out of concentric rings, starting with recreational middle, and spreading to education systems, residential, and waterfront "circles" with electronics industries and consumer shopping isolated outside the city.

In some ways the less imaginative teams met real social needs even less than Scheme 5 did: for example, Scheme 2 (also 1870) began its city with a colossal freeway, while Scheme 1 did not get much further than a consideration of how to park cars in downtown![37]

Unlike at Fort Worth, the participants were not asked to begin the planning session with a fantasy "starter" or "warm-up" score. Such fantasy activities were intended to loosen inhibitions and preconceptions and facilitate response based on intuitive immediacy. Perhaps this is why the participants' plans lacked innovation. It also may be why the firm, in later projects such as Cleveland, started workshops with role-playing exercises "to get people acting much freer together, and uncovering different perceptions of what they are doing through the 'eyes' of the role they are playing."[38]

The Master Score, in sum, was directed predominantly at environmental awareness— to trigger recognition of aspects of the physical environment to which participants—as residents—had become blindly habituated.[39] It presented a sequence of experiences carefully choreographed to progressively expose participants to environmental problems and opportunities foreseen by the firm. As one participant reported in an article in the *Everett Herald*:

> Have you ever heard of people moving around a city to a score—a bit like a musical score? This was the case at a community workshop Friday and Saturday at First Baptist Church. The score was a wide variety of assignments presented by "maestro" Lawrence Halprin where participants reacted and interacted within a given set of movements in the city of Everett and recorded their feelings.[40]

"Maestro" is a good term for Halprin, who wanted to confirm his plan was implementable by ensuring common understanding of the problems. Because each of the participants had the same two-day experience, despite their differences they could communicate based on this mutuality. The firm was able to pull out aspects of consensus to include in Nicholson's report for the workshop, including hopes for the recreational reclamation of the waterfront and "the consequent need for the city to broaden its economic base."

Nicholson criticized the firm's expectation that the participants make these observations then hand them over to the workshop leaders for analysis rather than have the participants synthesize the collective observations themselves.[41] In other words, though the score did structure a common experience it did not allow the participants to use their observations to generate their own conclusions. If the 1870 and 1970 score had been preempted by a fantasy "starter score" and had been followed up with a collective Planning Session for Everett, the participants could have actually become involved in the analytical or Valuaction (V) aspects of the process. However, Nicholson also noted that this possibility might have been hampered by the conflicting group dynamics consisting of "1. those lacking sufficient data in the form of decision–alternatives on which to base decisions, and 2. those feeling they knew all about the problems (ie: planners, consultants, etc.) and therefore already knew the answers (the 'we've cruised Colby before' set)." This latter note suggests the detrimental outcome of including too many participants from the power structure who might be resistant to release their preconceptions and practice the kind of immediacy Halprin hoped the workshop would stimulate. To generate such a change in attitude would require more "starter scores" and perhaps more generalized awareness exercises to initiate the process.

Nicholson's major criticism of the score or the workshop participants' response to it was their lack of social awareness. He reports that one Downtown Walk intersection along Colby was considered by participants as "beautiful," "better, cleaner, neater," and yet Nicholson notes this area "was in fact a social disaster-area . . . It seems clear . . . that most participants were more aware of their subjective perception and feelings than they were of the social fabric of the city." These comments suggest a gap between the emphases of Halprin and some of his associates, especially Simon Nicholson who actively wrote for social science journals. Halprin's scores were structured to stimulate an immediate physical and emotional response to the environment, not necessarily to trigger social awareness. He mainly considered aesthetic deficiencies, though often he attributed physical degradation to social inequities and vice versa.

Less than a month after the workshop, Halprin with Mendelsohn, Guthrie, and Gordon Cultum (of Everett's office of the mayor) sent a letter to the participants accompanied by Nicholson's "raw evaluation of Workshop participants' notes; a general and preliminary interpretation of the basic points in the notes; and preliminary observations regarding those common problems about which most seem to be in agreement." The firm presented these items as "working documents" and sent them to the members of the workshop to perpetuate the participatory process by asking for some of their feedback and requesting their willingness to lead a small local workshop of their own to "multiply the beneficial effects of the Community Workshop."[42]

The workshop and this follow-up letter initiated a longer-term process based entirely on participation and utmost transparency. The whole three-year process could be considered a fairly open score itself in the sense that objectives were to adjust according to continued participation and feedback. After a series of "second generation workshops," led by some of the members of the power group, the firm issued its December 1970 Progress Report.[43] In this document, Halprin begins with an introductory note to the citizens of Everett: "We view ourselves more as teachers and guides than as 'planners' in the traditional sense—we hope to plan with you rather than for you." The use of the word "teachers" seems more accurate than "facilitators" (often used in *Taking Part*), since the firm guided Everett citizens to propose conclusions they had largely already formulated.

By March 1971 the Community Planning Office opened as "a common meeting place" for public exposure to the planning process.[44] It was situated at 2825 Wetmore Avenue, an accessible storefront next to Tom Johnson's Luggage and across from the Everett Trust & Savings Bank, in order to involve more community members in the planning process and to make widely visible all steps in the process. Gordon Cultum of the mayor's office was selected as the liaison between the study team and the community and was responsible for securing and running the Community Planning Office.[45]

Simultaneous with the development of the Community Planning Office, the firm began conducting extensive surveys targeted to specific groups, particularly merchants in the downtown. Surveys continued through May 1971 at the same time as "Specialized Workshops" were held at the Community Planning Office. These events were hardly workshops in the Halprin sense, but rather were more conventional brainstorming sessions to consider specific topics, such as downtown, river/bay, mall/alley, convention center, downtown beautification and street furniture, industry/Paine Field, and natural environment.[46] The Halprin study in progress was also presented to a number of special interest (predominantly women's) groups during this first half of 1971, including the Women's Book Club, the Everett Business and Professional Women's Club, Silver Lake Women's Club, and the League of Women Voters. Most likely, the firm and the planning officials recognized the effectiveness of gaining the support of women in the community since they had historically been active in civic beautification efforts in Everett.

In February 1971 a public meeting was held in the First Baptist Church to present the Interim Planning Report and invite community comment. Lawrence Halprin & Associates released the Final Preliminary Report in September 1971, integrating some of this feedback and ignoring some as well according to the firm's stance on the suggestions made. The South Everett Association, for instance, requested the final report be less restrictive to development practices in the southern portion of the city; however, the Halprin firm considered this area most vulnerable to sprawl, so the restrictions were not loosened in the final policy plan. The firm again announced in the Final Preliminary Report an invitation for participatory feedback from the community over the following year in order to finalize the plan. One transcribed document recording the February 16, 1972, Public Hearing on the Community Development Plan held in the Council Chambers of City Hall presents what was originally a collective process splintering into individualized interests, particularly those based on economic concerns. However, the hearing also created a forum for everyday citizens to participate, including Pat Johnson who was clearly interested in the quality of life in Everett rather than only economic gains:

> I address the Council today as a citizen of this city, a parent, and last but not least a housewife ... We've lived in Everett for four years and I've attempted to make it our home.

Living as close as we do to the center of town, we are very much aware of the potential that Everett has for being an enjoyable and very livable city. We are also aware that some progress in the past has been at the expense of livability . . . You should see what we have to do to get our . . . two kayaks into the water next to the Yacht Club so that we can get over to the jetty [to] enjoy the beach. That's a humorous process but it's hardly convenient. I feel that the Halprin Study, as a guideline for future development, has taken into consideration many of the aspects that make cities livable for citizens. As a mother of 4 children I cannot stress enough the need for open space and recreational developments. Although I can walk here and my husband can walk from our house to work and come home for lunch, and my children can walk to the library; they can walk to the Y, but they can't walk to a park. We're surrounded by water, but we have to drive out to it so we can walk out on the docks and go fishing. I do feel the Halprin Study offers an alternative to this predicament and in talking to the parents of my children's friends and to my neighbors, I know I'm not alone in my feelings. In my opinion primary consideration should be given to the people who live in the city, who make it their home. I think this report does that. I think it did from the very beginning when they took citizens, 50 of them, up in helicopters and on tours of alleys and beaches so they could see what we had . . . If it seems like there's an overbalance toward ecology now, then possibly it's because the word was never used before. Perhaps it's because we never took a look at the land that surrounds Everett and its possible uses to see whether they were suitable for recreation or industrial development . . . I'd like to see people like you elicit involvement from people like me and people actually come out and ask others what they want for their children, other than jobs, from Everett as a place to live.[47]

This report by Pat Johnson reflects the frustration experienced by the Halprin firm at this stage in the continuing participatory process. The Everett residents who willingly participated in the initial workshop continued to contribute to the process. Those less interested in a comprehensive quality of life or strengthening Everett as a community, however, attempted to assert themselves at this late stage in plan development, causing Tom Koenig to report to the Everett Planning Department as follows:

I've had to get a new handle on our procedure in Everett, particularly in light of all the conflicting interests of various groups in Everett. I think that in this Phase II effort—which is toward implementation and pulling all the loose ends together—we have to deal with solution-oriented approaches to things if we are to get rolling. I personally am very attached to Everett and this project and I become frustrated and weary with those groups who have a singular interest and little willingness to give-and-take in the interest of the community as a whole. This attitude has to change if anything positive is to take place. I don't look forward to dealing anymore with groups or individuals who have strictly a "me first" attitude and simply want to complain. I do look forward, however, to working with those groups who want to work on solutions and ideas; who want to talk about what we CAN do rather than listing reasons why we CAN'T DO. For these reasons, I believe that adoption of the Final Preliminary Report will be a very telling milestone. If it is not accepted I think it will indicate that the community is not ready to join in and work for the common good, but would rather stand back and hack apart in a nonconstructive way. I do, however, feel that this will not be the case. Adoption of the Report will indicate that perhaps now the community is ready to accept responsibility for its own future and pull together. It's easy to lay and criticize "The Planners" and hold them responsible for what may or may not happen, but that attitude is the very thing that will prevent successful change. Adoption of the Report would certainly help to create a more positive attitude. I know you understand this but I had to get it off my chest one more time because it's what is draining my energy.[48]

The Halprin firm therefore pushed forward, ignoring input from self-serving individuals exhibiting little interest in community or collective ideals. Ignoring these (typically powerful) individuals, however, certainly threatened the possibility of plan implementation. Though the project invited public input over the firm's three-year involvement, the devolution of the workshop process into a more traditional approach based on surveys, public hearings, and special interest meetings diminished the original collective energy.

The final report, the *Everett Community Plan* (issued in December 1972) was, in fact, accepted as a "Policy Plan," where each section concluded with a list of policies that would aid the community in achieving plan objectives. What is unique about the plan is the degree to which the firm incorporates the process used to derive recommendations. Alternative schemes that the firm considered are included along with conclusions regarding their projected level of effectiveness. In "Residential Patterns," the firm consistently presents recommendations as "a framework giving form and definition to the individual sectors so that their inhabitants might develop certain community relationships and responsibilities, and begin to enjoy the confidence of belonging to a specific piece of territory much bigger than that limited to the individual dwelling unit" (105). The emphasis for this section on residential development is the sprawling area of South Everett, and the suggested development framework is intended to foster a more community-oriented neighborhood. In the Implementation section, the firm clearly presents their study as a guide rather than a "plan" (a word they associated with imposition). They emphasize continued "community review and participation" in order to periodically update the final document "to prevent it from becoming obsolete or discredited" (118). The firm recommends the reestablishment of the Community Planning Office to sustain interest and to serve as a center for community organizing and "place where people could come to find out what to do, how to proceed and who to talk to, about their environmental ideas" (130).

The final plan presents one final culminating score, called "Spring Thing," and states clearly that it is a "closed score." The event was intended as a low-cost beautification of one of the alleys off Colby Avenue. Its score is closed because it was to be predesigned by the city and the merchants and only implemented (or performed) by the community. The intention of this final participatory exercise was to generate a collective interest in improving the public environment and to instill a sense of responsibility and commitment to the city's future. The firm concludes: "Most importantly we will have generated the kind of spirit that can act as a catalyst for further improvements at a local level by the people themselves."[49] Participation in Everett was comprehensive, transparent, and at times open ended, culminating in a set of guidelines rather than a fixed physical intervention. However, the process presented here in its lengthy entirety reveals some critical contradictions that continued to emerge in later applications of Taking Part.

CHARLOTTESVILLE, VIRGINIA

By the time Lawrence Halprin & Associates's involvement in Everett ended in 1972, the firm had formulated the workshop approach into the Take Part Process and published its structure in the document *Take Part: A Report on New Ways in Which People Can Participate in Planning Their Own Environments*. Jim Burns had joined the office after fifteen years working as senior editor of *Progressive Architecture* and participating in both the 1966 and 1968 "Experiments in Environment," which inspired him to redirect his career toward activating citizen involvement in environmental design. He became increasingly involved in the firm while leading his own workshops and writing the book *Arthropods: New Design Futures* (1972) on alternative planning methods. He was integral in the April 1971 leadership training workshop for Halprin firm employees conducted under the HUD demonstration grant that culminated in the Indianapolis training workshop, which he led. He was also seminal in the firm's study of the Willamette Valley in Oregon, which concluded with the report *The Willamette Valley: Choices for the Future* (October 1972) that featured a scenario-planning method meant to stimulate increased public involvement in decision-making.[50]

Burns also acted as "Workshop Leader" for the Take Part Process in Charlottesville, Virginia. The firm was commissioned in August 1972 by the city of Charlottesville after it had begun negotiating with the business community over a possible downtown pedestrian mall to counteract the draining effects of developing suburban shopping centers (Figure 5.6).[51] By December, the firm had submitted a proposal for both a Central Business District Master Plan and the plan for the Mall, which they considered entirely interrelated.[52] In it, they included a program of "Client and Community Participation," insisting on an early workshop to involve the decision-makers and the public from the beginning, thus avoiding future opposition and the possible shelving of the plan.

The March 1973 Charlottesville Take Part Workshop occurred only a couple weeks after the firm conducted another in Tulsa, Oklahoma, also led by Burns. Both workshop teams spent February undertaking a thorough Resource (R) gathering phase, including interviews with city officials and community representatives. After the Resources had

Figure 5.6. Aerial photograph of downtown Charlottesville, late 1960s. Photograph by Holsinger Studio; found in Lawrence Halprin Collection, The Architectural Archives, University of Pennsylvania (014.I.A.3823–3885).

been gathered, Dean Abbott and Norman Kondy of the firm generated the Charlottesville score according to the following parameters set by Burns:

> There are basically five types of scores to produce: walking awareness score in the CBD; driving awareness score around both cities; sharing score after awareness events ... ; planning score(s) for Saturday sessions; and the master score for both workshops.[53]

Seemingly, the process had become standardized in its basic framework and then made city specific according to the Resources collected.

Though Halprin reviewed and critiqued the activity scores for each workshop, during the Tulsa and Charlottesville workshops he made only "special appearances," notably attending the last day and the "wrap-up sessions" at the end. Burns indicates that Halprin would "assume a special role combining elements of Master of Ceremonies and Workshop Leader-Facilitator. He will make the final statement about the workshop at the end."[54] After he had conducted his Leadership Training Workshop in San Francisco for his staff members, Halprin felt confident, especially with the energy, passion, and experience of his friend and colleague Jim Burns, that his employees could generally lead their own workshops. However, that he felt he could direct the Valuaction sessions without having attended the entirety of the workshop suggests a certain disregard for the participatory immersion and makes him appear as the outside "expert" or authority who controls the final outcome.

Despite the mixed message conveyed by Halprin's involvement, the firm thoroughly dissected previous workshops to continue to improve the experience and its effects. In the same February 1973 letter, Burns had the workshop teams consider previous Take Part approaches applied to earlier projects. Under the heading "Types of Workshops/Selection of Participants," Burns states:

> Both for these workshops and for the future, team members should consider several varieties of ways to form workshop groups to answer needs of specific kinds of workshops. Here are some of the areas we have identified.
>
> *General Community Participation*—Workshop, such as Everett and Wilmington, where a broad-based representation of community groups and interests is included.
>
> *Emphasis on Specific Neighborhood Problem*—The Morningside Park workshop in Harlem illustrates working with a neighborhood problem and neighborhood groups . . .
>
> *Decision-Making Groups for Immediate Action*—This can be called workshopping the

"power structure" of a city, or the people who traditionally have made decisions about the city and have the clout to have them implemented. Fort Worth is the example.

Community Group Learning Situations—Workshops, such as Indianapolis, where we instruct community-contact groups and people in ways to structure and conduct on-going processes in their areas of interest in the community . . .

Combination of Interests—If we extrapolate our work with the Task Forces in the Willamette Valley into a workshop situation, we see that a form of workshopping is possible wherein special interests or expert groups can workshop together, then combine objectives and solutions with other groups to evolve a comprehensive approach to their problems . . .

Awareness Experiences—These might be described as little workshops designed simply to let people learn about their environments by experiencing them through our scored situations. They would be done with school groups, neighborhood groups, and might be particularly useful in getting together and understanding workshop successes before getting into full-scale, lengthy planning workshop.[55]

According to another letter from Burns to Kondy and Abbott, Halprin considered the Tulsa workshop the best one they had conducted thence far. From that positive experience, Burns reminded his colleagues to remember to address certain issues in order to avoid problems they experienced in Tulsa, including:

Time the awareness scores precisely . . . Do not, however, give too *loose* a score and allow people to just wander around without proper guidance.

Alert people specifically to the *nature* of the workshop *and* its *objectives*. The Tulsa steering committee got some people on board who didn't, as it turned out, know exactly why they were there or what we were hoping to accomplish. These items should be impressed on everyone during the interview/selection process.

Ascertain equipment and props to be utilized early on. In Tulsa, we simply used base maps, magic markers, etc. It was rather difficult getting them to think and work in other than verbal terms, and we finally had to give a rather closed score requiring them to express themselves in other ways . . .

If you interview people who are not ultimately invited to be in the workshop, you should make this acceptable to them . . . In Tulsa, there were feelings from this situation—the client required us to cut back on minority representation and there were bad vibes that we had to take the time to deal with. (Incidentally, most of the people from the client group said they were wrong at workshop's end).[56]

These reminders have been included to demonstrate the maturation of the process from the firm's early experiences in Fort Worth and Everett.

The resource-gathering phase was also evidently streamlined by the time the firm was tackling the problems of Charlottesville. This part of the process was extensive, with Kondy and Abbott collecting and generating maps indicating current conditions of land use, development history, demographics, topography, and so forth. Many of these materials were made available to workshop participants as part of the workshop "Resource Center." From the early compilation of these materials, Burns was able to offer suggestions to the Charlottesville scorers on possible issues to emphasize in the awareness activities, including "the nature of the strip between downtown and University of Virginia, the demolished renewal areas, . . . relation of downtown and shopping center (Barracks Road), feelings of people who are in areas they ordinarily don't visit (blacks at University; whites across the railroad tracks)." He concludes this list with a reminder: "Don't be afraid to score in things that might surprise people; we have been asked to open eyes, and scores properly done are non-judgmental and receptive to the feelings of the performer. Don't hold back because you might step on some toes."[57] The awareness scores were therefore not intended to avoid discomfort, but by making participants face situations head on they were forced to confront the cause of their unease.

In addition to using tangible conditions to feed into the score development, Kondy and Abbott also conducted extensive interviews with major city players to understand the issues and tensions that could not necessarily be mapped or measured and to understand the power dynamics of different groups within the city. Most of these individuals did participate in the workshop, including Drewary Brown, a black community leader of the Neighborhood Youth Corps, who clearly represented an alienated minority and acted as an advocate for the black community.[58] Mary Williams was another individual interviewed who might not have been considered an official "power broker" but had community clout as the owner of The Nook restaurant, a downtown institution along Main Street.[59]

All these resource-generating activities fed into the development of appropriate scores and clarified who might represent a suitable cross-section of Charlottesville to invite to participate. In the weeks leading up the workshop, the Charlottesville team devoted themselves to testing scores and interviewing potential workshop participants to ensure commitment and to introduce the process.[60] The firm had learned from instances such as the Colby Cruise in Everett that individuals had to commit to full participation in all activities of the Master Score in order to experience the cumulative situations that the firm decided would best generate the common language from which to move forward collectively. These interviews were therefore essential in explaining the process and the reason why such dedication was necessary. In addition to the interview, Mayor Francis Fife sent out a letter to participants reminding them of their commitment to "prompt and complete attendance for the duration of each of the three sessions."[61]

The workshop of thirty-two participants was, in fact, fairly diverse, incorporating the typical city and business representatives, some downtown merchants, a number of African American participants including a hospital technician and a "housewife," a number of male and female students, and a retiree, among others.[62] The "neutral" space of the National Guard Armory building, one block north of Main Street, served as the workshop headquarters.

The Master Score was structured similarly to that of Everett with the addition of an initial evening of activities to explain Taking Part as it applied to Charlottesville, to introduce the participants and organizers to one another, and to jump-start the process of sharing feelings, as well as of expectations and hopes for the following two days (Figure 5.7). After members of the firm conducted a "Hopes Score" to understand participant anticipations, they led an activity called "Charlottesville Is . . ." in which participants were asked to write their individual perceptions of the city and then share them with the group. This activity clarified for the firm the participants' varied priorities, whether they were living conditions, pollution control, history, commerce, or social inequities.

The first evening also included a short "Downtown Experience," which was choreographed to make participants comfortable with interacting with their environment and observing their surroundings "with fresh eyes": "For the next ½ hour we ask you to go into downtown Charlottesville and experience the city as though you are a visitor here . . . not a resident or connected with the university. You might be someone attending a convention at the new Hilton in the future, a tourist, or a traveling businessman or woman. . . . Please do this walk alone."[63] The firm attempted to rid participants of their environmental preconceptions by organizing this role-playing exercise. In the Wilmington, Delaware, workshop that occurred the year before, the firm asked the participants to "attempt to cast away all . . . your background, and your experiences, and your knowledges that you do have, and relate to the city as if you were a newcomer who had just stepped off the bus in Wilmington, and for the first time saw it and saw its people and its physical configuration and its social makeup."[64]

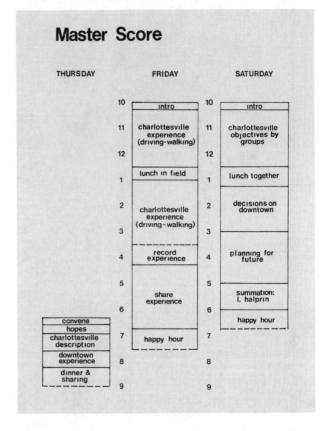

Figure 5.7. Master score for the Charlottesville Take Part Workshop, 1973. Lawrence Halprin Collection, The Architectural Archives, University of Pennsylvania (014.I.A.3831).

Figure 5.8. Driving Score map for the Charlottesville Take Part Workshop, 1973. Lawrence Halprin Collection, The Architectural Archives, University of Pennsylvania (014.I.A.3831).

Such requests directly emerged from Anna Halprin's attempts to uncover "authentic movement" response through the Gestalt therapy exercises she conducted with Fritz Perls. Asking citizens to release long-standing preconceptions without rigorous training, however, seems unrealistic and rather naive. Nonetheless, this initial awareness score in Charlottesville allowed the participants to walk on a route they devised themselves and, imagining they were "out-of-towners," find a place for a drink or a cup of coffee and engage someone in conversation about what there was to do for entertainment at night in the downtown. Obviously, from these instructions the firm had clearly predetermined the lack of downtown nightlife and, unsurprisingly, the participants concluded that the downtown "lacks animation and vitality" and that it "definitely looks dead at night."[65]

The following day was devoted to awareness scores—driving and walking. The participants were given a general list of items of which to remain conscious, including the nature of vehicular and pedestrian movement, open spaces, and cultural activities, and were given basic scores to perform at each stop along the processional routes. The "Driving Score" (Figure 5.8) sequenced the participants, in automobile teams of four, through thirteen locations in the city that varied in character and quality. The most significant of these locations included a drive along Main Street; a visit to the Barracks Road Shopping Center, which seemed to be the major cause for the Main Street drain; Thomas Jefferson's Lawn at the University of Virginia; the urban renewal areas; the neglected open spaces along Moore's Creek; the prolifer-

ating strip development; and some of the more established residential neighborhoods. The Driving Score, though supposedly "nonjudgmental," asked the participants to record their feelings in response to the issues the firm had identified, such as the weak connection between Main Street and the University of Virginia by means of the deteriorated West Main Street commercial corridor.

The "Walking Score" (Figure 5.9) was a choreographed route through downtown Charlottesville, which the firm organized to expose the participants to many aspects of the central business district that they intended to address in their plan. The sequence included a walk through the historic district north of Main Street; along the length of Main Street; through the razed neighborhood of Vinegar Hill slated for urban renewal but that remained vacant; to a high point just south of this area to get a view of the city and sketch it; along Water Street to consider the backs of buildings that faced Main Street and the surface

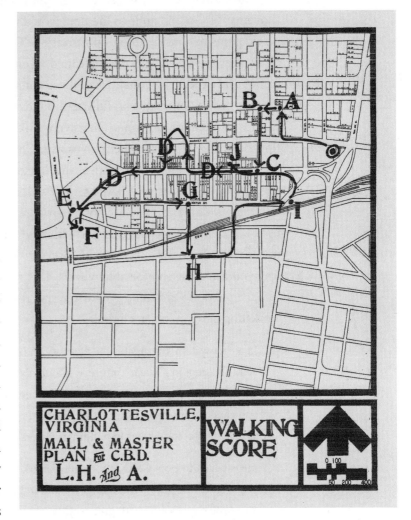

Figure 5.9. Walking Score map for the Charlottesville Take Part Workshop, 1973. Lawrence Halprin Collection, The Architectural Archives, University of Pennsylvania (014.I.A.3831).

parking lots that lined the street's south side; through the Garrett Street redevelopment area; to the freight railroad (C&O) station for which participants were asked to imagine alternative uses; and finally to another high point—the fifth floor terrace of Miller & Rhoads department store on Main Street to observe and sketch the activity on the street below.

The entirety of the walking score emphasized relationships, where the choreographed movement from one node to the next would reveal links and interconnections and force participants to consider their optimization. Throughout both awareness scores, the participants were asked to remain attuned to circulatory movement patterns and the efficiency and experiential qualities of these connections. The scores also guided movement in three dimensions with careful attention to directing workshop members to high points from which they could comprehensively observe views, understand environmental relationships, and familiarize themselves with Charlottesville's unique topographic situation.

After the awareness activities, the Master Score presented a "Record Experience" and a "Share Experience" (Figure 5.10). Participants were instructed as follows: "Don't be timid about drawing if you are not an artist, writing if you're not a writer, talking if you're not used to public speaking, or performing if you're not an actor. The aim of this session is to make everyone's experiences, observations, and feelings visible to the group in any way you are most comfortable with."[66] This session, according to the workshop report, "uncovered profound feelings of discovery" revealed in some of the printed statements of workshop participants, including:

> In an ecosystem, the greater the diversity, the greater the stability. It is also more aesthetically pleasing. In a *mono*-culture, it is a highly productive, but less stable, less humanistic environment. Example: Barracks Rd, monoculture productive environment with asphalt and cars omnipresent. Contrast to Jefferson's lawn: continuity, trees, arcade, lawn, diversity of architectural types in buildings. Diversity but continuity; an ecosystem.

> Ideas began to pop. C&O Stn—a great market place. The little green area around Murphy's Travel—a mini park. Hide cars and improve the view. This and many other small areas could be treated with greenery.[67]

Figure 5.10. Participants in the Charlottesville Take Part workshop, 1973.
Lawrence Halprin Collection, The Architectural Archives, University of
Pennsylvania (slide A-J435, unstamped).

Such statements reveal that the participants became aware of the diversity of their city
and the opportunity for choice it provided, especially once it was developed to its fullest
potential. Therefore, the score appears successful at achieving the firm's objectives aimed
at choreographing a progressive sequence that highlighted problems and opportunities
within a city that had rich experiential potential and was situated in a landscape of topo-
graphic distinction.

Day three was devoted to "Group Sessions in Planning for Charlottesville," initiated by a "Fantasy Score" for which participants were asked to imagine for five minutes that they were Thomas Jefferson and "invent something to cure a condition or solve a problem" that they noted the previous day. This short exercise was intended to loosen creativity and imagination by role-playing. To represent their inventions, the participants drew on long scrolls of paper that were tacked to the walls of the Armory. The exercise seemed to successfully stimulate participants' thoughts about the problems of their town, how to address them, and how nonverbal means of expression were sometimes optimal for generating innovative ideas.[68]

After this brief activity, Halprin led a score called "Charlottesville Scenarios" to sustain the energy level and intensify "collective creativity" by asking participants to work in groups to imagine what might happen given the situations of an assigned scenario; for example "Riding in automobiles has been found to cause mass impotence . . . Plan the city with this condition in mind," and "Moore's Creek has overflowed in a devastating flood that has wiped out 90% of Charlottesville. Replan the city the way you would like it to be."[69] According to Halprin's notes, each of the scenario groups considered transportation and interconnection, especially between the downtown, the university, and Barracks Road Shopping Center, thus assuring the firm that their score was suitably choreographed.

The same groups were then asked to consider Main Street and the downtown as a whole. The emphasis for the latter was equally on planning and implementation, or how one might institute ideas and make them reality. The summary for this session reported that "the interconnections and potential mutual interdependence of many areas of Charlottesville emerged as the chief concern of all members of the workshop," again assuring the firm that the workshop was progressing appropriately since environmental relationships were the firm's fundamental priority.[70]

From the summary of these "Valuaction" (or analysis) sessions, Halprin recognized a "remarkable consensus," which he listed to the participants to ensure they were not misrepresented:

> There should be areas for pedestrians only, without autos . . . People want to live downtown . . . People want a diversity of things to do downtown . . . for a variety of age groups

... Downtown needs urban amenities at least as good as the suburban shopping center ... fountains, benches, trees, lighting ... Buildings must have mixed uses ... Older buildings should be recycled and given new uses ... The Vinegar Hill development should be seen as an integral part of Main Street and downtown planning.[71]

The Halprin firm prided itself on the compilation of all sixteen consensus items, as well as the integration of all of them in their final report. Yet this example again illustrates that although Halprin wished to foster "collective creativity," the consensus items were not particularly innovative, controversial, or specific. From this example, however, it seems possible that the workshop was not really intended to generate unique ideas but rather to ensure that the community was included and the process was transparent in order to avoid obstacles to ultimate implementation.

At the conclusion of the workshop, therefore, the firm imparted on the group the responsibility for continued work as "communicators" and consultants to the city to ensure representation and timely implementation. However, the degree to which this workshop group remained involved is not entirely clear, since the client group—the City Council, the Central City Commission, and the City Staff—seems to have asserted their authority by this time to make sure the plan did not lose momentum. After this, the public was kept informed of progress through more traditional public presentations.

By October 1973, the firm had generated their Central Business District Master Plan, founded on the sixteen consensus items it derived from the workshop. The document embodies all of the firm's philosophies on participatory planning and design—emphasizing choices, connections, and movement choreography. In fact, one of the drawings in the plan presents a Motation Sequence or procession through the proposed form of downtown depicted by arrows along which "terminal points" and "sequential events" are marked. For each of the forty-two "sequential events," Kondy sketched a perspective view to illustrate the vertical dimension of the proposed urban interventions (Figure 5.11). The future of Main Street itself was conceived "neither as a mall nor a place but a continuous meandering path which interconnects primary, secondary and tertiary spaces into a kind of maze pattern. The downtown would thus be composed of a series of experiences along a network rather than a single experience along a spine."[72] The *Downtown Planning Report* continues, using the vocabulary of nodes, networks, anchor points, and magnets to identify environmental connections, and it suggests that this maze pattern might even structure the experience of downtown as "A Treasure Hunt"—inspiring playful environmental engagement. The document proposes a series of recommendations that perfectly embody Halprin's theories on design presented in part I of this book, "Built Work."

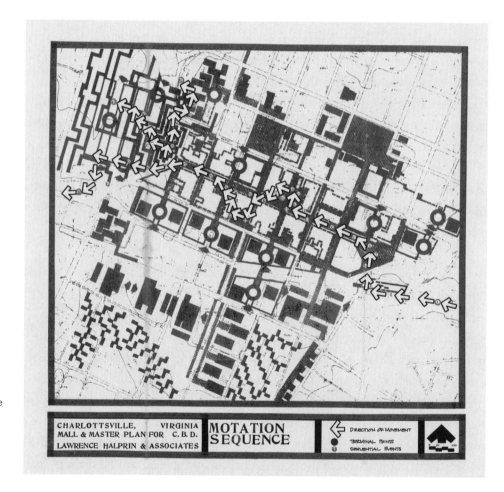

Figure 5.11.
Motation Sequence for downtown Charlottesville, c. 1973. Sequential sketches by Norman Kondy of Lawrence Halprin & Associates. Lawrence Halprin Collection, The Architectural Archives, University of Pennsylvania (014.I.A.3834).

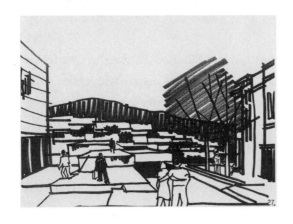 

Pedestrian movement and providing a "structure or system . . . to link experiences together to form sequences which increase anticipation" is integral to the downtown plan (28).

In spite of the generally positive result of the report, the firm hit a major obstacle to implementation in early 1974 when a group of downtown merchants decided they would not support the mall. In "An Open Letter to the People of Charlottesville and to the City Council," printed in *The Daily Progress*, the group expressed its reasons for not support-ing it.[73] The city had conducted a downtown business survey in December 1973, and the final report of the survey seemed to indicate a general acceptance of the mall plan.[74] The dissidents, however, strongly opposed the pedestrianization of Main Street in the as-sumption that it would make shopping "inconvenient" and be ultimately "detrimental to the downtown business community." In order to get the city to approve the mall after this controversy, the Halprin firm had to interview each merchant and then agree to certain stipulations presented by the city.[75] This major obstacle is mentioned to demonstrate that even conducting the workshop did not prevent the project from facing challenges to implementation. Ultimately, as in Everett, economic concerns determined the final directions and the process devolved. The eventual development of the urban renewal areas, particularly Vinegar Hill, also reveals this subordination of the participatory pro-cess to economic interests. The firm had designed elaborate plans for the transformation of Vinegar Hill into a dense mixed-use area, with ample housing, "serv[ing] as the key-stone or connective link between downtown and the western parts of Charlottesville."[76] Ultimately, however, the site remained vacant until 1983 when the city lent a developer money to build a luxury hotel.

Therefore, though the firm designed a pedestrian mall that now thrives in Charlottes-ville's downtown with cultural and entertainment venues and restaurants endowing it with a round-the-clock activity, the process to make that initial idea a reality was not en-tirely reliant on the participation of the community. Yet the firm proclaimed the project a success, stating: "The Charlottesville Workshop was a superb example of its kind—just enuf 'V' [Valuaction] allowed to overcome the Tulsa problem where people felt they were being led by the nose too much. No energy sag occurred—good build-up—good relationship between perceived objectives *and* the scores and the performance of scores—particularly Main Street and entire CBD."[77] Thus the firm seemed to be gauging success by the experience of the process—or really, the workshop itself—rather than by the ultimate outcome or how the city decided to deploy (or not deploy) the plan.

CLEVELAND, OHIO

In a culminating example of Taking Part, judging success became a lot more complicated. Just after Halprin began negotiations with officials in Charlottesville, he was invited to apply the Take Part Process to the even larger and more complex city of Cleveland, Ohio. The industrial city was suffering from the typical ills of 1960s and 1970s urban America, including racial tensions, a significant segregation between the suburbs and a dying downtown, and redevelopment and urban renewal projects that had failed to solve the city's "acute urban crisis."[78] Cleveland had historically served as a urban planning laboratory: Daniel Burnham designed a civic plan in 1905 based on City Beautiful ideals; the city instituted a more functionalist plan in 1949, laying the foundation for the largest urban renewal program in the country; and, simultaneous with Halprin's involvement, the planning director from 1969 to 1979, Norman Krumholz, began developing the famous *Cleveland Policy Planning Report* (1974) based on the new strategy of equity planning.[79]

In February 1973, the charitable community organization called the Cleveland Foundation invited Halprin, along with associate Barry Wasserman, to perform an "urban diagnosis" to evaluate the problems, potentials, and opportunities for downtown.[80] Subsequently, the Cleveland Foundation sponsored a Take Part Workshop to involve the community in the future of their downtown development. Very few people actually resided in downtown at this time, so the Halprin team focused on creating a group microcosmic of the entire city of Cleveland, a task that proved challenging. Minority representation seemed to be the most sensitive issue, especially the inclusion of a suitable number of African Americans.[81] Everett had a much smaller and more homogenous population, and Charlottesville, though certainly racially charged, especially after the displacement of the African American community of Vinegar Hill, had not experienced anything like

Cleveland's Hough neighborhood race riots of 1966. Cleveland was also much more ethnically diverse than the other cities in which the Halprin firm had previously applied the process. The final group of thirty-seven participants involved the expected power players, including Norman Krumholz, as well as representatives from various neighborhood groups; individuals from the arts, the police department, the university student body, the Department of Public Health & Welfare, and the media; and active citizens including a series of housewives, local factory workers, and a resident in one of the new senior citizen towers constructed downtown.[82] The group certainly did seem like a diverse mix if not a true cross-section.

The firm conducted the May 31–June 2, 1973, workshop in the Chesterfield Apartment Tower, one of the first residential high-rises built downtown. Wasserman, the Project Manager, was the workshop "Master of Ceremonies" and Jim Burns the "Workshop Leader." Halprin again made his "special appearance" on the third and last day of the workshop in order to, "based on notes and observations of the rest of the workshop team, [give] a summary of discoveries, decisions, and workshop activities."[83] The firm structured the Master Score similarly to previous workshops (Figure 5.12), though the starter exercises began even before the participants gathered together for the first time. In a letter informing them of the workshop time and place, the group was asked to do the following:

1. In Downtown Cleveland, between 6 pm and 7:30 pm ... go to a restaurant or café where you have never been before and have your dinner.

2. Spend less than $3 for your meal.

3. Observe your surroundings and the city as you walk to the restaurant and to the workshop. Engage your waitress or waiter in conversation about downtown at night.[84]

From the recorded responses, it seems that the group was not particularly familiar with downtown at night. They expressed mixed reactions but, as Halprin summarized, generally recognized that "there is something to build on," whether it was the ethnic restaurants or the Euclid Avenue retail. However, the bleakness, desolation, and perception of danger in the area were repeatedly noted as well.[85]

The most unique (and open-ended) activity was the Thursday evening Mini-Workshop for which participants were asked to play the roles of specific citizens of a made-up city called Clintonia to determine its future. The firm created a map (Figure 5.13), as well as a Clintonia community "Data Sheet" including the fabricated history of a city that could have been nearly any aged industrial city in the United States with a declining core caused by middle-class flight to the suburbs and urban renewal clearance.[86] Participants became "the mayor of Clintonia, the proprietor of the Mexicali Chili Parlor, students, directors of the Clintonia Cultural Center and the Afro-American Culture Center, the manager of an X-Rated movie house, suburban housewives, ethnic representatives, blue-collar workers, and a wide variety of other Clintonia citizens."[87]

Wasserman presented a slideshow of this "mythical city" in order for the

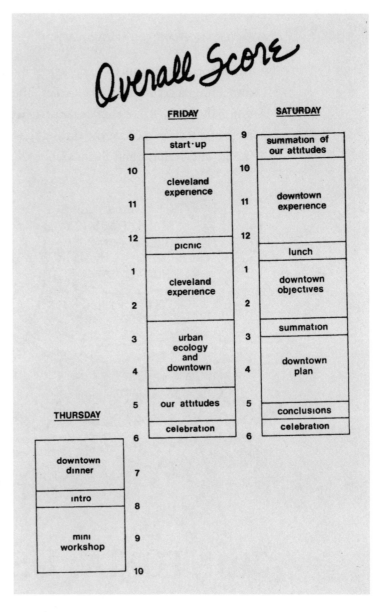

Figure 5.12. "Overall Score" (Master Score) for the Cleveland Take Part Workshop, 1973. Published in Halprin and Burns, *Taking Part*, 226. Lawrence Halprin Collection, The Architectural Archives, University of Pennsylvania.

workshop participants to "experience" it. In four groups, participants were asked to plan for Clintonia according to their roles. The intention of this "mini-workshop" was to condition the group to collaborate constructively and creatively before tackling the real problems of downtown Cleveland during the following two days. According to the workshop report and Halprin and Burns's book *Taking Part*, in which this workshop is featured,

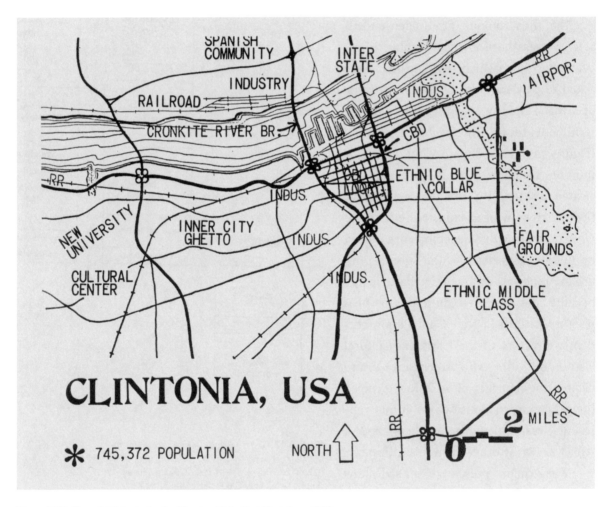

Figure 5.13. Map of Clintonia for the Cleveland Take Part Workshop, 1973. Published in Halprin and Burns, *Taking Part*, 231. Lawrence Halprin Collection, The Architectural Archives, University of Pennsylvania.

"role-playing freed people from harboring their day-to-day concerns and prejudices . . . and freed up communications between workshop members."[88] However, from summary accounts of the actual score, the group seemed somewhat unable to let go of their own realities. For instance, as the firm's recorder noted about one group: "preoccupied with own situation—couldn't care less about downtown." Halprin's "General Conclusion" for Clintonia indicated that, to the participants, "neighborhood problems in many instances overweigh downtown," and "jobs were a consistently high issue." These were clearly the priorities in Cleveland, and it was these pressing social issues that Krumholz's plan attempted to address. However, as physical planners first and foremost, hired to consider only downtown, the Halprin firm attempted to gain support for the notion that the downtown was the "glue" binding the city and its disparate parts together.[89]

On Friday the firm scored a bus tour throughout the city (Figure 5.14). The objective for this activity was to establish "a group understanding of the urban ecology of Cleveland and what the position of downtown is in that system." The participants were asked to share their personal experiences of their own neighborhoods as the bus traveled through them, and to think about "how the neighborhoods connect to or do not connect to the downtown and how they have an effect on what happens to downtown." Traveling first through the predominantly black Hough neighborhood, then the wealthier areas on the east side, through downtown, over to the west side to see the ethnic neighborhoods and the market, and then back into the downtown, revealed to the participants what the firm had concluded—that downtown was the "keystone" holding all these neighborhoods together. The firm obviously considered Cleveland's diversity an asset that would contribute to a unique urban character. During the bus tour, the firm enabled participants to discover that diversity by exposing them to unfamiliar parts of their own city. Halprin subsequently reported that "everyone found there were strong neighborhood characteristics in most parts of Cleveland—ethnic, cultural, social, racial—and that this diversity gives Cleveland a unique flavor."[90]

After the bus tour, the firm presented the "Urban Ecology and Downtown" activity, for which participants broke up into groups to discuss the relationships of downtown to the neighborhoods visited during the bus tour. Specific questions included: How do they have impact on each other? What are the ways of getting from one to the other? Are there walls separating them real or imaginary? Do the people get together or not? What are the provisions for many kinds of life styles?[91] Each group was asked to graphically present their findings. Acknowledging that most had generally ignored downtown to focus their attention on the neighborhoods in the Clintonia mini-workshop, Halprin stated that "every group Friday afternoon agreed that the health of the downtown is important and is related to the health of the city as a living entity made up of many parts (or neighborhoods)."[92]

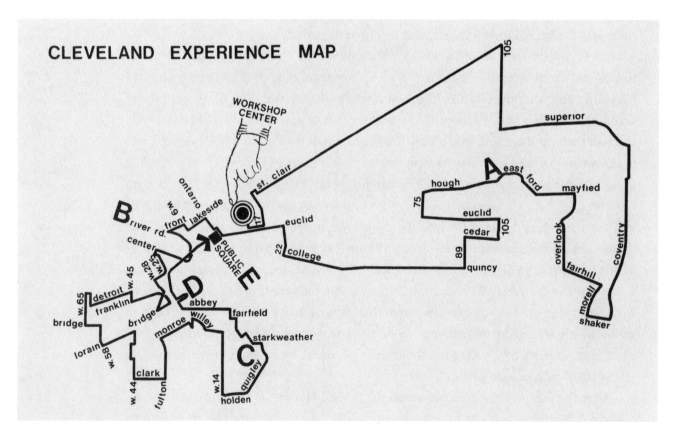

Figure 5.14. Cleveland Experience Map for the Cleveland Take Part Workshop, 1973. Published in Halprin and Burns, *Taking Part*, 234. Lawrence Halprin Collection, The Architectural Archives, University of Pennsylvania.

At the conclusion of this activity, the Halprin team stated:

> We now have . . . an overall view of how we as a workshop group see Cleveland and some
> of the general things that we think might be undertaken for its future. Individual feelings
> and opinions are important in this respect also, because they ultimately combine into
> a community attitude that is more than the sum of the parts . . . To get a picture of the
> attitudes of this community, the workshop group, we would like to read to you a num-
> ber of statements about Cleveland and its downtown. Please write down on the paper
> whether you consider each statement true or false. It's that simple but the overview that
> will emerge will be, we think you will agree, fascinating.[93]

Some of the statements are extremely leading, emphasizing the firm's obvious main con-
cerns: open space, river and lakefront development, transportation, pedestrian amenities,
and activities for different ages. Despite the Clintonia score results, the majority of the
workshop participants responded "false" to the following statement: "My neighborhood
is most important to me. If there is a change, I want it to start there." Either participants
were attempting to appease the Halprin team or the workshop had been scored carefully
enough to change participants' priorities. Similarly, the majority considered it "false" that
"We should spend our money on social programs instead of physical development" and
"true" that "The health of all the neighborhoods depends on the health of downtown,"
which the firm had hoped to impress on the workshop participants.[94] Such activities
allowed the firm to gauge how successfully they had "guided" the group to make conclu-
sions they found acceptable and productive to their cause.

At the beginning of day three, Halprin introduced himself and presented a summary
of each of the scores performed on the two previous days to open up discussions and
ensure agreement. After the summary presentation and subsequent group discussion,
the firm choreographed a three-hour solitary awareness walk, called "Downtown Experi-
ence" (Figure 5.15). At each of the fourteen downtown locations, the participants were
asked to observe, record, feel, sense, sketch, imagine, interact with others, and think
about specific issues. Such an explicit list of "issues" had not been provided in previous

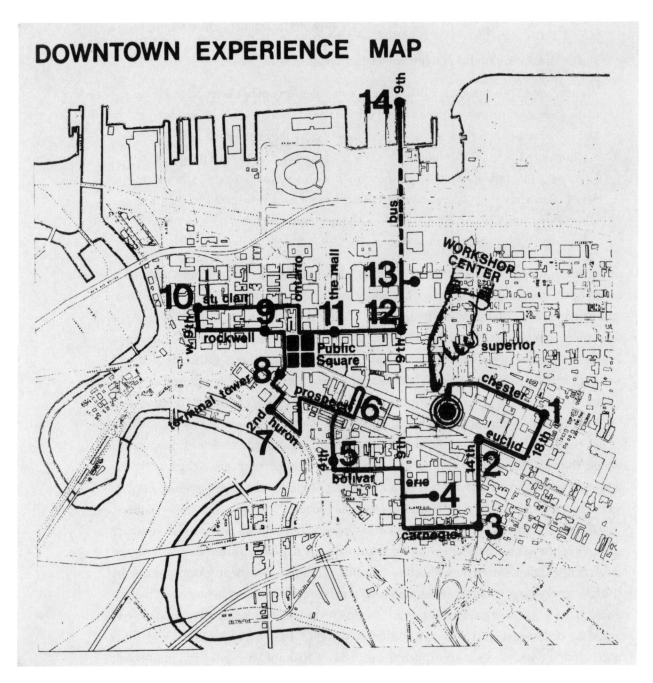

Figure 5.15. Downtown Experience Map for the Cleveland Take Part Workshop, 1973. Published in Halprin and Burns, *Taking Part*, 243. Lawrence Halprin Collection, The Architectural Archives, University of Pennsylvania.

workshops, thus demonstrating the firm's increasing desire to ensure that participants focused on what they deemed most critical.

Revealing documents in the Halprin Archive, generated most likely by Wasserman, list the preliminary walking score locations with a corresponding column indicating what kind of perceptual experience each location would provide, whether it was enclosed space, views, open space, city structure, movement, or sound (Figure 5.16). Clearly the rhythm of these types of experiences was considered carefully as part of the choreography so that they would not be repetitive or monotonous but constantly shifting.

The prescribed walk brought participants through Playhouse Square, Erie Cemetery, the Central Market, and the historic downtown shopping arcades.[95] From there they were directed to views of the river that they discovered were obstructed, to Terminal Tower for which they were asked to imagine a new use, then to the Illuminating Company Building Plaza, to attempt to seek access to the Flats, to the Mall, and then to Erieview Plaza, part of I. M. Pei's failed renewal scheme, which participants considered lonely, cold, and deserted. They were finally asked to take public transit as far out on the Municipal Pier as possible to consider its future possibilities. The firm had obviously selected areas that would expose participants to their previously unrecognized potential.

At this point the "Objectives for Downtown" score challenged the group to "put this awareness into action."[96] The compiled objectives were not particularly inventive, but seem to appropriately reflect the values of the Halprin firm. However, the workshop report does include a few novel suggestions such as helicopter rides from the waterfront, "a Playboy-type club for 'dirty old men,'" and a ski run from the top of Terminal Tower down to the Flats.[97] None of these ideas were considered any further.

The final activity requested that groups make a plan for all of downtown and present it graphically. The drawings generated, which have been reproduced in *Taking Part*, represent the most inventive documentation emerging from the workshop, demonstrating how valuable nonverbal expression is to innovatively imagining future possibilities. One group even proposed a geodesic dome over downtown "for environmental control."

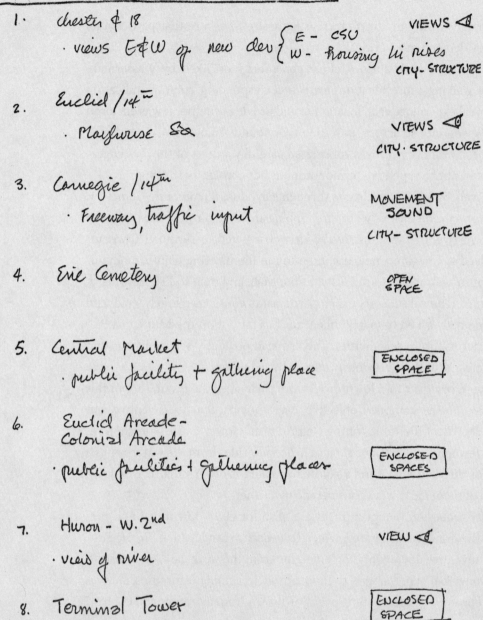

WALKING SCORE... CLEVELAND WORKSHOP.

1. Chester & 18   VIEWS ◁
   · views E&W of new dev { E - CSU
                           { W - housing hi rises
                                                       CITY- STRUCTURE

2. Euclid / 14ᵗʰ
   · Mayfurise Sq   VIEWS ◁
                                                       CITY · STRUCTURE

3. Carnegie / 14ᵗʰ   MOVEMENT
   · Freeway, traffic input   SOUND
                                                       CITY- STRUCTURE

4. Erie Cemetery   OPEN
                                                       SPACE

5. Central Market
   · public facility + gathering place   ENCLOSED
                                                       SPACE

6. Euclid Arcade -
   Colonial Arcade
   · public facilities + gathering places   ENCLOSED
                                                       SPACES

7. Huron - W. 2ⁿᵈ
   · view of river   VIEW ◁

8. Terminal Tower   ENCLOSED
   - walk thru public space   SPACE

Figure 5.16. Sample notes from the "Walking Score—Cleveland Workshop" document indicating the type of perceptual experience intended at each location, 1973. Lawrence Halprin Collection, The Architectural Archives, University of Pennsylvania (014.I.A.5644).

Ignoring some of the most extreme suggestions, Halprin devised a consensus summary, which he read back to the group to again confirm agreement:

> Downtown is the *glue* that brings Cleveland's variegated neighborhoods together . . . It should be *fun*. It should be *profitable* for many people. It must provide ease of access through *transit*. It must offer opportunities for people of many kinds and many ages. *Families* must be as welcome there as students or bankers or merchants or shoppers or conventioneers . . . Downtown must have more than the nine-to-five life it has in most parts right now . . . Downtown must be the province of the pedestrian, not the automobile . . . Parking should arrest the car at the periphery and public transit conduct people into the city core . . . Buildings must have more than one use so that they are not slab-sided gravestones after dark . . . Older buildings (even as young as half-a-dozen years old) should be recycled into new uses when their former uses are outdated . . . Cleveland's great resource of multiethnic and multiracial strains should be utilized positively and be reflected in public entertainment and cultural events . . . Communications between citizens and our elected officials is also a top priority.[98]

Clearly, this consensus summary was not especially groundbreaking, despite some of the participants' offbeat ideas. Similar to summaries emerging from other Take Part workshops they reflected the values of the Halprin firm, but they also remained general and could have been devised for any number of American cities.

From this "First Will and Testament" of the members of the first Cleveland Take Part Community Workshop,[99] the Halprin team structured a year-long process for the actual development of a concrete plan for downtown Cleveland, titled "Concept for Cleveland." This initial workshop became a source of foundational resource gathering for a much longer and more complex process of planning for development. "The Client Group" for the "Concept for Cleveland" was composed of representatives from three dominant decision-making groups: the city government, the quasi-public Cleveland Foundation, and the private Downtown Council. The long-term plan called for a series of four workshops that no longer included the "microcosmic" community group, but rather those who were more directly involved in the economy and politics of downtown, such as government officials, businessmen, developers, school officials, hospital directors, hotel managers, policemen, small business owners, the press, and representatives from special interest groups and nonprofit and cultural organizations. This "Planning Team" was intended to represent "a true cross section of the downtown decisionmakers and their constituents."[100] Such a transition from community microcosm to "power structure" was the opposite strategy to that applied in Everett, where the firm began with a workshop of powerful figures and then permeated the larger community through "follow-up" workshops for the public.

Cleveland residents were invited to stay abreast of the project through the firm's establishment of a Downtown Workshop center, as the tangible "symbol of the Downtown Plan."[101] This was situated on Euclid Avenue, in a vacant storefront where the public could view a display of models, slide shows, and graphics, making visible the planning process as it unfolded. Similar to the establishment of Everett's Community Planning Office, the firm and the city organized the center staff, composed of city personnel and public volunteers, who welcomed feedback and questions by the public. Printed advertisements for the Downtown Workshop center invited citizens to share their own responses to simple awareness scores.[102]

What is interesting (though not surprising) about the progression of this process as applied to such a large-scale environment as Cleveland is that the long-term planning became less creative and more "linear and didactic," an approach Halprin consistently criticized. In addition, notes by the Halprin team become increasingly more cynical about the public process in such a large-scale application. Associate Tom Koenig, who grew up in Cleveland, starts revealing frustration when he writes in the office notes:

> I would like to have a program of citizen involvement, with a clear understanding that the topic is DOWNTOWN CLEVELAND, not neighborhoods or social programs . . . I would like to make it clear that we are physical planners and designers—not social planners . . . One major problem when we lead the public to believe they have that power [during] the

process is that we are not able to fulfill that promise . . . When that becomes evident, they become disgruntled and negative . . . We are obliged to be aware of the citizen input and use it as we see fit during the planning process. That's all.[103]

The complexity of the city's problems and the limited timeframe and funding clearly caused frustrations regarding the degree to which community input could be accommodated.

The final document, *Concept for Cleveland: A Report to the People of Cleveland on Their Downtown* (1975), demonstrated how the firm was able to use the initial workshop as a foundation from which to develop more specific recommendations. It culminated with "A Score for Participation in Downtown" intended to generate enthusiasm for the downtown's potential at achieving plan recommendations. Clevelanders were not entirely sold, however, as indicated by one ambiguous article in the *Plain Dealer*:

> Some say that not many of the ideas presented at the [initial] workshop were ever used . . . Some say it was mainly a way of making people *feel* they had a part in the planning . . . But the plan has substance. Cleveland at last has a unified downtown development scheme with an unprecedented chance for materialization . . . What do Cleveland architects think of the Halprin Plan? Virtually all agree that nothing in it really is inventive . . . Campaigners for Cleveland's dying neighborhoods feel that they are being sacrificed for downtown glamour . . . Halprin is a man of charisma, vision and talent, and very good indeed for Cleveland, though perhaps in some respects, insufficiently acquainted with its problems.[104]

A sense of the fierce tensions of 1960s and 1970s Cleveland is not conveyed in the Halprin findings. While Norm Krumholz was issuing the *Cleveland Policy Planning Report*, which focused on social equity and neighborhood development, the Halprin firm seemed to gloss over the social injustices of the time and place.[105] Even the initial workshop, which was intended to represent a community cross-section, quite obviously did not include those who did not have the time, means, or awareness to participate, so concerns over race relations and unemployment did not inform the process as much as one might expect. Additionally, while the firm's initial workshop was deliberately scored to convince the participants of the value of downtown development as necessarily related to neighborhood improvement and social programs, it did not involve more of the public in these awareness scores which only cumulatively and progressively generated this change of attitude. Therefore, the final plan was not comfortably digested by all.

Though retrospective reports on the Halprin plan indicate it generated public interest and enthusiasm for the potentials of downtown, the Downtown Cleveland Corporation became the party responsible for its implementation. At the end of 1975, a *Cleveland Magazine* article, "No Commitment to Halprin Plan," declared:

> The Downtown Cleveland Corp. is committed to the concept of revitalizing downtown but not necessarily to the specifics of the so-called Halprin plan, President Francis A. Coy said today . . . , "We're in the process of implementing that plan . . . This may mean changes, revisions, deletions, but we're still in the housekeeping stage."[106]

Therefore, even this well-funded and innovative planning process was stalled by the ultimate decision-makers.[107] The scored workshop process had been intended to invite participation in order to generate enough support and consensus to ensure the possibility of implementation. After applying the Take Part Process in Cleveland and other cities, using previous experiences to continuously fine-tune the workshop scores, by 1975 Halprin had yet to see a city dedicate itself to full implementation. Perhaps this is one reason he disbanded his firm the following year to focus on smaller design projects.

THE PARTICIPATORY CITY

In sum, one of the major questions the Take Part projects provoke is the issue of Halprin's choreographic authority and the degree to which he actually had control over the process. The workshop leaders were clearly not passive "facilitators" or "intermediaries" but rather teachers and guides. If the scores were not choreographed properly and the participants began considering ideas the leaders felt inappropriate, scores would be adjusted accordingly. Similarly, consensus plans that the workshop participants produced had a general consistency, implying that Halprin had more of a preconceived "goal" than his theory proposes. In most of these studies the workshops derived a similar "kit of parts" that were considered alleviants to the aesthetic deprivation of the redeveloping urban core. The landscape architect and community organizer Randy Hester, in a 1999 published interview with Halprin on the Take Part Process, asked: "What about situations in which you are fairly certain that something needs to be done, but the consensus is not to do it, or that it's a low priority?" To which Halprin responded:

> We always have a resolution workshop at the end where we report back to people. If there are things that still need to be resolved, or some things that I think ought to be resolved, we bring them up again . . .
>
> If someone on this project had said, well, "It's very important to keep this parking," I would have felt that's wrong. I would have said, "Let's look at this more carefully and see what the implications are of keeping the parking where it is and what other possibilities there are . . ." You're not passive in that sense during the workshop . . . All you really have to do is get people to see what this looks like in reality on the ground. Sometimes we'll want to emphasize something because it doesn't feel right, or change the score to ask people to look at it more carefully because of the implications of what they are doing.[108]

This quotation is absolutely fundamental to understanding the true motivation of the Take Part Process. Though Halprin did genuinely have interest in collective participation, he was also devoted to the rehumanization of the urban experience and the restoration of ecological relationships. Because he was the "expert" (a word he disliked) in achieving these fundamental objectives to which he had dedicated his life, his process was more an instructional or "situational learning" exercise than an open-ended event like a "Happening."

Halprin's carefully choreographed sequence of activities and programs was thus deliberately organized to progressively transform people's environmental values based on the firm's long-established principles in environmental responsibility and enriched human experience in the city. Despite what some might consider "engineered" consensus, through this transformative experience-based process Halprin was able to open the eyes and minds of people with myopic interests, which (occasionally) led to heightened commitment.

I would thus like to propose that besides Halprin's relatively controlling personality, the only flaw in the process is his belief in "universal man" bound together by "archetypal needs"—a belief that is perhaps naive but also appropriate to his background, particularly the early exposure to the collective and communal ideals of the kibbutz and his design training under individuals like Walter Gropius and Marcel Breuer, who sought standardized solutions to widespread social challenges. Rather than acknowledge the American reality of multiple publics and endless pluralities of experience, Halprin relied on this idealistic belief in our common humanity and the ability to unearth this common bond through the experience-based process.

Though in practical application Taking Part may be deemed more placatory or even manipulative than open-ended, it offers much to be mined for its transformative potential.[109] Most of today's planning and design professionals either disregard citizen participation as a frivolous nuisance to their professional expertise or rely on normative methodologies like Arnstein's "Informing" and "Consultation" or meetings in institutional venues where concerned citizens may voice their concerns or respond to surveys. Taking Part is a unique comprehensive process that not only provides opportunities for community building and development but for taking action. It is an exemplary attempt at integrating participation into the creative process, as a transformative and generative tool that enriches the design challenge. In addition, it provides a methodology that links social justice and high-end design, or physical interventions made from the bottom-up (where there is little room for the professional) and from the top-down (where there is little room for the public). More recently, landcape architect Walter Hood's observation-based methodology, which he proposes in his *Urban Diaries* (1997) and his built works such as Lafayette Square in Oakland (completed 2001), also make that link, yet Taking Part is a compelling experiment in structuring a shared experience to facilitate communication between diverse constituents who saw their lives in new contexts.

In order for Taking Part to achieve a higher rung on Arnstein's ladder and be better adapted to applications today, it would have to be deployed closer to its theoretical intentions, as more open to unexpected input. One might also question how it could reach a larger public. Because Hood's process is not actually participatory but based on observation and accommodation of existing social patterns and practices, he is perhaps able to integrate the values of a wider cross-section including the disenfranchised. Like most participatory processes, Taking Part remains unresolved on how to reach this section of the population. Finally, rather than relying on the idealism of reaching consensus, perhaps integrating the notion that negotiation, and even conflict, is a healthy component of the public realm would best guarantee the applicability of Taking Part today.

CHOREOGRAPHY AND THE CONTEMPORARY CITY

THOUGH SOME MIGHT CLAIM that Lawrence Halprin's work is outdated, there is much to be learned from his ability to translate social consciousness into design action, particularly at a time that is again defined by discontinuity, disturbance, and unrest. With today's renewed global insistence on participatory democracy expressed in events such as the Arab Spring and the Occupy Movement, much of which has been catalyzed by the explosive growth of social media, the city once again has become a proper stage for public performance and collective ritual, making Halprin's relevance even more acute.

Scores, implying movement, process, and change, are what distinguish Halprin's pivotal contribution to 1960s and 1970s urban America; and this distinction can be attributed to Larry's artistic symbiosis with Anna. The creative process that emerged from this lifetime exchange challenged the Modernist (as devolved from its avant-garde origins) imposition of reductive formal values based on techno-bureaucratic rationalism applied in totalizing and fixed "master plans." These "master plans" claimed they would generate "urban renewal," but by the late 1960s this phrase evoked more distrust than hope amid much of the urban public. Halprin's creative process served to counteract the alienating effects of this massive urban restructuring. As these chapters have demonstrated, he mitigated the degradation of public life by attempting to reintegrate the scale, rhythm, and phenomena of the natural world and the inherited or historic city to counterbalance the "disclimax" conditions of urban renewal America. Instead of resisting the forces of change inherent to modernity, Halprin welcomed them as sources of creativity and ideation. With this acceptance of change, movement, and flux, the city became more than a spatial problem to be *fixed* in master plans but rather a spatiotemporal field of processes and interactions that could be structured to stimulate heightened creativity and socialization.

Though we might say we have learned from the mistakes of urban renewal, disinvested areas of American cities continue to experience widespread eminent domain seizure and wholesale clearance, often for land-banking in hopeful anticipation of future investment. Halprin's willingness to work with social scientists, community members, and city officials to remediate the social and psychological effects of such circumstances should serve as an example for today's designers (not just city planners).

While Halprin critiqued these impositional practices of top-down physical planning, he insists he is a Modernist, having trained under Bauhaus émigrés who shaped his attitude toward design. However, the "Modernism" of the European avant-garde was quite different from what devolved into a spatial translation of corporate power in the United States. The Bauhaus, and Halprin's exposure to it at Harvard, represented a confrontational attempt at dissolving social and artistic divides. His studies at Harvard were soon further nourished by the countercultural forces of the 1960s Bay Area, reacting to imposed values and standards of behavior deemed obsolete. Halprin, in a handwritten statement, defines Modernism as:

Dealing existentially with issues of OUR times

Making function & need a vital incentive of design

Asking forms to emerge from the above & stand overtly without being covered up by decoration . . . to speak for themselves!

To address social & community issues & to make them a focus of design

To *not* have preconceived design solutions

To forge a link between out of doors & architecture @ all scales

To emphasize people & their use & enjoyment as the major purpose of design

To include *all* people as the medium for design—ie: Design as non-elitism

To accept change & anticipate it

A view which addresses problems at many different scales: house/garden, neighborhood, street, region, country, etc etc

To view landscape architecture (as well as architecture) as an art form interactive with & influenced by the other art forms[1]

In a fierce reply to a 1988 essay by Patrick Condon in which he situates Halprin in the discourse "Postmodernism," Halprin rejects the evaluation again and proclaims himself a Modernist. However, his conception of Modernism differs from the "modernist paradigm" that Condon defines as "profoundly idealistic (mind centered), abstract (the conceptual over the self-evident), and tends to separate humans from any visceral connection with the phenomenon of nature."[2] Halprin, in his published reply, however, claims in contrast that Modernism is about "a whole appreciation of environmental design as a holistic approach to the matter of making places for people to live." He continues:

> It was as part of a Modern approach to design that I included Ecology, Psychology, and social values in my process. What is most important is that you describe Modernism as a rejection of environmental holism. That is quite inaccurate. Post Modernism perhaps! But Modernism, as I define it and practice it, *includes* and is based on the vital archetypal needs of human beings as individuals as well as social groups. This is far more important to me than any formulae for designing spaces. In all designs for humans the primary task for the designer is to discover the inherent biologic, social, and economic human needs,

with a good leavening of value systems for a democratic form of life. Then you can design spaces to make a holistic life achievable. For that reason the real issue in design is . . . what you design for and your views about humanism and how to achieve it.[3]

Halprin considered Scores a reassertion of Modernist values after they had devolved. The comprehensive qualities he attributes to Modernism developed from his interdisciplinary experience at Harvard. Archetypes and universal abstractions are clearly residual from this experience and remain the foundation of his process; thus he never fully accepts the "Postmodern" notion of diverse pluralities of experience and reference, while Anna does. Rather than pluralism, he held on to collectivism as his ideal.

Andreas Huyssen, in his 1984 essay "Mapping the Postmodern," attempts to reconcile what was a larger debate over the contrast between the 1960s counterculture and 1970s Postmodernism. Though he conceives of those who followed the "Duchamp–Cage–Warhol axis" in the 1960s as "Postmodern" (a term Halprin clearly resents), he claims that these individuals were different than their counterparts one decade later, because, instead of trying to assert a "culture of eclecticism," they "tried to revitalize the heritage of the European avantgarde and give it an American form" and to "recapture the adversary ethos which had nourished modern art in its earlier stages."[4] Halprin fits well within this characterization.

Yet Halprin and his choreographic process are still harder to categorize. His comprehensive environmental approach also emerged from the ecological planning tradition with Ian McHarg remaining a close and allied contemporary. Scores were emergent from both avant-garde performance and natural process. Halprin is a pivotal figure because he builds on and propels the ecological discourse pervasive in the field at this time, but he was also a physical designer making a direct and assertive impact on the city through built form. He brought nature (largely metaphorically) into the city as a powerful force rather than passive, pastoral, or static palliative (yet only rarely do his urban spaces have an ecologically performative function; the stormwater retention and controlled release of Skyline Park in downtown Denver is one of the few exceptions).[5] His forms serve as dynamic counterpoints to their dramatically shifting urban surrounds. Additionally, he exhibits no passivity in the structuring of the "Master Scores" of the Take Part Process—the choreography is extremely deliberate and the range of potential responses is clearly premeditated.

In terms of written theory, Halprin's texts such as *The RSVP Cycles*, *Freeways*, and his 1960 lecture "The Role of the Twentieth-Century Landscape Architect" given to the International Federation of Landscape Architects,[6] could have been seamlessly included in the seminal publications attempting to provide a theoretical framework for current process-based practice founded on principles of ecology, or comprehensive and dynamic relationships between humans and their environment. Today's designers who extol the principles of "Landscape Urbanism" challenge the Modernist practice of imposing fixed physical plans on the city by reframing urban design as strategic, adaptable to continuous input and indeterminate futures. The contemporary premise of conceiving the city through the infrastructural potentials of landscape—or a "continuous matrix that effectively binds the increasingly disparate elements of our environment together"—is based on staging surfaces that can accommodate or remain open to evolving performance (P).[7] These current practitioners frame and shape urban landscape as strategic, infrastructural, and organizational. For instance, James Corner, in his essay "Terra Fluxus" in the *Landscape Urbanism Reader*, proclaims that to conceive the city through the lens of landscape

> stages the surface with orders and infrastructures permitting a vast range of accommodations and is indicative of an urbanism that eschews formal object-making for the tactical work of choreography, a choreography of elements and materials in time that extends new networks, new linkages, and new opportunities ... Landscape Urbanism is here both instigator and accelerator ... The thrust of this work is less toward formal resolution and more toward public processes of design and future appropriation. Concerned with a working surface over time, this is a kind of urbanism that anticipates change, open-endedness, and negotiation.[8]

This statement bears strong resemblance to the words of his predecessor. Halprin's process invited and responded to participatory input and, by using the language and ideas of archetypes and addressing fundamental (acultural) human needs (such an essentialist attitude distinguishing him from today's Landscape Urbanists), he hoped his spaces would withstand cultural change as "interactive containers for life." His designs were intended to be infrastructural and his process strategic. Yet as the studies of both his "Built Work" and his "Workshops" should reveal—the projects emerge from fierce tension between openness and control, enabling and imposing, catalyzing and designing—a tension that arguably strengthens the body of work as a provocative manifestation of the essential idea that design is an act of inquiry rather than a set of solutions.

Thus, to close, it is important to recognize that Halprin's work has a richer dimensionality than much of today's theoretical discourse within landscape architecture, since he was not only interested in the urban organizational scale, but also made significant and meaningful physical interventions at the human scale. To Anna, any experience had the potential for being an aesthetic one. Larry attempted to enrich life in the city by infusing it with such aesthetic opportunities. His choreographic approach thus both enhanced environmental connections and generated tangible sensuous experiences.

NOTES

INTRODUCTION

1. For a good comprehensive review of these evolving performance practices and their early predecessors (Futurists, Dadaists, etc.), see Kirby, "The New Theatre," 23–43.

2. Of course, Halprin's participatory methodology may easily be situated as a counterpoint to the paradigms of Modernism, yet it is important to acknowledge that he remained resistant to the term "Postmodern" and unresolved about moving beyond the metanarrative. If one tries to situate Halprin's work within Hassan's chart "Schematic Differences between Modernism and Postmodernism" this lack of resolution becomes particularly acute (chart printed as Table 1.1 in Harvey, *The Condition of Postmodernity*, 43).

3. The unpublished manuscript titled "Environment as Art Experience" was completed in July 1974 and was later revised and retitled as "The New Modernism: Art of the Environment." The former title is clearly inspired by John Dewey's *Art as Experience*, which influenced both of the Halprins tremendously. This manuscript by Larry Halprin is more or less a presentation of all his complex and somewhat convoluted theories on design and reception of the environment. The manuscript's confused assertions are partially a result of Halprin's free interpretation of a wide range of fields in these texts—psychology (Jungian and Gestalt), anthropology, religion, music, the history of his own profession (and so on)—to conveniently illustrate or support his theories.

4. Ross, "Anna Halprin's Urban Rituals," 57.

5. Halprin, "Intuition and Improvisation," 11.

6. Ross, *Anna Halprin*, 154–55, 174–80. In fact, Anna became a regular workshop leader at Perls's Esalen Institute in Big Sur, according to Ross, "Anna Halprin and the 1960s," 47.

7. Ross, *Anna Halprin*, 177. Quotation from Ross's interview with Anna, July 19, 1999.

8. Roszak, *The Making of a Counter Culture*, 183. In *Communitas*, Paul Goodman and Percival Goodman consider how best to enable a "choreography of society in motion and in rest, an arrangement for society to live out its habits and ideals and do its work" (1).

9. Halprin, *The RSVP Cycles*, 89.

10. Quotations from Roszak, *The Making of a Counter Culture*, 188–98.

11. See Halprin, *A Life Spent Changing Places*, for more on *Parades and Changes* (128–29) and for more sketches of fountain notations from 1962 (135, Figures 83–84).

12. He does, however, admire the innovative work of Rudolf Laban in "Motation," 126–33, though more extensively in earlier drafts (see "Insert A" as part of a series of 1964 drafts included in a folder dedicated to Motation in the Lawrence Halprin Collection, The Architectural Archives, University of Pennsylvania, 014.I.A.6091 [hereafter cited as the Halprin Collection]). Rudolf Laban (1879–1958) studied architecture at L'Ecole des Beaux Arts and soon became interested in spatial dynamics of the moving body, sharing some parallel interests with Oskar Schlemmer. Laban was known for his unique use of the vertical staff to represent the body, a tool that Halprin adopts in Motation. Yet Laban's system is limited only to the movement of the body—its direction, timing, and simultaneous gestures of its many parts. Thus it lacked the capability to convey the body's shifting relationship to the environment.

13. "Motation," 126–28.

14. See Thiel, "Notes on the Description, Scaling, Notation, and Scoring of Some Perceptual and Cognitive Attributes of the Physical Environment," 594.

15. Since at the time (1967) Thiel was studying in Japan where landscape as sequenced approaches to temples or shrines or gardens of religious significance was an embedded cultural tradition, he proposed they consider a Japanese site. As he states in his letter: "Dear Larry, I'm spending a year in Japan in the further development of this space–sequence notation bit, and have found so far that interest here is very strong on this. Groups at Tokyo University, and at Tokyo Institute of Technology have both done a lot in using this tool: in highway planning, and in planning for new regional parks. It seems now that there are at least 7 systems in use: your 'Motation,' Lynch's, mine, Stuart Rose's, and 3 systems I have seen here! The thought has occurred to me that it would be worthwhile to all of us, in this healthy situation, to work up a direct comparison: that is, for each of us to notate the *same* sequence–environment. If I provided you with a detailed topo map and a set of wide-angle photos, would you be interested in writing out the notation in your system? A possible example I have in mind is part of the Tokyo Korakura Garden (see *Landscape Architecture*, July 1962, for an indication). Another possibility is a temple or shrine approach. Please let me have your feelings on this—Sincerely, Philip Thiel" (Halprin Collection, 014.I.A.6091; italics appear in the original). Divya Rao Heffley in her doctoral dissertation, *Vision in Motion: Architectural Space Time Notation and Urban Design, 1950–1970*, examines the work of Thiel, Halprin, and Lynch among others.

16. Though the architect Gordon Cullen does not propose a symbolic language to generate form, he uses sequential sketches and photography generatively to "mould the city into a coherent drama." In his book

Townscape (1961, 9–15), Cullen proposes this idea of "serial vision." Using the sequential method of recording progressive scenes throughout the city, he is able to propose manipulative ways to heighten the drama between the "existing view" and the "emerging view" by prolonging anticipation and juxtaposing contrasting spatial experiences, such as compression and release. The Halprin firm experimented with these sequential sketching techniques in their plans for Charlottesville's pedestrian mall in the 1970s (see Figure 6.11). Halprin would have known Cullen originally for his sketches in Tunnard's *Gardens in the Modern Landscape* (1938). Cullen's cartoonish drawings had obvious impact on Halprin's drawing style, particularly evident in the perspective illustrations of his early gardens.

17. In an article in *Progressive Architecture* entitled "Urbanography," (1966) the journal editors present further research attempts at the "notation of sequential experience in cities" by faculty within the architecture department of the University of Cincinnati. Two assignments by Samuel Noe, B. L. Abernathy, and Goetzman demonstrate the further development of the notational schemes of Halprin, Lynch, Thiel, and others to accommodate a full range of sensory stimuli and to use the process and symbolic language to design spatial sequences.

18. Landscape scholars and activists Anuradha Mathur and Dilip da Cunha harness representation techniques—drawing, modeling, etc.—as active agents of design. This is exemplified in their books *Mississippi Floods* (2001), *Deccan Traverses* (2006), and *SOAK: Mumbai in an Estuary* (2009). In April 2011, Mathur organized the "In the Terrain of Water" conference at the University of Pennsylvania, which was accompanied by an exhibition of designers, including Halprin, who use drawing (in mixed media) as a dynamic vehicle of creativity. James Corner's 1992 essay "Representation and Landscape: Drawing and Making in the Landscape Medium" introduced this idea into the theoretical discourse, citing Halprin as a point of reference.

19. Roszak, *Where the Wasteland Ends*, 400–4. McHarg's quotation is from *Design with Nature*, 29.

20. Cook, "Do Landscapes Learn?" 119–20. The influential 1953 textbook by Eugene Odum titled *Fundamentals of Ecology* perpetuates this paradigm. See McHarg's essay "Ecological Determinism."

21. Cook, "Do Landscapes Learn?" 118–21.

22. Description and photograph of the event are in Halprin, *The RSVP Cycles*, 91.

23. Halprin, in an essay entitled "The Artist and His/Her Community," part of the unpublished manuscript for the book called *The Environment as Art Experience*, compiled in July 1974 (Halprin Collection, 014.I.B.2302).

24. John Dewey distinguishes "the difference between the esthetic and the intellectual" by noting that "because of the comparative remoteness of his end, the scientific worker operates with symbols, words and mathematical signs. The artist does his thinking in the very qualitative media he works in, and the terms lie so close to the object that he is producing that they merge directly into it" (*Art as Experience*, 15–16).

25. Huyssen, "Mapping the Postmodern," 6.

26. Dewey, *Art as Experience*, 10.

27. Eco, *Opera Aperta* (1962), translated into English as *The Open Work* (1989). Michael Kirby makes the

distinction between indeterminacy and improvisation, which are both central parts of the "new theatre." As he explains, "Indeterminacy means that limits within which performers are free to make choices are provided by the creator of the piece: a range of alternatives is made available from which the performer may select" ("The New Theatre," 33).

1. THE CREATIVE ORIGINS OF LARRY AND ANNA HALPRIN

1. Ross, *Anna Halprin*, 38–40. The recollections about the trip abroad are from Ross's interview with Sydney Luria in November 2000.

2. Steinberg, interview with Larry Halprin, San Francisco, 1988. See also Halprin, *A Life Spent Changing Places*, 11–13, for his recollections of Arab wheat-harvesting rituals.

3. Quotation from July 10, 1992, interview with Ross, in *Anna Halprin*, 41. About the kibbutz experience, see Steinberg, interview with Larry Halprin, San Francisco, 1988; and Halprin, *A Life Spent Changing Places*, 26–31.

4. October 7, 1977, interview with Suzanne B. Riess, in *Thomas D. Church*, 727.

5. Steinberg, interview with Larry Halprin, San Francisco, 1988.

6. Quoted in Forgey, "Lawrence Halprin," 162.

7. Halprin, "Christopher Tunnard's Influence on Halprin," 466.

8. From Tunnard, *Gardens in the Modern Landscape*, 166; quoted in *Lawrence Halprin: Changing Places*, 10.

9. Halprin, "Christopher Tunnard's Influence on Halprin," 466.

10. Riess interview with Halprin, *Thomas D. Church*, 729.

11. See "The All-Europe House," 813–19.

12. After he joined Yale's city planning department, Halprin and Tunnard's views started to diverge. For instance, Halprin, in a book review of Tunnard and Boris Pushkarev's *Man-Made America: Chaos or Control?* (1963), praises the authors' broader view of the urban landscape and especially their attention to urban freeways, yet he criticizes the polar choice presented between "chaos or control." Halprin claims that the utopian quest for control actually "frightens" him. He calls the "green utopia" "sterile unto dullness, classical and formalistic in its order, uneventful and lacking in those tensions and diversities, freedoms of choice and contrasts, which in my view make for creative living . . . There are great virtues to be gained from recognizing the excitement of chance occurrence, of the value of what Tunnard and Pushkarev pejoratively call 'haphazard results' . . . [Environments] need to grow and evolve, sometimes haphazardly, in an organic way, so that they reflect our lives with all their variegations and conflicts and involvements. The notion that our choice is between 'chaos or control,' as stated in the subtitle of this important work (and the implication that chaos is all bad), is a choice I do not wish to make. What we need, I believe, for an exciting and creative environment, is both" (Halprin, "Over-Ordering the Environment," 180, 192, 194, 198).

13. See their collaborative essays appearing in *Architectural Record* in 1939–1940: "Landscape Design in the Urban Environment" (May 1939), "Landscape Design in the Rural Environment" (August 1939), and "Landscape Design in the Primeval Environment" (February 1940). Their theories emphasize rational

landscape planning and "dominance" and "control" by humans over their environment, thus differing significantly from Halprin's interest in humans' experience as part of the environment.

14. Ross interview with Halprin, August 1, 1995. Quoted in Ross, *Anna Halprin*, 52.

15. Riess interview with Halprin, *Thomas D. Church*, 730.

16. See Gropius's description of the "Total Theater" in his introduction to *The Theater of the Bauhaus*, 12.

17. Ibid., 8

18. Moholy-Nagy, "Theater, Circus, Variety," in *The Theater of the Bauhaus*, 60. "Gestaltung," implying the whole, was part of the everyday language of the Bauhaus.

19. See Moholy-Nagy, "The Mechanized Eccentric (Die mechanische Exzentrik)," and his ambiguous arguments on man's role in "The Theater of Totality," in his essay "Theater, Circus, Variety," 52–64.

20. Moholy-Nagy, "Theater, Circus, Variety," 67–68.

21. The quotation on "formation" is from a 1922 text reprinted in *The Thinking Eye*, 454. His comparison of form and Gestalt is from page 17.

22. The "Creative Credo," and *The Thinking Eye* more generally, also had direct impact on Edmund Bacon, who uses Klee's diagrams as a framework through which to interpret historical sources in his seminal study *Design of Cities* (47). For the garden design comparison and passage on multidimensional projections see pages 151–56 under the section "Synthesis of Spatio-plastic Representation and Movement." Klee's sketches dissecting two bars of Bach's Sonata no. VI are included in *The RSVP Cycles* (13) to, according to Halprin, enhance the expressive dimensionality of Bach's "controlling" score.

23. Ross, interview with Anna, March 12, 1994, *Anna Halprin*, 60–61.

24. Sibyl Moholy-Nagy, "Modern Art and Modern Dance," in *Impulse* (3–5), the annual dance magazine cofounded by Anna. Clearly the latter quotation was in direct response to her husband's work "The Mechanized Eccentric." Sibyl Moholy-Nagy is a fascinating art historian who wrote a biography of her husband, *Moholy-Nagy: Experiment in Totality* (1950; with a foreword by Gropius). Yet in the 1960s she fiercely criticized her husband's colleagues, including Gropius, for celebrating science and technology to the detriment of human values and urban experience. Her book *Matrix of Man* (1968), included in Halprin's bibliography for *The RSVP Cycles*, parallels Halprin's interests in urban structure, historic preservation, ecology, and participation.

25. Gropius, introduction to *The Scope of Total Architecture*, 15.

26. Gropius, "Education of Architects and Designers," in *The Scope of Total Architecture*, 51.

27. Ibid., 28.

28. Gropius, *The Scope of Total Architecture*, 146.

29. Ibid., 15.

30. Riess interview with Halprin, *Thomas D. Church*, 736–37.

31. Quoted in Ross, *Anna Halprin*, 68–69. April 1945 letter to "Julie," found in Papers of Anna Halprin, San Francisco Performing Arts Library and Museum.

32. Quotations from Anna Halprin in Kaplan, ed., *Anna Halprin, Moving Toward Life*, 73.

33. Duncan, *My Life*, 30, quoted in Starr, *Americans and the California Dream*, 383.

34. Lecture to the University of California Extension in San Francisco, December 10–12, 1957 (manuscript in the Halprin Collection, 014.I.A.5134).

35. Starr, *Americans and the California Dream*, 180.

36. Quoted in Ross, *Anna Halprin*, 71, from her interview with Daria Halprin, September 20, 1991.

37. Lewis Mumford, "The Architecture of the Bay Region," n.p.

38. Quoted in Ross, *Anna Halprin*, 72 (from Steinberg, interview with Larry Halprin, San Francisco, 1988).

39. Ross, *Anna Halprin*, 71.

40. See Halprin, "Angles for Economy," H13.

41. Riess interview with Halprin, *Thomas D. Church*, 740.

42. "A Garden Can Banish Subdivision Monotony," *House Beautiful* (March 1950), 78. The quotation is from Joseph Barry, "Free Taste: The American Style of the Future," *House Beautiful* (October, 1952), 178; quoted in Harris, "Making Your Private World," 202.

43. Church, "The Small California Garden," 17.

44. Riess interview with Halprin, *Thomas D. Church*, 741.

45. Halprin, interview with the author, February 14, 2008.

46. Eckbo, *Landscape for Living*, 1–2.

47. Ibid., 41–42, 238. To Halprin, design is related to "mysticism" or the myths and rituals of ancient and contemporaneous culture, which he and his wife attempted to elevate to art throughout their respective careers.

48. According to Marc Treib and Dorothée Imbert, Eckbo was also particularly impressed by the Tachard garden in La Celle-Saint-Cloud designed by Pierre-Emile Legrain in 1924. This garden's zigzag path became one of Eckbo's favorite design motifs (*Garrett Eckbo*, 22 and 24). For a comprehensive analysis of the 1925 exposition, see Imbert, *The Modernist Garden in France*.

49. Riess interview with Halprin, *Thomas D. Church*, 734.

50. Ibid., 751. In a later instance, Halprin, again praising the "brilliant" work of Burle Marx, describes the effect of this type of "painterly" work on the profession: "Roberto Burle Marx . . . exercised great influence on two dimensional patterning in America during the 50's and early 60's . . . In lesser hands his influence in America and elsewhere for that matter, has resulted in superficially decorative and overly complex parterres with very little organic relation to the landscape or relation to the functioning use of the landscape" (Halprin, "The Last 40 Years," 5).

51. Halprin, "Education for a Landscape Aesthetic," February 5, 1955, unpublished essay (Halprin Collection, 014.I.A.6099).

52. Dailey, "The Post-War House," n.p.

53. See Halprin, "Nature into Landscape into Art," 349; "Education for a Landscape Architect" (Halprin Collection, 014.I.A.6099); and Halprin's speech "The Human Community as an Ecosystem," presented to the AIA Northwest Regional Conference in Tacoma on September 9, 1963 (Halprin Collection, 014.I.A.6035).

54. Elizabeth Meyer, "Situating Modern Landscape Architecture," 21–31.

55. Tunnard, *Gardens in the Modern Landscape*, 106.

56. Halprin, *Cities*, 194.

57. Harris, "Thomas Church as Author," 161.

58. Riess interview with Halprin, *Thomas D. Church*, 752.

59. Halprin, "The Choreography of Gardens," 32–33. As early as July 1947, *Sunset* published an article by Halprin called "Good Theater in the Garden" in which he offers suggestions regarding how one might "set the stage" for entertaining "or just plain living" in the outdoors: "To use plants in a dramatic manner, to spotlight exceptional features, to introduce art forms are some of the good theater techniques. You can bring music to your garden stage with the trickle of water, bird songs, tinkle of glass bells. You can bring action with fountains, the flight of birds, or an open fire at night" (44–45).

60. Halprin, "Structure and Garden Spaces Related in Sequence," 95–103.

61. Halprin, "Dance Deck in the Woods," 24.

62. See the catalogue of Halprin's drawings for these early garden designs in Hirsch, "Lawrence Halprin."

63. This statement is according to the chronology in *Lawrence Halprin: Changing Places*, 117.

64. In Nilo Lindgren's 1971 article "Riding a Revolution," he describes Halprin's first assistants who became his associates, then principals: "Don Carter's strong architectural designs, Sat Nishita's soft and subtle designs, Jean Walton's work with living plants, Richard Vignolo's planning and design of urban complexes, all contributed to the firm's solid reputation. Later Sue Yung Li Ikeda [who joined the firm in 1959] brought a wider intellectual scope, keying in closely to Halprin's eternal seeking for new ideas, and Jerry Rubin [who also joined in 1959] brought a deep concern about the office administration" (48).

65. In 1952 he developed the Master Plan and Report for the University of California, Davis, and in 1953 he began the Landscape Master Plan for University of California, Berkeley (completed in 1960). See Temko's "'Planned Chaos' on the Piazza," and Halprin's response "Rebuttal: Chaos on the Piazza."

66. Hardwick, *Mall Maker*, 151. The latter quotation was originally taken from "A Break-Through for Two-Level Shopping Centers: Two-Level Southdale," *Architectural Forum* (December 1956).

67. Draft document from November 1968 on shopping centers by Halprin to Jim Burns, then editor of *Progressive Architecture*, for a possible article (Halprin Collection, 014.I.A5192). The following quotations in this paragraph are taken from the same document.

68. As Halprin explained: "It was the first time that gardens in the shopping centers became the major elements . . . Up until that time it was a series of buildings on both sides of a kind of narrow walkway. And there we centered the parks in between the buildings, and brought walkways in from parking and planted parking areas heavily" (Steinberg, interview with Larry Halprin, San Francisco, 1988).

69. Document from Halprin to Burns, November 1968 (Halprin Collection, 014.I.A.5192).

70. "Conversation with Lawrence Halprin, Urban Planner," 18. Halprin is probably this critical because he was then working on a downtown plan for Cleveland, which had suffered tremendously from middle-class flight to the suburbs. He is most likely being sensitive to his audience in order to sustain public and client relations.

71. See "New Standard of Quality in Urban Design Housing," *House & Home* (February 1964), 90–97.

72. As early as the 1950s, the firm, with architect Vernon DeMars, designed the low-income housing development called Easter Hill Village in Richmond, California. It was situated within an abandoned rock quarry; Halprin used the outcroppings to structure the development and imbue a sense of place-identity. By the 1970s, the development experienced significant decline, which was partially attributed to the design (see Marcus, *Easter Hill Village*).

73. Halprin, *Process Architecture*, 11–12.

74. Halprin, "The Human Community as an Ecosystem," presented to the AIA Northwest Regional Conference, in Tacoma, Washington, September 9, 1963 (Halprin Collection, 014.I.A.6035).

75. Lawrence Halprin & Associates, "Peacock Gap: A Preliminary Report on Its Oecological Development," for Draper Companies, 1960 (Halprin Collection, 014.I.B.2654).

76. Quotation in an article by Carol Nuckols, "Halprin Discusses Fort Worth, Design Ideas," *Fort Worth Star Telegram*, May 28, 1978 (unpaginated clipping in the Halprin Collection, 014.I.B.1317).

77. From the unpublished essay "The Sensuous Environment," which was discovered as part of an unpublished manuscript for a book entitled *The Environment as Art Experience* compiled in July 1974 (Halprin Collection, 014.I.B.2302).

78. Lindgren, "Riding a Revolution," 51. Unless otherwise indicated, this paragraph and the next references the Lindgren article.

79. *Lawrence Halprin & Associates: Our Office, Our Work*, "Philosophy & Process," c. 1972 (Halprin Collection library).

2. FRAMING CIVIC RITUALS

1. Halprin's manuscript for the 1960 IFLA conference can be found in the Halprin Collection, 014.I.A.6141 (italics in the original).

2. "Crisis of the Object: Predicament of Texture" is a chapter in Colin Rowe and Fred Koetter's *Collage City*, 50–85, in which they argue for the reintegration of the object back into its field, or the Modernist architectural monument back into the fabric of the existing city. Frampton's essay appeared in *Columbia Documents of Architecture and Theory*, 83–94. Many publications on landscape urbanism have emerged since the late 1990s. See, for instance, Waldheim, ed., *Landscape Urbanism Reader*. Camillo Sitte, it might be argued, was the real pioneer of such a view, but his *City Planning According to Artistic Principles* (1889) remains focused on aesthetics rather than on the operative potential of open space or the "field" as a structuring or organizational matrix.

3. Roy A. Rappaport, "Ritual," 255 (quoted in Ross, *Anna Halprin*, 158).

4. The following quotations are taken from this article, appearing in *Impulse* (1951): 1–2.

5. See www.planetarydance.org. The dance, established to reclaim Mt. Tamalpais after six women were murdered there from 1979 to 1981, was originally called *In and On the Mountain*. In 1985 it was renamed *Circle the Earth*, before it was renamed again.

6. *The RSVP Cycles*, 31. The quotation originated with Larry Halprin in 1962, in his "A Discussion of 'The

Five-Legged Stool,'" 3, in which he makes a similar statement as his opening remarks: "Today's performing artist profoundly wants a partnership which will involve the audience as much as himself. To do this he has had to go back to some of the fundamental principles of his art—back to its basic, ritualistic beginnings when men were simpler and art was only a sharpened expression of life."

7. Quotation from a page of Larry Halprin's notebook reproduced in *Notebooks: 1959–1971*, 127. For *Parades and Changes*, Subotnick introduced his "cell-block method," where each collaborating artist, musician, dancer, and lighting designer developed a numbered series of "sound actions, movement actions, light actions, environmental or sculptural actions in discrete thematic ideas called cell-blocks," which could be visually represented in a chart. The cell-blocks were intended to be entirely interchangeable so that selecting actions from the matrix would always yield different results (a description of Subotnick's involvement can be seen in *The RSVP Cycles*, 36; see also Ross, *Anna Halprin*, 181–88). This scoring methodology emphasized choice rather than pure chance or complete control, thus appealing to Larry, who defined creativity as "freedom of choice."

8. Halprin, *Taking Part*, 175, in chapter by Anna under the section "What Is Ritual?"

9. For a description by Anna on each of the "Myths," see "Mutual Creation," 163–75. The postcard announcement declared *Ten Myths* "an experiment in mutual creation."

10. Kaplan, ed., *Moving Toward Life*, 130–31.

11. Quote is from the undated (1970s) essay "The City as a Spiritual Center for Modern Myths and Rituals," found in the Papers of Anna Halprin, housed at the San Francisco Performing Arts Library and Museum, Box 3, Folder 1.

12. From "Nature into Landscape into Art," 350. The final quotation is from Joseph Campbell's *The Masks of God: Primitive Mythology*.

13. Halprin in "The Sensuous Environment," included in the unpublished manuscript for *The Environment as Art Experience* (1974).

14. Henderson, "Psychology and the Roots of Design," 70. The following quotations in this paragraph are from the same source.

15. Halprin, "The Collective Perception of Cities," 4.

16. *The RSVP Cycles*, 89–92 (italics in the original).

17. Halprin used the term "recycling" as distinguished from "preservation," which he considered resistant to future change rather than open to continuous adaptation.

18. See Halprin Collection, 014.I.A.6221 and 014.I.A.5910, for notes on the controversy, including Halprin's "Statement on the New Sculpture in the Fountain at Ghirardelli Square," summarized below. The historian Alison Isenberg has covered this controversy in fascinating depth, considering gender implications in particular. Apparently the abstract form that Halprin had in mind was a fifteen-foot "shaft" of metal, making those implications quite clear. See Isenberg, "'Culture-a-Go-Go.'"

19. "What to Do about Market Street? A Prospectus for a Development Program," prepared for the Market Street Development Project, an affiliate of the San Francisco Planning and Urban Research Association

(SPUR), by Livingston & Blayney, City and Regional Planning, in association with Lawrence Halprin & Associates and Rockrise & Watson, architects, and Larry Smith & Co., real estate consultants, October 1962. Halprin Collection, 014.I.A.1463.

20. Or, if construction limited this option, a series of seven-hundred-foot mezzanines radiating from the subway stations.

21. "What to Do about Market Street" and "Market Street Study, Draft #2, 29 August 1962" by Halprin and Don Ray Carter (Halprin Collection, 014.I.A.1463).

22. See *Market Street Design Plan, Summary Report* of November 6, 1967, for all illustrations and basic data.

23. The quotation "knit together all the various uses" is from the interviews with S. Steinberg in 1988. The street also linked corporate plazas at the bases of some of the new buildings along Market Street, including that at the foot of the Crown Zellerbach Building, built in 1959 by Skidmore, Owings & Merrill. The 1962 study heralded this project as "the finest development ever built on Market Street; its plaza is a precious gift to the City." The Yerba Buena Center development, a project Halprin worked on beginning in 1967, is also linked in to the hierarchical spine of Market Street (see Figure 2.3).

24. "California to Come," 72. Many currently argue for the dismantling of the fountain, since the freeway was demolished after its irreparable damage by the 1989 Loma Prieta earthquake. It serves as a curious memorial to the freeway now that it has lost its *raison d' être.*

25. See Halprin's "Statement to Sculptors" (1966), reproduced in *Cities*, 2nd edition, 228.

26. Temko, "The 'New' Market Street—An Unfulfilled Promise"; and Goldberger, "Will a 'New' Market Street Mean a New San Francisco?" C15.

27. Lawrence Halprin & Associates, "United Nations Plaza," found in the Halprin Collection, 014.I.A.5147, with note: "used for *Architectural Forum* article sent on 14 Feb 1973."

28. The project "fact sheet" states that "on the sidewalks the brick will be laid in a herringbone pattern, in the crosswalks, a running bond, and in the plazas, various patterns" with all gutters and curbs delineated by grey granite, See Transit Task Force, City & County of San Francisco, document from the "Office of the Project Manager," "Market Street Reconstruction, Fact Sheet" (Halprin Collection, 014.I.B.2968).

29. The existing Path of Gold lamp standards, installed during the 1898 Panama Pacific Exposition, were retained and refurbished.

30. According to the *Hennepin County History* bulletin featuring "The Nicollet Mall," "Nicollet Avenue has always been a parade street. In 1891 a gigantic parade spectacle was staged to celebrate that year's great harvest . . . This most important street was platted as an 80-foot-wide street, bordered on either side by a 15-foot wide sidewalk. In the past circus parades always used this great street; fire lads used to race their fire engines down the Avenue to display shiny-red new equipment; returning soldiers of the several wars—Spanish-American, First and Second World Wars—and Civil War veterans, all paraded here to the joy of 1000s of spectators! The greatest display of humanity on Nicollet Avenue . . . was the celebration of the end of WWI on Nov 11, 1918" (issued as a quarterly bulletin by the Hennepin County Historical Society, Summer 1968, 14, found in the Halprin Collection, 014.I.B.2978).

31. The other is the Student Union Plaza on Berkeley's campus recorded February 10, 1965, and included in Halprin's article "Motation" (see Figure I.5). The vertical track for this project is additionally keyed into a series of photographs showing sequential views. The photographs in this case include other people within the frame of view while the Motational sequence does not include moving objects.

32. In practical application, Halprin's Motational System, rather than beginning with abstract movement to generate form, essentially became a "testing-out device" in the early 1970s. Halprin claims these notations "allow us to see—in our mind's eye—possible changes in the environment before actually carrying them out. They are a way to test our innumerable alternate futures" ("Calligraphy as a Structuring Device" essay draft found in the Halprin Collection, 014.I.B.2479).

33. Nicollet Avenue, prior to the Downtown Council's formation in 1955, was actually performing fine, though it had just started to experience losses to suburban shopping centers. Most likely the project was such an immediate success partially due to the fact that the city, or its business people, did not allow its further deterioration before initiating the process. According to one article, "The impetus for this change came in the mid-1950's. At that time General Mills announced that it would move its headquarters from downtown Minneapolis to the suburbs, and a $20-million shopping center was opened in the outlying community of Edina. Astonished and troubled, leading businessmen formed the Downtown Council of Minneapolis, to find ways of keeping the city's core vital and prosperous" ("The Merchants' High Hopes in Minnesota," *Fortune*, June 1966, clipping in the Halprin Collection, 014.I.A.5934). Apparently, however, until this point the northern end of Nicollet Avenue had remained neglected as a marginal industrial and flophouse area, which had sparked the first phase of urban renewal in downtown Minneapolis through the construction of the four-acre Gateway Center. Photographs in the Halprin Collection documenting the preexisting condition of the street reveal a well-populated daytime environment overwhelmed with automobiles (Halprin Collection, 014.IV.A.105). The photographs capture a particular drabness in the wide, straight asphalt lined with parked cars and narrow concrete sidewalks. Apparently, most of the major shopping facilities had managed to stay contained on this one street throughout the city's development, including the department stores Dayton's, Donaldson's, J. C. Penney, Power's, Kresge's, and Woolworth's, as well as a large number of specialty shops, eateries, and offices.

34. "The Sensuous Environment" in *The Environment as Art Experience*, 1974 (Halprin Collection, 014.I.B.2302). Unfortunately, cities typically did not have the same budgets as private mall developers, yet, in this case, the mall was funded by property owners over a period of years and offered the unique opportunity for high-quality design.

35. Aschman, "Nicollet Mall," 4. The other caveat was that "the mall would be of top quality construction or not come into existence at all."

36. Sketches and notes from 1962 and 1963 pulled from Halprin's notebooks present his immediate impressions of existing conditions and ideas for intervention (reproduced in "Lawrence Halprin," *Process Architecture* [1978]).

37. Halprin's Nicollet Mall dedication speech (Halprin Collection, 014.I.A.5934). Halprin and his associates

reference Germany and Scandinavia as precedents in their notations on various schematic plans for the mall. In his speech, he also cites existing pedestrian malls in Copenhagen, Stockholm, Amsterdam, and Fresno (the latter of which was designed by Victor Gruen with Eckbo Dean Williams and dedicated in 1964). The walled city of Jerusalem had the most lasting effect on him. In his autobiography, he reflects on his endless walks there: "The entire walled city of Jerusalem was like a wonderful piece of theater . . . It was a pedestrian city devoted to the daily lives of its people" (88).

38. Halprin's interest in the separation of pedestrian and vehicle, despite its later indictment as a "Modernist" failure, is best illustrated by his love for Venice, a city that he references repeatedly throughout his career. For instance, in *Cities* he states: "Venice, centuries ago, established some of the principles of traffic separation we now realize are so important. The watery canals carry the traffic and service vehicles and the pedestrians and trees are on the ground" (17).

39. As early as September 1973, one reporter noted that the "popular acceptance of the first bridge, plus the increased rentals from the newly created second level, led to the construction of five more bridges, linking a total of 16 downtown buildings. The heated walkways are especially inviting during Minneapolis' cold winters, but an estimated 200,000 pedestrians use the 10 skyways *every* day. Although the skyways cost up to $300,000 each, current plans call for a total of 64 bridges connecting 54 blocks of the downtown CBD, virtually all by private financing" (Fruin, "Pedway Systems in Urban Centers," 64).

40. This development was part of the Gateway Center, which was Phase I of what was originally a "five phase program for renewal": Phase I: Gateway Center, Phase II: Nicollet Mall, Phase III: Hennepin Avenue (design studies by Halprin), Phase IV: Civic Center, Phase V: Convention Center (see Martin, "Exciting Start with Nicollet Mall").

41. See the section "Transportation Characteristics" in "The Nicollet Avenue Mall & Transitway—General Description" found in the Halprin Collection, 014.I.B.2979. All cross streets would carry normal traffic, but only public buses (in addition to service vehicles and occasional taxis) would be permitted on the length of the mall.

42. Published in "Lawrence Halprin," *Process Architecture* (1978), 121.

43. Tom Brown quoted in "Downtown Minneapolis' Urban Renaissance," 28.

44. "The Design of Nicollet Mall" draft document (Halprin Collection, 014.I.A.5934).

45. Though Halprin never cited Kevin Lynch, this insertion of orienting "landmarks" might be situated in the context of Lynch's *The Image of the City* (1960). Lynch reported that urban residents understood their surroundings in consistent and predictable ways, forming "mental maps" with five basic elements (paths, edges, districts, nodes, and landmarks), which, when arranged appropriately, increase human ability to see and remember patterns.

46. Though each block was granted its "special feature," nothing along the mall was given particularly monumental treatment despite the extravagant materials used (in early drawings, each "feature" was situated on top of a base or pedestal). Halprin scored an even rhythm along the eight blocks to establish continuity and encourage movement along the mall's full length.

47. Halprin Collection, 014.I.A.2979. Halprin makes the same statement in "The Design of Nicollet Mall" draft document (Halprin Collection, 014.I.A.5934).

48. See photographs by Paul Ryan in the Halprin Collection, 014.IV.A.105–106. See the section "The Floor of the City" in *Cities*, 93–94.

49. *Hennepin County History* bulletin, 8, 14

50. "The Design of Nicollet Mall" draft document (Halprin Collection, 014.I.A.5934).

51. Dedication speech manuscript (Halprin Collection, 014.I.A.5934).

52. For instance, Halprin considered the police and firecall boxes, mailboxes, and signal controllers incompatible with his comprehensive "master plan" and had them relocated to the side streets. In addition, he allowed phone booths in bus stops only. See his notes reproduced in "Lawrence Halprin," *Process Architecture* (1978), 121.

53. According to O. D. Gay, executive vice president of the Downtown Council, quoted in Wright, "Mall Stirs Downtown Minneapolis Revival," 43, 45.

54. Amundsen quoted in Christianson, "Nicollet Mall Redux," 30.

55. Amundsen, "Tomorrow's Nicollet Mall," 36.

56. Amundsen, "The New Nicollet Mall, 70.

57. Christianson, "Nicollet Mall Redux," 30, 32. The quotations following are from this article.

58. Though significant funds were raised by the Bicentennial Committee, the city still had to depend on federal grants, in addition to generous contributions from the Amon Carter Foundation and the Sid Richardson Foundation (according to Steve Blow, "We're One Hurdle Away from Park on Bluffs," 5). By 1974, the city was waiting for a federal grant to provide half the projected $1.2 million needed for the park. By 1979, nearly 80 percent of what was ultimately a $2 million budget was paid by private contributions primarily from these two sources (according to Svacina, "It Began Here, Pilgrim, Nearly Finished Park Honors Pioneers").

59. According to Pat Svacina ("It Began Here, Pilgrim"), the water that directs the visitor's experience within the site was pumped from the Trinity River.

60. Ruth Carter Stevenson, Amon Carter Sr.'s daughter, played a major role in the development of the committee. The Carter Foundation was, and still is, active in local philanthropy, with particular focus on the arts and culture. The foundation has historically commissioned the best designers from all over the country to work on the projects they were funding. For example, Phillip Johnson designed the Amon Carter Museum, which opened in 1961. The Carter Foundation has also historically funded parks in the Fort Worth system, including Heritage Park and Philip Johnson's Water Garden.

61. Halprin was commissioned for this study by the Fort Worth City Center Sector Planning Council and the City of Fort Worth. *The Fort Worth Central Business District Sector Report* was released in October 1971 (Halprin Collection, 014.box.362).

62. The levee system really began as early as 1910, but after a devastating flood in 1949 the Fort Worth Floodway program, established by the Army Corps of Engineers and the Tarrant County Water Control and

Improvement District no. 1, channeled the West and Clear forks and expanded and strengthened the levee system.

63. See documents by Lawrence Halprin & Associates, as part of the "resource-gathering" phase, entitled "Fort Worth Studies," including "Why the Gruen Plan Failed." This list is followed by a document entitled "Fort Worth Studies, Gruen Plan, Comments on Report" that summarizes and criticizes it (Halprin Collection, 014.I.A.4162). See also "A Preliminary Study for Fort Worth, Texas, Prepared by Lawrence Halprin & Associates" by the "Design Team" of associates: Alexander Cuthbert, George McLaughlin, and Felix Warburg, who also comment on the Gruen Plan. Documentation from Halprin Collection, 014.I.B.2603. For an assessment of the Gruen plan, see Jacobs, *The Death and Life of Great American Cities*, 344–45.

64. See the document "Outline of Steps for Implementation of the Six Major Projects Selected by the Sector Council" generated by Lawrence Halprin & Associates, located in the Halprin Collection, 014.I.A.4163, as well as the "6 immediate action programs" listed in the "City Center Design for Fort Worth" brochure found in the archives of Historic Fort Worth, Inc. The report describes both the Long Range Growth Framework and the Short Range Growth Program, or "action program," which was instituted to act as the "stimulus, incentive and direction for private and public investment in Fort Worth's future" (5–12).

65. The "Intermediate and Long-Range Programs" listed in the brochure include Transit Systems, Open Spaces, Residential Development along the bluffs, and Trinity River Development, meaning the full implementation of Halprin's Trinity River Report.

66. CBD report, 12.

67. Trinity River report, 19, and "City Center Design for Fort Worth" brochure. At the current plaza site, now to the west of the viaduct, the CBD plan included a proposed Riverfront Residential Development of "a variety of clustered and courted townhouses, rowhouses, patio houses, terrace houses, and medium rise apartments" (87).

68. Through the current development campaign called the Trinity River Vision many of Halprin's ideas are finally being implemented, such as the development of an urban lake, increased recreational opportunities along the river, and the encouragement of downtown businesses to turn to face the river and embrace it.

69. "Building the River Dream, Bit by Bit," 1. Regarding the 1973 Mayfest, see "Mayfest and Park Make Happy Pair," 6-C; Lawrence Halprin & Associates, "Fort Worth: A City Rediscovers Its River" (Halprin Collection, 014.I.A.4159); and "Halprins to Assist in Festival Activities," 6F. See the photograph of dancers around the Maypole in the Halprin Collection, 014.IV.A.42.

70. Letter from July 11, 1970. See Blow, "We're One Hurdle Away from Park on Bluffs" (Letters from Streams and Valleys Committee, Halprin Collection, 014.I.A.4172).

71. Therefore, when Lawrence Halprin & Associates disbanded in 1976, much of the correspondence indicates there was confusion regarding whom Fort Worth officials should consult. In spite of this, CHNMB seems to have been the primary contact after the breakup. Perhaps due to this final confusion, little

reference to this design exists in the Halprin Collection. In a report summary titled "Meeting with Lawrence Halprin concerning the Heritage Park Plaza and Fountain Design," April 1, 1976, with the participants Lawrence Halprin, Ruth Johnson, Phyllis Tilley, Poly Phillips, James Toal, Jack Tuomey, and Uria Lester, it is stated: "Mr. Halprin sketched out a plaza concept which he envisioned appropriate for the bluff overlook area. In summary, his sketch included a series of plaza levels with a sequence of water cascades running along and down the various plaza levels" (see slide B-J432 of Halprin's initial sketch in the Halprin Collection slide collection). The short document in its entirety was extremely informative in understanding how Halprin became involved in the project. A local engineering firm, Carter & Burgess, Inc., had initially proposed a design that Halprin rejected. The engineering firm eventually became the local consultants to Halprin's design. This document can be found in the City of Fort Worth Parks and Community Services Department's files on Heritage Park. Another city document from James Toal to Jack Graham, public works director, dated January 25, 1977, with the subject heading "Heritage Park—Phase II Plaza Design and Engineering Work," conveys Halprin's specific role in design: "Lawrence Halprin ["the person"] shall perform design development, design supervision and design critique at the *conceptual* and *detailed levels* of the project. The contract with Carter and Burgess and Halprin and Associates [what eventually became Carter Hull Nishita McCulley Baxter (CHNMB)] should reflect Lawrence Halprin's involvement as stated above, however, the contract need not be a three party contract" (Halprin Collection, 014.I.B.1255).

72. See Halprin, *Cities*, 11. The Water Gardens and adjacent Convention Center were placed right on top of what was once the city's red-light district, "Hell's Half Acre," which made saloons, brothels, casinos, and dance halls available to cowboys passing through along the historic Chisholm Trail that led to meat markets in the north. The redevelopment of this area was meant to erase this aspect of the city's fabric and history. Though the city did not want to perpetuate this seedy component of its identity, it is now trying to economically capitalize on its image as "Cowtown" through such caricatured tourist attractions as the stockyards. By scraping Hell's Half Acre, however, it erased a significant chapter of this history. Of course, the redevelopment was encouraged by Halprin himself in his 1970 plan, which praised the progress of the Water Gardens and played a role in the then-evolving image of the city from "Cowtown" to "Nowtown."

73. In an e-mail Junji Shirai actually calls the pavilion a "water temple" (May 8, 2010, e-mail to blogger with name "Durango Texas," reprinted on the blog on May 9, 2010, under the heading "The Demise of Heritage Park in Fort Worth Texas" http://durangotexas.blogspot.com/2010/05/demise-of-heritage-park-in-fort-worth.html).

74. As is additionally noted by the designer and critic Kevin Sloan. Because these drawings demonstrate the firm's interest in quality of experience, Sloan claims that "today, when image is everything and experience counts for very little, these drawings are vivid reminders of a time when the experience of a place was more highly valued in the design of public spaces" ("Second Man Missing,"85). According to the Cultural Landscape Foundation's website, the dedication-day program for the park states that "it is a pilgrimage site, visited by those who pursue understanding of the city's founding and origins. The

opportunity to experience the spirituality of the site in solitude intensifies the power of the environment" (http://www.tclf.org/landslide/2008/heritage/history3.html; accessed November 18, 2008).

75. This information is based on a letter dated August 5, 1976, from Sat Nishita to Presten M. Geren, chairman of the Streams and Valleys Committee (City of Fort Worth Parks and Community Services Department, Heritage Park files).

76. Quotations from *Trinity River Report*, 17, and 7. The plant was recently acquired by Tarrant County College as part of the Trinity River Vision; the implosion of the stacks by the new owner seriously undermined the commemorative park's historic viewshed.

77. Sloan, "Second Man Missing," 84. The article includes comparative photographs of the site's trestle bridge and stockyard structures.

78. See, for instance, the August 5, 1976, letter from Sat to Presten Geren, Chairman of the Streams and Valleys Committee, indicating that Mr. Bradford of Curtis and Burgess had "chauffer[ed] me around to see the many points of interest" (Halprin Collection, file unknown).

79. Saucer magnolias (*Magnolia soulangiana*) (grown as multistemmed shrubs) were originally planted in front of the terminal grotto, once enclosing the intimate space within. The plants, however, either died or the space they enclosed was considered unsafe, and they were pulled out. These magnolias are pictured in Svacina, "It Began Here Pilgrim."

80. See the "Light/Sun Score," "Sound Score," "Images Score," and "Activities Score" Halprin derived as "Motation Scores for FDR Experience" on July 5, 1975, reproduced in *Sketchbooks of Lawrence Halprin*, 90.

81. See Jung, "Approaching the Unconscious," 95.

82. This quotation and those above are from the July 1, 1976, document "Heritage Park/Related Fort Worth Facts for NBC" (Halprin Collection, file unknown).

3. DESIGNING WITH NATURE AS "ARCHETYPAL PRECEDENT"

1. Cage and Cunningham, as early as the 1940s, experimented with the idea of chance in relation to the indeterminacy of life. Working independently at first, each would overlay the autonomously constructed dance and music, producing unpredictable collisions. Cunningham applied the *I Ching* text quite literally by using random methods similar to the casting of yarrow sticks to decide how to sequence his choreography. Though Anna was strongly influenced by Cunningham, who appears in published photographs performing on the Halprins' Dance Deck (see Figure 1.2), she remained skeptical of such external chance procedures. In a 2001 interview with her biographer, Janice Ross, Anna states: "I thought with Merce and John it's so odd to throw the dice or I Ching to make a decision—why torture it? All you have to do is sit on my deck and feel nature" (November 15, 2001, interview; quoted in Ross, *Anna Halprin*, 237–38).

2. *The RSVP Cycles*, 26.

3. Quotation from Halprin, "Nature into Landscape into Art," 243. See also Halprin, "The Gardens of the High Sierra."

4. *Sketchbooks of Lawrence Halprin*, 20.

5. Essay located in the Halprin Collection, 014.I.B.2479.

6. Halprin, "The Shape of Erosion," 87–88.

7. Amirkhanian's comments from *KPFA Folio* on "Serenade II Janice Wentworth" of 1967–68, which he developed with Ted Greer, are included in *The RSVP Cycles*, 14–15. KPFA is a progressive listener-supported Bay Area radio station. Amirkhanian was the main composer for the San Francisco Dancers' Workshop performance piece called *Ceremony of Us* (1968). See the 1990 interview with Charles Amirkhanian published in Zurbrugg, ed., *Art, Performance, Media*, 17–23 (see pages 19–20 for his descriptions of collaborations with Ted Greer).

8. *The RSVP Cycles*, 14.

9. The former quotation is from *Cities*, 11, and the latter is from "Nature into Landscape into Art," 354.

10. "Wildness" is a term that Halprin defines in his essay "Wildness as Art," in the unpublished manuscript *The Environment as Art Experience* of 1974 (Halprin Collection, 014.I.B.2302). He begins: "Wildness or wild nature, if you will, *is* where we can perceive the pure world and react to it in a state unmodified as yet by our technological changes. It is the last pure stronghold on earth of '*what is*,' without *our* value system imposed . . . 'Wildness' is a state of being . . . an effable quality existing in those places in our world in which humans have not made changes . . . in which natural forces have created all that exists without our intervention. It is not nature but 'nature unaffected by humans' that creates the quality of wildness. Wildness is different than wilderness—wilderness is a place, an area, a situation in which wildness may exist. Wildness is the quality, the experience, the essence of wilderness . . . Everything we are has origins in wildness. And only there can we see *undisturbed process at work*."

11. *Sketchbooks of Lawrence Halprin*, 30–31.

12. "Nature into Landscape into Art," 352.

13. See the 1968 notebook page reproduced in Gragg, ed., *Where the Revolution Began*, 16.

14. Halprin, *Cities*, 134.

15. See, for instance, Craig Wollner, John Provo, and Julie Schablitsky's "A Brief History of Urban Renewal in Portland, Oregon" (August 2001), 6, in which they cite a 1962 promotional flyer issued by the Bureau of Buildings distributed to property owners entitled "Meet Creepy Blight."

16. It was so named because the Civic Auditorium was just north of its original boundaries. This original project area was bounded by SW Market Street, SW Harbor Drive, SW Arthur Street, and SW Fourth Avenue. By 1965, the South Auditorium Urban Renewal Area had expanded to include the Civic Auditorium (as Area II). See South Auditorium Urban Renewal Project Area I & II issued by PDC on November 22, 1965 (Halprin Collection, 014.I.A.4998).

17. See PDC, *South Auditorium Redevelopment Plan*, September 29, 1961, amended plan.

18. Huxtable, "In Portland, Ore., Urban Decay Is Masked by Natural Splendor," 39, 75.

19. Huxtable, "Critic Lauds Auditorium Forecourt," 1. This article also appeared in the *New York Times* on the same day with the title "Coast Fountain Melds Art & Environment."

20. The Design Advisory Council consisted of a board of design experts whose function was to be available for consultation on proposals submitted by developers for "Portland's urban renaissance," as well as

more general design policy issues for the city. The group, formed in 1962, then included Pietro Belluschi of Boston, Paul Hayden Kirk of Seattle, and George Rockrise of San Francisco. Halprin was recommended most aggressively by Rockrise, since the two had collaborated successfully together since the late 1940s on gardens, including the Donnell Garden, and later on larger projects, including Market Street in San Francisco.

21. See the June 11, 1963, letter from Kenward to Halprin found in the Halprin Collection, 014.I.A.2087, and the contract documents found in 014.I.A.2088. David Thompson was retained as the "resident landscape architect."

22. Lawrence Halprin & Associates, *South Auditorium, Portland, Oregon*, prepared for the PDC. While this report is undated, all original drawings for it are dated November 1963 (Halprin Collection, 014.I.B.2656).

23. *Sketchbooks of Lawrence Halprin*, 60–61 (italics and capitalization in the original). These two pages were clearly generated *after* the firm's interventions in Portland. The whole graphic sequence is presented on pages 60–72 and is predominantly composed of selected process documents from Halprin's sketchbooks. They have been cleaned up and colored for the 1981 publication.

24. See also the project description included in "Lawrence Halprin," *Process Architecture*, in which he states that the malls were the most important part of the project: "They are a progression of walkways, fountains, little places to sit, benches, plazas—I think that all cities based on this principle would become beautiful cities . . . It is what in my view a whole city should be like" (67).

25. Halprin, *Cities*, 2nd edition, 232–33.

26. See the drawings in the Halprin Collection, 014.II.A.144–151. Though the built paths remain relatively straight and unobstructed, a few early schematic drawings for the master plan include a sculpted "water wall" around which pedestrians would have to move to reach lateral steps to the continuing path, thus diversifying movement. In the firm's early master plan, the malls are punctuated by sculptures and other focal points and the full extension of Montgomery Street Mall, which crosses the east length of Pettygrove Park (or "North Park"), follows a serpentine progression ultimately extending east to a recreation grounds on Block J also planned by the firm.

27. Along Second Avenue, one brick crosswalk over Lincoln Street was intended to link the open space within the private residential and motel development on Block C (south of Lincoln Street) to the block containing Lovejoy Plaza. Block C, bounded by Stadium Freeway, SW First Avenue, and SW Fourth Avenue, was zoned for a motel to the west of an extended Second Avenue Mall and for apartments to the east of it in the urban renewal plan as updated through the consultation by SOM (September 29, 1961, and adopted October 18, 1961).

28. Halprin's experimentation with capturing the essence of a natural watercourse and its source began in the private garden in the late 1950s. In one drawing in 1959 for the Dollar residence in Marin, for instance, he situates a series of local boulders at the peak of the upper garden and notes "water to gush from among rocks." See "Preliminary Garden Plan, Mr. and Mrs. Jack Dollar," June 22, 1959 (Halprin Collection, 014.II.A.43).

29. The source fountain was actually built after Lovejoy Plaza, according to Randy Gragg, ed., *Where the*

Revolution Began, 9. In Halprin's landscape master plan for the redevelopment area, he had situated a similar such fountain not off Lincoln Street but within the "quiet residential square" at the end of College Avenue Mall, which was a "short one-block long pedestrian way leading from a major traffic street." For this proposed fountain, "the stone floor of the square abruptly rises into a mound from which squirts a pencil-thin water jet." Therefore, one may question whether the firm originally intended the source fountain to be located off the "major traffic street" of Barbur Boulevard and Fourth Avenue (in a more topographically suitable position at the base of the hills to the southwest), as a transitional space from the disquieting urban environment into the introverted experience of the superblocks. Once one reached this "pencil-thin water jet," the visitor would have been forced, by lack of any other choice, to turn left along the Third Avenue Mall, which leads to the apex of the elaborate fountain proposed for what became Lovejoy Plaza.

30. The "Portland Downtown Plan" of 1972 refers to this type of shopping area as "convenience retailing" (See Portland City Planning Commission, "Planning Guidelines—Portland Downtown Plan," 22).

31. The few shops that do exist in this southeast portion of the development face the external street (First Street) and are fronted by a surface parking lot. The area, otherwise, is filled with small offices.

32. Halprin writes that "both sites sloped at an angle across the space more than 20 feet . . which gave us an initial impetus for FALLING WATER and dropping planes" (capitalization in the original). Because Kepes was particularly impressed with Halprin's *The RSVP Cycles*, he invited Halprin to contribute an essay to his edited book, *Arts of the Environment*. The intended essay was entitled "The Interface of Nature and Man," according to one letter from the publisher pressuring Halprin to complete it. The material Halprin provides to the publisher, however, is a series of handwritten notes including this personal letter to Kepes (correspondence in the Halprin Collection, 014.I.A.5095). Kepes, who was impacted by the Berlin-based development of Gestalt psychology, authored *Language of Vision* (1944) while teaching at the new Bauhaus in Chicago, asserting that "visual communication is universal and international; it knows no limits of tongue, vocabulary, or grammar, and it can be perceived by the illiterate as well as by the literate" (13; a notion clearly appealing to Larry). Kepes wrote a series of books called "Vision and Value" (1965–66), including *The Nature and Art of Motion*, and in 1967 he founded the Center for Advanced Visual Studies at MIT where he collaborated with Kevin Lynch. This information is included to demonstrate the understandable professional alliance between Halprin and Kepes. Information on Kepes is from Heffley, *Vision in Motion*.

33. Halprin was working on the Sea Ranch with Charles Moore and his firm Moore & Turnbull simultaneous to his work in Portland. Because he knew that Moore had written his dissertation, "Water in Architecture," as a historical survey tracing the use of water to shape the experience of place, Halprin invited Moore to participate in the design of the "South Park" fountain. The fountain, as many critics have noted, embodies a kind of hybrid between the monumental fountains of Italian public squares and rugged mountain topography. Halprin recalls repeatedly showing Moore images of High Sierra rock forms and watercourses, clearly indicating what he had in mind (Gragg, "Urban Plazas that Set Portland's Modern Landscape Get some TLC," A1). In "Portland's Plaza: It's Like Wow" the author

claims that "while the designers were working on the fountain, they were subjected to countless slides of water formations in the mountains, until the way water acts in nature became almost subliminal with them."

34. Moore, "Still Pools and Crashing Waves," 22. Moore continues: "There was only one part of the design that (probably fortunately) he didn't persuade them to accept: originally, after the water had cascaded to the lower level and had flowed between stepping stones that were meant to let participants walk out into the middle of things, it swept around the lower basin into a swirling whirlpool straight out of Edgar Allan Poe. It was feared by the clients that this exciting maelstrom might suck up every detached infant in Portland, and it subsequently became a pool of quiet water. Probably just as well" (22).

35. *The RSVP Cycles*, 58.

36. In "Portland's Plaza: It's Like Wow," the author claims: "[The] fountain and plaza . . . has turned on the entire hippie population of Portland and not a few of its over-30 inhabitants. They treat it as a public place should be treated, reveling in it, eating in it, making music in it, resting in it, being loose and open and free in it, even getting married in it, as a hippie couple did last summer. This free behavior does not go down well with everyone, needless to say, particularly some of the inhabitants of the buttoned-down SOM-designed apartment buildings that form an up-tight backdrop to the fountain, plaza, and Moore-Turnbull pavilion. Inaccurately considering the plaza their front yard, some of these citizens have sought surcease from hippiedom at City Hall, with, we are happy to report, small success (an evening curfew in the park was imposed). With any luck, when architects get here in June [for the AIA conference], the place will still be swinging and alive" (164).

37. Lyndon, "Concrete Cascade in Portland," 78.

38. "Living rituals" was apparently a term coined by Halprin and printed in the article "Water Plaza" in *Architectural Review*.

39. Halprin Collection, 014.I.A.2115. Most of the letter's contents were printed in "Portland's Plaza: It's Like Wow." The firm's office files (Halprin Collection, 014.I.B.3003) also include a poem written for the cover of the Lewis & Clark College newspaper, celebrating the life-giving qualities of the fountain (see St. John, "The Fountain").

40. See Gragg, ed., *Where the Revolution Began*, 9 (quotation from Bowes taken from "Portland Council Rewrites Park Curfew Ordinance," *Oregonian*, August 23, 1963).

41. Halprin, *Cities*, 2nd edition, 232–33. Maples, beeches, sweetgums, tulip trees, lindens, cherries, saucer magnolias, northern catalpas, and Japanese zelkovas forested the mounds along with a sprinkling of other species, while rhododendrons and azaleas contributed to the shrub layer at the park's perimeter. See "North Park Irrigation & Planting Plan," dated February 22, 1965, Halprin Collection, 014.II.A.144–151.

42. Benches are interspersed within the mounded knolls. At the end of the more primary approach to Pettygrove Park along the Second Avenue Mall, Halprin situated a simple circular fountain basin for the later placement of sculpture (the bronze "Dreamer" by Manuel Izquierdo was commissioned by the PDC in

1979). The drawings in the master plan document indicate that the full development of the proposed park would have required more funding and attention than it was evidently given. Proposed pavilions on the northwest would have balanced the fountain and anticipated sculpture to the southeast. A children's play area, which was centrally located, would have enlivened the space and would have fit well into the park's protective enclosure, which was predominantly composed of residences. Additionally in the landscape master plan document, the firm originally intended for the Montgomery Street Mall to continue east from this plaza in rounded serpentine curves to a pedestrian bridge over Front Avenue and into Block J, which was planned to serve as a traditional recreation grounds with prescriptive programs like tennis, handball, and swimming but never materialized. The design of this "leftover" space, situated between a major downtown traffic artery and a freeway near the riverfront, also integrated mounds and curvilinear paths, continuing the themes of Pettygrove.

43. For instance, in the Woerner Garden, designed in 1951–52 in the hills of Marin County, he created different material effects to generate a more "varied garden choreography." Two such spaces defined the opposing qualities of the garden "edge" (see Halprin, "Hill Garden," 99).

44. See his description of the SOM proposal in an "Interview with Dennis Buchanan" with Ernie Bonner of Urbsworks, Inc., transcribed on July 30, 2001, in a memo to Marcy McInelly, also of Urbsworks, Inc. (Halprin Collection, 014.I.C.1595).

45. According to John Kenward in an interview with Ernie Bonner also transcribed on July 30, 2001, in the same memo.

46. By 1967, Halprin had completed the document "Report to Mrs. Lyndon B. Johnson's Committee for a More Beautiful Capital," which was predominantly concerned with the East Capitol Area of low-rise, low-income housing and business. Its only criticism regarded Halprin's heavy hand in design: "One of the possible drawbacks of the proposal to Mrs. Johnson's committee, were it to be adopted and implemented in toto . . . is that it would leave so little possibility for undesigned chance. Practically every aspect of open urban space is examined and suggested for improvement" (see Burns, "Positive Proposals on 'Beauty,'" 178; Burns actually later joined the Halprin firm). Finally, as Richard Lakeman, head of urban design for the City of Portland from 1967 to 1973, claimed: "Ira Keller (ironic) wanted the site to be a taxi circle for the Auditorium and did not want a public park. John Kenward was really the shrewd and political fellow who made it all happen as it stands today" (as part of the series of interviews done and transcribed by Ernie Bonner on June 30, 2001, in his memo to Marcy McInelly).

47. Halprin Collection, Portland office files: 014.I.A.2085–2123.

48. Bonner interview with Kenward.

49. Halprin, *Cities*, 2nd edition, 232–33.

50. Engels, "L. Halprin: 'Tomorrow's Architect,'" 12.

51. Danadjieva studied architecture at the State University in Sofia, Bulgaria, and at the École Nationale Supérieure des Beaux-Arts. Quotation from Danadjieva, "Seattle's Freeway Park II," 405. Halprin himself had long demonstrated an interest in film as a way of both designing and recording landscape. In his

article "Motation" he uses sequential photographic stills to depict processional movement, while one year later, in *Freeways*, he claims: "Motion picture techniques are an obvious and very useful tool and should be widely used" (23). Danadjieva sometimes refers to herself as Angela Danadjieva Tzvetin while she was married to Ivan Tzvetin.

52. According to a January 2009 conversation with John Beardsley, author of "Being in Space," in Gragg, ed., *Where the Revolution* Began, 31.

53. See the various photos of ballerinas in the Forecourt Fountain in "Portland . . . a City for the Good Life," issued by the PDC for the Department of Development and Civic Promotion of the city of Portland, c. December 1972 (Halprin Collection, 014.I.B.3002). See also "Lawrence Halprin," *Process Architecture*, 179, for an image of what looks like a musical performance in front of the fountain, which has been turned off for the performers to be heard. In September 2008, the fountain sequence was again enlivened through a performance event entitled "The City Dance of Lawrence & Anna Halprin," funded by the National Endowment for the Arts and the Oregon Arts Commission (event brochure, http://www .tclf.org/pioneers/halprin_citydance/index.htm; accessed June 2009). The firm considered acoustics and theatrical lighting both for the structured performances and to enhance the evening drama of the space itself as Performance (P). The cascading water and twisted pines were originally uplit and underwater lights illuminated the pools and falls so that the water would glow through the surrounding darkness, producing an ethereal effect. The Portland Auditorium Forecourt "Fact Sheet" lists the equipment as follows: "221 mercury vapor & incandescent lights for trees & water areas, plus 20 pole-mounted spots and floods. Programmed sequence with multiple dimmers & cross connected sys for theatrical lighting" (Halprin Collection, 014.I.A.2115). See also the nighttime photographs reproduced in "Portland . . . a City for the Good Life," n.p. (Halprin Collection, 014.I.B.3002); "Portland's Walk-In Waterfall," 57; and Von Eckardt, "A Beautiful Plaza, Designed for Fun," 54.

54. See photograph with railings drawn in 1971 (Halprin Collection, 014.I.A.2118). The firm had ingeniously dealt with the safety codes of the day, which required a thirty-six-inch barrier at each ledge, by situating the thirty-six-inch-deep pools on the highest precipices.

55. "Portland's Walk-In Waterfall," 58.

56. Lawrence Halprin Landscape Conservancy, "Where the Revolution Began: Lawrence Halprin and the Reinvention of Portland Public Space," generated to distribute during the NEA-funded "City Dance" event (September 2008). The Forecourt was thus immediately embraced by a wide spectrum of the Portland community—from children and hippies to local office workers and top city officials. A series of citizen-motivated rejuvenation campaigns have since been generated around Auditorium Forecourt, which was renamed Ira Keller Fountain in 1972 when the first chairman of the PDC finished his term. In 1972, for instance, the Committee to Save the Fountain formed when a high-rise development adjacent to the park threatened to cast shadows over it for most of the day. In June 8, 1972, Bruce R. Bonine, the architect of the Committee to Save the Fountain, wrote to the Halprin firm requesting a statement. In "Lawrence Halprin's Position Statement" response he states: "The design execution of the Portland Fountain was an intense effort we performed for the people of Portland. It now belongs to them! It is

vital that they *now* take the lead in preserving this unique gift they received . . . Naturally, I am upset, not only about the shadow pattern, which diminishes usability of the plaza; there is also a moral and ethical issue involved. The developers are benefiting from the resource of a public amenity. They had not contributed in the effort of bringing about the fountain and plaza, but they are capitalizing on it. They owe the public a great deal! In addition, I oppose the arrogant lack of concern for the visual environment. The two buildings are using the Forecourt as foreground to enhance themselves, but not relating to it as an element of enclosure for this magnificent urban space; the relation of the building bases to the Forecourt is not resolved, and only detract from it" (correspondence from the Halprin Collection, 014.I.A.5129. See also "Oregonians Fight to Save Fountain," 27, in which Halprin is quoted as saying, "The fountain has been recognized throughout the world as one of the most important urban things in recent times. It deserves special attention, should have its own space and should not be just a frieze for a large building"). Though Halprin participated in the struggle, the condominium tower, called Portland Plaza, was erected on the west block and remains one of the tallest buildings in the city, benefiting greatly from the public amenity at its base. In the 1990s, a businessman and property owner, John Russell, initiated another campaign for the rejuvenation of the park. For this campaign, Halprin inspected the park in its twenty-year maturity, and developed the report "Ira Keller Fountain: Recapturing the Magic" (see his notes and this January 1992 report in the Halprin Collection, 014.I.B.1501). Efforts to achieve his recommendations continue by the Halprin Landscape Conservancy, which is dedicated to all three parks with particular focus on the Forecourt.

57. Quotation from *Cities*, 2nd edition, 232–33.

58. Portland City Planning Commission et al., "Planning Guidelines—Portland Downtown Plan." Halprin's influence is detectable throughout the plan.

59. Gragg, "Urban Plazas that Set Portland's Modern Landscape get some TLC," A1. The city is building another open space sequence to the north, in the gentrified "Pearl District," comprising Jamison Square and Tanner Springs Park, each intended to evoke Tanner Creek, which once existed in this area but is now buried in pipes below, as well as the Fields Neighborhood Park, which opened in May 2013. The parks create a spine and amenity for a new neighborhood that the Portland Development Commission is calling the "River District."

60. In "Two Portland Fountains Come of Age," Portland urban planning historian Carl Abbott claims: "Although Portlanders have certainly not forgotten the [Forecourt] fountain, their attention has been drawn to newer public spaces in other parts of downtown. Inauguration of the new Performing Arts Center reduced use of the Civic Auditorium. Tom McCall Waterfront Park has recaptured the space previously preempted by a six-lane riverbank freeway. The parks offer spaces that range from the Japanese–American Historical Plaza to a busy housing–marina–shopping complex, from a sidewalk-level fountain that invites squealing kids to open lawns that crawl with food-and-drink festivals nearly every summer weekend. Pioneer Courthouse Square, a formally designed block in the heart of Portland's retail district, has become the venue of choice for programmed outdoor activities" (48).

61. Letter to Kepes (Halprin Collection, 014.I.A.5095).

62. In 1974, when Halprin was working on the Transit Mall, his firm created a "Pedestrian Crosswalks and Intersections" study for the PDC (original study drawings are dated January 1974 and the "Preliminary Working Drawings" were executed in August 1974; see Halprin Collection, 014.II.A.144–151). In July 1971, the Halprin firm had been invited to review the open space sequence. In the report of the inspection, the firm states under the section "All Streets" that the "Crosswalks are not well delineated—should be remedied" (report sent by Byron McCulley of Lawrence Halprin & Associates to John Kenward, July 16, 1971, regarding the visit on July 20, 1971, Halprin Collection, 014.I.A.2114). The designed crosswalks proposed in the 1974 study not only link Portland Center to Auditorium Forecourt but continue both from the Forecourt to the waterfront and north to the heart of downtown toward the Transit Mall. Simultaneous with the crosswalks study, drawings in the Halprin Collection indicate that a way-finding system was initiated for this area, primarily directing pedestrians toward the Transit Mall and the Auditorium (see "Furniture Location" plan dated November 11, 1974, in the Halprin Collection, 014.II.A.144–151). Unfortunately, other than the Second Avenue Mall crosswalk over Lincoln Street, neither the crosswalks nor the elaborate way-finding system materialized. Both would have greatly enhanced Halprin's desire to connect these spaces to the downtown and the waterfront, thus facilitating an expanded network to create an urban-scale matrix.

63. Davis, "Portland Center, Portland, Oregon," 128–29.

64. Quotation from Ira Keller Fountain "Fact Sheet" developed by Urbsworks, Inc. working on the preservation of the Halprin fountain, c. 2002 (Halprin Collection, 014.I.C.1597).

65. Halprin, "Ira Keller Fountain: Recapturing the Magic" (1992; Halprin Collection, 014.I.B.1501).

66. Report sent by Byron McCulley of Lawrence Halprin & Associates to John Kenward, July 16, 1971, regarding the visit on July 20, 1971 (Halprin Collection, 014.I.A.2114).

67. The analysis of Skyline Park in Denver, Seattle Freeway Park in Seattle, and Heritage Park Plaza in Fort Worth grows forth from a previous study by the author arguing for their preservation, published as "Lawrence Halprin's Public Spaces: Design, Experience, and Recovery. Three Case Studies," 258–355.

68. Forward Thrust had formulated a $2 billion list of civic improvements, proposing that $800 million come from local contributions. In 1968, voters of King County approved $334 million in bond resolutions, $65 million of which was dedicated to parks and park facilities in Seattle. Remediating the schism created by the twelve-lane depressed freeway, completed in 1966, had become a priority even before the Forward Thrust funds became available. Though the city did not have funds or expertise enough to implement Thiry's lid, it was able to develop a small plaza on the west side of the Seneca Street off-ramp, completed in 1967. The plaza was funded by a $75,000 donation from Floyd Naramore of Naramore Bain Brady Johanson Architects (NBBJ), who designed it, with the landscape architect William Teufel, around a central fountain by local sculptor George Tsutakawa. The architect Perry Johanson subsequently proposed the extension of the park to the block bounded by Seneca, Sixth, University, and the freeway, but due to a lack of immediate funds this proposal was absorbed into the Forward Thrust measure (this synopsis of the pre-Halprin plans comes largely from the October 6, 1969, "Script for Slide

Program on Proposed Freeway Park in the Central Business District of Seattle" to be presented in the mayor's conference room on the following day (document in Construction and Maintenance, Department of Parks and Recreation, Facilities Maintenance Division, series 5804–05, box 23, folder 2 in the Seattle Municipal Archives). Local attorney James Ellis, often called "the father of Forward Thrust" (see, for instance, "Seattle Freeway Park," 1976 publicity brochure issued by Your Seattle Parks and Recreation, Seattle Municipal Archives), thenceforth committed himself to seeing a linear park along the freeway fully realized, partly since he had watched the freeway construction from his office windows within the IBM Building at Fifth Avenue and Seneca Street.

69. Other firms considered were Sasaki Dawson DeMay Associates and the local Sakuma & James and Paul Thiry. Richard Haag and Paul Friedberg were also briefly considered (see August 13, 1970, letter from Hans A. Thompson, Superintendent of Seattle's Department of Parks and Recreation, to Al Bumgardner, Chairman of the Seattle Design Commission, re: "Freeway Park—Selection of Landscape Architect," and the August 4, 1970, memo from J. Wm. Dimmich, Director of Architectural Design and Construction at the City of Seattle's Department of Building, to Hans Thompson with the "Designer List" for Freeway Park, both found in the Seattle Municipal Archives).

70. Angela Danadjieva was appointed principal designer owing to her impressive contribution to the Auditorium Forecourt in Portland. According to the Seattle Freeway Park "Factsheet," Danadjieva was project designer, Byron McCulley project manager, and Dai Williams job captain (see page 3 of the undated "Seattle Freeway Park Factsheet," Halprin Collection, 014.I.B.1251). The factsheet does not mention Robert (Bob) Mendelsohn, who quite clearly played a role in project administration and is listed as a member of the team in other Halprin firm documents (including an earlier document entitled "Seattle Freeway Park: New Dimensions for Freeways," Halprin Collection, 014.box.70), or Jean Walton, associate and horticulturalist within the firm, who was referenced in numerous sources as a major player in the development of the planting plan. Consultants included Sakuma & James (which became Sakuma James Peterson), landscape architects, Seattle; Edward McLeod & Associates, landscape architects, Seattle; Gilbert Forsberg, Diekmann & Schmidt (GFDS), structural engineers, San Francisco; Beamer Wilkinson and Associates, mechanical and electrical engineers, San Francisco; Richard Chaix, mechanical engineer, park's fountain consultant, Oakland; Engineering Enterprise, lighting consultant, electrical design of fountains, and site lighting, Berkeley; Elisabeth C. Miller, horticultural consultant, Seattle; and George Bell, irrigation design. Also, Peter Keiwit Sons built the bridge and park structures south of Seneca, and David A. Mowat Company built the bridge and park north of Seneca. Prior to park development, in addition to the creation of Naramore Plaza, which was integrated into the Halprin firm's design, Naramore Bain Brady Johanson Architects "was responsible for the design of the East Garage, coordinated the park design with the state Department of Highways' bridge design and provided coordination and construction management assistance to the City of Seattle" (according to "Seattle Freeway Park Factsheet," 3). Van Slyck, Callison, Nelson of Seattle designed and built the Park Place Building, garage, and associated plaza. Structural engineers with Victor Gray of Seattle consulted Naramore Bain Brady Johanson

Architects on the construction of the East Garage and the Washington State Highway Department Bridge Division oversaw the construction of the structural portion of the park built over the freeway.

71. Specifically for "Ecological and Environmental" resources, the firm conducted studies of the noise, climate, microclimate, pollution, shadow patterns, and silviculture. See January 25, 1971, letter from Robert Mendelsohn of Lawrence Halprin & Associates to James Hornell of Seattle's Office of Community Development, Seattle Municipal Archives, series 5804–05, box 23, folder 4.

72. Lawrence Halprin & Associates document entitled "Seattle Freeway Park—Work to be Performed by Lawrence Halprin & Associates (draft), October 13, 1970," (Halprin Collection, 014.I.A.4655a; see also views study, 014.II.A.261a).

73. Letter report to the city's project coordinator for Freeway Park, Jim Hornell of the Department of Community Development, dated January 25, 1971, Seattle Municipal Archives, series 5804–05, box 23, folder 4.

74. Including *The Captured Squadron*, for which she won a "Golden Rose" (the Bulgarian equivalent of an Oscar), according to Schurch, "Angela Danadjieva," 72.

75. Danadjieva, "Seattle's Freeway Park II," 405. Nicollet Mall represented an early attempt at addressing these two scale impressions—the rhythm of pedestrian paving patterns were more condensed than the medallions marking the intersections of each cross street.

76. This portion of the park is referred to as the "Great Box Garden" in *Sunset* magazine's cover story "Seattle's 'Tomorrow Park' Opens July 4," 52–55.

77. January 12, 1971, memo with the subject heading "Design Notes on Freeway Park" from Danadjieva (she refers to herself here with her earlier married name, Angela Tvetzin) to "Seattle Freeway Park Design Team," 2–4 (Halprin Collection, 014.I.A.4655a).

78. One approaches the site from downtown by crossing over Seneca and the freeway's off-ramp, and enters West Plaza situated above the Park Place Building's garage. Because this property is privately owned, its rotating horticultural displays are more elaborate and better maintained, making it somewhat "aesthetically and economically disjunct from the rest of the park" (according to Brice Maryman and Liz Birkholz, "City of Seattle Landmark Nomination: Freeway Park," March 11, 2005, 11). The park critic John Pastier, in an article written in 1983, claims that "Halprin now finds [the West Plaza] weak as a passage between the city and the park center." The article further notes, quoting Halprin: "'If I were designing it today, I would celebrate the way in better—now you ooze in'" ("Evaluation: Park Atop a Freeway," 46). As an entry, there is little indication of the pleasures within. However, the brilliantly colored horticultural displays do attempt to entice.

79. See page 3 of the January 12, 1971, memo where Danadjieva suggests the café. Another reference to the planned café is in "New Dimensions for Freeways" (Halprin Collection, 014.I.A.4655a).

80. The initial park brochure states 27,000 gallons per minute, and the figure is also on a sign mounted on the fountain itself as well as in a variety of articles covering the park's opening. However, the "Seattle Freeway Park Factsheet" (Halprin Collection, 014.I.B.1251) states: "The central plaza fountain's water is

recirculated by three-125 horsepower pumps which have a total capacity to circulate water at a rate of more than 30 million gallons/day (or 22,650 gallons/minute). Normal operation, however, uses two of the three pumps for a recirculation rate of 15,100 gallons/minute."

81. Steinberg, interview with L. Halprin, 1988.

82. Danadjieva, "Seattle's Freeway Park II," 405.

83. See January 25, 1971, letter from Bob Mendelsohn to Jim Hornell on the "several moods" the firm hopes to achieve (Seattle Municipal Archives, series 5804–05, box 23, folder 4).

84. Quotations from Halprin's essay "Fantasy Environments" as part of the unpublished manuscript *The Environment as Art Experience*, 1974 (Halprin Collection, 014.I.B.2302). Additionally, associate Jim Burns's essay on the park, titled "The Hanging Gardens of Seattle," evokes ancient legends and mysteries (Halprin Collection, 014.I.B.1251).

85. See *Sketchbooks of Lawrence Halprin*, 31.

86. "Seattle Freeway Park: New Dimensions for Freeways" (Halprin Collection, 014.box.70).

87. Quotation from Burns, "The Hanging Gardens of Seattle," 2 (Halprin Collection, 014.I.B.1251).

88. As Danadjieva claims, "The texture of the cityscape is dominated by concrete. The Freeway itself appears like a dry concrete riverbed that flows through the City," memo of January 12, 1971 (Halprin Collection, 014.I.A.4655a).

89. Ibid.

90. Ibid.

91. See also Richard Haag's groundbreaking integration of the coal gasification plant on Lake Union in Seattle in a new form of public space (opened 1975), which has inspired other parks that adopt and adapt industrial relics such as Landschaftspark Duisburg-Nord in Germany (designed by Latz & Partner).

92. The Washington State Convention and Trade Center is a sprawling mass that also uses the same formal and material language as the original park. In 1988, Danadjieva & Koenig, working as associate architects for the Convention Center, another air-rights development over I-5, designed the plaza extending from the American Legion portion of the park as well as the interior landscaping of the glass-encased structure.

93. The Pigott Corridor was funded by Paul Pigott, former chief officer of the PACCAR Corporation, to honor his mother who was a resident of the adjacent Horizon House retirement community and enjoyed the park. Though designed and constructed with positive intentions to improve access into the park, the corridor is somewhat dizzying owing to blind corners resulting from concrete obstructions and tall, dense vegetation.

94. Burns, "The Hanging Gardens of Seattle," 2 (Halprin Collection, 014.I.B.1251).

95. Undated document found in the Halprin Collection, 014.box.70.

96. The former quotation is from Burns, "The Hanging Gardens of Seattle," 3 (Halprin Collection, 014.I.B.1251); the latter is from Danadjieva, "Seattle's Freeway Park II," 406.

97. January 14, 1971, document in the Halprin Collection, 014.I.A.4655a.

98. The "lid" over I-5 is proposed again in this open space campaign. From "The Blue Ring: Connecting Places, 100-Year Vision, Seattle's Open Space Strategy for the Center City," revised draft June 2002, publicity brochure, www.seattle.gov/dpd/stellent/groups/pan/@pan/@plan/@citydesign/documents/web_informational/dpds_006516.pdf (accessed March 2005).

99. The Seattle Symphony Orchestra once held annual concerts in the park (see Charles Brown, "Menu at Freeway Park: Sandwiches and Sousa," A12). On St. Patrick's Day in 1977, the water in the fountains was dyed green (see the *Seattle Times* article "Waterfall to Flow Green"). A Japanese folk art performance was hosted at Freeway Park as part of the Smithsonian Institution on Tour program (see "Japan's Ancient Past Lives at Freeway Park," A14).

100. Burns, "The Hanging Gardens of Seattle," 3 (Halprin Collection, 014.I.B.1251).

101. Midtown Plaza (at Clinton Avenue S. and Main Street E.) was the first downtown indoor shopping mall built in the United States. It was designed by Victor Gruen and completed in 1962 as the initial step to regenerate the city's downtown. Over the years, it served as a kind of all-season "town square" (see the fascinating account of this mall in Hardwick, *Mall Maker*, 198–205). It was torn down in 2008 for a telecommunication company headquarters (PAETEC). Midtown Plaza generated increased investment downtown, resulting in the construction of several towers nearby, including the Xerox tower (Welton Becket & Associates, 1967–68) and Marine Midland plaza (SOM, 1970), both in close proximity to the park (the latter immediately across E. Broad Street from the park's fountain plaza). For more on the architecture of Rochester during the time of park construction, see Paul Malo, *Landmarks of Rochester and Monroe County*, 93–137.

102. See Hirsch, "Lawrence Halprin's Public Spaces," on Denver. See Marvin Hatami and Associates and Tanaka and Associates, *Urban Design and Development Study* (1970) for design guidelines that were eventually abandoned.

103. See the extensive office correspondence with lists of activities that each park element could generate in the Halprin Collection, 014.I.A.6251–6272. Also, see the *Southeast Loop Park* report in 014.I.B.box 367.

104. For more on the park's "contextualism," see the thoughtful account of the park by the landscape architect Ken Smith in "Case Study: Manhattan Square Park, Rochester, New York," 50–55. In addition, the construction photographs of the park in the Halprin Collection, 014.IV.A.146 show the gradual disappearance of George Street.

105. See slides in the Halprin Collection (Dc. 4, 5, 6, 7, Dd. 1, 2, 3, 4, 5, 6, 7, De. 1, 2, 3) for images of the no-longer-extant "space frame."

106. See the reproduction in "Lawrence Halprin," *Process Architecture*, 35, in which he diagrams the range of control possible within the scoring process (the original diagram without the summary appears in the first few pages of *The RSVP Cycles*). Halprin summarizes the different degrees and examples that apply to each: "Closed score for complete control—score as vehicle—as precise as possible to accomplish a mission (Seminary South Fountain, Street Movement); No control during performance—score energizes (Seattle Center Fountain, Lovejoy Plaza, Nicollet Motation); Some control, very little feedback

or selectivity during performance (Tidal graph, Earthquake faults, Sea Ranch Ecoscore); full process potential: Some: control, selectivity, feedback, change, growth (YBC, 24-day Workshop)."

107. Halprin, *Notebooks*, 249–52.

108. Ibid., 81, as part of "Thoughts on Design," dated Sunday, March 24.

109. See Halprin's unpublished essay "Calligraphy as a Structuring Device" (Halprin Collection, 014.I.B.2479; italics in the original).

110. Halprin's enthusiasm for "megastructures" most likely stemmed from Jim Burns's studies of them. See Burns, *Arthropods*, and the section "Multi-Dimensional Urban Systems" in Halprin, *New York, New York*, 104. In 1969, Halprin, with Kenzo Tange and others, was commissioned by the San Francisco Redevelopment Agency to devise a master plan for the thirty-five-acre Yerba Buena Center just south of Market Street. Halprin considers it an optimized embodiment of the RSVP Cycles method. See his diagram of the project in "Lawrence Halprin," *Process Architecture*, (35), and *The RSVP Cycles* (96–97), which, he claims, "does not preclude change or the vagaries of chance over time." For a critical account of the Yerba Buena redevelopment, see Hartman, *Yerba Buena: Land Grab and Community Resistance in San Francisco*.

111. A term Halprin uses in a March 19, 1992, letter response to a Landscape Design student at Radcliffe who compared his work to Christo's (Halprin Collection, 014.I.B.2479).

4. THE TAKE PART PROCESS

1. Written criticism of urban renewal in the early to mid-1960s is vast, but the most thoughtful evaluations include Scott Greer's *Urban Renewal and American Cities*, and Charles Abrams's *The City Is the Frontier*. See Herbert Gans's sociological response to the displacement and inadequate relocation of Italian Americans in the West End of Boston in *The Urban Villagers*, as well as the essays included in his *People and Plans*, such as "The Failure of Urban Renewal" 260–77. Similarly, see urban planner Chester Hartman's "The Housing of Relocated Families," and psychologist Marc Fried's "Grieving for a Lost Home: Psychological Costs of Relocation" (the latter two essays were reprinted in Wilson, ed., *Urban Renewal*).

2. Sherry R. Arnstein, "A Ladder of Citizen Participation," 216–24. In the article, she breaks down participation policies into eight levels: Manipulation, Therapy, Informing, Consultation, Placation, Partnership, Delegated Power, and Citizen Control. She is highly critical of Model Cities participation policies. See also *Between the Idea and the Reality* by Charles Haar, who served on the president's task force that designed the model cities program, and then served as the assistant secretary in the Department of Housing and Urban Development (HUD). In the book, Haar describes how the program "rejected the idea of funding an OEO [Office of Economic Opportunity]-styled 'direct democracy' of the poor," limiting their power to effect decisions (48).

3. "Downtown Is for People" originated as a speech Jacobs gave at Harvard in 1956. It later was published in *Fortune* magazine.

4. See *Taking Part*, 12–13, and *A Life Spent Changing Places*, 138–40. See also Halprin's position piece "Why

I Am in Favor of the Panhandle Freeway," which appeared in the *San Francisco Chronicle* on May 3, 1964 (9). (A clipping of this article is in Halprin's scrapbooks, Halprin Collection, 1960s volume). His plan recommended that the freeway run underneath Golden Gate Park, but he claims the media incorrectly implied the freeway would cut *through* the park, thus sparking public outcry.

5. "Community Workshops = CW," 6 (Halprin Collection, 014.I.B.2515–31).

6. *Taking Part*, 106–7.

7. "Leadership Training Workshop, General Statement of Objectives," March 11, 1971 (Halprin Collection, 014.I.B.2531; italics in the original). The Leadership Training Workshop was conducted to train employees of Lawrence Halprin & Associates how to lead their own workshops (April 12–13, 1971). It was funded by a HUD demonstration grant and would culminate in an actual community leadership training workshop in Indianapolis involving trainees from the city and state planning agencies.

8. See Ross, *Anna Halprin*, 266–84, on *Ceremony of Us*, along with an interview with Anna Halprin about this performance published in *Tulane Drama Review* as "Ceremony of Us." Worth noting is the Watts participant Wanda Coleman's reflection on the workshop (Ross, *Anna Halprin*, 274), where she claims Anna and Jim Woods "ran scared" when they got close to the "nastiness of what racism really is," and that this emerged from Anna's "naive" belief that the group could find common ground, "peace and love." Just after *Ceremony of Us*, Anna developed her Reach Out program in which a multiracial ensemble of dancers, funded by the National Endowment for the Arts, would gather for a training workshop and apprenticeships. See also the 1970 performance of *New Time Shuffle* performed in Northern California's Soledad State Prison.

9. Lawrence Halprin & Associates, *New York, New York*, 2.

10. *Taking Part*, 294.

11. See Halprin's vague recognition of "community-designed playgrounds" in *Taking Part*, 226. In Philadelphia beginning in 1959, Linn instituted a program that transformed municipally owned tax-delinquent land into what he called "Neighborhood Commons," for which he and his University of Pennsylvania students would work directly with communities to build outdoor gathering places from salvaged local and donated materials. He extended this program to Washington, D.C., and Baltimore (see Lisa Rubens interview of Karl Linn in *Karl Linn: Landscape Architect in Service of Peace, Social Justice, Commons, and Community*). In 1964, Paul Friedberg designed Jacob Riis Plaza, most renowned for its interactive playground, between the public housing towers in lower Manhattan. Also that year, he worked with Pratt Institute to transform a vacant lot in Brooklyn's Bedford–Stuyvesant neighborhood into a vest-pocket park as a demonstration project (see Friedberg's book *Play and Interplay* [1970] on his theoretical method and its application). He designed the park pro bono according to neighborhood needs and the residents did most of the work cleaning the lot, installing the infrastructure, and planting. See Thomas Hoving, "Think Big about Small Parks"; see also Alison Hirsch, "Activist Landscape Architects of the 1960s," *Places* (forthcoming).

12. As Hester in "Interview with Lawrence Halprin," states: "Most of us who came into participation from

civil rights came in from very different concerns. It was about empowerment, about activism. If you hadn't been doing participation already, it would have been much more difficult for us to convince cities to use it to address issues of justice and injustice. But we came at participation from a different angle, and I think that is why, in the end, that you, Larry, still get extraordinary pieces of landscape or city built that touch people's hearts, and the rest of us are still out here going over the next social issue or whatever" (50).

13. See, for instance, Alan Atshuler's critique *The City Planning Process* and "The Goals of Comprehensive Planning."

14. Keyes and Teitcher, "Limitations of Advocacy Planning," 225.

15. *Lawrence Halprin: Changing Places*, 134.

16. He most likely had such expectations since Halprin had just completed the "Report to Mrs. Lyndon B. Johnson's Committee for a More Beautiful Capital" (1967). About the study, Mayor Lindsay claimed: "We have given new emphasis to the quality of living in New York by stressing the vital necessity for high quality design. The careful placement of buildings, tree planting, lighting, and street furniture will create a more intimate and beautiful environment. The study will assist us in meeting these goals" (quoted in Bennett, "City Plans Study on Use of Spaces," 27).

17. Ada Louise Huxtable, "Nobody Here but Us New Yorkers," D34.

18. *New York, New York*, 110. The Halprin Collection includes a massive "Paste-Up" document with hundreds of pages of text responding to the multiplicity of issues addressed by the study, including pasted comments by each of the diverse consultants. It served as a tangible reflection of the interdisciplinary approach to this complex project (Halprin Collection, 014.I.A.4386).

19. Gans studies how new housing destroyed the Italian American community by neglecting to respond to their long-established domestic patterns. See Glazer and Moynihan, *Beyond the Melting Pot* in which they raise doubts about the belief in the great city as "the solvent of previous identity" (quotation from Charles Tilly's review of the book in the *Journal of the American Institute of Planners*, February 1965, 69). Hall insisted that "there is no melting pot in American cities" since ethnic groups maintain distinct identities for several generations, and the only way to avoid disrupting their communities was to plan for their accustomed scale and density (*The Hidden Dimension*, 156).

20. Halprin, *Changing Places*, 132.

21. Halprin, *Taking Part*, 178–79.

22. Day one quotations from Halprin, *The RSVP Cycles*, 79 (capitalization in the original).

23. Day two quotations from *Taking Part*, 182–83.

24. "Lawrence Halprin," *Process Architecture*, 45.

25. Halprin, *Taking Part*, 186.

26. Ibid., 202–3; see also page 275 for Halprin's explanation of the "Our Community" score.

27. Ibid., 204.

28. Halprin Collection, 014.I.A.970 (capitalization in the original).

29. Hester, "Interview with Lawrence Halprin," 50.

5. FACILITATION AND/OR MANIPULATION

1. This workshop was led by Halprin in 1973 and is particularly interesting because of the heatedness of the conflict and the racial implications. See Halprin Collection, 014.I.A.5066, for workshop documents.

2. For documents related to the organization of the staff training workshop in San Francisco, April 12–25, 1971, see Halprin Collection, 014.I.B.2531. According to a March 11, 1971, document in this folder on the workshop, Halprin states: "Much work will be based on accumulated experiences and problems and techniques that have arisen out of earlier workshop sessions not only in real-life environmental city workshops such as Fort Worth, etc., but also the experimental ones upon which *these* were based, i.e., 1966 and 1968 experiments in environment; MIT, 1969 [*The RSVP Cycles*]; early Kentfield studies of scoring and Dancers' Workshop workshops; RSVP Cycles." See Halprin Collection, 014.I.A.5524, for Jim Burns's notebook and miscellaneous documents on the 1971 Indianapolis workshop. See also Halprin Collection, 014.I.A.5071 and 014.I.A.4255, for the summary of the Indianapolis five-day workshop. See the document "Take Part Community Planning Workshops Planned and Conducted by Lawrence Halprin & Associates" in the Halprin Collection, 014.I.A.5485. The 1972 report *Take Part* also offers a summary of various workshops. Finally, the article by Barbara Goldstein, "Participation Workshops," includes Halprin's summary of some of the smaller workshops, such as those in Yountville, California, and Marin County, California, as well as workshops in educational institutions.

3. According to a report in 1969, Halprin "no longer had a sense that the office was 'his' office . . . What he really wanted to do was take his name and three of four trusted Associates and set up a small office in which he could be directly involved in every project. He felt he had also been holding back for years on the feeling of really not wanting to work with a number of people in the office" ("Jim Creighton's Report on the Office Re-Organization," 10, Halprin Collection, 014.I.B.2630).

4. Halprin's quotation appeared in "Community Development: Mendelsohn's New Job," *San Francisco Chronicle*, June 10, 1970, page unknown (clipping from Halprin Collection, 014.I.B.2911).

5. In Nilo Lindgren's article "Riding a Revolution: A Radical Experiment in Reorganization," he explains: "One more recent arrival to the firm who hews to traditional views of management, Bob Mendelsohn, argues that the Policy Council should basically act as an elected advisory body to Halprin who is president of the firm. This he sees as a correct form of community *participation* in decisions but not community *control*" (55).

6. Document entitled "Fort Worth Community Workshops, June 26–27, 1970" found in the Halprin Collection, 014.I.A.4156. See "List of Members Participating in the Community Workshop" document found in the Halprin Collection, 014.I.A.4158. In the "Fort Worth Workshop—Notes from Tapes and Discussions" document generated by the Halprin firm, the list of "Observations" includes: "5. As business leaders they viewed the city in terms of private enterprise—a means of making money first. (I think solutions to their problems will be examined in that light) . . . 8. The group acknowledged the fact that they represented only one social-economic level and that a realistic user need profile should be based on similar workshops for other citizens. Some felt that they as the power and decision makers in Fort

Worth had very little to do with the city as participants, and their conception of need was based more on speculation, in some areas" (Halprin Collection, 014.I.A.5071).

7. See the February 4, 1969, letter from "Charlie" to "Stew," labeled "Ft. Worth Background" and filed with the project documents, in which he identifies the "power structure in Fort Worth" (Halprin Collection, 014.I.A.4162).

8. Under the section "The Fort Worth CBD Workshop, June 1970, Purpose of the Workshop," 96. See the "Fort Worth CBD Community Workshop Score, June 1970" reproduced in *Taking Part*, 19. It is also reproduced in the CBD Sector Report, 99–100.

9. Memorandum from Peter Vandine to Bob Stadelman, Bob Mendelsohn, and Byron McCulley, July 14, 1971 (Halprin Collection, 014.I.A.4157). Vandine was most active in the Trinity River study.

10. See the section "Experience Situation" in *Taking Part*, 106–7. Subsequent quotations are from the same pages.

11. See "A Preliminary Study for Fort Worth, Texas, Prepared by Lawrence Halprin & Associates" by the "Design Team" of associates: Alexander Cuthbert, George McLaughlin, and Felix Warburg (Halprin Collection, 014.I.B.2603).

12. Not all of Halprin's employees were equipped to handle this jump in environmental scale. In fact, in Jim Creighton's report on the reorganization he claims: "The three Design Principals (Vig, Don, and Sat) were excellent in physical design, but had no especial competence in these new fields [of urban planning and ecology]. In many cases the expertise of the Associates exceeded that of the Principals in these fields, and the Associates resented receiving direction from people who 'knew less about the problems' than they did" ("Jim Creighton's Report on Office Re-Organization," 2–3, Halprin Collection, 014.I.B.2630).

13. "Everett Comprehensive Design Study Progress Report," December 8, 1970. The document continues by noting that "the layman can simply substitute 'criticism and creativity' for 'valuation' without significant loss of meaning" (Halprin Collection, 014.I.B.2552).

14. See Lawrence Halprin & Associates, *Everett Community Plan*. One interesting technique presented is "Sieve Mapping" (14–15), which is directly adopted from Ian McHarg's overlay mapping methodology.

15. The funding came out of HUD's Comprehensive Planning Assistance program authorized under Section 701 of the Housing Act of 1954. In a Halprin firm document, spelling out the "reasons" for the participatory process, and especially the Community Planning Office (to be discussed), it is stated that this process was instituted "to satisfy FEDERAL LAW: Urban Planning grants for the Department of Housing and Urban Development, under provisions of the Housing Act of 1954, as amended require Citizen Participation" (Halprin Collection, 014.I.A.4091).

16. See Mendelsohn's recorded statements in the "Public Hearing Community Development Plan" transcription, taking place on February 16, 1972 (Halprin Collection, 014.I.A.4092).

17. According to Mendelsohn in the February 16, 1972, public hearing.

18. "Reconnaissance Report & Planning Program, City of Everett, Washington," submitted by Felix M.

Warbug, Project Director of Lawrence Halprin & Associates, with consultants Livingston & Blayney, City and Regional Planners, San Francisco, July 21, 1969 (Halprin Collection, 014.I.A.4086).

19. See the "Project History" section of Koenig's "Presentation Outline for Council/Commission Work Session," in which he summarizes the input of individuals in the firm. The comprehensive nature of the project made it so that Koenig claimed in this document that "on this project alone we've used almost everyone in the office at one point or another" (Halprin Collection, 014.I.A.4080). See also the April 10, 1972, list (directed to Ed Wilbur of the Everett Planning Department) of those Halprin firm members who worked on the Everett study from July 1971 through March 1972 (Halprin Collection, 014.I.A.4080). After receiving a master's degree in city and regional planning from University of California, Berkeley, Tom Koenig worked with local advocacy groups and participated in Halprin's Bay Area Leadership Training workshop in 1971. He was subsequently hired by Halprin & Associates to work on community and regional planning projects (according to his biography in the Halprin Collection, 014.I.A.5526).

20. Lawrence Halprin & Associates, "Final Preliminary Report," September 1971 (Halprin Collection, 014.I.B.2552).

21. See the document "Presentation Outline for Council/Commission Work Session" (Halprin Collection, 014.I.A.4080, capitalization in the original).

22. Both quotations are from the memorandum from Creighton to Guthrie, Mendelsohn, and Halprin, "RE: Everett Community Participation Program," August 1970 (Halprin Collection, 014.I.A.4078).

23. In Creighton's August 1970 memo he declares the "homogeneity of the community." See also Appendices 5 and 6 in the final document, *Everett Community Plan* (December 1972). The firm's initial interest in the utmost cross-sectional diversity diminished when they realized that the city was relatively homogenous. See the two early 1970 drafts of the "City of Everett Planning Program" that state: "Workshops will involve representatives of every facet of Everett's population and ethnic groups as well as differing interests and professions" (3; date not recorded). In the March 12, 1970, revised version they state that the workshops will be supplemented by "The Committee of 100," which would "be appointed to advise and assist in implementation of the study results. The composition of this group will include a cross section of the total citizenry of Everett and will include all segments of the social and economic structure of the community" (Halprin Collection, 014.I.A.4086). Creighton later writes of a "Citizen Committee" in his August 1970 memo, yet the program seems to have been subsequently abandoned. Though the reports speak about the "younger generation" included in the workshop, no children or teenagers seem to have been represented in this initial workshop. Simon Nicholson suggests a separate workshop for Everett community members ages sixteen to twenty-one, which did not occur (see Simon Nicholson's September 28, 1970, "Preliminary Notes on Everett Community Workshop," Halprin Collection, 014.I.A.4077). Unfortunately, a list of participants which would indicate the number of men and women was never located. Though a number of women are cited as participants in documents (Judy Blake and Jeanne Metzger, both staff writers for the *Everett Herald*, and Mrs. Bryce Hausmann), the workshops

did not include equal numbers of women. Perhaps this is why in 1971 the study was presented to so many women's groups (Women's Book Club, Everett Business & Professional Women's Club, Silver Lake Women's Club, League of Women Voters).

24. October 14, 1970, letter from Judy Baker to Gordon Cultum, then representing the office of the mayor. The letter was carbon copied to Halprin (Halprin Collection, 014.I.A.4089; italics and capitalization in the original).

25. Quotations from Lawrence Halprin & Associates, "Everett Workshop," September 11, 1970 (Halprin Collection, 014.I.A.4078); see also the August 1970 memo from Creighton to Guthrie, Mendelsohn, and Halprin "RE: "Everett Community Participation Program" (Halprin Collection, 014.I.A.4078).

26. Simon Nicholson, "Preliminary Notes on Everett Community Workshop," September 28, 1970 (Halprin Collection, 014.I.A.4077). The document continues: "They include: 1. Pollution and impossibility of recreation use of waterfront and Snohomish river. 2. City not pedestrian-oriented: streets wide and bare: Evergreen Way, in particular because it has no walkway. 3. The incredible proximity of docks, (an interesting place), yet no-one goes there."

27. As Judy Blake, participant and staff writer for the *Everett Herald*, writes in "Impressionistic Tour of Everett": "The sense of smell also reminded the workshoppers that Everett is a mill town. A deep breath as the 'copter flew over the city's smokestacks made this fact readily evident, as did the haze hanging over the valley" (3A).

28. The paste-up document compiled by Simon Nicholson is in the Halprin Collection, 014.I.B.2552.

29. In "Impressionistic Tour of Everett," Judy Blake reports: "Despite the sound of traffic . . . and a view of industrialization all around, the river had a lazy quality reminiscent of earlier times. It was something that some participants had never noticed before" (3A).

30. See Halprin's handwritten "Notes from people's description of their reaction to Colby" (Halprin Collection, 014.I.B.2552). See also Jeanne Metzger's article "Over-30 Crowd Experiences 'Cruising Colby' Routine" in the *Everett Herald*.

31. Claudia D. Hansen, "Cruising Colby," clipping from the *Everett Herald* (undated; Halprin Collection, 014.I.A.4088).

32. "Shooting the Gut" comes from Metzger's "Over-30 Crowd Experiences 'Cruising Colby' Routine." One policeman in Hansen's article only reports "some traffic and noise problems on Friday night" (3A).

33. See "E1 'April Park' Experimental Mall, Everett, Washington, April–May 1971," document compiled by Gordon Cultum of the Community Planning Office in July 1971 (Halprin Collection, 014.I.A.4090).

34. See *Everett Community Plan*, "Commerce and Finance" section, 42–47.

35. "E1 'April Park' Experimental Mall" (Halprin Collection, 014.I.A.4090). Teenagers also did not pose the kind of threat to implementation that other groups might have. Clearly the firm recommended such physical alterations to the city in anticipation of future commissions.

36. In the "Preliminary Notes on Everett Community Workshop" (September 28, 1970), Nicholson asks: "The workshop was good insofar as the participants did feel that they could generate solutions, but there was

not the optimism of the younger generation that they could improve on the 'planners': the youngest representatives at the workshop tended to agree with their elders . . . What would the results be if we could schedule a second workshop identical to the first . . . but for young people between . . . 16 and 21?" (Halprin Collection, 014.I.A.4077). One undated clipping from the *Everett Herald* by workshop participant Judy Blake included in the Halprin Collection reports on the organization of a workshop for eighth graders in St. Mary Magdalen School by the original workshop participant Mrs. Bryce Hausmann: "While the students' involvement is aimed in large at helping them learn about city government, problems and planning, they will also be contributing to the growing collection of information which will become part of the comprehensive plan . . . Yesterday the students elected a 'mayor,' 'city executive' and 'city planner' to lead them in their project. Later on, they will be talking to community leaders, observing various parts of the city and gathering data in an effort to help determine which direction Everett's development should take in the future" ("Eighth Graders Helping Draw Plans for City," Halprin Collection, 014.I.A.4091).

37. "Preliminary Notes on Everett Community Workshop" (September 28, 1970). Participant Jeanne Metzger reported: "The 1870 group came up with the most imaginative ideas that had no impediments. The 1970 teams were frustrated with tackling the problems of working with what we have and ended up by spending their time tackling ways to solve immediate problems" ("Workshop Participants Follow 'Score' Prepared by Planning 'Maestro' for Unusual Tour of City," 3A).

38. *Taking Part*, 298.

39. Judy Blake, in "Impressionistic Tour of Everett," reports: " 'I've never been here before.' It was a comment heard over and over during the Halprin workshop. Leading citizens who had lived and worked in Everett for many years were seeing areas and details of the city that they had never noticed before" (3A).

40. Metzger, "Workshop Participants Follow 'Score' Prepared by Planning 'Maestro' for Unusual Tour of City"(3A).

41. Nicholson considered the lack of collective analysis "an inherent defect in the Everett Workshop."

42. Letter dated October 21, 1970 (Halprin Collection, 014.I.A.4078).

43. "Everett Comprehensive Design Study Progress Report" (Halprin Collection, 014.I.B.2552). The Halprin Collection included no records of this second-generation process, which occurred in October 1970; the firm only mentions it briefly in various documentation. This is probably due to the fact that "some of the leaders were disappointed because the results did not contribute any ideas beyond those of the first workshop" ("L1 Citizen Participation," Halprin Collection, 014.I.A.4091). In a November 9, 1970, document by Nicholson, "The Everett Community Workshops," he indicates that the "workshop generated, given, and evaluated by the community, and subsequently submitted in written, taped, and photographic form, to LH&A" was undertaken in mid-October (Halprin Collection, 014.I.A.5066). A document entitled "Everett Community Workshops and Community Planning Office, 1970–1971" states that some of the participants of the first workshop "proceeded to organize and develop—with planning guidance from Lawrence Halprin & Associates—*workshops of their own*. The benefits of this snowball effect were twofold. First, it was found that community participation in planning and conducting workshops . . . had great educational benefits. Secondly, this process naturally helped to achieve the four major objectives of

workshops, since greater numbers of the community could become involved in the development of the Everett plan" (Halprin Collection, 014.I.A.4080).

44. "L1 Citizen Participation" (Halprin Collection, 014.I.A.4091).

45. Everett resident Tom Sullivan was appointed director of community planning for the Halprin study effort in Everett. He and Cultum had the joint responsibility to organize workshops and events out of the Community Planning Office. According to one clipping included in the Halprin Collection, 014.I.A.4091: "Sullivan is in the US Navy, which continues to pay his salary. A former student of city planning at CA Polytechnic College, he is participating in a Navy program which allows men to hold certain types of civilian jobs during their final months of their military terms. The purpose is to provide training and to help in the transformation from military to civilian life" ("Everett Community Workshops and Community Planning Office," Halprin Collection, 014.I.A.4080).

46. All these workshops took place in May 1971. See the list of participants and items discussed for each of these meetings in the Halprin Collection, 014.I.A.4089. According to the "L1 Citizen Participation" document generated by the Community Planning Office (Halprin Collection, 014.I.A.4091), these workshops were advertised in the papers and in mailings to all the workshop participants, yet they were not well attended and those who did attend "preferred to 'express ideas' rather than structure themselves into working committees."

47. Transcription of the "Public Hearing Community Development Plan," February 16, 1972 (Halprin Collection, 014.I.A.4092).

48. Letter from Koenig to Frank Bennett of the Everett Planning Department, February 26, 1972 (Halprin Collection, 014.I.A.4080; capitalization in the original).

49. Lawrence Halprin & Associates, *Everett Community Plan*, 130.

50. Prepared for Willamette Valley Environmental Protection & Development Planning Council by Lawrence Halprin & Associates, October 1972. This report for a region with a similar ecology to that of Everett was instituted as an open-ended instigator of planning "Foresight" and an example of providing alternatives as a means in which to involve more people in decision-making.

51. See the letter from Thomas A. Conger to Jim Coleman, director of the New York office of Lawrence Halprin & Associates, August 8, 1972 (Halprin Collection, 014.I.A.3846). In the letter, he claims: "We have a new city manager and council who are willing to push hard to get the project off the ground. We also have a business community that is willing to work together to pull this thing off (for example, all of the bankers are agreeable with the general concept of the mall—see enclosed map. It is not every day that they get together on an idea)." See the document entitled "Background and Neighborhood Analysis, Part of the Comprehensive Plan for Charlottesville, Virginia" produced by Harland Bartholomew and Associates and submitted to the City Planning Commission in June 1971 for a neighborhood analysis of the city's physical and economic conditions at the time of Halprin's interventions.

52. The proposed work was broken down week by week in "A Proposal to the City of Charlottesville for the Development of a Central Business District Master Plan and the Design of a Mall" (Halprin Collection, 014.I.A.3836).

53. In a letter from Burns to the Charlottesville team, dated February 2, 1973, he asks Abbott in the New York office to generate the walking and driving scores, and Kondy to create the introductory meeting scores, the score for the sharing session after the awareness walk and drive, and the planning and sharing sessions on Saturday (Halprin Collection, 014.I.A.3841).

54. Ibid.

55. Ibid.

56. March 13, 1973, memo from Burns to Kondy and Abbott (Halprin Collection, 014.I.A.3841).

57. February 2, 1973, letter from Burns to the Charlottesville team.

58. The most heated tension was the city's decision to entirely demolish the Vinegar Hill neighborhood west of Main Street, which was a healthy and vibrant African American community designated as "blighted" by city officials. What made it such a contentious issue was that after the land was cleared it remained vacant for over a decade while the city tried to secure an investor to develop it.

59. See the series of interview notes compiled as "Notes from Charlottesville Interview (February 7, 8, & 9) with Civic Leaders, Community Representatives, City Staff, Merchants, Financers, etc." (Halprin Collection, 014.I.A.3854).

60. In a February 26, 1973, letter from Abbott to Harold Baxter, Kondy, and Burns, he explains that this time would be devoted to "test scores" and "interview workshop participants" (Halprin Collection, 014.I.A.3841).

61. March 23, 1973, letter (Halprin Collection, 014.I.A.3846).

62. See the "Participants in the 'Take Part Community Workshop'" document (Halprin Collection, 014.I.A.4907) for preliminary names and occupations, as well as the final list of names included on page 58 of "Charlottesville Take Part Community Workshop Actions & Recommendations" generated by Lawrence Halprin & Associates (Halprin Collection, 014.I.A.3831).

63. "Charlottesville Workshop Scores" (Halprin Collection, 014.I.A.3826).

64. Transcribed audiotapes of Wilmington Workshop (Halprin Collection, 014.I.A.5071).

65. "Charlottesville Take Part Community Workshop Actions & Recommendations," 12–14 (Halprin Collection, 014.I.A.3831).

66. "Charlottesville Workshop Scores" (Halprin Collection, 014.I.A.3826).

67. "Charlottesville Take Part Community Workshop Actions & Recommendations," 20–28 (Halprin Collection, 014.I.A.3831).

68. See some of these drawings in the Halprin Collection slide archive (section catalogued under AJ400–AJ700).

69. Listed in "Charlottesville Workshop Scores" (Halprin Collection, 014.I.A.3826) and "Charlottesville Take Part Community Workshop Actions & Recommendations," 31–32 (Halprin Collection, 014.I.A.3831).

70. "Charlottesville Take Part Community Workshop Actions & Recommendations," 50 (Halprin Collection, 014.I.A.3831)

71. Ibid., 56–57.

72. *Downtown Planning Report*, Charlottesville, Virginia, 11 (Halprin Collection, 014.I.A.3832).

73. The letter was published on March 28, 1974, on page A8. Other articles and correspondence about this controversy are included in the Halprin Collection, 014.I.A.3861.

74. See the December 19, 1973, memorandum to City Manager Cole Hendrix from Satyendra S. Huja, Director of Planning, Department of Community Development, in which he claims "the overall response was positive" (Halprin Collection, 014.I.A.3861).

75. See the March 22, 1974, letter from City Manager Cole Hendrix to Project Manager Bill Hull listing those stipulations (Halprin Collection, 014.I.A.3861). In fact, only two of the five City Council members, all of whom had participated in the workshop, voted in favor of the mall in February 1974, while three abstained because of "conflicts of interest" (see Yellig, "Downtown Mall: Charlottesville's Public Square" for a good history of the mall development).

76. *Downtown Planning Report*, 40.

77. From the document "Take Part Participatory Workshops for People's Involvement in Planning Their Environment Mini-Workshop for LH&A Workshop Leaders, 10 April 1973" (Halprin Collection, 014.I.A.3826).

78. See Hirt, "Toward Postmodern Urbanism? Evolution of Planning in Cleveland, Ohio," 33. Citing Norman Krumholz's "City Planning for Greater Equity," Hirt claims that "from 1950 to 1980, manufacturing jobs declined in Cleveland by 60 percent, population fell by more than a third, incomes fell to 70 percent of those of the country, and poverty reached a quarter of residents." In 1969, the polluted Cuyahoga River burned, and in 1978, according to Hirt, Cleveland became the first American city since the Depression to default on its debt.

79. The *Cleveland Policy Planning Report*, generated by the Cleveland City Planning Commission, pioneered this new social-policy driven strategy, which was a relative of advocacy planning focused on the needs of the poor in Cleveland's disenfranchised neighborhoods. In the report "Concept for Cleveland, Scope of Work for a Concept Plan for Downtown Cleveland," 2, Halprin acknowledges the equity-planning efforts of Krumholz (Halprin Collection, 014.I.A.5631). Sonia Hirt tellingly does not include Halprin's innovative plan for the downtown in her article on the evolution of cutting-edge planning in Cleveland.

80. Wasserman was the West Coast office manager who had previously run an architecture firm in San Francisco committed to low-income housing. See the manuscript "Cleveland Downtown, Urban Diagnosis Speech" for Wasserman's slide presentation (Halprin Collection, 014.I.A.5430). The *Plain Dealer* published a number of articles on this early process (see Halprin's scrapbooks in the Halprin Collection).

81. As indicated in various notes documents in the Halprin Collection, 014.I.A.5644.

82. See the list of workshop participants in "Cleveland Take Part Workshop, Objectives for Downtown, Report & Recommendations" (June 1973), 10–12 (Halprin Collection, 014.I.A.5644). Notes in the Halprin Collection reveal the firm's initial interest in finding representatives of different neighborhoods such as Chinatown, Hough, Fairfax, and the inner-ring suburbs of Cleveland and Shaker Heights, as well as of various social programs, community development corporations, schools, the library, the universities, and the "young people." Find these various handwritten notes documents in the Halprin Collection, 014.I.A.5644. See Halprin Collection, 014.I.A.5644, for notes on Wasserman's preworkshop planning

interviews with community leaders, including the director of the Hough Area Development Corporation and the planning director Norman Krumholz, and for the document "Guidelines for Conversations with Cleveland Workshop Prospects."

83. "Cleveland Take Part Workshop, Objectives for Downtown, Report & Recommendations," 29.

84. "Community Workshop: Scores for Downtown Cleveland Take Part Workshop" (Halprin Collection, 014.I.A.5643). All the activities explained in this section are from this document unless otherwise noted.

85. In fact, Halprin noted the emphasis of the group, claiming that "safety more than had thought," in his handwritten document "Summary of Score 1—Eating Score" (Halprin Collection, 014.I.A.5643), reproduced in "Cleveland Take Part Workshop, Objectives for Downtown, Report & Recommendations."

86. See "Take Part Participatory Workshops for People's Involvement in Planning Their Environment Mini Workshop for LH&A Workshop Leaders, 10 April 1973" (Halprin Collection, 014.I.A.3826), and *Taking Part*, 233. The founding date of the city, 1796, matches that of Cleveland.

87. "Cleveland Take Part Workshop, Objectives for Downtown," 16.

88. Ibid., 20, and *Taking Part*, 232.

89. All the quotations for this paragraph came from various handwritten notes contained in the Halprin Collection, 014.I.A.5643.

90. "Cleveland Take Part Workshop, Objectives for Downtown," 24.

91. "Scores for Downtown Cleveland Take Part Workshop" (Halprin Collection, 014.I.A.5643).

92. "Cleveland Take Part Workshop, Objectives for Downtown," 26.

93. "Scores for Downtown Cleveland Take Part Workshop" (Halprin Collection, 014.I.A.5643).

94. The statements and the tabulated results are reproduced in *Taking Part*, 241–42.

95. Lawrence Halprin & Associates, "Concept for Cleveland: A Report to the People of Cleveland on Their Downtown," 6.

96. "Scores for Downtown Cleveland Take Part Workshop" (Halprin Collection, 014.I.A.5643).

97. "Cleveland Take Part Workshop, Objectives for Downtown," 51–61; see also "Turn Downtown into Funtown, Planners Urge," clipping in the Halprin Collection, 014.I.A.5644, which highlights these more innovative ideas.

98. *Taking Part*, 260–61 (italics in the original).

99. As it was called on the final page of "Cleveland Take Part Workshop, Objectives for Downtown."

100. "Concept for Cleveland, Scope of Work for a Concept Plan for Downtown Cleveland," prepared by Lawrence Halprin & Associates for the Downtown Council of the Greater Cleveland Growth Association, January 1974, 8.

101. Tom Koenig notes: "We must understand from the start, the importance of the center as the main SYMBOL of the DOWNTOWN PLAN. Because a planning project, unlike architecture, offers no specific tangible visible thing to see being built, the Center will be that visible symbol. It will be 'place' associated with the plan" (Halprin Collection, 014.I.A.5638).

102. See the February 1975 article "Be a City Planner, Tell Halprin What You Want Downtown," in *Cleveland*

Magazine. The score states: "Tomorrow, pay close attention to how you got to work, how you move around the city during your day, how you get home. Make a map of your day's movements and your method of transportation. Say how you liked it. And bring to the Downtown Workshop."

103. Handwritten document by "TK," dated August 14, 1974 (Halprin Collection, 014.I.A.5638; capitalization in the original).

104. Cullinan, "Halprin's Plan: Give People Shops, Restaurants, Trees, Arcades and *Joie di vivre*," 1.

105. It is particularly telling that Norman Krumholz, in an e-mail correspondence with the author in 2007, did not mention the Take Part Process when he described Halprin's work in Cleveland. Krumholz only focused on Halprin's proposal for the "rejuvenation" of the lake and riverfront, adding that he "didn't think [Halprin's] work here was particularly innovative."

106. Julian Krawcheck, "No Commitment to Halprin Plan for City Coy Says," unknown press source, October 31, 1975, B12. Clipping found in the Halprin Collection, 014.I.A.3805.

107. Halprin was awarded an honorary grant from the Cleveland Foundation to return to Cleveland in 1985 for a "retrospective review" (the Cleveland Foundation was then referred to as the "Cleveland Development Foundation"). See the letter from Herbert E. Strawbridge to Halprin dated October 2, 1985 (Halprin Collection, 014.I.B.1479). In his short document dated October 24, 1985, Halprin stated that although downtown Cleveland was undergoing some redevelopment, his recommendations were still quite valid.

108. Hester, "Interview with Lawrence Halprin," 47–48.

109. See Jeremy Till, "The Negotiation of Hope," on what he calls "transformative participation."

CONCLUSION

1. Halprin's notes on "Modernism," dated April 22, 1992, directed to Peter Walter and Melanie Simo in preparation for their book *Invisible Gardens*. The notes can be found in the Halprin Collection, 014.I.B.2479 (italics and capitalization in the original).

2. Condon in his January 1, 1989, reply in *Landscape Journal* to Halprin's response to "Cubist Space, Volumetric Space, and Landscape Architecture."

3. Halprin's response (*Landscape Journal*, Fall 1989) to Condon's "Cubist Space, Volumetric Space, and Landscape Architecture."

4. Andreas Huyssen, "Mapping the Postmodern," 16, 22.

5. See Spirn, *The Granite Garden*, 161–63, on the ecological performance of Skyline Park, which was built as a depressed space to retain stormwater to prevent the destructive recurrence of the Platte River Flood of 1965.

6. Halprin's 1960 lecture can be found in the Halprin Collection, 014.I.A.6141.

7. Wall, "Programming the Urban Surface," 246.

8. Corner, "Terra Fluxus," 31.

BIBLIOGRAPHY

ARCHIVAL COLLECTIONS

Halprin, Anna. Papers. San Francisco Performing Arts Library and Museum (now the Museum of Performance and Design). San Francisco, California.

Halprin, Lawrence. Collection. The Architectural Archives, University of Pennsylvania. Philadelphia, Pennsylvania.

Heritage Park Files. City of Fort Worth Parks and Community Services Department. Fort Worth, Texas.

Historic Fort Worth, Inc. Archives. Fort Worth, Texas.

Seattle Municipal Archives. Seattle, Washington.

REFERENCES

Abbott, Carl. *Portland: Planning, Politics, and Growth in a Twentieth-Century City.* Lincoln: University of Nebraska Press, 1983.

———. "Two Portland Fountains Come of Age." *Landscape Architecture* 83, no. 3 (March 1993): 46–48.

Abrams, Charles. *The City Is the Frontier.* New York: Harper Row, 1965.

Alinsky, Saul. *Rules for Radicals.* New York: Vintage Books, 1971.

"The All-Europe House." *RIBA Journal* 46, no. 3 (June 26, 1939): 813–19.

Amundsen, Craig A. "The New Nicollet Mall." *Urban Land* 52, no. 4 (April 1993): 70–71.

———. "Tomorrow's Nicollet Mall." *Architecture Minnesota* 14, no. 4 (July–August 1988): 34–39.

Anderson, Martin. *The Federal Bulldozer: A Critical Analysis of Urban Renewal, 1949–1962.* Cambridge, Mass.: MIT Press, 1964.

Appleyard, Donald, Kevin Lynch, and John R. Myer. *The View from the Road.* Cambridge, Mass.: MIT Press, 1964.

Arnstein, Sherry R. "A Ladder of Citizen Participation." *Journal of the American Institute of Planners* 35, no. 4 (July 1969): 216–24.

Aschman, Frederick T. "Nicollet Mall: Civic Cooperation to Preserve Downtown's Vitality." *Planners Notebook* 1, no. 6 (Sept 1971): entire issue.

Atshuler, Alan. *The City Planning Process: A Political Analysis*. Ithaca, N.Y.: Cornell University Press, 1965.

———. "The Goals of Comprehensive Planning." *Journal of the American Institute of Planners* 31, no. 3 (1965): 186–97.

Auther, Elissa, and Adam Lerner, eds. *West of Center: Art and the Counterculture Experiment in America, 1965–1977*. Minneapolis: University of Minnesota Press, 2012.

Bacon, Edmund. *Design of Cities*. New York: Viking Press, 1967.

Balloon, Hilary, and Kenneth Jackson, eds. *Robert Moses and the Modern City: The Transformation of New York*. New York: Norton, 2007.

Banes, Sally, ed. *Reinventing Dance in the 1960s: Everything Was Possible*. Madison: University of Wisconsin Press, 2003.

Bauer, Catherine. *Modern Housing*. Boston: Houghton Mifflin, 1934.

Beardsley, John. "Being in Space: Lawrence Halprin's Urban Ecologies and the Reconciliation of Modernism's Ideals." In *Where the Revolution Began*, ed. Randy Gragg. Washington, D.C.: Spacemaker Press, 2009.

Bennett, Charles G. "City Plans Study on Use of Spaces." *New York Times*, August 12, 1967, 27.

Berleant, Arnold. *Art and Engagement*. Philadelphia: Temple University Press, 1991.

Bernstein, David W. *The San Francisco Tape Music Center: 1960s Counterculture and the Avant-Garde*. Berkeley: University of California Press, 2008.

Birnbaum, Charles A., ed. *Preserving Modern Landscape Architecture: Papers from the Wave Hill—National Park Service Conference*. Cambridge, Mass.: Spacemaker Press, 1999.

Birnbaum, Charles A. with Jane Brown Gillette and Nancy Slade, eds. *Preserving Modern Landscape Architecture II: Making Postwar Landscapes Visible*. Cambridge, Mass.: Spacemaker Press, 2004.

Blake, Judy. "Impressionistic Tour of Everett." *Everett Herald*, September 28, 1970, 3A.

Blofeld, John, ed. and trans. *I Ching: The Book of Change*. New York: E. P. Dutton, 1965.

Blow, Steve. "We're One Hurdle Away from Park on Bluffs." *Fort Worth Press*, October 1, 1974, 5.

"The Blue Ring: Connecting Places, 100-year Vision, Seattle's Open Space Strategy for the Center City." Revised draft of publicity brochure generated by the City of Seattle. June 2002. www.seattle.gov/dpd/stellent/groups/pan/@pan/@plan/@citydesign/documents/web_informational/dpds_006516.pdf (accessed March 2005).

Blumenthal, Ralph. "See, Hear, Taste, Smell Used in New Urban Planning Method." *New York Times*, January 10, 1972, 18.

Brown, Charles. "Menu at Freeway Park: Sandwiches and Sousa," *Seattle Times*, September 16, 1978, A12.

"Building the River Dream, Bit by Bit." *Fort Worth Star–Telegram*, January 21, 1996, editorial section, 1.

Burns, Jim. *Arthropods: New Design Futures*. New York: Praeger, 1972.

———. *Connections: Ways to Discover and Realize Community Potentials.* Stroudsburg, Penn.: Dowden, Hutchinson and Ross, 1979.

———. "Positive Proposals on 'Beauty.'" *Progressive Architecture* 48 (March 1967): 176–79.

"California to Come." *Interiors* (July 1971): 72.

Campbell, Joseph. *The Masks of God: Primitive Mythology.* New York: Viking Press, 1959.

Carson, Rachel. *Silent Spring.* New York: Houghton Mifflin, 1962.

Christianson, Kate. "Nicollet Mall Redux." *Inland Architect* 35, no. 2 (March/April 1991): 30–32.

Church, Thomas. *Gardens Are for People.* New York: Reinhold, 1955.

———. "The Small California Garden, Chapter One: A New Deal for the Small Lot." *California Arts and Architecture* (May 1933): 16–17, 32.

———. *Your Private World: A Study of Intimate Gardens.* San Francisco: Chronicle Books, 1969.

Church, Thomas, and Lawrence Halprin. "You Have a Gold Mine in Your Backyard." *House Beautiful* 91, no.1 (January 1949): 37–53.

Ciampi, Mario et al. *The Market Street Design Plan Summary Report.* Prepared for the City and County of San Francisco, November 1967.

Cleveland City Planning Commission. *Cleveland Policy Planning Report.* Cleveland: City Planning Commission, 1974.

Conan, Michel, ed. *Environmentalism in Landscape Architecture.* Washington, D.C.: Dumbarton Oaks Research Library and Collection, 2000.

———, ed. *Landscape Design and the Experience of Motion.* Washington, D.C.: Dumbarton Oaks Research Library and Collection, 2003.

Condon, Patrick. "Cubist Space, Volumetric Space, and Landscape Architecture." *Landscape Journal* 7, no. 1 (Spring 1988): 1–14.

"Conversation with Lawrence Halprin, Urban Planner." *Cleveland Magazine* (February 1975): 16–28.

Cook, Robert E. "Do Landscapes Learn? Ecology's 'New Paradigm' and Design in Landscape Architecture." In *Environmentalism in Landscape Architecture*, ed. Michel Conan. Washington, D.C.: Dumbarton Oaks, 2000.

Cooper-Hewitt Museum. *Urban Open Spaces.* Revised edition. New York: Rizzoli, 1981.

Corner, James, ed. *Recovering Landscape: Essays in Contemporary Landscape Architecture.* New York: Princeton Architectural Press, 1999.

———. "Representation and Landscape: Drawing and Making in the Landscape Medium." *Word and Image* 8, no. 3 (July–September 1992): 243–75.

———. "Terra Fluxus." In *The Landscape Urbanism Reader*, ed. Charles Waldheim. New York: Princeton Architectural Press, 2006.

Cullen, Gordon. *Townscape.* New York: Reinhold, 1961.

Cullinan, Helen. "Halprin's Plan: Give People Shops, Restaurants, Trees, Arcades and *Joie di vivre.*" *Plain Dealer*, September 14, 1975, 5: 1, 3, 9.

Dailey, Gardner. "The Post-War House." In *Domestic Architecture of the San Francisco Bay Region*. San Francisco: San Francisco Museum of Art, 1949.

Danadjieva, Angela. "Seattle's Freeway Park II: Danadjieva on the Creative Process." *Landscape Architecture* 67, no. 5 (September 1977): 404–6.

Davidoff, Paul. "Advocacy and Pluralism in Planning." *Journal of the American Institute of Planners* 31, no. 4 (November 1965): 331–38.

Davis, Douglas. "Planning Spaces for People, Not Buildings." *National Observer* (June 23, 1969).

Davis, Howard. "Portland Center, Portland, Oregon: Skidmore, Owings and Merrill; Lawrence Halprin." *Center: A Journal for Architecture in America* 5 (1989): 128–29.

Denver Renewed: Denver Urban Renewal Authority, History of DURA 1958–1983. Denver: Denver Foundation, 1992.

Dewey, John. *Art as Experience*. New York: Minton, Balch and Co., 1934.

"Downtown Minneapolis' Urban Renaissance." *Grounds Maintenance* 3, no. 11 (November 1968): 24–28.

Doyle, Michael William, and Peter Braunstein, eds. *Imagine Nation: The American Counterculture of the 1960s and '70s*. New York: Routledge, 2002.

Duhl, Leonard J., ed. *The Urban Condition: People and Policy in the Metropolis*. New York: Simon and Schuster, 1963.

Duncan, Isadora. *My Life*. New York: Boni and Liveright, 1927.

Eckbo, Garrett. *Landscape for Living*. New York: Duell, Sloan, and Pearce, 1950.

Eckbo, Garrett, Dan Kiley, and James C. Rose. "Landscape Design in the Primeval Environment." *Architectural Record* 87 (February 1940): 73–79.

———. "Landscape Design in the Rural Environment." *Architectural Record* 86 (August 1939): 68–74.

———. "Landscape Design in the Urban Environment." *Architectural Record* 85 (May 1939): 70–77.

Eco, Umberto. *Opera Aperta*. Milan: Fabri, 1962. Translated into English as *The Open Work*. Cambridge, Mass.: Harvard University Press, 1989.

Ehrlich, Susan. *Pacific Dreams: Currents of Surrealism and Fantasy in California Art, 1934–1957*. Los Angeles: UCLA at the Armand Hammer Museum of Art and Cultural Center, 1995.

Engels, B. "L. Halprin: 'Tomorrow's Architect.'" *Evening News* (Newark, N.J.), July 14, 1972, 12.

Forgey, Benjamin. "Lawrence Halprin: Maker of Places and Living Spaces." *Smithsonian* 19, no. 9 (December 1988): 160–70.

Foster, Paul J., and Barbara Gibson. *Denver's Skyline Park: A History*. Denver: City and County of Denver, 2000.

Frampton, Kenneth. "Toward an Urban Landscape." *Columbia Documents* 4 (1995): 83–93.

Fried, Marc. "Grieving for a Lost Home." In *The Urban Condition: People and Policy in the Metropolis*, ed. Leonard J. Duhl. New York: Basic Books, 1963.

Friedberg, Paul. *Play and Interplay: A Manifesto for New Design in Urban Recreational Environment*. New York: Macmillan, 1970.

Frieden, Bernard J. *The Future of Old Neighborhoods: Rebuilding for a Changing Population.* Cambridge, Mass.: MIT Press, 1964.

Frieden, Bernard J., and Lynne B. Sagalyn. *Downtown, Inc.: How America Rebuilds.* Cambridge, Mass.: MIT Press, 1989.

Fruin, "Pedway Systems in Urban Centers," *Civil Engineering–ASCE* 43, no. 9 (September 1973): 63–66.

Gans, Herbert. *People and Plans: Essays on Urban Problems and Solutions.* New York: Basic Books, 1968.

———. *The Urban Villagers: Group and Class in the Life of Italian-Americans.* New York: Free Press, 1962.

"Garden Setting Lends Charm to Chicago's Newest Center." *Architectural Forum* 107 (September 1957): 227.

Geddes, Patrick. *Cities in Evolution: An Introduction to the Town Planning Movement and to the Study of Civics.* London: Williams and Norgate, 1915.

Gelfand, Mark. *A Nation of Cities: The Federal Government and Urban America, 1933–1965.* New York: Oxford University Press, 1975.

Glazer, Nathan, and Daniel Patrick Moynihan. *Beyond the Melting Pot: The Negroes, Puerto Ricans, Jews, Italians, and Irish of New York City.* Cambridge, Mass.: MIT Press, 1963.

Goffman, Erving. *Behavior in Public Places: Notes on the Social Organization of Gatherings.* New York: Free Press of Glencoe, 1963.

———. *The Presentation of Self in Everyday Life.* Edinburgh: University of Edinburgh, Social Science Research Centre, 1956.

———. *Relations in Public.* New York: Basic Books, 1971.

Goldberger, Paul. "Will a 'New' Market Street Mean a New San Francisco?" *New York Times,* April 2, 1979, C15.

Goldstein, Barbara. "Participation Workshops." *Architectural Design* 44, no. 4 (April 1974): 207–12.

Goodman, Paul, and Percival Goodman. *Communitas: Means of Livelihood and Ways of Life.* Chicago: University of Chicago Press, 1947.

Goodman, Robert. *After the Planners.* New York: Simon and Schuster, 1972.

Gragg, Randy. "Urban Plazas that Set Portland's Modern Landscape Get Some TLC." *Oregonian,* June 29, 2003, A1.

———, ed. *Where the Revolution Began: Lawrence and Anna Halprin and the Reinvention of Public Space.* Washington, D.C.: Spacemaker Press, 2009.

"The Grand Plans for Market Street, by Day and Night, Avenue of Sights to Please the Eye." *San Francisco Examiner,* October 19, 1969, 33.

Greer, Scott. *Urban Renewal and American Cities: The Dilemma of Democratic Intervention.* Indianapolis: Bobbs-Merrill, 1965.

Gropius, Walter. *The Scope of Total Architecture.* New York: Collier Books, 1962.

———, ed. *The Theatre of the Bauhaus.* Middletown, Conn.: Wesleyan University Press, 1961.

Gruen, Victor. *Centers for the Urban Environment: Survival of the Cities*. New York: Van Nostrand Reinhold, 1973.

———. *The Heart of Our Cities. The Urban Crisis: Diagnosis and Cure*. New York: Simon and Schuster, 1964.

Gruen, Victor, and Larry Smith. *Shopping Towns USA: The Planning of Shopping Centers*. New York: Van Nostrand Reinhold, 1960.

Guest, Ann Hutchinson. *Labanotation: The System of Analyzing and Recording Movement*. New York: Routledge, 2013.

Haar, Charles. *Between the Idea and the Reality: A Study in the Origin, Fate, and Legacy of the Model Cities Program*. Boston: Little, Brown, 1975.

Habermas, Jürgen. *Structural Transformation of the Public Sphere: An Inquiry into a Category of Bourgeois Society*. Cambridge, Mass.: MIT Press, 1989.

H'Doubler, Margaret. *Dance: A Creative Art Experience*. New York: F. S. Crofts, 1940.

Hall, Edward T. *The Hidden Dimension*. Garden City, N.Y.: Doubleday, 1966.

———. *The Silent Language*. Greenwich, Conn.: Fawcett, 1959.

Halprin, Anna. "Intuition and Improvisation in Dance." *Impulse: Annual of Contemporary Dance* (1955): 10–15.

———. "Mutual Creation." *Tulane Drama Review* 13, no. 1 (Fall 1968): 163–74.

Halprin, Anna, and Jim Burns. "Ceremony of Us." *Tulane Drama Review* 13, no. 4 (Summer 1969): 131–43.

"Halprin Firm Named Skyline Park Designers." *Denver Post*, April 24, 1970, 28.

Halprin, Lawrence. "Angles for Economy." *Los Angeles Times*, February 6, 1949, H13.

———. "The Choreography of Gardens." *Impulse: Annual of Contemporary Dance* (1949): 32–33.

———. "Christopher Tunnard's Influence on Halprin." *Landscape Architecture* 50 (September 1979): 466.

———. *Cities*. New York: Reinhold Publishing Corporation, 1963. Second edition, Cambridge, Mass.: MIT Press, 1972.

———. "The Collective Perception of Cities." In *Urban Open Spaces*. Revised edition. New York: Rizzoli, 1981.

———. "Commentary." *Landscape Journal* 8, no. 2 (Fall 1989): 151–52.

———. "Dance Deck in the Woods." *Impulse: Annual of Contemporary Dance* (1956): 22–25.

———. "Design as a Value System." *Places* 6, no. 1 (Fall 1989): 60–67.

———. "A Discussion of 'The Five-Legged Stool.'" *San Francisco Chronicle*, April 29, 1962, 3.

———. *Freeways*. New York: Reinhold Publishing Corporation, 1966.

———. "The Gardens of the High Sierra." *Landscape* 11, no. 2 (Winter 1961–1962): 26–28.

———. "Good Theater in the Garden." *Sunset: The Magazine of Western Living* (July 1947): 44–45.

———. "Hill Garden: The Importance of Edge." *Landscape Architecture* 50, no. 2 (Winter 1959–1960): 96–99.

———. "How to Score." *Royal Institute of British Architects Journal* 78 (July 1971): 290–94.

———. "The Last 40 Years: A Personal Overview of Landscape Architecture in America." *Space Design*, no. 235 (April 1984): 118–21.

———. *A Life Spent Changing Places*. Philadelphia: University of Pennsylvania Press, 2011.

———. "Motation." *Progressive Architecture* 46 (July 1965): 126–33.

———. "Nature into Landscape into Art." *Ekistics* 333 (November–December 1988): 349–54.

———. *Notebooks: 1959–1971*. Cambridge, Mass.: MIT Press, 1972.

———. "Over-Ordering the Environment." *Progressive Architecture* 45 (March 1964): 180–198.

———. "Point of View." *Landscape Architecture* 76, no. 6 (November–December 1986): 78–79.

———. "Preserving the Modern Landscape: The Views of Lawrence Halprin." *Cultural Landscape Foundation*, http://www.tclf.org/view_halprin.htm (accessed June 2009).

———. "Rebuttal: Chaos on the Piazza." *Architectural Forum* 116 (January 1962).

———. *The RSVP Cycles: Creative Processes and the Human Environment*. New York: G. Braziller, 1969.

———. "The Shape of Erosion." *Landscape Architecture* 52, no. 1 (January 1962): 87–88.

———. *Sketchbooks of Lawrence Halprin*. Tokyo: Process Architecture, 1981.

———. "Structure and Garden Spaces Related in Sequence." *Progressive Architecture* 39 (May 1958): 95–103.

———, and Jim Burns. *Taking Part: A Workshop Approach to Collective Creativity*. Cambridge, Mass.: MIT Press, 1974.

Halprin, Lawrence et al. "5-Legged Stool." *Impulse: Annual of Contemporary Dance* (1962): 37.

"Halprins to Assist in Festival Activities." *Fort Worth Star–Telegram*, April 29, 1973, 6F.

Hardwick, M. Jeffrey. *Mall Maker: Victor Gruen, Architect of an American Dream*. Philadelphia: University of Pennsylvania Press, 2004.

Harris, Dianne. "Making Your Private World: Modern Landscape Architecture and *House Beautiful*. In T*he Architecture of Landscape, 1940–1960*, ed. Marc Treib. Philadelphia: University of Pennsylvania Press, 2002.

———. "Thomas Church as Author: Publicity and the Professional at Mid-Century." *Studies in the History of Gardens and Designed Landscapes* 20, no. 2 (Summer 2000): 157–70.

Hartman, Chester. "The Housing of Relocated Families." *Journal of American Institute of Planners* 30, no. 4 (November 1964): 266–86.

———. *Yerba Buena: Land Grab and Community Resistance in San Francisco*. Berkeley: University of California Press, 1974.

Harvey, David. *The Condition of Postmodernity: An Enquiry into the Origins of Cultural Change*. New York: Blackwell, 1989.

———. *Social Justice and the City*. Baltimore: Johns Hopkins University Press, 1973.

Heffley, Divya Rao. "Vision in Motion: Architectural Space Time Notation and Urban Design, 1950–1970." Ph.D. diss., Brown University, 2011.

Henderson, Joseph. "Dance in Relation to the Individual and Society." *Impulse: Annual of Contemporary Dance* (1951): 1–2.

———. "Psychology and the Roots of Design." In *Lawrence Halprin: Changing Places*. San Francisco: San Francisco Museum of Modern Art, 1986.

Hester, Randy. "Interview with Lawrence Halprin." *Places* 12, no. 2 (Winter 1999): 42–51.

———. *User Needs as Design Determinants: Eight Case Studies.* Raleigh: North Carolina State University, 1975.

Hirsch, Alison B. "Activist Landscape Architects of the 1960s," *Places* (forthcoming).

———. "Facilitation and/or Manipulation? Participatory Planning During Urban Renewal." *Landscape Journal* 31, nos. 1–2 (Winter 2012): 119–36.

———. "Lawrence Halprin: The Choreography of Private Gardens." *Studies in the History of Gardens and Designed Landscapes* 27, no. 4 (October–December 2007): 258–355.

———. "Lawrence Halprin's Public Spaces: Design, Experience, and Recovery. Three Case Studies." *Studies in the History of Gardens and Designed Landscapes* 26, no. 1 (January–March 2006): 1–97.

———. "Scoring the Participatory City: Lawrence (and Anna) Halprin's Take Part Process." *Journal of Architectural Education* 64, no. 2 (March 2011): 127–40.

Hirt, Sonia. "Toward Postmodern Urbanism? Evolution of Planning in Cleveland, Ohio." *Journal of Planning Education and Research* 25, no. 1 (2005): 27–42.

Hood, Walter. *Urban Diaries.* Washington, D.C.: Spacemaker Press, 1997.

Hoving, Thomas. "Think Big about Small Parks." *New York Times,* April 10, 1966, 13, 68–72.

Huizinga, Johan. *Homo Ludens: A Study of the Play-Element in Culture.* Boston: Beacon Press, 1950.

Huyssen, Andreas. "Mapping the Postmodern." *New German Critique,* no. 33 (August 1984): 5–52.

Huxtable, Ada Louise. "Coast Fountain Melds Art and Environment." *New York Times,* June 21, 1970, 53.

———. "Critic Lauds Auditorium Forecourt." *Sunday Oregonian,* June 21, 1970 1.

———. "In Portland, Ore., Urban Decay Is Masked by Natural Splendor." *New York Times,* June 19, 1970, 39, 75.

———. "Nobody Here but Us New Yorkers." *New York Times,* May 19, 1968, D34.

Imbert, Dorothée. *The Modernist Garden in France.* New Haven, Conn.: Yale University Press, 1993.

Isenberg, Alison. "'Culture-a-Go-Go': The Arts of Redevelopment in 1960s San Francisco." *Journal of Social History* 44, no. 2 (Winter 2010): 379–412.

———. *Downtown America: A History of the Place and the People Who Made It.* Chicago: University of Chicago Press, 2005.

Jacobs, Jane. *The Death and Life of Great American Cities.* New York: Random House, 1961.

———. "Downtown Is for People." *Fortune* 57, no. 4 (April 1958): 133–39.

Jacques, David, and Jan Woudstra. *Landscape Modernism Renounced: The Career of Christopher Tunnard.* New York: Routledge, 2009.

Jameson, Fredric. "Periodizing the 60s." *Social Text* 9/10 (Spring–Summer 1984): 178–209.

"Japan's Ancient Past Lives at Freeway Park." *Seattle Post–Intelligencer,* August 28, 1976, A14.

Jones, Peter Blundell, Doina Petrescu, and Jeremy Till, eds. *Architecture and Participation.* London: Spon Press, 2005.

Jung, Carl G. "Approaching the Unconscious." In *Man and His Symbols,* ed. Carl G. Jung. Garden City, N.Y.: Doubleday, 1964.

——, ed. *Man and His Symbols.* Garden City, NY: Doubleday, 1964.

Kaplan, Rachel, ed., and Anna Halprin. *Anna Halprin, Moving Toward Life: Five Decades of Transformational Dance.* Hanover, N.H.: University Press of New England and Wesleyan University Press, 1995.

Kepes, Gyorgy, ed. *Arts of the Environment.* New York: Braziller, 1972.

——. *Language of Vision.* Chicago: P. Theobald, 1944.

——. *Nature and Art of Motion.* New York: Braziller, 1965.

Keyes, Langley, and Edward Teitcher. "Limitations of Advocacy Planning: A View from the Establishment." *Journal of the American Institute of Planners* (July 1970): 225.

Kirby, Michael. "The New Theatre." *Tulane Drama Review* 10, no. 2 (Winter 1965): 23–43.

Klee, Paul. *The Thinking Eye: The Notebooks of Paul Klee.* New York: Wittenborn, 1961.

Krumholz, Norman. "City Planning for Greater Equity." *Journal of Architectural and Planning Research* 3, no. 4 (1986): 163–74.

Lawrence Halprin & Associates. *Concept for Cleveland: A Report to the People of Cleveland on Their Downtown.* Prepared for the City of Cleveland, the Greater Cleveland Growth Association, and the Cleveland Foundation, 1975.

——. *Everett Community Plan.* Prepared for the City of Everett, Washington, Mayor Robert Anderson, and the City Council, December 1972.

——. *New York, New York: A Study of the Quality, Character, and Meaning of Open Space in Urban Design.* New York: Prepared for the City of New York, Housing and Development Administration, 1968.

——. *Take Part: A Report on New Ways in Which People Can Participate in Planning Their Own Environments.* San Francisco/New York, 1972.

——. *The Willamette Valley: Choices for the Future.* Prepared for the Willamette Valley Environmental Protection and Development Planning Council, October 1972.

"Lawrence Halprin." *Process Architecture,* no. 4 (February 1978): entire issue. Third edition, March 1984.

Lawrence Halprin: Changing Places. San Francisco: San Francisco Museum of Modern Art, 1986.

Lawrence Halprin Landscape Conservancy. *Where the Revolution Began: Lawrence Halprin and the Reinvention of Portland Public Space* (publicity pamphlet). Portland, Ore.: Lawrence Halprin Landscape Conservancy, 2008.

Lefebvre, Henri. *Rhythmanalysis: Space, Time, and Everyday Life.* London: Continuum, 2004.

Lindgren, Nilo. "A Radical Experiment in Reorganization: A 'Spectacular and Poignant Attempt at Management Reform' within Lawrence Halprin and Associates." *Landscape Architecture* 64, no. 3 (April 1974): 133–39, 190–91.

——. "Riding a Revolution: A Radical Experiment in Reorganization." *Innovation* 18 (1971): 46–60.

Livingston and Blayney et al. *What to Do about Market Street: A Prospectus for a Development Program.* San Francisco, October 1962.

Lynch, Kevin. *The Image of the City.* Cambridge, Mass.: MIT Press, 1960.

——. *What Time Is This Place?* Cambridge, Mass.: MIT Press, 1972.

Lyndon, Donlyn. "Concrete Cascade in Portland." *Architectural Forum* 125, no. 1 (July–August 1966): 74–79.

MacKaye, Benton. *The New Exploration: A Philosophy of Regional Planning.* New York: Harcourt, Brace and Co., 1928.

Malo, Paul. *Landmarks of Rochester and Monroe County.* Syracuse, N.Y.: Syracuse University Press, 1974.

Marcus, Clare Cooper. *Easter Hill Village: Some Social Implications of Design.* New York: Free Press, 1975.

Marshall, Margaret. "Seattle Freeway Park I: How the Impossible Came to Be." *Landscape Architecture* 67, no. 5 (September 1977): 399–402.

Martin, Roger. "Exciting Start with Nicollet Mall." *Landscape Architecture* 59, no. 4 (July 1969): 299–304.

Marvin Hatami and Associates and Tanaka and Associates. *Urban Design and Development Study: Skyline Urban Renewal Project.* Denver, Colo.:Prepared for the Denver Urban Renewal Authority, 1970.

Mathur, Anuradha, and Dilip da Cunha. *Deccan Traverses: The Making of Bangalore's Terrain.* New Delhi: Rupa and Co., 2006.

———. *Mississippi Floods: Designing a Shifting Landscape.* New Haven, Conn.: Yale University Press, 2001.

———. *SOAK: Mumbai in an Estuary.* New Delhi: Rupa and Co., 2009.

"Mayfest and Park Make Happy Pair." *Fort Worth Star–Telegram,* May 8, 1973, 6-C.

McHarg, Ian. *Design with Nature.* New York: Natural History Press, 1969.

———. "Ecological Determinism." In *The Future Environments of North America,* ed. John P. Milton. New York: National History Press, 1966.

McInelly, Marcy. "The Lawrence Halprin Landscapes Conservancy, Restoration Master Plan & Tree Rejuvenation Project, Portland, Oregon." Cultural Landscape Foundation, http://www.tclf.org/halprin_portland.htm (accessed June 2007).

Merleau-Ponty, Maurice. *Phenomenology of Perception.* New York: Humanities Press, 1962.

Metzger, Jeanne. "Over-30 Crowd Experiences 'Cruising Colby' Routine." *Everett Herald,* September 28, 1970, 3A.

———. "Workshop Participants Follow 'Score' Prepared by Planning 'Maestro' for Unusual Tour of City." *Everett Herald,* September 28, 1970, 3A.

Meyer, Elizabeth. "Post-Earth Day Conundrum: Translating Environmental Values into Landscape Design." In *Environmentalism in Landscape Architecture,* ed. Michel Conan. Washington, D.C.: Dumbarton Oaks Research Library and Collection, 2000.

———. "Situating Modern Landscape Architecture" (1992). In *Theory in Landscape Architecture,* ed. Simon Swaffield. Philadelphia: University of Pennsylvania Press, 2002.

Moholy-Nagy, Lázló. "Theater, Circus, Variety." In *The Theater of the Bauhaus,* ed. Walter Gropius. Middletown, Conn.: Wesleyan University Press, 1961.

———. *Vision in Motion.* Chicago: Paul Theobald and Co., 1947.

Moholy-Nagy, Sibyl. *Matrix of Man: An Illustrated History of the Urban Environment.* New York: Praeger, 1968.

———. "Modern Art and Modern Dance." *Impulse: Annual of Contemporary Dance* (1951): 3–5.

Moore, Charles. "Still Pools and Crashing Waves." In *Lawrence Halprin: Changing Places*. San Francisco: San Francisco Museum of Modern Art, 1986.

Mumford, Lewis. "The Architecture of the Bay Region." In *Domestic Architecture of the San Francisco Bay Region*. San Francisco: San Francisco Museum of Art, 1949.

———. *The City in History: Its Origins, Its Transformations, and Its Prospects*. New York: Harcourt, Brace and World, 1961.

———. "The Fourth Migration." *Survey Graphic* 54, no. 6 (May 1, 1925): 130–33.

Museum of Modern Art. *The New City: Architecture and Urban Renewal*. New York: Museum of Modern Art, 1967.

Neckar, Lance M. "Christopher Tunnard: The Garden in the Modern Landscape." In *Modern Landscape Architecture: A Critical Review*, ed. Marc Treib. Cambridge, Mass.: MIT Press, 1993.

Noe, Samuel, and B. L. Abernathy. "Urbanography." *Progressive Architecture* 47 (April 1966): 184–90.

Odum, Eugene. *Fundamentals of Ecology*. Philadelphia: Saunders, 1953.

"Oregonians Fight to Save Fountain." *New York Times*, July 11, 1972, 27.

Pastier, John. "Evaluation: Park Atop a Freeway." *AIA Journal* 72, no. 6 (June 1983): 43–47.

Pearson, Charles, and Joan Saffa. *Lawrence and Anna Halprin: Inner Landscapes*. VHS. San Francisco: KQED–TV, 1991.

Perls, Frederick S., Ralph F. Hefferline, and Paul Goodman. *Gestalt Therapy: Excitement and Growth in the Human Personality*. New York: Dell, 1951.

Phillips, Lisa. *Beat Culture and the New America, 1950–1965*. New York: Whitney Museum of Art, 1995.

Portland City Planning Commission et al. "Planning Guidelines—Portland Downtown Plan." Report for the City of Portland, Oregon, 1972.

"Portland's Plaza: It's Like Wow." *Progressive Architecture* 49 (May 1968): 163–65.

"Portland's Walk-In Waterfall." *Architectural Forum* 133, no. 3 (October 1970): 56–59.

Proshansky, Harold, William Ittelson, and Leanne Rivlin. *Environmental Psychology: Man and his Physical Setting*. New York: Holt, Rinehart and Winston, 1970.

Rainer, Yvonne, and Anna Halprin. "Yvonne Rainer Interviews Anna Halprin." *Tulane Drama Review* 10, no. 2 (Winter 1965): 142–67.

Rappaport, Roy. "Ritual." In *Folklore, Cultural Performances, and Popular Entertainments*, ed. R. Bauman. New York: Oxford University Press, 1992.

Relph, Edward. *Place and Placelessness*. London: Pion, 1976.

Riess, Suzanne B., interviewer. *Thomas D. Church, Landscape Architect*. 2 volumes. Berkeley: Regional Oral History Office, Bancroft Library, University of California, 1978.

Ross, Janice. "Anna Halprin and the 1960s: Acting in the Gap between the Personal, the Public, and the Political." In *Reinventing Dance in the 1960s: Everything was Possible*, ed. Sally Banes. Madison: University of Wisconsin, 2003.

———. *Anna Halprin: Experience as Dance*. Berkeley: University of California Press, 2007.

———. "Anna Halprin's Urban Rituals." *Tulane Drama Review* 48, no. 2 (Summer 2004): 49–67.

Roszak, Theodore. *The Making of a Counter Culture: Reflections of the Technocratic Society and Its Youthful Opposition*. Garden City, N.Y.: Doubleday, 1969.

———. *Where the Wasteland Ends: Politics and Transcendence in Postindustrial Society*. Garden City, N.Y.: Doubleday, 1972.

Rowe, Colin, and Fred Koetter. *Collage City*. Cambridge, Mass.: MIT Press, 1978.

Rubens, Lisa, interviewer. *Karl Linn: Landscape Architect in Service of Peace, Social Justice, Commons, and Community*. Berkeley: Regional Oral History Office, Bancroft Library, University of California, 2005.

San Francisco Museum of Art. *Contemporary Landscape Architecture and Its Sources*. San Francisco: San Francisco Museum of Art, 1937.

———. *Domestic Architecture of the San Francisco Bay Region*. San Francisco: San Francisco Museum of Art, 1949.

Sanoff, Henry, ed. *Designing with Community Participation*. Stroudsburg, Penn.: Dowden, Hutchinson and Ross, 1978.

Schurch, Thomas W. "Angela Danadjieva: Reshaping the American Urban Center." *Landscape Architecture* 78, no. 3 (April–May 1988): 72–77.

Sears, Paul B. "Ecology—A Subversive Subject." *Bioscience* 14, no. 7 (July 1964): 11–13.

"Seattle's 'Tomorrow Park' Opens July 4: It's Built on Top of a Freeway." *Sunset: The Magazine of Western Living* (July 1976): 52–55.

Sennett, Richard. *The Fall of Public Man*. New York: Knopf, 1976.

Shepard, Paul. *The Subversive Science: Essays Toward An Ecology of Man*. New York: Houghton Mifflin, 1969.

Sitte, Camillo. *City Planning According to Artistic Principles* (1889). Translated by George R. Collins and Christiane Crasemann Collins. London: Phaidon Press, 1965.

Sloan, Kevin W. "Second Man Missing: Lawrence Halprin and Associates' 1970s Heritage Plaza in Fort Worth remains Uncompleted and Undermaintained." *Landscape Architecture* 93, no. 4 (April 2003): 82–89.

Smith, Ken. "Case Study: Manhattan Square Park, Rochester, New York." In *Preserving Modern Landscape Architecture II: Making Postwar Landscapes Visible*, ed. C. Birnbaum et al. Washington, D.C.: Spacemaker Press, 2004.

Sommer, Robert. *Design Awareness*. San Francisco: Rinehart Press, 1972.

Spirn, Anne Whiston. *The Granite Garden*. New York: Basic Books, 1984.

Starr, Kevin. *Americans and the California Dream, 1850–1915*. New York: Oxford University Press, 1973.

Steinberg, Stephen. Interviews with Lawrence and Anna Halprin. 1988. Transcripts provided by Janice Ross.

St. John, Primus. "The Fountain." *Pioneer Log* (Lewis & Clark College, Portland, Oregon), 28, no. 37, April 3, 1970 (cover).

Svacina, Pat. "It Began Here, Pilgrim; Nearly Finished Park Honors Pioneers." *Dallas Morning News*, September 30, 1979, Fort Worth Metro section, cover page.

Swaffield, Simon. *Theory in Landscape Architecture: A Reader*. Philadelphia: University of Pennsylvania Press, 2002.

Teaford, Jon C. *The Rough Road to Renaissance: Urban Revitalization in America, 1940–1985*. Baltimore: Johns Hopkins University Press, 1990.

Temko, Allan. "The 'New' Market Street—An Unfulfilled Promise." *San Francisco Chronicle*, March 21, 1979.

———. "'Planned Chaos' on the Piazza." *Architectural Forum* 115 (October 1961): 112–17.

Thiel, Philip. "Notes on the Description, Scaling, Notation, and Scoring of Some Perceptual and Cognitive Attributes of the Physical Environment." In *Environmental Psychology: Man and His Physical Setting*, ed. Harold Proshansky, William Ittelson, and Leanne Rivlin. New York: Holt, Rinehart and Winston, 1970.

———. "A Sequence-Experience Notation." *Town Planning Review* 32, no. 1 (April 1961): 33–52.

Thompson, J. William. "Master of Collaboration." *Landscape Architecture* 82, no. 7 (July 1992): 60–69.

Till, Jeremy. "The Negotiation of Hope." In *Architecture and Participation*, ed. Peter Blundell Jones, Doina Petrescu, and Jeremy Till. London: Spon Press, 2005.

Treib, Marc, ed. *The Architecture of Landscape, 1940–1960*. Philadelphia: University of Pennsylvania Press, 2002.

———, ed. *Modern Landscape Architecture: A Critical Review*. Cambridge, Mass.: MIT Press, 1989.

Treib, Marc, and Dorothée Imbert. *Garrett Eckbo: Modern Landscapes for Living*. Berkeley: University of California Press, 1997.

Tuan, Yi-Fu. *Topophilia: A Study of Environmental Perception, Attitudes, and Values*. Englewood Cliffs, N.J.: Prentice Hall, 1974.

Tunnard, Christopher. *Gardens in the Modern Landscape*. London: Architectural Press, 1938. Second edition, 1948.

Tunnard, Christopher, and Boris Pushkarev. *Man-Made America: Chaos or Control?* New Haven, Conn.: Yale University Press, 1963.

Turner, Victor. *The Ritual Process: Structure and Anti-Structure*. Chicago: Aldine, 1969.

Von Eckardt, Wolf. "A Beautiful Plaza, Designed for Fun." *Smithsonian* (November 1970): 52–56.

Waldheim, Charles, ed. *Landscape Urbanism Reader*. New Brunswick, N.J.: Princeton Architectural Press, 2006.

Walker, Peter, and Melanie Simo. *Invisible Gardens: The Search for Modernism in the American Landscape*. Cambridge, Mass.: MIT Press, 1996.

Wall, Alex. "Programming the Urban Surface." In *Recovering Landscape*, ed. James Corner. New York: Princeton Architectural Press, 1999.

"Water Plaza." *Architectural Review* 144 (December 1968): 326–27.

Whyte, William Hollingsworth. *City: Rediscovering the Center*. New York: Doubleday, 1988.

———. *The Social Life of Small Urban Spaces.* Washington, D.C.: Conservation Foundation, 1980.

Wick, Rainer. *Teaching at the Bauhaus.* Ostfildern-Ruit, Germany: Hatje Cantze, 2000.

Wilson, James Q., ed. *Urban Renewal: The Record and the Controversy.* Cambridge, Mass.: MIT Press, 1966.

Wollner, Craig, John Provo, and Julie Schablitsky. "A Brief History of Urban Renewal in Portland, Oregon." August 2001. *Portland Development Commission,* www.pdc.us/pdf/about/urban_renewal_history.pdf (accessed June 2009).

Wright, Robert A. "Mall Stirs Downtown Minneapolis Revival." *New York Times,* March 24, 1973, 43, 45.

Yellig, John. "Downtown Mall: Charlottesville's Public Square." *Daily Progress,* June 25, 2006. www.daily progress.com/news/downtown-mall-charlottesville-s-public-square/article_f6e0f0cf-644c-5fd3-a87e-7d45b7be1acb.html.

Zurbrugg, Nicholas, ed. *Art, Performance, Media: 31 Interviews.* Minneapolis: University of Minnesota Press, 2004.

INDEX

ALISON BICK HIRSCH is a landscape and urban designer, as well as an urban historian and theorist. She is assistant professor of landscape architecture at the University of Southern California and is cofounder and partner of Foreground design agency, a transdisciplinary practice operating between the fields of architecture, landscape architecture, urbanism, and the visual arts.